ROBERT LOUIS STEVENSON

Vol. XXII

SKETCHES ✿ ✿ ✿ ✿
CRITICISMS, ETC.

THE HOUSE AT VAILIMA

Drawn from a photograph

LETTERS AND MISCEL-LANIES OF ROBERT LOUIS STEVENSON

SKETCHES ❧ ❧ ❧ CRITICISMS, ETC.

PUBLISHED IN ❧
NEW YORK BY
CHARLES SCRIBNER'S
SONS ❧ ❧ 1919 ❧

CONTENTS

v

CONTENTS

vi

CONTENTS

SKETCHES

The following "Sketches" (so named by the writer) are from unpublished MSS. of 1870 to 1871.

SKETCHES

I

THE SATIRIST

MY companion enjoyed a cheap reputation for wit and insight. He was by habit and repute a satirist. If he did occasionally condemn anything or anybody who richly deserved it, and whose demerits had hitherto escaped, it was simply because he condemned everything and everybody. While I was with him he disposed of St. Paul with an epigram, shook my reverence for Shakespeare in a neat antithesis, and fell foul of the Almighty himself, on the score of one or two out of the ten commandments. Nothing escaped his blighting censure. At every sentence he overthrew an idol, or lowered my estimation of a friend. I saw everything with new eyes, and could only marvel at my former blindness. How was it possible that I had not before observed A's false hair, B's selfishness, or C's boorish manners? I and my companion, methought, walked the streets like a couple of gods among a swarm of vermin; for every one we saw seemed to bear openly upon his brow the mark of the apocalyptic

beast. I half expected that these miserable beings, like
the people of Lystra, would recognise their betters and
force us to the altar; in which case, warned by the fate
of Paul and Barnabas, I do not know that my modesty
would have prevailed upon me to decline. But there
was no need for such churlish virtue. More blinded
than the Lycaonians, the people saw no divinity in our
gait; and as our temporary godhead lay more in the
way of observing than healing their infirmities, we
were content to pass them by in scorn.

I could not leave my companion, not from regard or
even from interest, but from a very natural feeling,
inseparable from the case. To understand it, let us
take a simile. Suppose yourself walking down the
street with a man who continues to sprinkle the crowd
out of a flask of vitriol. You would be much diverted
with the grimaces and contortions of his victims; and
at the same time you would fear to leave his arm until
his bottle was empty, knowing that, when once among
the crowd, you would run a good chance yourself of
baptism with his biting liquor. Now my companion's
vitriol was inexhaustible.

It was perhaps the consciousness of this, the knowledge that I was being anointed already out of the vials
of his wrath, that made me fall to criticising the critic,
whenever we had parted.

After all, I thought, our satirist has just gone far
enough into his neighbours to find that the outside is
false, without caring to go farther and discover what
is really true. He is content to find that things are not
what they seem, and broadly generalises from it that
they do not exist at all. He sees our virtues are not

what they pretend they are; and, on the strength of that, he denies us the possession of virtue altogether. He has learnt the first lesson, that no man is wholly good; but he has not even suspected that there is another equally true, to wit, that no man is wholly bad. Like the inmate of a coloured star, he has eyes for one colour alone. He has a keen scent after evil, but his nostrils are plugged against all good, as people plugged their nostrils before going about the streets of the plague-struck city.

Why does he do this? It is most unreasonable to flee the knowledge of good like the infection of a horrible disease, and batten and grow fat in the real atmosphere of a lazar-house. This was my first thought; but my second was not like unto it, and I saw that our satirist was wise, wise in his generation, like the unjust steward. He does not want light, because the darkness is more pleasant. He does not wish to see the good, because he is happier without it. I recollect that when I walked with him, I was in a state of divine exaltation, such as Adam and Eve must have enjoyed when the savour of the fruit was still unfaded between their lips; and I recognise that this must be the man's habitual state. He has the forbidden fruit in his waistcoat pocket, and can make himself a god as often and as long as he likes. He has raised himself upon a glorious pedestal above his fellows; he has touched the summit of ambition; and he envies neither King nor Kaiser, Prophet nor Priest, content in an elevation as high as theirs, and much more easily attained. Yes, certes, much more easily attained. He has not risen by climbing himself, but by pushing others down. He

has grown great in his own estimation, not by blowing himself out, and risking the fate of Æsop's frog,
but simply by the habitual use of a diminishing glass
on everybody else.   And I think altogether that his is
a better, a safer, and a surer recipe than most others.

After all, however, looking back on what I have
written, I detect a spirit suspiciously like his own.   All
through, I have been comparing myself with our Satirist, and all through, I have had the best of the comparison.   Well, well, contagion is as often mental as physical; and I do not think my readers, who have all been
under his lash, will blame me very much for giving the
headsman a mouthful of his own sawdust.

II

NUITS BLANCHES

IF any one should know the pleasure and pain of a sleepless night, it should be I. I remember, so long ago, the sickly child that woke from his few hours' slumber with the sweat of a nightmare on his brow, to lie awake and listen and long for the first signs of life among the silent streets. These nights of pain and weariness are graven on my mind; and so when the same thing happened to me again, everything that I heard or saw was rather a recollection than a discovery.

Weighed upon by the opaque and almost sensible darkness, I listened eagerly for anything to break the sepulchral quiet. But nothing came, save, perhaps, an emphatic crack from the old cabinet that was made by Deacon Brodie, or the dry rustle of the coals on the extinguished fire. It was a calm; or I know that I should have heard in the roar and clatter of the storm, as I have not heard it for so many years, the wild career of a horseman, always scouring up from the distance and passing swiftly below the window; yet always returning again from the place whence first he came, as though, baffled by some higher power, he had retraced his steps to gain impetus for another and another attempt.

As I lay there, there arose out of the utter stillness the rumbling of a carriage a very great way off, that drew near, and passed within a few streets of the house, and died away as gradually as it had arisen. This, too, was a reminiscence.

I rose and lifted a corner of the blind. Over the black belt of the garden I saw the long line of Queen Street, with here and there a lighted window. How often before had my nurse lifted me out of bed and pointed them out to me, while we wondered together if, there also, there were children that could not sleep, and if these lighted oblongs were signs of those that waited like us for the morning.

I went out into the lobby, and looked down into the great deep well of the staircase. For what cause I know not, just as it used to be in the old days that the feverish child might be the better served, a peep of gas illuminated a narrow circle far below me. But where I was, all was darkness and silence, save the dry monotonous ticking of the clock that came ceaselessly up to my ear.

The final crown of it all, however, the last touch of reproduction on the pictures of my memory, was the arrival of that time for which, all night through, I waited and longed of old. It was my custom, as the hours dragged on, to repeat the question, "When will the carts come in?" and repeat it again and again until at last those sounds arose in the street that I have heard once more this morning. The road before our house is a great thoroughfare for early carts. I know not, and I never have known, what they carry, whence they come, or whither they go. But I know that, long ere dawn, and for hours together, they stream continuously past, with the same rolling and jerking of wheels and the same clink of horses' feet. It was not for nothing that they made the burthen of my wishes all night through. They are really the first throbbings of life, the harbingers of day; and it pleases you as much to hear them as it must please a shipwrecked seaman once again to grasp a hand of flesh and blood after years of miserable solitude. They have the freshness of the daylight life about them. You can hear the carters cracking their whips and crying hoarsely to their horses or to one another; and sometimes even a peal of healthy, harsh horse-laughter comes up to you through the darkness. There is now an end of mystery and fear. Like the knocking at the door in *Macbeth*,[1] or the cry of the watchman in the *Tour de Nesle*, they show that the horrible cæsura is over and the nightmares have fled away, because the day is breaking and the ordinary life of men is beginning to bestir itself among the streets.

In the middle of it all I fell asleep, to be awakened by the officious knocking at my door, and I find myself twelve years older than I had dreamed myself all night.

[1] See a short essay of De Quincey's.

III

THE WREATH OF IMMORTELLES

IT is all very well to talk of death as "a pleasant potion of immortality"; but the most of us, I suspect, are of "queasy stomachs," and find it none of the sweetest.[1] The graveyard may be cloak-room to Heaven; but we must admit that it is a very ugly and offensive vestibule in itself, however fair may be the life to which it leads. And though Enoch and Elias went into the temple through a gate which certainly may be called Beautiful, the rest of us have to find our way to it through Ezekiel's low-bowed door and the vault full of creeping things and all manner of abominable beasts. Nevertheless, there is a certain frame of mind to which a cemetery is, if not an antidote, at least an alleviation. If you are in a fit of the blues, go nowhere else. It was in obedience to this wise regulation that the other morning found me lighting my pipe at the entrance to Old Greyfriars', thoroughly sick of the town, the country, and myself.

Two of the men were talking at the gate, one of them carrying a spade in hands still crusted with the soil of graves. Their very aspect was delightful to me;

[1] *Religio Medici*, Part ii.

8

and I crept nearer to them, thinking to pick up some snatch of sexton gossip, some "talk fit for a charnel,"[1] something, in fine, worthy of that fastidious logician, that adept in coroner's law, who has come down to us as the patron of Yaughan's liquor, and the very prince of gravediggers. Scots people in general are so much wrapped up in their profession that I had a good chance of overhearing such conversation: the talk of fishmongers running usually on stockfish and haddocks; while of the Scots sexton I could repeat stories and speeches that positively smell of the graveyard. But on this occasion I was doomed to disappointment. My two friends were far into the region of generalities. Their profession was forgotten in their electorship. Politics had engulfed the narrower economy of gravedigging. "Na, na," said the one, "ye 're a' wrang." "The English and Irish Churches," answered the other, in a tone as if he had made the remark before, and it had been called in question—"The English and Irish Churches have *impoverised* the country."

"Such are the results of education," thought I as I passed beside them and came fairly among the tombs. Here, at least, there were no commonplace politics, no diluted this-morning's leader, to distract or offend me. The old shabby church showed, as usual, its quaint extent of roofage and the relievo skeleton on one gable, still blackened with the fire of thirty years ago. A chill dank mist lay over all. The Old Greyfriars' churchyard was in perfection that morning, and one could go round and reckon up the associations with no fear of vulgar interruption. On this stone the Covenant was signed.

[1] *Duchess of Malfi.*

In that vault, as the story goes, John Knox took hiding in some Reformation broil. From that window Burke the murderer looked out many a time across the tombs, and perhaps o' nights let himself down over the sill to rob some new-made grave. Certainly he would have a selection here. The very walks have been carried over forgotten resting-places; and the whole ground is uneven, because (as I was once quaintly told) " when the wood rots it stands to reason the soil should fall in," which, from the law of gravitation, is certainly beyond denial. But it is round the boundary that there are the finest tombs. The whole irregular space is, as it were, fringed with quaint old monuments, rich in death's-heads and scythes and hour-glasses, and doubly rich in pious epitaphs and Latin mottoes—rich in them to such an extent that their proper space has run over, and they have crawled end-long up the shafts of columns and ensconced themselves in all sorts of odd corners among the sculpture. These tombs raise their backs against the rabble of squalid dwelling-houses, and every here and there a clothes-pole projects between two monuments its fluttering trophy of white and yellow and red. With a grim irony they recall the banners in the Invalides, banners as appropriate perhaps over the sepulchres of tailors and weavers as these others above the dust of armies. Why they put things out to dry on that particular morning it was hard to imagine. The grass was grey with drops of rain, the headstones black with moisture. ·Yet, in despite of weather and common-sense, there they hung between the tombs; and beyond them I could see through open windows into miserable rooms where whole families were born and

fed, and slept and died. At one a girl sat singing
merrily with her back to the graveyard; and from another came the shrill tones of a scolding woman. Every
here and there was a town garden full of sickly flowers,
or a pile of crockery inside upon the window-seat.
But you do not grasp the full connection between these
houses of the dead and the living, the unnatural marriage of stately sepulchres and squalid houses, till, lower
down, where the road has sunk far below the surface
of the cemetery, and the very roofs are scarcely on a
level with its wall, you observe that a proprietor has
taken advantage of a tall monument and trained a
chimney-stack against its back. It startles you to see
the red, modern pots peering over the shoulder of the
tomb.

A man was at work on a grave, his spade clinking
away the drift of bones that permeates the thin brown
soil; but my first disappointment had taught me to
expect little from Greyfriars' sextons, and I passed him
by in silence. A slater on the slope of a neighbouring
roof eyed me curiously. A lean black cat, looking as
if it had battened on strange meats, slipped past me.
A little boy at a window put his finger to his nose in so
offensive a manner that I was put upon my dignity,
and turned grandly off to read old epitaphs and peer
through the gratings into the shadow of vaults.

Just then I saw two women coming down a path,
one of them old, and the other younger, with a child
in her arms. Both had faces eaten with famine and
hardened with sin, and both had reached that stage of
degradation, much lower in a woman than a man,
when all care for dress is lost. As they came down

they neared a grave, where some pious friend or relative had laid a wreath of immortelles, and put a bell glass over it, as is the custom. The effect of that ring of dull yellow among so many blackened and dusty sculptures was more pleasant than it is in modern cemeteries, where every second mound can boast a similar coronal; and here, where it was the exception and not the rule, I could even fancy the drops of moisture that dimmed the covering were the tears of those who laid it where it was. As the two women came up to it, one of them kneeled down on the wet grass and looked long and silently through the clouded shade, while the second stood above her, gently oscillating to and fro to lull the muling baby. I was struck a great way off with something religious in the attitude of these two unkempt and haggard women; and I drew near faster, but still cautiously, to hear what they were saying. Surely on them the spirit of death and decay had descended: I had no education to dread here: should I not have a chance of seeing nature? Alas! a pawnbroker could not have been more practical and commonplace, for this was what the kneeling woman said to the woman upright—this and nothing more: " Eh, what extravagance! "

O nineteenth century, wonderful art thou indeed— wonderful, but wearisome in thy stale and deadly uniformity. Thy men are more like numerals than men. They must bear their idiosyncrasies or their professions written on a placard about their neck, like the scenery in Shakespeare's theatre. Thy precepts of economy have pierced into the lowest ranks of life; and there is now a decorum in vice, a respectability among the disreputable, a pure spirit of Philistinism among the waifs and strays of thy Bohemia. For lo! thy very gravediggers talk politics; and thy castaways kneel upon new graves, to discuss the cost of the monument and grumble at the improvidence of love.

Such was the elegant apostrophe that I made as I went out of the gates again, happily satisfied in myself, and feeling that I alone of all whom I had seen was able to profit by the silent poem of these green mounds and blackened headstones.

IV

I KNEW one once, and the room where, lonely and old, she waited for death. It was pleasant enough, high up above the lane, and looking forth upon a hillside, covered all day with sheets and yellow blankets, and with long lines of underclothing fluttering between the battered posts. There were any number of cheap prints, and a drawing by one of "her children," and there were flowers in the window, and a sickly canary withered into consumption in an ornamental cage. The bed, with its checkered coverlid, was in a closet. A great Bible lay on the table; and her drawers were full of "scones," which it was her pleasure to give to young visitors such as I was then.

You may not think this a melancholy picture; but the canary, and the cat, and the white mouse that she had for a while, and that died, were all indications of the want that ate into her heart. I think I know a little of what that old woman felt; and I am as sure as if I had seen her, that she sat many an hour in silent tears, with the big Bible open before her clouded eyes.

If you could look back upon her life, and feel the great chain that had linked her to one child after another, sometimes to be wrenched suddenly through, and sometimes, which is infinitely worse, to be torn gradually off through years of growing neglect, or perhaps growing dislike! She had, like the mother, overcome that natural repugnance—repugnance which no man can conquer—towards the infirm and helpless mass of putty of the earlier stage. She had spent her best and happiest years in tending, watching, and learning to love like a mother this child, with which she has no connection and to which she has no tie. Perhaps she refused some sweetheart (such things have been), or put him off and off, until he lost heart and turned to some one else, all for fear of leaving this creature that had wound itself about her heart. And the end of it all,— her month's warning, and a present perhaps, and the rest of the life to vain regret. Or, worse still, to see the child gradually forgetting and forsaking her, fostered in disrespect and neglect on the plea of growing manliness, and at last beginning to treat her as a servant whom he had treated a few years before as a mother. She sees the Bible or the Psalm-book, which with gladness and love unutterable in her heart she had bought for him years ago out of her slender savings, neglected for some newer gift of his father, lying in dust in the lumber-room or given away to a poor child, and the act applauded for its unfeeling charity. Little wonder if she becomes hurt and angry, and attempts to tyrannise and to grasp her old power back again. We are not all patient Grizzels, by good fortune, but the most of us human beings with feelings and tempers of our own.

And so in the end, behold her in the room that I described. Very likely and very naturally, in some fling of feverish misery or recoil of thwarted love, she has quarrelled with her old employers and the children are forbidden to see her or to speak to her; or at best she gets her rent paid and a little to herself, and now and then her late charges are sent up (with another nurse, perhaps) to pay her a short visit. How bright these visits seem as she looks forward to them on her lonely bed! How unsatisfactory their realisation, when the forgetful child, half wondering, checks with every word and action the outpouring of her maternal love! How bitter and restless the memories that they leave behind! And for the rest, what else has she?—to watch them with eager eyes as they go to school, to sit in church where she can see them every Sunday, to be passed some day unnoticed in the street, or deliberately cut because the great man or the great woman are with friends before whom they are ashamed to recognise the old woman that loved them.

When she goes home that night, how lonely will the room appear to her! Perhaps the neighbours may hear her sobbing to herself in the dark, with the fire burnt out for want of fuel, and the candle still unlit upon the table.

And it is for this that they live, these quasi-mothers —mothers in everything but the travail and the thanks. It is for this that they have remained virtuous in youth, living the dull life of a household servant. It is for this that they refused the old sweetheart, and have no fireside or offspring of their own.

I believe in a better state of things, that there will be no more nurses, and that every mother will nurse her own offspring; for what can be more hardening and demoralising than to call forth the tenderest feelings of

a woman's heart and cherish them yourself as long as
you need them, as long as your children require a nurse
to love them, and then to blight and thwart and destroy
them, whenever your own use for them is at an end?
This may be Utopian; but it is always a little thing if
one mother or two mothers can be brought to feel more
tenderly to those who share their toil and have no part
in their reward.

V

A CHARACTER

THE man has a red, bloated face, and his figure is short and squat. So far there is nothing in him to notice, but when you see his eyes, you can read in these hard and shallow orbs a depravity beyond measure depraved, a thirst after wickedness, the pure, disinterested love of Hell for its own sake. The other night, in the street, I was watching an omnibus passing with lit-up windows, when I heard some one coughing at my side as though he would cough his soul out; and turning round, I saw him stopping under a lamp, with a brown greatcoat buttoned round him and his whole face convulsed. It seemed as if he could not live long; and so the sight set my mind upon a train of thought, as I finished my cigar up and down the lighted streets.

He is old, but all these years have not yet quenched his thirst for evil, and his eyes still delight themselves in wickedness. He is dumb; but he will not let that hinder his foul trade, or perhaps I should say, his yet fouler amusement, and he has pressed a slate into the service of corruption. Look at him, and he will sign to you with his bloated head, and when you go to him in answer to the sign, thinking perhaps that the poor dumb man has lost his way, you will see what he writes upon his slate. He haunts the doors of schools, and shows such inscriptions as these to the innocent children that come out. He hangs about picture-galleries, and makes the noblest pictures the text for some silent homily of vice. His industry is a lesson to ourselves. Is it not wonderful how he can triumph over his infirmities and do such an amount of harm without a tongue? Wonderful industry—strange, fruitless, pleasureless toil? Must not the very devil feel a soft emotion to see his disinterested and laborious service? Ah, but the devil knows better than this: he knows that this man is penetrated with the love of evil and that all his pleasure is shut up in wickedness. he recognises him, perhaps, as a fit type for mankind of his satanic self, and watches over his effigy as we might watch over a favourite likeness. As the business man comes to love the toil, which he only looked upon at first as a ladder towards other desires and less unnatural gratifications, so the dumb man has felt the charm of his trade and fallen captivated before the eyes of sin. It is a mistake when preachers tell us that vice is hideous and loathsome; for even vice has her Hörsel and her devotees, who love her for her own sake.

COLLEGE PAPERS

Originally printed :

    i. *Edinburgh University Magazine, January, 1871.*

    ii. *Ibid., February, 1871.*

    iii. *Ibid., March, 1871.*

    iv. *Ibid., February, 1871.*

    v. *Ibid., April, 1871.*

For the history of the short-lived periodical to which these papers (now reprinted for the first time) were contributed, see the Author's essay "A College Magazine" in "Memories and Portraits" (Travel and Essays, vol. xiii. of this edition). A sixth paper contributed to the same publication, "An Old Scots Gardener," is omitted in this place, having been reprinted with corrections by the Author himself in "Memories and Portraits."

COLLEGE PAPERS

I

EDINBURGH STUDENTS IN 1824

ON the 2nd of January, 1824, was issued the pro-
spectus of the *Lapsus Linguæ; or, the College
Tatler;* and on the 7th the first number appeared.   On
Friday the 2nd of April "*Mr. Tatler* became speechless."
Its history was not all one success; for the editor (who
applies to himself the words of Iago, "I am nothing if
I am not critical") overstepped the bounds of caution,
and found himself seriously embroiled with the powers
that were.   There appeared in No. XVI. a most bitter
satire upon Sir John Leslie, in which he was compared
to Falstaff, charged with puffing himself, and very
prettily censured for publishing only the first volume of
a class-book, and making all purchasers pay for both.
Sir John Leslie took up the matter angrily, visited Car-
frae the publisher, and threatened him with an action,
till he was forced to turn the hapless *Lapsus* out of
doors.   The maltreated periodical found shelter in the
shop of Huie, Infirmary Street; and No. XVII. was duly
issued from the new office.   No. XVII. beheld *Mr.*

23

Tatler's humiliation, in which, with fulsome apology
and not very credible assurances of respect and admiration, he disclaims the article in question, and advertises
a new issue of No. xvi. with all objectionable matter
omitted. This, with pleasing euphemism, he terms in
a later advertisement, "a new and improved edition."
This was the only remarkable adventure of *Mr. Tatler's*
brief existence; unless we consider as such a silly
Chaldee manuscript in imitation of *Blackwood*, and a
letter of reproof from a divinity student on the impiety
of the same dull effusion. He laments the near approach
of his end in pathetic terms. "How shall we summon
up sufficient courage," says he, "to look for the last
time on our beloved little devil and his inestimable
proof-sheet? How shall we be able to pass No. 14
Infirmary Street and feel that all its attractions are over?
How shall we bid farewell for ever to that excellent man,
with the long greatcoat, wooden leg and wooden board,
who acts as our representative at the gate of *Alma
Mater?*" But alas! he had no choice: *Mr. Tatler*,
whose career, he says himself, had been successful,
passed peacefully away, and has ever since dumbly
implored "the bringing home of bell and burial."

Alter et idem. A very different affair was the *Lapsus
Linguæ* from the *Edinburgh University Magazine*.
The two prospectuses alone, laid side by side, would
indicate the march of luxury and the repeal of the paper
duty. The penny bi-weekly broadside of session 1823–4
was almost wholly dedicated to Momus. Epigrams,
pointless letters, amorous verses, and University grie-
vances are the continual burthen of the song. But *Mr.
Tatler* was not without a vein of hearty humour; and

24

his pages afford what is much better: to wit, a good picture of student life as it then was. The students of those polite days insisted on retaining their hats in the class-room. There was a cab-stance in front of the College; and "Carriage Entrance" was posted above the main arch, on what the writer pleases to call "coarse, unclassic boards." The benches of the "Speculative" then, as now, were red; but all other Societies (the "Dialectic" is the only survivor) met down-stairs, in some rooms of which it is pointedly said that "nothing else could conveniently be made of them." However horrible these dungeons may have been, it is certain that they were paid for, and that far too heavily for the taste of session 1823–4, which found enough calls upon its purse for porter and toasted cheese at Ambrose's, or cranberry tarts and ginger-wine at Doull's. Duelling was still a possibility; so much so that when two medicals fell to fisticuffs in Adam Square, it was seriously hinted that single combat would be the result. Last and most wonderful of all, Gall and Spurzheim were in every one's mouth; and the Law student, after having exhausted Byron's poetry and Scott's novels, informed the ladies of his belief in phrenology. In the present day he would dilate on "*Red as a rose is she,*" and then mention that he attends Old Greyfriars', as a tacit claim to intellectual superiority. I do not know that the advance is much.

But *Mr. Tatler's* best performances were three short papers in which he hit off pretty smartly the idiosyncrasies of the "*Divinity,*" the "*Medical,*" and the "*Law*" of session 1823–4. The fact that there was no notice of the "*Arts*" seems to suggest that they stood in the same intermediate position as they do now—the epitome of student-kind. *Mr. Tatler's* satire is, on the whole, good-humoured, and has not grown superannuated in *all* its limbs. His descriptions may limp at some points, but there are certain broad traits that apply equally well to session 1870–71. He shows us the *Divinity* of the period—tall, pale, and slender—his collar greasy, and his coat bare about the seams—"his white neckcloth serving four days, and regularly turned the third,"—"the rim of his hat deficient in wool,"—and "a weighty volume of theology under his arm." He was the man to buy cheap "a snuff-box, or a dozen of pencils, or a six-bladed knife, or a quarter of a hundred quills," at any of the public sale-rooms. He was noted for cheap purchases, and for exceeding the legal tender in halfpence. He haunted "the darkest and remotest corner of the Theatre Gallery." He was to be seen issuing from "aerial lodging-houses." Withal, says mine author, "there were many good points about him: he paid his landlady's bill, read his Bible, went twice to church on Sunday, seldom swore, was not often tipsy, and bought the *Lapsus Linguæ*."

The *Medical*, again, "wore a white greatcoat, and consequently talked loud"—(there is something very delicious in that *consequently*). He wore his hat on one side. He was active, volatile, and went to the top of Arthur's Seat on the Sunday forenoon. He was as quiet in a debating society as he was loud in the streets. He was reckless and imprudent: yesterday he insisted on your sharing a bottle of claret with him (and claret was claret then, before the cheap-and-nasty treaty), and to-morrow he asks you for the loan of a penny to buy the last number of the *Lapsus*.

The student of *Law*, again, was a learned man. "He had turned over the leaves of Justinian's *Institutes*, and knew that they were written in Latin. He was well acquainted with the title-page of *Blackstone's Commentaries*, and *argal* (as the gravedigger in *Hamlet* says) he was not a person to be laughed at." He attended the Parliament House in the character of a critic, and could give you stale sneers at all the celebrated speakers. He was the terror of essayists at the Speculative or the Forensic. In social qualities he seems to have stood unrivalled. Even in the police-office we find him shining with undiminished lustre. "If a *Charlie* should find him rather noisy at an untimely hour, and venture to take him into custody, he appears next morning like a Daniel come to judgment. He opens his mouth to speak, and the divine precepts of unchanging justice and Scots Law flow from his tongue. The magistrate listens in amazement, and fines him only a couple of guineas."

Such then were our predecessors and their College Magazine. Barclay, Ambrose, Young Amos, and Fergusson were to them what the Café, the Rainbow, and Rutherford's are to us. An hour's reading in these old pages absolutely confuses us, there is so much that is similar and so much that is different; the follies and amusements are so like our own, and the manner of frolicking and enjoying are so changed, that one pauses and looks about him in philosophic judgment. The muddy quadrangle is thick with living students; but in our eyes it swarms also with the phantasmal white

27

greatcoats and tilted hats of 1824. Two races meet: races alike and diverse. Two performances are played before our eyes; but the change seems merely of impersonators, of scenery, of costume. Plot and passion are the same. It is the fall of the spun shilling whether seventy-one or twenty-four has the best of it.

In a future number we hope to give a glance at the individualities of the present, and see whether the cast shall be head or tail—whether we or the readers of the *Lapsus* stand higher in the balance.

THE MODERN STUDENT CONSIDERED GENERALLY

WE have now reached the difficult portion of our task. *Mr. Tatler*, for all that we care, may have been as virulent as he liked about the students of a former day; but for the iron to touch our sacred selves, for a brother of the Guild to betray its most privy infirmities, let such a Judas look to himself as he passes on his way to the Scots Law or the Diagnostic, below the solitary lamp at the corner of the dark quadrangle. We confess that this idea alarms us. We enter a protest. We bind ourselves over verbally to keep the peace. We hope, moreover, that having thus made you secret to our misgivings, you will excuse us if we be dull, and set that down to caution which you might before have charged to the account of stupidity.

The natural tendency of civilisation is to obliterate those distinctions which are the best salt of life. All the fine old professional flavour in language has evaporated. Your very gravedigger has forgotten his avocation in his electorship, and would quibble on the Franchise over Ophelia's grave, instead of more appropriately discussing the duration of bodies under ground. From this tendency, from this gradual attrition of life, in which everything pointed and characteristic is being

29

rubbed down, till the whole world begins to slip between our fingers in smooth undistinguishable sands,
from this, we say, it follows that we must not attempt
to join *Mr. Tatler* in his simple division of students
into *Law*, *Divinity*, and *Medical*. Nowadays the
faculties may shake hands over their follies; and, like
Mrs. Frail and Mrs. Foresight (in *Love for Love*), they
may stand in the doors of opposite class-rooms, crying:
" Sister, Sister—Sister everyway! " A few restrictions,
indeed, remain to influence the followers of individual
branches of study. The *Divinity*, for example, must
be an avowed believer; and as this, in the present day,
is unhappily considered by many as a confession of
weakness, he is fain to choose one of two ways of gild-
ing the distasteful orthodox bolus. Some swallow it
in a thin jelly of metaphysics; for it is even a credit to
believe in God on the evidence of some crack-jaw philosopher, although it is a decided slur to believe in Him
on His own authority. Others again (and this we think
the worst method), finding German grammar a somewhat dry morsel, run their own little heresy as a proof
of independence; and deny one of the cardinal doctrines that they may hold the others without being
laughed at.

Besides, however, such influences as these, there is
little more distinction between the faculties than the tra-
ditionary ideal, handed down through a long sequence of
students, and getting rounder and more featureless at
each successive session. The plague of uniformity has
descended on the College. Students (and indeed all
sorts and conditions of men) now require their faculty
and character hung round their neck on a placard, like

the scenes in Shakespeare's theatre. And in the midst of all this weary sameness, not the least common feature is the gravity of every face. No more does the merry medical run eagerly in the clear winter morning up the rugged sides of Arthur's Seat, and hear the church bells begin and thicken and die away below him among the gathered smoke of the city. He will not break Sunday to so little purpose. He no longer finds pleasure in the mere output of his surplus energy. He husbands his strength, and lays out walks, and reading, and amusement with deep consideration, so that he may get as much work and pleasure out of his body as he can, and waste none of his energy on mere impulse, or such flat enjoyment as an excursion in the country.

See the quadrangle in the interregnum of classes, in those two or three minutes when it is full of passing students, and we think you will admit that, if we have not made it "an habitation of dragons," we have at least transformed it into "a court for owls." Solemnity broods heavily over the enclosure; and wherever you seek it, you will find a dearth of merriment, an absence of real youthful enjoyment. You might as well try

"To move wild laughter in the throat of death,"

as to excite any healthy stir among the bulk of this staid company.

The studious congregate about the doors of the different classes, debating the matter of the lecture, or comparing note-books. A reserved rivalry sunders them. Here are some deep in Greek particles : there, others are already inhabitants of that land

> " Where entity and quiddity,
>   Like ghosts of defunct bodies fly—
>   Where Truth in person does appear
>   Like words congealed in northern air."

But none of them seem to find any relish for their studies—no pedantic love of this subject or that lights up their eyes—science and learning are only means for a livelihood, which they have considerately embraced and which they solemnly pursue. "Labour's pale priests," their lips seem incapable of laughter, except in the way of polite recognition of professorial wit. The stains of ink are chronic on their meagre fingers. They walk like Saul among the asses.

The dandies are not less subdued. In 1824 there was a noisy dapper dandyism abroad. Vulgar, as we should now think, but yet genial—a matter of white greatcoats and loud voices—strangely different from the stately frippery that is rife at present. These men are out of their element in the quadrangle. Even the small remains of boisterous humour, which still cling to any collection of young men, jar painfully on their morbid sensibilities; and they beat a hasty retreat to resume their perfunctory march along Princes Street. Flirtation is to them a great social duty, a painful obligation, which they perform on every occasion in the same chill official manner, and with the same commonplace advances, the same dogged observance of traditional behaviour. The shape of their raiment is a burden almost greater than they can bear, and they halt in their walk to preserve the due adjustment of their trouser-knees, till one would fancy he had mixed in a procession of Jacobs. We speak, of course, for ourselves; but we would as soon associate with a herd of sprightly apes as with these gloomy modern beaux. Alas, that our Mirabels, our Valentines, even our Brummels, should have left their mantles upon nothing more amusing!

Nor are the fast men less constrained. Solemnity, even in dissipation, is the order of the day; and they go to the devil with a perverse seriousness, a systematic rationalism of wickedness that would have surprised the simpler sinners of old. Some of these men whom we see gravely conversing on the steps have but a slender acquaintance with each other. Their intercourse consists principally of mutual bulletins of depravity; and, week after week, as they meet they reckon up their items of transgression, and give an abstract of their downward progress for approval and encouragement. These folk form a freemasonry of their own. An oath is the shibboleth of their sinister fellowship. Once they hear a man swear, it is wonderful how their tongues loosen and their bashful spirits take enlargement, under the consciousness of brotherhood. There is no folly, no pardoning warmth of temper about them; they are as steady-going and systematic in their own way as the studious in theirs.

Not that we are without merry men. No. We shall not be ungrateful to those whose grimaces, whose ironical laughter, whose active feet in the *College Anthem* have beguiled so many weary hours and added a pleasant variety to the strain of close attention. But even these are too evidently professional in their antics. They go about cogitating puns and inventing tricks. It is their vocation, Hal. They are the gratuitous jesters of the class-room; and, like the clown when he leaves the stage, their merriment too often sinks as the bell rings the hour of liberty, and they pass forth by the Post-Office, grave and sedate, and meditating fresh gambols for the morrow.

This is the impression left on the mind of any observing student by too many of his fellows. They seem all frigid old men; and one pauses to think how such an unnatural state of matters is produced. We feel inclined to blame for it the unfortunate absence of *University feeling* which is so marked a characteristic of our Edinburgh students. Academical interests are so few and far between—students, as students, have so little in common, except a peevish rivalry—there is such an entire want of broad college sympathies and ordinary college friendships, that we fancy that no University in the kingdom is in so poor a plight. Our system is full of anomalies. A, who cut B whilst he was a shabby student, curries sedulously up to him and cudgels his memory for anecdotes about him when he becomes the great so-and-so. Let there be an end of this shy, proud reserve on the one hand, and this shuddering fine-ladyism on the other; and we think we shall find both ourselves and the College bettered. Let it be a sufficient reason for intercourse that two men sit together on the same benches. Let the great A be held excused for nodding to the shabby B in Princes Street, if he can say, "That fellow is a student." Once this could be brought about, we think you would find the whole heart of the University beat faster. We think you would find a fusion among the students, a growth of common feelings, an increasing sympathy between

34

class and class, whose influence (in such a heterogeneous company as ours) might be of incalculable value in all branches of politics and social progress. It would do more than this. If we could find some method of making the University a real mother to her sons—something beyond a building full of class-rooms, a Senatus and a lottery of somewhat shabby prizes—we should strike a death-blow at the constrained and unnatural attitude of our Society. At present we are not a united body, but a loose gathering of individuals, whose inherent attraction is allowed to condense them into little knots and coteries. Our last snowball riot read us a plain lesson on our condition. There was no party spirit—no unity of interests. A few, who were mischievously inclined, marched off to the College of Surgeons in a pretentious file; but even before they reached their destination the feeble inspiration had died out in many, and their numbers were sadly thinned. Some followed strange gods in the direction of Drummond Street, and others slunk back to meek good-boyism at the feet of the Professors. The same is visible in better things. As you send a man to an English University that he may have his prejudices rubbed off, you might send him to Edinburgh that he may have them ingrained—rendered indelible—fostered by sympathy into living principles of his spirit. And the reason of it is quite plain. From this absence of University feeling it comes that a man's friendships are always the direct and immediate results of these very prejudices. A common weakness is the best master of ceremonies in our quadrangle: a mutual vice is the readiest introduction. The studious associate with the studious

alone—the dandies with the dandies. There is nothing
to force them to rub shoulders with the others; and
so they grow day by day more wedded to their own
original opinions and affections. They see through the
same spectacles continually. All broad sentiments, all
real catholic humanity expires; and the mind gets gradually stiffened into one position—becomes so habituated
to a contracted atmosphere, that it shudders and withers
under the least draught of the free air that circulates in
the general field of mankind.

Specialism in Society, then, is, we think, one cause of
our present state. Specialism in study is another. We
doubt whether this has ever been a good thing since
the world began; but we are sure it is much worse
now than it was. Formerly, when a man became a
specialist, it was out of affection for his subject. With
a somewhat grand devotion he left all the world of
Science to follow his true love; and he contrived to
find that strange pedantic interest which inspired the
man who

> " Settled *Hoti's* business—let it be—
> Properly based *Oun*—
> Gave us the doctrine of the enclitic *De*,
> Dead from the waist down."

Nowadays it is quite different. Our pedantry wants
even the saving clause of Enthusiasm. The election is
now matter of necessity and not of choice. Knowledge
is now too broad a field for your Jack-of-all-Trades;
and, from beautifully utilitarian reasons, he makes his
choice, draws his pen through a dozen branches of
study, and behold—John the Specialist. That this is
the way to be wealthy we shall not deny; but we hold

that it is *not* the way to be healthy or wise. The whole mind becomes narrowed and circumscribed to one " punctual spot " of knowledge. A rank unhealthy soil breeds a harvest of prejudices. Feeling himself above others in his one little branch—in the classification of toadstools, or Carthaginian history—he waxes great in his own eyes and looks down on others. Having all his sympathies educated in one way, they die out in every other; and he is apt to remain a peevish, narrow, and intolerant bigot. Dilettante is now a term of reproach; but there is a certain form of dilettantism to which no one can object. It is this that we want among our students. We wish them to abandon no subject until they have seen and felt its merit—to act under a general interest in all branches of knowledge, not a commercial eagerness to excel in one.

In both these directions our sympathies are constipated. We are apostles of our own caste and our own subject of study, instead of being, as we should, true men and *loving* students. Of course both of these could be corrected by the students themselves; but this is nothing to the purpose: it is more important to ask whether the Senatus or the body of alumni could do nothing towards the growth of better feeling and wider sentiments. Perhaps in another paper we may say something upon this head.

One other word, however, before we have done. What shall we be when we grow really old ? Of yore, a man was thought to lay on restrictions and acquire new deadweight of mournful experience with every year, till he looked back on his youth as the very summer of impulse and freedom. We please ourselves with think-

ing that it cannot be so with us. We would fain hope
that, as we have begun in one way, we may end in
another; and that when we *are* in fact the octogena-
rians that we *seem* at present, there shall be no merrier
men on earth. It is pleasant to picture us, sunning
ourselves in Princes Street of a morning, or chirping
over our evening cups, with all the merriment that we
wanted in youth.

III

DEBATING SOCIETIES

A DEBATING society is at first somewhat of a disappointment. You do not often find the youthful Demosthenes chewing his pebbles in the same room with you; or, even if you do, you will probably think the performance little to be admired. As a general rule, the members speak shamefully ill. The subjects of debate are heavy; and so are the fines. The Ballot Question—oldest of dialectic nightmares—is often found astride of a somnolent sederunt. The Greeks and Romans, too, are reserved as sort of *general-utility* men, to do all the dirty work of illustration; and they fill as many functions as the famous waterfall scene at the *Princess's*, which I found doing duty on one evening as a gorge in Peru, a haunt of German robbers, and a peaceful vale in the Scottish borders. There is a sad absence of striking argument or real lively discussion. Indeed, you feel a growing contempt for your fellow-members; and it is not until you rise yourself to hawk and hesitate and sit shamefully down again, amid eleemosynary applause, that you begin to find your level and value others rightly. Even then, even when failure has damped your critical ardour, you will see many things to be laughed at in the deportment of your rivals.

Most laughable, perhaps, are your indefatigable strivers after eloquence. They are of those who " pursue with eagerness the phantoms of hope," and who, since they expect that " the deficiencies of last sentence will be supplied by the next," have been recommended by Dr. Samuel Johnson to " attend to the History of Rasselas, Prince of Abyssinia." They are characterised by a hectic hopefulness. Nothing damps them. They rise from the ruins of one abortive sentence, to launch forth into another with unabated vigour. They have all the manner of an orator. From the tone of their voice, you would expect a splendid period—and lo! a string of broken-backed, disjointed clauses, eked out with stammerings and throat-clearings. They possess the art (learned from the pulpit) of rounding an uneuphonious sentence by dwelling on a single syllable—of striking a balance in a top-heavy period by lengthening out a word into a melancholy quaver. Withal, they never cease to hope. Even at last, even when they have exhausted all their ideas, even after the would-be peroration has finally refused to perorate, they remain upon their feet with their mouths open, waiting for some further inspiration, like Chaucer's widow's son in the dung-hole, after

" His throat was kit unto the nekké bone,"

in vain expectation of that seed that was to be laid upon his tongue, and give him renewed and clearer utterance.

These men may have something to say, if they could only say it—indeed they generally have; but the next class are people who, having nothing to say, are cursed with a facility and an unhappy command of words, that makes them the prime nuisances of the society they affect. They try to cover their absence of matter by an unwholesome vitality of delivery. They look triumphantly round the room, as if courting applause, after a torrent of diluted truism. They talk in a circle, harping on the same dull round of argument, and returning again and again to the same remark with the same sprightliness, the same irritating appearance of novelty.

After this set, any one is tolerable; so we shall merely hint at a few other varieties. There is your man who is pre-eminently conscientious, whose face beams with sincerity as he opens on the negative, and who votes on the affirmative at the end, looking round the room with an air of chastened pride. There is also the irrelevant speaker, who rises, emits a joke or two, and then sits down again, without ever attempting to tackle the subject of debate. Again, we have men who ride pick-a-pack on their family reputation, or, if their family have none, identify themselves with some well-known statesman, use his opinions, and lend him their patronage on all occasions. This is a dangerous plan, and serves oftener, I am afraid, to point a difference than to adorn a speech.

But alas! a striking failure may be reached without tempting Providence by any of these ambitious tricks. Our own stature will be found high enough for shame. The success of three simple sentences lures us into a fatal parenthesis in the fourth, from whose shut brackets we may never disentangle the thread of our discourse. A momentary flush tempts us into a quotation; and we may be left helpless in the middle of one of Pope's couplets, a white film gathering before our eyes, and our kind friends charitably trying to cover our disgrace by a feeble round of applause. *Amis lecteurs*, this is a painful topic. It is possible that we too, we, the " potent, grave, and reverend " editor, may have suffered these things, and drunk as deep as any of the cup of shameful failure. Let us dwell no longer on so delicate a subject.

In spite, however, of these disagreeables, I should recommend any student to suffer them with Spartan courage, as the benefits he receives should repay him an hundredfold for them all. The life of the debating society is a handy antidote to the life of the class-room and quadrangle. Nothing could be conceived more excellent as a weapon against many of those *peccant humours* that we have been railing against in the Jeremiad of our last *College Paper*—particularly in the field of intellect. It is a sad sight to see our heather-scented students, our boys of seventeen, coming up to College with determined views—*roués* in speculation—having gauged the vanity of philosophy or learned to shun it as the middleman of heresy—a company of determined, deliberate opinionists, not to be moved by all the sleights of logic. What have such men to do with study ? If their minds are made up irrevocably, why burn the " studious lamp " in search of further confirmation ? Every set opinion I hear a student deliver I feel a certain lowering of my regard. He who studies, he who is yet employed in groping for his premises, should keep his mind fluent and sensitive, keen to mark flaws, and willing to surrender untenable positions. He should keep himself teachable, or cease the expensive farce of being taught. It is to further this docile spirit that we desire to press the claims of debating societies. It is as a means of melting down this museum of premature petrifactions into living and impressionable soul that we insist on their utility. If we could once prevail on our students to feel no shame in avowing an uncertain attitude towards any subject, if we could teach them that it was unnecessary for every lad to have his *opinionette* on every topic, we should have gone a far way towards bracing the intellectual tone of the coming race of thinkers; and this it is which debating societies are so well fitted to perform.

We there meet people of every shade of opinion, and make friends with them. We are taught to rail against a man the whole session through, and then hob-a-nob with him at the concluding entertainment. We find men of talent far exceeding our own, whose conclusions are widely different from ours; and we are thus taught to distrust ourselves. But the best means of all towards catholicity is that wholesome rule which some folk are most inclined to condemn,—I mean the law of *obliged speeches*. Your senior member commands; and you must take the affirmative or the negative, just as suits his best convenience. This tends to the most perfect liberality. It is no good hearing the arguments of an opponent, for in good verity you rarely follow them; and even if you do take the trouble to listen, it is merely in a captious search for weaknesses. This is proved, I fear, in every debate; when you hear each speaker arguing out his own prepared *spécialité* (he never intended speaking, of course, until some remarks of, etc.), arguing out, I say, his own *coached-up* subject without

43

the least attention to what has gone before, as utterly at sea about the drift of his adversary's speech as Panurge when he argued with Thaumaste, and merely linking his own prelection to the last by a few flippant criticisms. Now, as the rule stands, you are saddled with the side you disapprove, and so you are forced, by regard for your own fame, to argue out, to feel with, to elaborate completely, the case as it stands against yourself; and what a fund of wisdom do you not turn up in this idle digging of the vineyard! How many new difficulties take form before your eyes! how many superannuated arguments cripple finally into limbo, under the glance of your enforced eclecticism!

Nor is this the only merit of Debating Societies. They tend also to foster taste, and to promote friendship between University men. This last, as we have had occasion before to say, is the great requirement of our student life; and it will therefore be no waste of time if we devote a paragraph to this subject in its connection with Debating Societies. At present they partake too much of the nature of a *clique*. Friends propose friends, and mutual friends second them, until the society degenerates into a sort of family party. You may confirm old acquaintances, but you can rarely make new ones. You find yourself in the atmosphere of your own daily intercourse. Now, this is an unfortunate circumstance, which it seems to me might readily be rectified. Our Principal has shown himself so friendly towards all College improvements that I cherish the hope of seeing shortly realised a certain suggestion, which is not a new one with me, and which must often have been proposed and canvassed heretofore—I mean, a real *University Debating Society*, patronised by the Senatus, presided over by the Professors, to which every one might gain ready admittance on sight of his matriculation ticket, where it would be a favour and not a necessity to speak, and where the obscure student might have another object for attendance besides the mere desire to save his fines: to wit, the chance of drawing on himself the favourable consideration of his teachers. This would be merely following in the good tendency, which has been so noticeable during all this session, to increase and multiply student societies and clubs of every sort. Nor would it be a matter of much difficulty. The united societies would form a nucleus: one of the class-rooms at first, and perhaps afterwards the great hall above the library, might be the place of meeting. There would be no want of attendance or enthusiasm, I am sure; for it is a very different thing to speak under the bushel of a private club on the one hand, and, on the other, in a public place, where a happy period or a subtle argument may do the speaker permanent service in after life. Such a club might end, perhaps, by rivalling the "Union" at Cambridge or the "Union" at Oxford.

IV

THE PHILOSOPHY OF UMBRELLAS[1]

It is wonderful to think what a turn has been given to our whole Society by the fact that we live under the sign of Aquarius,—that our climate is essentially wet. A mere arbitrary distinction, like the walking-swords of yore, might have remained the symbol of foresight and respectability, had not the raw mists and dropping showers of our island pointed the inclination of Society to another exponent of those virtues. A ribbon of the Legion of Honour or a string of medals may prove a person's courage; a title may prove his birth; a professorial chair his study and acquirement; but it is the habitual carriage of the umbrella that is the stamp of Respectability. The umbrella has become the acknowledged index of social position.

Robinson Crusoe presents us with a touching instance of the hankering after them inherent in the civilised and educated mind. To the superficial, the hot suns of Juan Fernandez may sufficiently account for his quaint choice of a luxury; but surely one who had borne the hard labour of a seaman under the tropics for all

[1] "This paper was written in collaboration with James Walter Ferrier, and if reprinted this is to be stated, though his principal collaboration was to lie back in an easy-chair and laugh."—[R. L. S., *Oct.* 25, 1894.]

these years could have supported an excursion after goats or a peaceful *constitutional* arm in arm with the nude Friday. No, it was not this: the memory of a vanished respectability called for some outward manifestation, and the result was—an umbrella. A pious castaway might have rigged up a belfry and solaced his Sunday mornings with the mimicry of church bells; but Crusoe was rather a moralist than a pietist, and his leaf-umbrella is as fine an example of the civilised mind striving to express itself under adverse circumstances as we have ever met with.

It is not for nothing, either, that the umbrella has become the very foremost badge of modern civilisation —the Urim and Thummim of respectability. Its pregnant symbolism has taken its rise in the most natural manner. Consider, for a moment, when umbrellas were first introduced into this country, what manner of men would use them, and what class would adhere to the useless but ornamental cane. The first, without doubt, would be the hypochondriacal, out of solicitude for their health, or the frugal, out of care for their raiment; the second, it is equally plain, would include the fop, the fool, and the Bobadil. Any one acquainted with the growth of Society, and knowing out of what small seeds of cause are produced great revolutions and wholly new conditions of intercourse, sees from this simple thought how the carriage of an umbrella came to indicate frugality, judicious regard for bodily welfare, and scorn for mere outward adornment, and, in one word, all those homely and solid virtues implied in the term RESPECTABILITY. Not that the umbrella's costliness has nothing to do with its great influence.

47

Its possession, besides symbolising (as we have already indicated) the change from wild Esau to plain Jacob dwelling in tents, implies a certain comfortable provision of fortune. It is not every one that can expose twenty-six shillings' worth of property to so many chances of loss and theft. So strongly do we feel on this point, indeed, that we are almost inclined to consider all who possess really well-conditioned umbrellas as worthy of the Franchise. They have a qualification standing in their lobbies; they carry a sufficient stake in the common-weal below their arm. One who bears with him an umbrella—such a complicated structure of whalebone, of silk, and of cane, that it becomes a very microcosm of modern industry—is necessarily a man of peace. A half-crown cane may be applied to an offender's head on a very moderate provocation; but a six-and-twenty shilling silk is a possession too precious to be adventured in the shock of war.

These are but a few glances at how umbrellas (in the general) came to their present high estate. But the true Umbrella-Philosopher meets with far stranger applications as he goes about the streets.

Umbrellas, like faces, acquire a certain sympathy with the individual who carries them: indeed, they are far more capable of betraying his trust; for whereas a face is given to us so far ready-made, and all our power over it is in frowning, and laughing, and grimacing, during the first three or four decades of life, each umbrella is selected from a whole shopful, as being most consonant to the purchaser's disposition. An undoubted power of diagnosis rests with the practised Umbrella-Philosopher. O you who lisp, and amble, and change

the fashion of your countenances—you who conceal all
these, how little do you think that you left a proof of
your weakness in our umbrella-stand—that even now,
as you shake out the folds to meet the thickening snow,
we read in its ivory handle the outward and visible sign
of your snobbery, or from the exposed gingham of its
cover detect, through coat and waistcoat, the hidden
hypocrisy of the *dickey!* But alas! even the umbrella is no certain criterion. The falsity and the folly
of the human race have degraded that graceful symbol
to the ends of dishonesty; and while some umbrellas,
from carelessness in selection, are not strikingly characteristic (for it is only in what a man loves that he
displays his real nature), others, from certain pruden-
tial motives, are chosen directly opposite to the person's disposition. A mendacious umbrella is a sign of
great moral degradation. Hypocrisy naturally shelters
itself below a silk; while the fast youth goes to visit
his religious friends armed with the decent and repu-
table gingham. May it not be said of the bearers of
these inappropriate umbrellas that they go about the
streets "with a lie in their right hand"?

The king of Siam, as we read, besides having a
graduated social scale of umbrellas (which was a good
thing), prevented the great bulk of his subjects from
having any at all, which was certainly a bad thing.
We should be sorry to believe that this Eastern legisla-
tor was a fool—the idea of an aristocracy of umbrellas
is too philosophic to have originated in a nobody,—and
we have accordingly taken exceeding pains to find out
the reason of this harsh restriction. We think we have
succeeded; but, while admiring the principle at which

he aimed, and while cordially recognising in the Siamese potentate the only man before ourselves who had taken a real grasp of the umbrella, we must be allowed to point out how unphilosophically the great man acted in this particular. His object, plainly, was to prevent any unworthy persons from bearing the sacred symbol of domestic virtues. We cannot excuse his limiting these virtues to the circle of his court. We must only remember that such was the feeling of the age in which he lived. Liberalism had not yet raised the war-cry of the working classes. But here was his mistake: it was a needless regulation. Except in a very few cases of hypocrisy joined to a powerful intellect, men, not by nature *umbrellarians*, have tried again and again to become so by art, and yet have failed—have expended their patrimony in the purchase of umbrella after umbrella, and yet have systematically lost them, and have finally, with contrite spirits and shrunken purses, given up their vain struggle, and relied on theft and borrowing for the remainder of their lives. This is the most remarkable fact that we have had occasion to notice; and yet we challenge the candid reader to call it in question. Now, as there cannot be any *moral selection* in a mere dead piece of furniture—as the umbrella cannot be supposed to have an affinity for individual men equal and reciprocal to that which men certainly feel towards individual umbrellas,—we took the trouble of consulting a scientific friend as to whether there was any possible physical explanation of the phenomenon. He was unable to supply a plausible theory, or even hypothesis; but we extract from his letter the following interesting passage relative to the physical peculiarities of umbrellas: "Not the least important, and by far the most curious property of the umbrella, is the energy which it displays in affecting the atmospheric strata. There is no fact in meteorology better established—indeed, it is almost the only one on which meteorologists are agreed—than that the carriage of an umbrella produces desiccation of the air; while if it be left at home, aqueous vapour is largely produced, and is soon deposited in the form of rain. No theory," my friend continues, "competent to explain this hygrometric law has yet been given (as far as I am aware) by Herschel, Dove, Glaisher, Tait, Buchan, or any other writer; nor do I pretend to supply the defect. I venture, however, to throw out the conjecture that it will be ultimately found to belong to the same class of natural laws as that agreeable to which a slice of toast always descends with the buttered surface downwards."

But it is time to draw to a close. We could expatiate much longer upon this topic, but want of space constrains us to leave unfinished these few desultory remarks—slender contributions towards a subject which has fallen sadly backwards, and which, we grieve to say, was better understood by the king of Siam in 1686 than by all the philosophers of to-day. If, however, we have awakened in any rational mind an interest in the symbolism of umbrellas—in any generous heart a more complete sympathy with the dumb companion of his daily walk,—or in any grasping spirit a pure notion of respectability strong enough to make him expend his six-and-twenty shillings—we shall have deserved well of the world, to say nothing of the many industrious persons employed in the manufacture of the article.

V

THE PHILOSOPHY OF NOMENCLATURE

"How many Cæsars and Pompeys, by mere inspirations of the names, have been rendered worthy of them? And how many are there, who might have done exceeding well in the world, had not their characters and spirits been totally depressed and Nicodemus'd into nothing?"— *Tristram Shandy*, vol. i. chap. xix.

SUCH were the views of the late Walter Shandy, Esq., Turkey merchant. To the best of my belief, Mr. Shandy is the first who fairly pointed out the incalculable influence of nomenclature upon the whole life—who seems first to have recognised the one child, happy in an heroic appellation, soaring upwards on the wings of fortune, and the other, like the dead sailor in his shotted hammock, haled down by sheer weight of name into the abysses of social failure. Solomon possibly had his eye on some such theory when he said that "a good name is better than precious ointment"; and perhaps we may trace a similar spirit in the compilers of the English Catechism, and the affectionate interest with which they linger round the catechumen's name at the very threshold of their work. But, be these as they may, I think no one can censure me for appending, in pursuance of the expressed wish of his son, the Turkey merchant's name to his system, and pronouncing, without further preface, a short epitome of the *Shandean Philosophy of Nomenclature*.

To begin, then: the influence of our name makes itself felt from the very cradle. As a schoolboy I remember the pride with which I hailed Robin Hood, Robert Bruce, and Robert le Diable as my name-fellows; and the feeling of sore disappointment that fell on my heart when I found a freebooter or a general who did not share with me a single one of my numerous *prænomina*. Look at the delight with which two children find they have the same name. They are friends from that moment forth; they have a bond of union stronger than exchange of nuts and sweetmeats. This feeling, I own, wears off in later life. Our names lose their freshness and interest, become trite and indifferent. But this, dear reader, is merely one of the sad effects of those " shades of the prison-house " which come gradually betwixt us and nature with advancing years; it affords no weapon against the philosophy of names.

In after life, although we fail to trace its working, that name which careless godfathers lightly applied to your unconscious infancy will have been moulding your character, and influencing with irresistible power the whole course of your earthly fortunes. But the last name, overlooked by Mr. Shandy, is no whit less important as a condition of success. Family names, we must recollect, are but inherited nicknames; and if the *sobriquet* were applicable to the ancestor, it is most likely applicable to the descendant also. You would not expect to find Mr. M'Phun acting as a mute, or Mr. M'Lumpha excelling as a professor of dancing. Therefore, in what follows, we shall consider names, independent of whether they are first or last. And to begin with, look what a pull *Cromwell* had over *Pym*—the one name full of a resonant imperialism, the other, mean, pettifogging, and unheroic to a degree. Who would expect eloquence from *Pym*—who would read poems by *Pym*—who would bow to the opinion of *Pym?* He might have been a dentist, but he should never have aspired to be a statesman. I can only won- der that he succeeded as he did. Pym and Habakkuk stand first upon the roll of men who have triumphed, by sheer force of genius, over the most unfavourable appellations. But even these have suffered; and, had they been more fitly named, the one might have been Lord Protector, and the other have shared the laurels with Isaiah. In this matter we must not forget that all our great poets have borne great names. Chaucer, Spenser, Shakespeare, Milton, Pope, Wordsworth, Shelley—what a constellation of lordly words! Not a single commonplace name among them—not a Brown, not a Jones, not a Robinson; they are all names that one would stop and look at on a door-plate. Now, imagine if *Pepys* had tried to clamber somehow into the enclosure of poetry, what a blot would that word have made upon the list! The thing was impossible. In the first place, a certain natural consciousness that men have would have held him down to the level of his name, would have prevented him from rising above the Pep- sine standard, and so haply withheld him altogether from attempting verse. Next, the booksellers would refuse to publish, and the world to read them, on the mere evidence of the fatal appellation. And now, be- fore I close this section, I must say one word as to *punnable* names, names that stand alone, that have a significance and life apart from him that bears them. These are the bitterest of all. One friend of mine goes bowed and humbled through life under the weight of this misfortune; for it is an awful thing when a man's name is a joke, when he cannot be mentioned without exciting merriment, and when even the intimation of his death bids fair to carry laughter into many a home.

So much for people who are badly named. Now for people who are *too* well named, who go top-heavy from the font, who are baptised into a false position, and find themselves beginning life eclipsed under the fame of some of the great ones of the past. A man, for instance, called William Shakespeare could never dare to write plays. He is thrown into too humbling an apposition with the author of *Hamlet*. His own name coming after is such an anticlimax. "The plays of William Shakespeare?" says the reader—"O no! The plays of William Shakespeare Cockerill," and he throws the book aside. In wise pursuance of such views, Mr. John Milton Hengler, who not long since delighted us in this favoured town, has never attempted to write an epic, but has chosen a new path, and has excelled upon the tight-rope. A marked example of triumph over this is the case of Mr. Dante Gabriel Rossetti. On the face of the matter, I should have advised him to imitate the pleasing modesty of the last-named gentleman, and confine his ambition to the sawdust. But Mr. Rossetti has triumphed. He has even dared to translate from his mighty name-father; and the voice of fame supports him in his boldness.

Dear readers, one might write a year upon this matter. A lifetime of comparison and research could scarce suffice for its elucidation. So here, if it please you, we shall let it rest. Slight as these notes have been, I would that the great founder of the system had been alive to see them. How he had warmed and brightened, how his persuasive eloquence would have fallen on the ears of Toby; and what a letter of praise and sympathy would not the editor have received before the month was out! Alas! the thing was not to be. Walter Shandy died and was duly buried, while yet his theory lay forgotten and neglected by his fellow-countrymen. But, reader, the day will come, I hope, when a paternal government will stamp out, as seeds of national weakness, all depressing patronymics, and when godfathers and godmothers will soberly and earnestly debate the interest of the nameless one, and not rush blindfold to the christening. In these days there shall be written a *Godfather's Assistant*, in shape of a dictionary of names, with their concomitant virtues and vices; and this book shall be scattered broadcast through the land, and shall be on the table of every one eligible for godfathership, until such a thing as a vicious or untoward appellation shall have ceased from off the face of the earth.

NOTES AND ESSAYS
CHIEFLY OF THE ROAD

Previously published :

III. *Portfolio, November, 1873.*

IV. *Ibid., August, 1874.*

V. *Ibid., November, 1874.*

VI. *Ibid., April and May, 1875.*

VII. (*posthumously*) *Illustrated London News, Summer Number, 1896.*

VIII. *Cornhill Magazine, May, 1876.*

IX. (*posthumously*) *The Studio, Winter Number, 1896.*

Nos. I. *and* II. *are printed from the Author's MSS. for the first time.*

NOTES AND ESSAYS
CHIEFLY OF THE ROAD

I

A RETROSPECT

(A Fragment : written at Dunoon, 1870)

IF there is anything that delights me in Hazlitt, beyond the charm of style and the unconscious portrait
of a vain and powerful spirit which his works present,
it is the loving and tender way in which he returns
again to the memory of the past.   These little recollections of bygone happiness were too much a part of the
man to be carelessly or poorly told.   The imaginary
landscapes and visions of the most ecstatic dreamer can
never rival such recollections, told simply perhaps, but
still told (as they could not fail to be) with precision,
delicacy, and evident delight.   They are too much
loved by the author not to be palated by the reader.
But beyond the mere felicity of pencil, the nature of
the piece could never fail to move my heart.   When I
read his essay " On the Past and Future," every word
seemed to be something I had said myself.   I could
have thought he had been eavesdropping at the door
of my heart, so entire was the coincidence between his

writing and my thought. It is a sign perhaps of a somewhat vain disposition. The future is nothing; but the past is myself, my own history, the seed of my present thoughts, the mould of my present disposition. It is not in vain that I return to the nothings of my childhood; for every one of them has left some stamp upon me or put some fetter on my boasted free-will. In the past is my present fate; and in the past also is my real life. It is not the past only, but the past that has been many years in that tense. The doings and actions of last year are as uninteresting and vague to me as the blank gulf of the future, the *tabula rasa* that may never be anything else. I remember a confused hotch-potch of unconnected events, a "chaos without form, and void"; but nothing salient or striking rises from the dead level of "flat, stale, and unprofitable" generality. When we are looking at a landscape we think ourselves pleased; but it is only when it comes back upon us by the fire o' nights that we can disentangle the main charm from the thick of particulars. It is just so with what is lately past. It is too much loaded with detail to be distinct; and the canvas is too large for the eye to encompass. But this is no more the case when our recollections have been strained long enough through the hour-glass of time; when they have been the burthen of so much thought, the charm and comfort of so many a vigil. All that is worthless has been sieved and sifted out of them. Nothing remains but the brightest lights and the darkest shadows. When we see a mountain country near at hand, the spurs and haunches crowd up in eager rivalry, and the whole range seems to have shrugged its shoulders to its ears, till we cannot tell the higher from the lower: but when we are far off, these lesser prominences are melted back into the bosom of the rest, or have set behind the round horizon of the plain, and the highest peaks stand forth in lone and sovereign dignity against the sky. It is just the same with our recollections. We require to draw back and shade our eyes before the picture dawns upon us in full breadth and outline. Late years are still in limbo to us; but the more distant past is all that we possess in life, the corn already harvested and stored for ever in the grange of memory. The doings of to-day at some future time will gain the required offing; I shall learn to love the things of my adolescence, as Hazlitt loved them, and as I love already the recollections of my childhood. They will gather interest with every year. They will ripen in forgotten corners of my memory; and some day I shall waken and find them vested with new glory and new pleasantness.

It is for stirring the chords of memory, then, that I love Hazlitt's essays, and for the same reason (I remember) he himself threw in his allegiance to Rousseau, saying of him, what was so true of his own writings: "He seems to gather up the past moments of his being like drops of honey-dew to distil some precious liquor from them; his alternate pleasures and pains are the bead-roll that he tells over and piously worships; he makes a rosary of the flowers of hope and fancy that strewed his earliest years." How true are these words when applied to himself! and how much I thank him that it was so! All my childhood is a golden age to me. I have no recollection of bad weather. Except one or two storms where grandeur had impressed itself on my mind, the whole time seems steeped in sunshine. "*Et ego in Arcadia vixi*" would be no empty boast upon my grave. If I desire to live long, it is that I may have the more to look back upon. Even to one, like the unhappy Duchess,

> " Acquainted with sad misery
> As the tamed galley-slave is with his oar,"

and seeing over the night of troubles no " lily-wristed morn" of hope appear, a retrospect of even chequered and doubtful happiness in the past may sweeten the bitterness of present tears. And here I may be excused if I quote a passage from an unpublished drama (the unpublished is perennial, I fancy) which the author believed was not all devoid of the flavour of our elder dramatists. However this may be, it expresses better than I could some further thoughts on this same subject. The heroine is taken by a minister to the grave, where already some have been recently buried, and where her sister's lover is destined to rejoin them on the following day.[1]

. . . .

What led me to the consideration of this subject, and what has made me take up my pen to-night, is the rather strange coincidence of two very different accidents—a prophecy of my future and a return into my past. No later than yesterday, seated in the coffee-room here, there came into the tap of the hotel a poor mad Highland woman. The noise of her strained, thin voice brought me out to see her. I could conceive that she

[1] The quotation here promised from one of the Author's own early dramatic efforts (a tragedy of Semiramis) is not supplied in the MS. —[ED.]

had been pretty once, but that was many years ago. She was now withered and fallen-looking. Her hair was thin and straggling, her dress poor and scanty. Her moods changed as rapidly as a weather-cock before a thunder-storm. One moment she said her "mutch" was the only thing that gave her comfort, and the next she slackened the strings and let it back upon her neck, in a passion at it for making her too hot. Her talk was a wild, somewhat weird, farrago of utterly meaningless balderdash, mere inarticulate gabble, snatches of old Jacobite ballads and exaggerated phrases from the drama, to which she suited equally exaggerated action. She "babbled of green fields" and Highland glens; she prophesied "the drawing of the claymore," with a lofty disregard of cause or common-sense; and she broke out suddenly, with uplifted hands and eyes, into ecstatic "Heaven bless hims!" and "Heaven forgive hims!" She had been a camp-follower in her younger days, and she was never tired of expatiating on the gallantry, the fame, and the beauty of the 42nd Highlanders. Her patriotism knew no bounds, and her prolixity was much on the same scale. This Witch of Endor offered to tell my fortune, with much dignity and proper oracular enunciation. But on my holding forth my hand a somewhat ludicrous incident occurred. "Na, na," she said; "wait till I have a draw of my pipe." Down she sat in the corner, puffing vigorously and regaling the lady behind the counter with conversation more remarkable for stinging satire than prophetic dignity. The person in question had "mair weeg than hair on her head" (did not the chignon plead guilty at these words?)—"wad be better if she had less tongue"—and would come at last to the grave, a goal which, in a few words, she invested with "warning circumstance" enough to make a Stoic shudder. Suddenly, in the midst of this, she rose up and beckoned me to approach. The oracles of my Highland sorceress had no claim to consideration except in the matter of obscurity. In "question hard and sentence intricate" she beat the priests of Delphi; in bold, unvarnished falsity (as regards the past) even spirit-rapping was a child to her. All that I could gather may be thus summed up shortly: that I was to visit America, that I was to be very happy, and that I was to be much upon the sea, predictions which, in consideration of an uneasy stomach, I can scarcely think agreeable with one another. Two incidents alone relieved the dead level of idiocy and incomprehensible gabble. The first was the comical announcement that "when I drew fish to the Marquis of Bute, I should take care of my sweetheart," from which I deduce the fact that at some period of my life I shall drive a fishmonger's cart. The second, in the middle of such nonsense, had a touch of the tragic. She suddenly looked at me with an eager glance, and dropped my hand, saying, in what were tones of misery or a very good affectation of them, "Black eyes!" A moment after she was at work again. It is as well to mention that I have not black eyes.[1]

This incident, strangely blended of the pathetic and

[1] "The old pythoness was right," adds the Author in a note appended to his MS. in 1887; "I have been happy: I did go to America (am even going again—unless——): and I have been twice and once upon the deep." The seafaring part of the prophecy remained to be fulfilled on a far more extended scale in his Pacific voyages of 1888–90.—[ED.]

the ludicrous, set my mind at work upon the future; but I could find little interest in the study. Even the predictions of my sibyl failed to allure me, nor could life's prospect charm and detain my attention like its retrospect.

Not far from Dunoon is Rosemore, a house in which I had spent a week or so in my very distant childhood, how distant I have no idea; and one may easily conceive how I looked forward to revisiting this place and so renewing contact with my former self. I was under necessity to be early up, and under necessity also, in the teeth of a bitter spring north-easter, to clothe myself warmly on the morning of my long-promised excursion. The day was as bright as it was cold. Vast irregular masses of white and purple cumulus drifted rapidly over the sky. The great hills, brown with the bloomless heather, were here and there buried in blue shadows, and streaked here and there with sharp stripes of sun. The new-fired larches were green in the glens; and " pale primroses " hid themselves in mossy hollows and under hawthorn roots. All these things were new to me; for I had noticed none of these beauties in my younger days, neither the larch woods, nor the winding road edged in between field and flood, nor the broad, ruffled bosom of the hill-surrounded loch. It was, above all, the height of these hills that astonished me. I remember the existence of hills, certainly, but the picture in my memory was low, featureless, and uninteresting. They seemed to have kept pace with me in my growth, but to a gigantic scale; and the villas that I remembered as half-way up the slope seemed to have been left behind like myself, and now only ringed their mighty feet, white among the newly kindled woods. As I felt myself on the road at last that I had been dreaming of for these many days before, a perfect intoxication of joy took hold upon me; and I was so pleased at my own happiness that I could let none past me till I had taken them into my confidence. I asked my way from every one, and took good care to let them all know, before they left me, what my object was, and how many years had elapsed since my last visit. I wonder what the good folk thought of me and my communications.

At last, however, after much inquiry, I arrive at the place, make my peace with the gardener, and enter. My disillusion dates from the opening of the garden door. I repine, I find a reluctation of spirit against believing that this is the place. What, is this kailyard that inexhaustible paradise of a garden in which M—— and I found " elbow-room," and expatiated together without sensible constraint ? Is that little tufted slope the huge and perilous green bank down which I counted it a feat, and the gardener a sin, to run ? Are these two squares of stone, some two feet high, the pedestals on which I walked with such a penetrating sense of dizzy elevation, and which I had expected to find on a level with my eyes ? Ay, the place is no more like what I expected than this bleak April day is like the glorious September with which it is incorporated in my memory. I look at the gardener, disappointment in my face, and tell him that the place seems sorrily shrunken from the high estate that it had held in my remembrance, and he returns, with quiet laughter, by asking me how long it is since I was there. I tell him, and he remembers me. Ah! I say, I was a great nuisance, I believe. But no, my good gardener will plead guilty to having kept no record of my evil-doings, and I find myself much softened towards the place and willing to take a kinder view and pardon its shortcomings for the sake of the gardener and his pretended recollection of myself. And it is just at this stage (to complete my re-establishment) that I see a little boy—the gardener's grandchild —just about the same age and the same height that I must have been in the days when I was here last. My first feeling is one of almost anger, to see him playing on the gravel where I had played before, as if he had usurped something of my identity; but next moment I feel a softening and a sort of rising and qualm of the throat, accompanied by a pricking heat in the eyeballs. I hastily join conversation with the child, and inwardly felicitate myself that the gardener is opportunely gone for the key of the house. But the child is a sort of homily to me. He is perfectly quiet and resigned, an unconscious hermit. I ask him jocularly if he gets as much abused as I used to do for running down the bank; but the child's perfect seriousness of answer staggers me—"O no, grandpapa does n't allow it—why should he?" I feel caught: I stand abashed at the reproof: I must not expose my child'shness again to this youthful disciplinarian, and so I ask him very stately what he is going to be—a good serious practical question, out of delicacy for his parts. He answers that he is going to be a missionary to China, and tells me how a missionary once took him on his knee and told him about missionary work, and asked him if he, too, would not like to become one, to which the child had simply answered in the affirmative. The child is altogether so different from what I have been, is so absolutely complementary to what I now am, that I turn away not a little abashed from the conversation, for there is always something painful in sudden contact with the good qualities that we do not possess. Just then the grandfather returns; and I go with him to the summer-house, where I used to learn my Catechism, to the wall which M—— and I thought it no small exploit to walk upon, and all the other places that I remembered.

In fine, the matter being ended, I turn and go my way home to the hotel, where, in the cold afternoon, I write these notes with the table and chair drawn as near the fire as the rug and the French polish will permit.

One other thing I may as well make a note of, and that is how there arises that strange contradiction of the hills being higher than I had expected, and everything near at hand being so ridiculously smaller. This is a question I think easily answered: the very terms of the problem suggest the solution. To everything near at hand I applied my own stature, as a sort of natural unit of measurement, so that I had no actual image of their dimensions but their ratio to myself; so, of course, as one term of the proportion changed, the other changed likewise, and as my own height increased my notion of things near at hand became equally expanded. But the hills, mark you, were out of my reach: I could not apply myself to them: I had an actual, instead of a proportional eidolon of their magnitude; so that, of course (my eye being larger and flatter nowadays, and so the image presented to me then being in sober earnest smaller than the image presented to me now), I found

the hills nearly as much too great as I had found the
other things too small.

[*Added the next morning.*]—He who indulges habitu-
ally in the intoxicating pleasures of imagination, for the
very reason that he reaps a greater pleasure than others,
must resign himself to a keener pain, a more intolerable
and utter prostration. It is quite possible, and even
comparatively easy, so to enfold oneself in pleasant
fancies that the realities of life may seem but as the
white snow-shower in the street, that only gives a relish to the swept hearth and lively fire within. By such
means I have forgotten hunger, I have sometimes eased
pain, and I have invariably changed into the most pleasant hours of the day those very vacant and idle seasons
which would otherwise have hung most heavily upon
my hand. But all this is attained by the undue prominence of purely imaginative joys, and consequently the
weakening and almost the destruction of reality. This
is buying at too great a price. There are seasons when
the imagination becomes somehow tranced and sur-
feited, as it is with me this morning; and then upon what
can we fall back? The very faculty that we have fostered and trusted has failed us in the hour of trial; and
we have so blunted and enfeebled our appetite for the
others that they are subjectively dead to us. It is just
as though a farmer should plant all his fields in potatoes,
instead of varying them with grain and pasture; and so,
when the disease comes, lose all his harvest, while his
neighbours, perhaps, may balance the profit and the loss.
Do not suppose that I am exaggerating when I talk
about all pleasures seeming stale. To me, at least, the

edge of almost everything is put on by imagination; and even nature, in these days when the fancy is drugged and useless, wants half the charm it has in better moments. I can no longer see satyrs in the thicket, or picture a highwayman riding down the lane. The fiat of indifference has gone forth: I am vacant, unprofitable: a leaf on a river with no volition and no aim: a mental drunkard the morning after an intellectual debauch. Yes, I have a more subtle opium in my own mind than any apothecary's drug; but it has a sting of its own, and leaves me as flat and helpless as does the other.

COCKERMOUTH AND KESWICK

(*A Fragment : 1871*)

VERY much as a painter half closes his eyes so that some salient unity may disengage itself from among the crowd of details, and what he sees may thus form itself into a whole; very much on the same principle, I may say, I allow a considerable lapse of time to intervene between any of my little journeyings and the attempt to chronicle them. I cannot describe a thing that is before me at the moment, or that has been before me only a very little while before; I must allow my recollections to get thoroughly strained free from all chaff till nothing be except the pure gold; allow my memory to choose out what is truly memorable by a process of natural selection; and I piously believe that in this way I ensure the Survival of the Fittest. If I make notes for future use, or if I am obliged to write letters during the course of my little excursion, I so interfere with the process that I can never again find out what is worthy of being preserved, or what should be given in full length, what in torso, or what merely in profile. This process of incubation may be unreasonably prolonged; and I am somewhat afraid that I have made this mistake with the present journey. Like a bad daguerreotype, great part of it has been entirely lost; I can tell you nothing about the beginning and nothing about the end; but the doings of some fifty or sixty hours about the middle remain quite distinct and definite, like a little patch of sunshine on a long, shadowy plain, or the one spot on an old picture that has been restored by the dexterous hand of the cleaner. I remember a tale of an old Scots minister, called upon suddenly to preach, who had hastily snatched an old sermon out of his study and found himself in the pulpit before he noticed that the rats had been making free with his manuscript and eaten the first two or three pages away; he gravely explained to the congregation how he found himself situated; "And now," said he, "let us just begin where the rats have left off." I must follow the divine's example, and take up the thread of my discourse where it first distinctly issues from the limbo of forgetfulness.

COCKERMOUTH

I was lighting my pipe as I stepped out of the inn at Cockermouth, and did not raise my head until I was fairly in the street. When I did so, it flashed upon me that I was in England; the evening sunlight lit up English houses, English faces, an English conformation of street,—as it were, an English atmosphere blew against my face. There is nothing perhaps more puzzling (if one thing in sociology can ever really be more unaccountable than another) than the great gulf that is set between England and Scotland—a gulf so easy in appearance, in reality so difficult to traverse. Here are two people almost identical in blood; pent up together on one small island, so that their intercourse (one would have thought) must be as close as that of prisoners who shared one cell of the Bastille; the same in language and religion; and yet a few years of quarrelsome isolation —a mere forenoon's tiff, as one may call it, in comparison with the great historical cycles—have so separated their thoughts and ways that not unions, not mutual dangers, nor steamers, nor railways, nor all the king's horses and all the king's men, seem able to obliterate the broad distinction. In the trituration of another century or so the corners may disappear; but in the meantime, in the year of grace 1871, I was as much in a new country as if I had been walking out of the Hotel St. Antoine at Antwerp.

I felt a little thrill of pleasure at my heart as I realised the change, and strolled away up the street with my hands behind my back, noting in a dull, sensual way how foreign, and yet how friendly, were the slopes of the gables and the colour of the tiles, and even the demeanour and voices of the gossips round about me.

Wandering in this aimless humour, I turned up a lane and found myself following the course of the bright little river. I passed first one and then another, then a third, several couples out love-making in the spring evening; and a consequent feeling of loneliness was beginning to grow upon me, when I came to a dam across the river, and a mill—a great, gaunt promontory of building,—half on dry ground and half arched over the stream. The road here drew in its shoulders, and crept through between the landward extremity of the mill and a little garden enclosure, with a small house

73

and a large sign-board within its privet hedge. I was pleased to fancy this an inn, and drew little etchings in fancy of a sanded parlour, and three-cornered spittoons, and a society of parochial gossips seated within over their churchwardens; but as I drew near, the board displayed its superscription, and I could read the name of Smethurst, and the designation of "Canadian Felt Hat Manufacturers." There was no more hope of evening fellowship, and I could only stroll on by the river-side, under the trees. The water was dappled with slanting sunshine, and dusted all over with a little mist of flying insects. There were some amorous ducks, also, whose love-making reminded me of what I had seen a little farther down. But the road grew sad, and I grew weary; and as I was perpetually haunted with the terror of a return of the tic that had been playing such ruin in my head a week ago, I turned and went back to the inn, and supper, and my bed.

The next morning, at breakfast, I communicated to the smart waitress my intention of continuing down the coast and through Whitehaven to Furness, and, as I might have expected, I was instantly confronted by that last and most worrying form of interference, that chooses to introduce tradition and authority into the choice of a man's own pleasures. I can excuse a person combating my religious or philosophical heresies, because them I have deliberately accepted, and am ready to justify by present argument. But I do not seek to justify my pleasures. If I prefer tame scenery to grand, a little hot sunshine over lowland parks and woodlands to the war of the elements round the summit of Mont Blanc; or if I prefer a pipe of mild tobacco, and the company of one or two chosen companions, to a ball where I feel myself very hot, awkward, and weary, I merely state these preferences as facts, and do not seek to establish them as principles. This is not the general rule, however, and accordingly the waitress was shocked, as one might be at a heresy, to hear the route that I had sketched out for myself. Everybody who came to Cockermouth for pleasure, it appeared, went on to Keswick. It was in vain that I put up a little plea for the liberty of the subject; it was in vain that I said I should prefer to go to Whitehaven. I was told that there was "nothing to see there"—that weary, hackneyed, old falsehood; and at last, as the handmaiden began to look really concerned, I gave way, as men always do in such circumstances, and agreed that I was to leave for Keswick by a train in the early evening.

AN EVANGELIST

Cockermouth itself, on the same authority, was a place with "nothing to see"; nevertheless I saw a good deal, and retain a pleasant, vague picture of the town and all its surroundings. I might have dodged happily enough all day about the main street and up to the castle and in and out of byways, but the curious attraction that leads a person in a strange place to follow, day after day, the same round, and to make set habits for himself in a week or ten days, led me half unconsciously up the same road that I had gone the evening before. When I came up to the hat manufactory, Smethurst himself was standing in the garden gate. He was brushing one Canadian felt hat, and several others had

75

been put to await their turn one above the other on his own head, so that he looked something like the typical Jew old-clothesman. As I drew near, he came sidling out of the doorway to accost me, with so curious an expression on his face that I instinctively prepared myself to apologise for some unwitting trespass. His first question rather confirmed me in this belief, for it was whether or not he had seen me going up this way last night; and after having answered in the affirmative, I waited in some alarm for the rest of my indictment. But the good man's heart was full of peace; and he stood there brushing his hats and prattling on about fishing, and walking, and the pleasures of convalescence, in a bright shallow stream that kept me pleased and interested, I could scarcely say how. As he went on, he warmed to his subject, and laid his hats aside to go along the water-side and show me where the large trout commonly lay, underneath an overhanging bank; and he was much disappointed, for my sake, that there were none visible just then. Then he wandered off on to another tack, and stood a great while out in the middle of a meadow in the hot sunshine, trying to make out that he had known me before, or, if not me, some friend of mine, merely, I believe, out of a desire that we should feel more friendly and at our ease with one another. At last he made a little speech to me, of which I wish I could recollect the very words, for they were so simple and unaffected that they put all the best writing and speaking to the blush; as it is, I can recall only the sense, and that perhaps imperfectly. He began by saying that he had little things in his past life that it gave him especial pleasure to recall; and that the faculty of receiving such sharp impressions had now died out in himself, but must at my age be still quite lively and active. Then he told me that he had a little raft afloat on the river above the dam which he was going to lend me, in order that I might be able to look back, in after years, upon having done so, and get great pleasure from the recollection. Now, I have a friend of my own who will forego present enjoyments and suffer much present inconvenience for the sake of manufacturing "a reminiscence" for himself; but there was something singularly refined in this pleasure that the hatmaker found in making reminiscences for others; surely no more simple or unselfish luxury can be imagined. After he had unmoored his little embarkation, and seen me safely shoved off into mid-stream, he ran away back to his hats with the air of a man who had only just recollected that he had anything to do.

I did not stay very long on the raft. It ought to have been very nice punting about there in the cool shade of the trees, or sitting moored to an overhanging root; but perhaps the very notion that I was bound in gratitude specially to enjoy my little cruise, and cherish its recollection, turned the whole thing from a pleasure into a duty. Be that as it may, there is no doubt that I soon wearied and came ashore again, and that it gives me more pleasure to recall the man himself and his simple, happy conversation, so full of gusto and sympathy, than anything possibly connected with his crank, insecure embarkation. In order to avoid seeing him, for I was not a little ashamed of myself for having failed to enjoy his treat sufficiently, I determined to continue up the river, and, at all prices, to find some other way back into the town in time for dinner. As I went, I was thinking of Smethurst with admiration; a look into that man's mind was like a retrospect over the smiling champaign of his past life, and very different from the Sinai-gorges up which one looks for a terrified moment into the dark souls of many good, many wise, and many prudent men. I cannot be very grateful to such men for their excellence, and wisdom, and prudence. I find myself facing as stoutly as I can a hard, combative existence, full of doubt, difficulties, defeats, disappointments, and dangers, quite a hard enough life without their dark countenances at my elbow, so that what I want is a happy-minded Smethurst placed here and there at ugly corners of my life's wayside, preaching his gospel of quiet and contentment.

ANOTHER

I was shortly to meet with an evangelist of another stamp. After I had forced my way through a gentleman's grounds, I came out on the highroad, and sat down to rest myself on a heap of stones at the top of a long hill, with Cockermouth lying snugly at the bottom. An Irish beggar-woman, with a beautiful little girl by her side, came up to ask for alms, and gradually fell to telling me the little tragedy of her life. Her own sister, she told me, had seduced her husband from her after many years of married life, and the pair had fled, leaving her destitute, with the little girl upon her hands. She seemed quite hopeful and cheery, and, though she was unaffectedly sorry for the loss of her husband's earnings, she made no pretence of despair at the loss of his affection; some day she would meet the fugitives, and the law would see her duly righted, and in the meantime the smallest contribution was gratefully received. While she was telling all this in the most matter-of-fact way, I had been noticing the approach of a tall man, with a high white hat and darkish clothes. He came up the hill at a rapid pace, and joined our little group with a sort of half-salutation. Turning at once to the woman, he asked her in a business-like way whether she had anything to do, whether she were a Catholic or a Protestant, whether she could read, and so forth; and then, after a few kind words and some sweeties to the child, he despatched the mother with some tracts about Biddy and the Priest, and the Orangeman's Bible. I was a little amused at his abrupt manner, for he was still a young man, and had somewhat the air of a navy officer; but he tackled me with great solemnity. I could make fun of what he said, for I do not think it was very wise; but the subject does not appear to me just now in a jesting light, so I shall only say that he related to me his own conversion, which had been effected (as is very often the case) through the agency of a gig accident, and that, after having examined me and diagnosed my case, he selected some suitable tracts from his repertory, gave them to me, and, bidding me God-speed, went on his way.

LAST OF SMETHURST

That evening I got into a third-class carriage on my way for Keswick, and was followed almost immediately by a burly man in brown clothes. This fellow-passenger was seemingly ill at ease, and kept continually putting his head out of the window, and asking the bystanders if they saw *him* coming. At last, when the train was already in motion, there was a commotion on the platform, and a way was left clear to our carriage door. *He* had arrived. In the hurry I could just see Smethurst, red and panting, thrust a couple of clay pipes into my companion's outstretched hand, and hear him crying his farewells after us as we slipped out of the station at an ever-accelerating pace. I said something about its being a close run, and the broad man, already engaged in filling one of the pipes, assented, and went on to tell me of his own stupidity in forgetting a necessary, and of how his friend had good-naturedly gone down-town at the last moment to supply the omission. I mentioned that I had seen Mr. Smethurst already, and that he had been very polite to me; and we fell into a discussion of the hatter's merits that lasted some time and left us quite good friends at its conclusion. The topic was productive of goodwill. We exchanged tobacco and talked about the season, and agreed at last that we should go to the same hotel at Keswick and sup in company. As he had some business in the town which would occupy him some hour or so, on our arrival I was to improve the time and go down to the lake, that I might see a glimpse of the promised wonders.

The night had fallen already when I reached the water-side, at a place where many pleasure-boats are moored and ready for hire; and as I went along a stony path, between wood and water, a strong wind blew in gusts from the far end of the lake. The sky was covered with flying scud; and, as this was ragged, there was quite a wild chase of shadow and moon-glimpse over the surface of the shuddering water. I had to hold my hat on, and was growing rather tired, and inclined to go back in disgust, when a little incident occurred to break the tedium. A sudden and violent squall of wind sundered the low underwood, and at the same time there came one of those brief discharges of moonlight, which leaped into the opening thus made, and showed me three girls in the prettiest flutter and disorder. It was as though they had sprung out of the ground. I accosted them very politely in my capacity of stranger, and requested to be told the names of all manner of hills and woods and places that I did not wish to know, and we stood together for a while and had an amusing little talk. The wind, too, made himself of the party, brought the colour into their faces, and gave them enough to do to repress their drapery; and one of them, amid much giggling, had to pirouette round and round upon her toes (as girls do) when some specially strong gust had got the advantage over her. They were just high enough up in the social order not to be afraid to speak to a gentleman; and just low enough to feel a little tremor, a nervous consciousness of wrong-doing—of stolen waters, that gave a considerable zest to our most innocent interview. They were as much discomposed and fluttered, indeed, as if I had been a wicked baron proposing to elope with the whole trio; but they showed no inclination to go away, and I had managed to get them off hills and waterfalls and on to more promising subjects, when a young man was descried coming along the path from the direction of Keswick. Now whether he was the young man of one of my friends, or the brother of one of them, or indeed the brother of all, I do not know; but they incontinently said that they must be going, and went away up the path with friendly salutations. I need not say that I found the lake and the moonlight rather dull after their departure, and speedily found my way back to potted herrings and whisky-and-water in the commercial room with my late fellow-traveller. In the smoking-room there was a tall dark man with a moustache, in an ulster coat, who had got the best place and was monopolising most of the talk; and, as I came in, a whisper came round to me from both sides, that this was the manager of a London theatre. The presence of such a man was a great event for Keswick, and I must own that the manager showed himself equal to his position. He had a large fat pocket-book, from which he produced poem after poem, written on the backs of letters or hotel-bills; and nothing could be more humorous than his recitation of these elegant extracts, except perhaps the anecdotes with which he varied the entertainment. Seeing, I suppose, something less countrified in my appearance than in most of the company, he singled me out to corroborate some statements as to the depravity and vice of the aristocracy, and when he went on to describe some gilded saloon experiences, I am proud to say that he honoured my sagacity with one little covert wink before a second time appealing to me for confirmation. The wink was not thrown away; I went in up to the elbows with the manager, until I think that some of the glory of that great man settled by reflection upon me, and that I was as noticeably the second person in the smoking-room as he was the first. For a young man, this was a position of some distinction, I think you will admit. . . .

ROADS

(1873)

No amateur will deny that he can find more pleasure in a single drawing, over which he can sit a whole quiet forenoon, and so gradually study himself into humour with the artist, than he can ever extract from the dazzle and accumulation of incongruous impressions that sends him, weary and stupefied, out of some famous picture-gallery. But what is thus admitted with regard to art is not extended to the (so-called) natural beauties: no amount of excess in sublime mountain outline or the graces of cultivated lowland can do anything, it is supposed, to weaken or degrade the palate. We are not at all sure, however, that moderation, and a regimen tolerably austere, even in scenery, are not healthful and strengthening to the taste; and that the best school for a lover of nature is not to be found in one of those countries where there is no stage effect—nothing salient or sudden,—but a quiet spirit of orderly and harmonious beauty pervades all the details, so that we can patiently attend to each of the little touches that strike in us, all of them together, the subdued note of the landscape. It is in scenery such as this that we find ourselves in

the right temper to seek out small sequestered loveliness. The constant recurrence of similar combinations
of colour and outline gradually forces upon us a sense
of how the harmony has been built up, and we become
familiar with something of nature's mannerism. This
is the true pleasure of your "rural voluptuary,"—not to
remain awe-stricken before a Mount Chimborazo; not
to sit deafened over the big drum in the orchestra, but
day by day to teach himself some new beauty—to experience some new vague and tranquil sensation that
has before evaded him. It is not the people who "have
pined and hungered after nature many a year, in the
great city pent," as Coleridge said in the poem that made
Charles Lamb so much ashamed of himself; it is not
those who make the greatest progress in this intimacy
with her, or who are most quick to see and have the
greatest gusto to enjoy. In this, as in everything else,
it is minute knowledge and long-continued loving industry that make the true dilettante. A man must have
thought much over scenery before he begins fully to
enjoy it. It is no youngling enthusiasm on hill-tops
that can possess itself of the last essence of beauty.
Probably most people's heads are growing bare before
they can see all in a landscape that they have the capa-
bility of seeing; and, even then, it will be only for one
little moment of consummation before the faculties are
again on the decline, and they that look out of the windows begin to be darkened and restrained in sight.
Thus the study of nature should be carried forward
thoroughly and with system. Every gratification should
be rolled long under the tongue, and we should be
always eager to analyse and compare, in order that we

may be able to give some plausible reason for our admirations. True, it is difficult to put even approximately into words the kind of feelings thus called into play. There is a dangerous vice inherent in any such intellectual refining upon vague sensation. The analysis of such satisfactions lends itself very readily to literary affectations; and we can all think of instances where it has shown itself apt to exercise a morbid influence, even upon an author's choice of language and the turn of his sentences. And yet there is much that makes the attempt attractive; for any expression, however imperfect, once given to a cherished feeling, seems a sort of legitimation of the pleasure we take in it. A common sentiment is one of those great goods that make life palatable and ever new. The knowledge that another has felt as we have felt, and seen things, even if they are little things, not much otherwise than we have seen them, will continue to the end to be one of life's choicest pleasures.

Let the reader, then, betake himself in the spirit we have recommended to some of the quieter kinds of English landscape. In those homely and placid agricultural districts, familiarity will bring into relief many things worthy of notice, and urge them pleasantly home to him by a sort of loving repetition; such as the wonderful life-giving speed of windmill sails above the stationary country; the occurrence and recurrence of the same church tower at the end of one long vista after another: and, conspicuous among these sources of quiet pleasure, the character and variety of the road itself, along which he takes his way. Not only near at hand, in the lithe contortions with which it adapts itself to the interchanges of level and slope, but far away also, when he sees a few hundred feet of it upheaved against a hill and shining in the afternoon sun, he will find it an object so changeful and enlivening that he can always pleasurably busy his mind about it. He may leave the riverside, or fall out of the way of villages, but the road he has always with him; and, in the true humour of observation, will find in that sufficient company. From its subtle windings and changes of level there arises a keen and continuous interest, that keeps the attention ever alert and cheerful. Every sensitive adjustment to the contour of the ground, every little dip and swerve, seems instinct with life and an exquisite sense of balance and beauty. The road rolls upon the easy slopes of the country, like a long ship in the hollows of the sea. The very margins of waste ground, as they trench a little farther on the beaten way, or recede again to the shelter of the hedge, have something of the same free delicacy of line—of the same swing and wilfulness. You might think for a whole summer's day (and not have thought it any nearer an end by evening) what concourse and succession of circumstances has produced the least of these deflections; and it is, perhaps, just in this that we should look for the secret of their interest. A foot-path across a meadow—in all its human waywardness and unaccountability, in all the *grata protervitas* of its varying direction—will always be more to us than a railroad well engineered through a difficult country.[1] No reasoned sequence is thrust upon our at-

[1] Compare Blake, in the *Marriage of Heaven and Hell* : "Improvement makes straight roads; but the crooked roads, without improvement, are roads of Genius."

tention: we seem to have slipped for one lawless little moment out of the iron rule of cause and effect; and so we revert at once to some of the pleasant old heresies of personification, always poetically orthodox, and attribute a sort of free-will, an active and spontaneous life, to the white riband of road that lengthens out, and bends, and cunningly adapts itself to the inequalities of the land before our eyes. We remember, as we write, some miles of fine wide highway laid out with conscious æsthetic artifice through a broken and richly cultivated tract of country. It is said that the engineer had Hogarth's line of beauty in his mind as he laid them down. And the result is striking. One splendid satisfying sweep passes with easy transition into another, and there is nothing to trouble or dislocate the strong continuousness of the main line of the road. And yet there is something wanting. There is here no saving imperfection, none of those secondary curves and little trepidations of direction that carry, in natural roads, our curiosity actively along with them. One feels at once that this road has not grown like a natural road, but has been laboriously made to pattern; and that, while a model may be academically correct in outline, it will always be inanimate and cold. The traveller is also aware of a sympathy of mood between himself and the road he travels. We have all seen ways that have wandered into heavy sand near the sea-coast, and trail wearily over the dunes like a trodden serpent: here we too must plod forward at a dull, laborious pace; and so a sympathy is preserved between our frame of mind and the expression of the relaxed, heavy curves of the roadway. Such a phenomenon, indeed, our reason

87

might perhaps resolve with a little trouble. We might reflect that the present road had been developed out of a track spontaneously followed by generations of primitive wayfarers; and might see in its expression a testimony that those generations had been affected at the same ground, one after another, in the same manner as we are affected to-day. Or we might carry the reflection further, and remind ourselves that where the air is invigorating and the ground firm under the traveller's foot, his eye is quick to take advantage of small undulations, and he will turn carelessly aside from the direct way wherever there is anything beautiful to examine or some promise of a wider view; so that even a bush of wild roses may permanently bias and deform the straight path over the meadow; whereas, where the soil is heavy, one is preoccupied with the labour of mere progression, and goes with a bowed head heavily and unobservantly forward. Reason, however, will not carry us the whole way; for the sentiment often recurs in situations where it is very hard to imagine any possible explanation; and indeed, if we drive briskly along a good, well-made road in an open vehicle, we shall experience this sympathy almost at its fullest. We feel the sharp settle of the springs at some curiously twisted corner; after a steep ascent, the fresh air dances in our faces as we rattle precipitately down the other side, and we find it difficult to avoid attributing something headlong, a sort of *abandon*, to the road itself.

The mere winding of the path is enough to enliven a long day's walk in even a commonplace or dreary country-side. Something that we have seen from miles back, upon an eminence, is so long hid from us, as we wan-

der through folded valleys or among woods, that on
expectation of seeing it again is sharpened into a violent
appetite, and as we draw nearer we impatiently quicken
our steps and turn every corner with a beating heart.
It is through these prolongations of expectancy, this
succession of one hope to another, that we live out long
seasons of pleasure in a few hours' walk. It is in following these capricious sinuosities that we learn, only bit
by bit and through one coquettish reticence after another,
much as we learn the heart of a friend, the whole loveliness of the country. This disposition always preserves
something new to be seen, and takes us, like a careful
cicerone, to many different points of distant view before
it allows us finally to approach the hoped-for destination.

In its connection with the traffic, and whole friendly
intercourse with the country, there is something very
pleasant in that succession of saunterers and brisk and
business-like passers-by, that peoples our ways and
helps to build up what Walt Whitman calls " the cheerful voice of the public road, the gay, fresh sentiment of
the road." But out of the great network of ways that
binds all life together from the hill-farm to the city,
there is something individual to most, and, on the
whole, nearly as much choice on the score of company
as on the score of beauty or easy travel. On some we
are never long without the sound of wheels, and folk
pass us by so thickly that we lose the sense of their
number. But on others, about little-frequented districts,
a meeting is an affair of moment; we have the sight far
off of some one coming towards us, the growing defi-
niteness of the person, and then the brief passage and
salutation, and the road left empty in front of us for

perhaps a great while to come. Such encounters have a wistful interest that can hardly be understood by the dweller in places more populous. We remember standing beside a countryman once, in the mouth of a quiet by-street in a city that was more than ordinarily crowded and bustling; he seemed stunned and bewildered by the continual passage of different faces; and after a long pause, during which he appeared to search for some suitable expression, he said timidly that there seemed to be a *great deal of meeting thereabouts.* The phrase is significant. It is the expression of town-life in the language of the long, solitary country highways. A meeting of one with one was what this man had been used to in the pastoral uplands from which he came; and the concourse of the streets was in his eyes only an extraordinary multiplication of such "meetings."

And now we come to that last and most subtle quality of all, to that sense of prospect, of outlook, that is brought so powerfully to our minds by a road. In real nature as well as in old landscapes, beneath that impartial daylight in which a whole variegated plain is plunged and saturated, the line of the road leads the eye forth with the vague sense of desire up to the green limit of the horizon. Travel is brought home to us, and we visit in spirit every grove and hamlet that tempts us in the distance. *Sehnsucht*—the passion for what is ever beyond—is livingly expressed in that white riband of possible travel that severs the uneven country; not a ploughman following his plough up the shining furrow, not the blue smoke of any cottage in a hollow, but is brought to us with a sense of nearness and attainability by this wavering line of junction. There is a passion-

ate paragraph in *Werther* that strikes the very key.
" When I came hither," he writes, " how the beautiful
valley invited me on every side, as I gazed down into it
from the hill-top!   There the wood—ah, that I might
mingle in its shadows! there the mountain summits—
ah, that I might look down from them over the broad
country! the interlinked hills! the secret valleys!   O,
to lose myself among their mysteries!   I hurried into
the midst, and came back without finding aught I hoped
for.   Alas! the distance is like the future.   A vast
whole lies in the twilight before our spirit; sight and
feeling alike plunge and lose themselves in the prospect,
and we yearn to surrender our whole being, and let it
be filled full with all the rapture of one single glorious
sensation; and alas! when we hasten to the fruition,
when *there* is changed to *here*, all is afterwards as it
was before, and we stand in our indigent and cramped
estate, and our soul thirsts after a still ebbing elixir."
It is to this wandering and uneasy spirit of anticipation
that roads minister.   Every little vista, every little
glimpse that we have of what lies before us, gives the
impatient imagination rein, so that it can outstrip the
body and already plunge into the shadow of the woods,
and overlook from the hill-top the plain beyond it, and
wander in the windings of the valleys that are still far
in front.   The road is already there—we shall not be
long behind.   It is as if we were marching with the
rear of a great army, and, from far before, heard the
acclamation of the people as the vanguard entered
some friendly and jubilant city.   Would not every man,
through all the long miles of march, feel as if he also
were within the gates ?

IV

(1874)

I WISH to direct the reader's attention to a certain quality in the movements of children when young, which is
somehow lovable in them, although it would be even
unpleasant in any grown person. Their movements
are not graceful, but they fall short of grace by something so sweetly humorous that we only admire them
the more. The imperfection is so pretty and pathetic,
and it gives so great a promise of something different
in the future, that it attracts us more than many forms
of beauty. They have something of the merit of a
rough sketch by a master, in which we pardon what is
wanting or excessive for the sake of the very bluntness
and directness of the thing. It gives us pleasure to see
the beginning of gracious impulses and the springs of
harmonious movement laid bare to us with innocent
simplicity.

One night some ladies formed a sort of impromptu
dancing-school in the drawing-room of an hotel in
France. One of the ladies led the ring, and I can recall
her as a model of accomplished, cultured movement.
Two little girls, about eight years old, were the pupils;

that is an age of great interest in girls, when natural grace comes to its consummation of justice and purity, with little admixture of that other grace of forethought and discipline that will shortly supersede it altogether. In these two, particularly, the rhythm was sometimes broken by an excess of energy, as though the pleasure of the music in their light bodies could endure no longer the restraint of regulated dance. So that, between these and the lady, there was not only some beginning of the very contrast I wish to insist upon, but matter enough to set one thinking a long while on the beauty of motion. I do not know that, here in England, we have any good opportunity of seeing what that is; the generation of British dancing men and women are certainly more remarkable for other qualities than for grace: they are, many of them, very conscientious artists, and give quite a serious regard to the technical parts of their performance; but the spectacle, somehow, is not often beautiful, and strikes no note of pleasure. If I had seen no more, therefore, this evening might have remained in my memory as a rare experience. But the best part of it was yet to come. For after the others had desisted, the musician still continued to play, and a little button between two and three years old came out into the cleared space and began to figure before us as the music prompted. I had an opportunity of seeing her, not on this night only, but on many subsequent nights; and the wonder and comical admiration she inspired was only deepened as time went on. She had an admirable musical ear; and each new melody, as it struck in her a new humour, suggested wonderful combinations and variations of movement. Now it would be a dance with which she would suit the music, now rather an appropriate pantomime, and now a mere string of disconnected attitudes. But whatever she did, she did it with the same verve and gusto. The spirit of the air seemed to have entered into her, and to possess her like a passion; and you could see her struggling to find expression for the beauty that was in her against the inefficacy of the dull, half-informed body. Though her footing was uneven, and her gestures often ludicrously helpless, still the spectacle was not merely amusing; and though subtle inspirations of movement miscarried in tottering travesty, you could still see that they had been inspirations; you could still see that she had set her heart on realising something just and beautiful, and that, by the discipline of these abortive efforts, she was making for herself in the future a quick, supple, and obedient body. It was grace in the making. She was not to be daunted by any merriment of people looking on critically; the music said something to her, and her whole spirit was intent on what the music said: she must carry out its suggestions, she must do her best to translate its language into that other dialect of the modulated body into which it can be translated most easily and fully.

Just the other day I was witness to a second scene, in which the motive was something similar; only this time with quite common children, and in the familiar neighbourhood of Hampstead. A little congregation had formed itself in the lane underneath my window, and was busy over a skipping-rope. There were two sisters, from seven to nine perhaps, with dark faces and dark hair, and slim, lithe little figures clad in lilac frocks. The elder of these two was mistress of the art of skipping. She was just and adroit in every movement; the rope passed over her black head and under her scarlet-stockinged legs with a precision and regularity that was like machinery; but there was nothing mechanical in the infinite variety and sweetness of her inclinations, and the spontaneous agile flexure of her lean waist and hips. There was one variation favourite with her, in which she crossed her hands before her with a motion not unlike that of weaving, which was admirably intricate and complete. And when the two took the rope together and whirled in and out with occasional interruptions, there was something Italian in the type of both—in the length of nose, in the slimness and accuracy of the shapes—and something gay and harmonious in the double movement, that added to the whole scene a Southern element, and took me over sea and land into distant and beautiful places. Nor was this impression lessened when the elder girl took in her arms a fair-haired baby, and while the others held the rope for her, turned and gyrated, and went in and out over it lightly, with a quiet regularity that seemed as if it might go on for ever. Somehow, incongruous as was the occupation, she reminded me of Italian Madonnas. And now, as before in the hotel drawing-room, the humorous element was to be introduced; only this time it was in broad farce. The funniest little girl, with a mottled complexion and a big, damaged nose, and looking for all the world like any dirty, broken-nosed doll in a nursery lumber-room, came forward to take her turn. While the others swung the rope for her as gently as it could be done—a mere mockery of move-

ment—and playfully taunted her timidity, she passaged
backwards and forwards in a pretty flutter of indecision,
putting up her shoulders and laughing with the embarrassed laughter of children by the water's edge, eager
to bathe and yet fearful.   There never was anything at
once so droll and so pathetic.   One did not know whether
to laugh or to cry.   And when at last she had made an
end of all her deprecations and drawings back, and summoned up heart enough to straddle over the rope, one
leg at a time, it was a sight to see her ruffle herself up
like a peacock and go away down the lane with her
damaged nose, seeming to think discretion the better
part of valour, and rather uneasy lest they should ask
her to repeat the exploit.   Much as I had enjoyed the
grace of the older girls, it was now just as it had been
before in France, and the clumsiness of the child seemed
to have a significance and a sort of beauty of its own,
quite above this grace of the others in power to affect
the heart.   I had looked on with a certain sense of
balance and completion at the silent, rapid, masterly
evolutions of the eldest; I had been pleased by these in
the way of satisfaction.   But when little broken-nose
began her pantomime of indecision I grew excited.
There was something quite fresh and poignant in the
delight I took in her imperfect movements.   I remember, for instance, that I moved my own shoulders, as
if to imitate her; really, I suppose, with an inarticulate
wish to help her out.

Now, there are many reasons why this gracelessness
of young children should be pretty and sympathetic to
us.   And, first, there is an interest as of battle.   It is
in travail and laughable *fiasco* that the young school

their bodies to beautiful expression, as they school their minds. We seem, in watching them, to divine antagonists pitted one against the other; and, as in other wars, so in this war of the intelligence against the unwilling body, we do not wish to see even the cause of progress triumph without some honourable toil; and we are so sure of the ultimate result, that it pleases us to linger in pathetic sympathy over these reverses of the early campaign, just as we do over the troubles that environ the heroine of a novel on her way to the happy ending. Again, people are very ready to disown the pleasure they take in a thing merely because it is big, as an Alp, or merely because it is little, as a little child; and yet this pleasure is surely as legitimate as another. There is much of it here; we have an irrational indulgence for small folk; we ask but little where there is so little to ask it of; we cannot overcome our astonishment that they should be able to move at all, and are interested in their movements somewhat as we are interested in the movements of a puppet. And again, there is a prolongation of expectancy when, as in these movements of children, we are kept continually on the very point of attainment and ever turned away and tantalised by some humorous imperfection. This is altogether absent in the secure and accomplished movements of persons more fully grown. The tight-rope walker does not walk so freely or so well as any one else can walk upon a good road; and yet we like to watch him for the mere sake of the difficulty; we like to see his vacillations; we like this last so much even, that I am told a really artistic tight-rope walker must feign to be troubled in his balance, even if he is not so really. And again,

we have in these baby efforts an assurance of sponta-
neity that we do not have often. We know this at least
certainly, that the child tries to dance for its own pleasure, and not for any by-end of ostentation and conformity. If we did not know it we should see it.
There is a sincerity, a directness, an impulsive truth,
about their free gestures that shows throughout all
imperfection, and it is to us as a reminiscence of primitive festivals and the Golden Age. Lastly, there is in
the sentiment much of a simple human compassion for
creatures more helpless than ourselves. One nearly
ready to die is pathetic; and so is one scarcely ready
to live. In view of their future, our heart is softened
to these clumsy little ones. They will be more adroit
when they are not so happy.

Unfortunately, then, this character that so much delights us is not one that can be preserved by any plastic
art. It turns, as we have seen, upon consideration not
really æsthetic. Art may deal with the slim freedom of
a few years later; but with this fettered impulse, with
these stammering motions, she is powerless to do more
than stereotype what is ungraceful, and, in the doing of
it, lose all pathos and humanity. So these humorous little
ones must go away into the limbo of beautiful things
that are not beautiful for art, there to wait a more perfect age before they sit for their portraits.

V

ON THE ENJOYMENT OF UNPLEASANT PLACES

(1874)

IT is a difficult matter to make the most of any given place, and we have much in our own power. Things looked at patiently from one side after another generally end by showing a side that is beautiful. A few months ago some words were said in the *Portfolio* as to an "austere regimen in scenery"; and such a discipline was then recommended as "healthful and strengthening to the taste." That is the text, so to speak, of the present essay. This discipline in scenery, it must be understood, is something more than a mere walk before breakfast to whet the appetite. For when we are put down in some unsightly neighbourhood, and especially if we have come to be more or less dependent on what we see, we must set ourselves to hunt out beautiful things with all the ardour and patience of a botanist after a rare plant. Day by day we perfect ourselves in the art of seeing nature more favourably. We learn to live with her, as people learn to live with fretful or violent spouses: to dwell lovingly on what is good, and shut our eyes against all that is bleak or inharmonious. We learn, also, to come to each place in the right spirit. The traveller, as Brantôme quaintly tells us, "*fait des discours en soi pour se soutenir en chemin*"; and into these discourses he weaves something out of all that he sees and suffers by the way; they take their tone greatly from the varying character of the scene; a sharp ascent brings different thoughts from a level road; and the man's fancies grow lighter as he comes out of the wood into a clearing. Nor does the scenery any more affect the thoughts than the thoughts affect the scenery. We see places through our humours as through differently coloured glasses. We are ourselves a term in the equation, a note of the chord, and make discord or harmony almost at will. There is no fear for the result, if we can but surrender ourselves sufficiently to the country that surrounds and follows us, so that we are ever thinking suitable thoughts or telling ourselves some suitable sort of story as we go. We become thus, in some sense, a centre of beauty; we are provocative of beauty, much as a gentle and sincere character is provocative of sincerity and gentleness in others. And even where there is no harmony to be elicited by the quickest and most obedient of spirits, we may still embellish a place with some attraction of romance. We may learn to go far afield for associations, and handle them lightly when we have found them. Sometimes an old print comes to our aid; I have seen many a spot lit up at once with picturesque imaginations, by a reminiscence of Callot, or Sadeler, or Paul Brill. Dick Turpin has been my lay figure for many an English lane. And I suppose the Trossachs would hardly be the Trossachs for most tourists if a man of admirable romantic instinct had not peopled it for them with harmonious figures, and brought them thither with minds rightly prepared for the impression. There is half the battle in this preparation. For instance: I have rarely been able to visit, in the proper spirit, the wild and inhospitable places of our own Highlands. I am happier where it is tame and fertile, and not readily pleased without trees. I understand that there are some phases of mental trouble that harmonise well with such surroundings, and that some persons, by the dispensing power of the imagination, can go back several centuries in spirit, and put themselves into sympathy with the hunted, houseless, unsociable way of life that was in its place upon these savage hills. Now, when I am sad, I like nature to charm me out of my sadness, like David before Saul; and the thought of these past ages strikes nothing in me but an unpleasant pity; so that I can never hit on the right humour for this sort of landscape, and lose much pleasure in consequence. Still, even here, if I were only let alone, and time enough were given, I should have all manner of pleasures, and take many clear and beautiful images away with me when I left. When we cannot think ourselves into sympathy with the great features of a country, we learn to ignore them, and put our head among the grass for flowers, or pore, for long times together, over the changeful current of a stream. We come down to the sermon in stones, when we are shut out from any poem in the spread landscape. We begin to peep and botanise, we take an interest in birds and insects, we find many things beautiful in miniature. The reader will recollect the little summer scene in *Wuthering Heights*—the one warm scene, perhaps, in all that powerful, miserable novel—and the great feature that is made therein by grasses and flowers and a little sunshine: this is in the spirit of which I now speak. And, lastly, we can go indoors; interiors are sometimes as beautiful, often more picturesque, than the shows of the open air, and they have that quality of shelter of which I shall presently have more to say.

With all this in mind, I have often been tempted to put forth the paradox that any place is good enough to live a life in, while it is only in a few, and those highly favoured, that we can pass a few hours agreeably. For, if we only stay long enough, we become at home in the neighbourhood. Reminiscences spring up, like flowers, about uninteresting corners. We forget to some degree the superior loveliness of other places, and fall into a tolerant and sympathetic spirit which is its own reward and justification. Looking back the other day on some recollections of my own, I was astonished to find how much I owed to such a residence; six weeks in one unpleasant country-side had done more, it seemed, to quicken and educate my sensibilities than many years in places that jumped more nearly with my inclination.

The country to which I refer was a level and treeless plateau, over which the winds cut like a whip. For miles on miles it was the same. A river, indeed, fell into the sea near the town where I resided; but the valley of the river was shallow and bald, for as far up as ever I had the heart to follow it. There were roads, certainly, but roads that had no beauty or interest; for, as there was no timber, and but little irregularity of surface, you saw your whole walk exposed to you from the beginning: there was nothing left to fancy, nothing to expect, nothing to see by the wayside, save here and there an unhomely-looking homestead, and here and there a solitary, spectacled stone-breaker; and you were only accompanied, as you went doggedly forward, by the gaunt telegraph-posts and the hum of the resonant wires in the keen sea-wind. To one who had learned to know their song in warm pleasant places by the Mediterranean, it seemed to taunt the country, and make it still bleaker by suggested contrast. Even the waste places by the side of the road were not, as Hawthorne liked to put it, "taken back to Nature" by any decent covering of vegetation. Wherever the land had the chance, it seemed to lie fallow. There is a certain tawny nudity of the South, bare sunburnt plains, coloured like a lion, and hills clothed only in the blue transparent air; but this was of another description— this was the nakedness of the North; the earth seemed to know that it was naked, and was ashamed and cold.

It seemed to be always blowing on that coast. Indeed, this had passed into the speech of the inhabitants, and they saluted each other when they met with "Breezy, breezy," instead of the customary "Fine day" of farther south. These continual winds were not like the harvest breeze, that just keeps an equable pressure against your face as you walk, and serves to set all the trees talking over your head, or bring round you the smell of the wet surface of the country after a shower. They were of the bitter, hard, persistent sort, that interferes with sight and respiration, and makes the eyes sore. Even such winds as these have their own merit in proper time and place. It is pleasant to see them brandish great masses of shadow. And what a power they have over the colour of the world! How they ruffle the solid woodlands in their passage, and make them shudder and whiten like a single willow! There is nothing more vertiginous than a wind like this among the woods, with all its sights and noises; and the effect gets between some painters and their sober eyesight, so that, even when the rest of their picture is calm, the foliage is coloured like foliage in a gale. There was nothing, however, of this sort to be noticed in a country where there were no trees and hardly any shadows, save the passive shadows of clouds or those of rigid houses and walls. But the wind was nevertheless an occasion of pleasure; for nowhere could you taste more fully the pleasure of a sudden lull, or a place of opportune shelter. The reader knows what I mean; he must remember how, when he has sat himself down behind a dyke on a hill-side, he delighted to hear the wind hiss vainly through the crannies at his back; how his body tingled all over with warmth, and it began to dawn upon him, with a sort of slow surprise, that the country was beautiful, the heather purple, and the far-away hills all marbled with sun and shadow. Wordsworth, in a beautiful passage of the "Prelude," has used this as a figure for the feeling struck in us by the quiet by-streets of London after the uproar of the great thoroughfares; and the comparison may be turned the other way with as good effect:

> "Meanwhile the roar continues, till at length,
>   Escaped as from an enemy, we turn
>   Abruptly into some sequester'd nook,
>   Still as a shelter'd place when winds blow loud!"

I remember meeting a man once, in a train, who told me of what must have been quite the most perfect instance of this pleasure of escape. He had gone up, one sunny, windy morning, to the top of a great cathedral somewhere abroad; I think it was Cologne Cathedral, the great unfinished marvel by the Rhine; and after a long while in dark stairways, he issued at last into the sunshine, on a platform high above the town. At that elevation it was quite still and warm; the gale was only in the lower strata of the air, and he had forgotten it in the quiet interior of the church and during his long ascent; and so you may judge of his surprise when, resting his arms on the sunlit balustrade and looking over into the *Place* far below him, he saw the good people holding on their hats and leaning hard against the wind as they walked. There is something, to my fancy, quite perfect in this little experience of my fellow-traveller's. The ways of men seem always very trivial to us when we find ourselves alone on a church-top, with the blue sky and a few tall pinnacles, and see far below us the steep roofs and foreshortened buttresses, and the silent activity of the city streets; but how much more must they not have seemed so to him as he stood, not only above other men's business, but above other men's climate, in a golden zone like Apollo's!

This was the sort of pleasure I found in the country of which I write. The pleasure was to be out of the wind, and to keep it in memory all the time, and hug oneself upon the shelter. And it was only by the sea that any such sheltered places were to be found. Between the black worm-eaten headlands there are little bights and havens, well screened from the wind and the commotion of the external sea, where the sand and weeds look up into the gazer's face from a depth of tranquil water, and the sea-birds, screaming and flicker-

ing from the ruined crags, alone disturb the silence and
the sunshine. One such place has impressed itself on
my memory beyond all others. On a rock by the
water's edge, old fighting men of the Norse breed had
planted a double castle; the two stood wall to wall like
semi-detached villas; and yet feud had run so high between their owners, that one, from out of a window,
shot the other as he stood in his own doorway. There is
something in the juxtaposition of these two enemies full
of tragic irony. It is grim to think of bearded men and
bitter women taking hateful counsel together about the
two hall-fires at night, when the sea boomed against the
foundations and the wild winter wind was loose over
the battlements. And in the study we may reconstruct
for ourselves some pale figure of what life then was.
Not so when we are there; when we are there such
thoughts come to us only to intensify a contrary impression, and association is turned against itself. I remember walking thither three afternoons in succession, my
eyes weary with being set against the wind, and how,
dropping suddenly over the edge of the down, I found
myself in a new world of warmth and shelter. The
wind, from which I had escaped, "as from an enemy,"
was seemingly quite local. It carried no clouds with it,
and came from such a quarter that it did not trouble
the sea within view. The two castles, black and ruin-
ous as the rocks about them, were still distinguishable
from these by something more insecure and fantastic in
the outline, something that the last storm had left im-
minent and the next would demolish entirely. It would
be difficult to render in words the sense of peace that
took possession of me on these three afternoons. It

was helped out, as I have said, by the contrast. The shore was battered and bemauled by previous tempests; I had the memory at heart of the insane strife of the pigmies who had erected these two castles and lived in them in mutual distrust and enmity, and knew I had only to put my head out of this little cup of shelter to find the hard wind blowing in my eyes; and yet there were the two great tracts of motionless blue air and peaceful sea looking on, unconcerned and apart, at the turmoil of the present moment and the memorials of the precarious past. There is ever something transitory and fretful in the impression of a high wind under a cloudless sky; it seems to have no root in the constitution of things; it must speedily begin to faint and wither away like a cut flower. And on those days the thought of the wind and the thought of human life came very near together in my mind. Our noisy years did indeed seem moments in the being of the eternal silence: and the wind, in the face of that great field of stationary blue, was as the wind of a butterfly's wing. The placidity of the sea was a thing likewise to be remembered. Shelley speaks of the sea as "hungering for calm," and in this place one learned to understand the phrase. Looking down into these green waters from the broken edge of the rock, or swimming leisurely in the sunshine, it seemed to me that they were enjoying their own tranquillity; and when now and again it was disturbed by a wind ripple on the surface, or the quick black passage of a fish far below, they settled back again (one could fancy) with relief.

On shore too, in the little nook of shelter, everything was so subdued and still that the least particular struck in me a pleasurable surprise. The desultory crackling of the whin-pods in the afternoon sun usurped the ear. The hot, sweet breath of the bank, that had been saturated all day long with sunshine, and now exhaled it into my face, was like the breath of a fellow-creature. I remember that I was haunted by two lines of French verse; in some dumb way they seemed to fit my surroundings and give expression to the contentment that was in me, and I kept repeating to myself—

> " Mon cœur est un luth suspendu,
> Sitôt qu'on le touche, il résonne."

I can give no reason why these lines came to me at this time; and for that very cause I repeat them here. For all I know, they may serve to complete the impression in the mind of the reader, as they were certainly a part of it for me.

And this happened to me in the place of all others where I liked least to stay. When I think of it I grow ashamed of my own ingratitude. "Out of the strong came forth sweetness." There, in the bleak and gusty North, I received, perhaps, my strongest impression of peace. I saw the sea to be great and calm; and the earth, in that little corner, was all alive and friendly to me. So, wherever a man is, he will find something to please and pacify him: in the town he will meet pleasant faces of men and women, and see beautiful flowers at a window, or hear a cage-bird singing at the corner of the gloomiest street; and for the country, there is no country without some amenity—let him only look for it in the right spirit, and he will surely find.

VI

AN AUTUMN EFFECT

(1875)

"Nous ne décrivons jamais mieux la nature que lorsque nous nous efforçons d'exprimer sobrement et simplement l'impression que nous en avons reçue."—M. ANDRÉ THEURIET, "L'Automne dans les bois," *Revue des Deux Mondes*, 1st Oct., 1874, p. 562.[1]

A COUNTRY rapidly passed through under favourable auspices may leave upon us a unity of impression that would only be disturbed and dissipated if we stayed longer. Clear vision goes with the quick foot. Things fall for us into a sort of natural perspective when we see them for a moment in going by; we generalise boldly and simply, and are gone before the sun is overcast, before the rain falls, before the season can steal like a dial-hand from his figure, before the lights and shadows, shifting round towards nightfall, can show

[1] I had nearly finished the transcription of the following pages, when I saw on a friend's table the number containing the piece from which this sentence is extracted, and, struck with a similarity of title, took it home with me and read it with indescribable satisfaction. I do not know whether I more envy M. Theuriet the pleasure of having written this delightful article, or the reader the pleasure, which I hope he has still before him, of reading it once and again, and lingering over the passages that please him most.

us the other side of things, and belie what they showed us in the morning. We expose our mind to the landscape (as we would expose the prepared plate in the camera) for the moment only during which the effect endures; and we are away before the effect can change. Hence we shall have in our memories a long scroll of continuous wayside pictures, all imbued already with the prevailing sentiment of the season, the weather, and the landscape, and certain to be unified more and more, as time goes on, by the unconscious processes of thought. So that we who have only looked at a country over our shoulder, so to speak, as we went by, will have a conception of it far more memorable and articulate than a man who has lived there all his life from a child upwards, and had his impression of to-day modified by that of to-morrow, and belied by that of the day after, till at length the stable characteristics of the country are all blotted out from him behind the confusion of variable effect.

I began my little pilgrimage in the most enviable of all humours: that in which a person, with a sufficiency of money and a knapsack, turns his back on a town and walks forward into a country of which he knows only by the vague report of others. Such an one has not surrendered his will and contracted for the next hundred miles, like a man on a railway. He may change his mind at every finger-post, and, where ways meet, follow vague preferences freely and go the low road or the high, choose the shadow or the sunshine, suffer himself to be tempted by the lane that turns immediately into the woods, or the broad road that lies open before him into the distance, and shows him the far-off spires of some city, or a range of mountain-tops, or a rim of sea, perhaps, along a low horizon. In short, he may gratify his every whim and fancy, without a pang of reproving conscience, or the least jostle to his self-respect. It is true, however, that most men do not possess the faculty of free action, the priceless gift of being able to live for the moment only; and as they begin to go forward on their journey, they will find that they have made for themselves new fetters. Slight projects they may have entertained for a moment, half in jest, become iron laws to them, they know not why. They will be led by the nose by these vague reports of which I spoke above; and the mere fact that their informant mentioned one village and not another will compel their footsteps with inexplicable power. And yet a little while, yet a few days of this fictitious liberty, and they will begin to hear imperious voices calling on them to return; and some passion, some duty, some worthy or unworthy expectation, will set its hand upon their shoulder and lead them back into the old paths. Once and again we have all made the experiment. We know the end of it right well. And yet if we make it for the hundredth time to-morrow, it will have the same charm as ever; our heart will beat and our eyes will be bright, as we leave the town behind us, and we shall feel once again (as we have felt so often before) that we are cutting ourselves loose for ever from our whole past life, with all its sins and follies and circumscriptions, and go forward as a new creature into a new world.

It was well, perhaps, that I had this first enthusiasm to encourage me up the long hill above High Wycombe; for the day was a bad day for walking at best, and now began to draw towards afternoon, dull, heavy, and life-less. A pall of grey cloud covered the sky, and its colour reacted on the colour of the landscape. Near at hand, indeed, the hedgerow trees were still fairly green, shot through with bright autumnal yellows, bright as sunshine. But a little way off, the solid bricks of wood-land that lay squarely on slope and hill-top were not green, but russet and grey, and ever less russet and more grey as they drew off into the distance. As they drew off into the distance, also, the woods seemed to mass themselves together, and lie thin and straight, like clouds, upon the limit of one's view. Not that this massing was complete, or gave the idea of any extent of forest, for every here and there the trees would break up and go down into a valley in open order, or stand in long Indian file along the horizon, tree after tree relieved, foolishly enough, against the sky. I say foolishly enough, although I have seen the effect employed clev-erly in art, and such long line of single trees thrown out against the customary sunset of a Japanese picture with a certain fantastic effect that was not to be despised; but this was over water and level land, where it did not jar, as here, with the soft contour of hills and valleys. The whole scene had an indefinable look of being painted, the colour was so abstract and correct, and there was something so sketchy and merely impressional about these distant single trees on the horizon that one was forced to think of it all as of a clever French land-scape. For it is rather in nature that we see resem-blance to art, than in art to nature; and we say a hundred times, "How like a picture!" for once that we say, "How like the truth!" The forms in which we learn to think of landscape are forms that we have got from painted canvas. Any man can see and understand a picture; it is reserved for the few to separate anything out of the confusion of nature, and see that distinctly and with intelligence.

The sun came out before I had been long on my way; and as I had got by that time to the top of the ascent, and was now treading a labyrinth of confined by-roads, my whole view brightened considerably in colour, for it was the distance only that was grey and cold, and the distance I could see no longer. Overhead there was a wonderful carolling of larks which seemed to follow me as I went. Indeed, during all the time I was in that country the larks did not desert me. The air was alive with them from High Wycombe to Tring; and as, day after day, their "shrill delight" fell upon me out of the vacant sky, they began to take such a prominence over other conditions, and form so integral a part of my conception of the country, that I could have baptised it "The Country of Larks." This, of course, might just as well have been in early spring; but everything else was deeply imbued with the sentiment of the later year. There was no stir of insects in the grass. The sunshine was more golden, and gave less heat than summer sunshine; and the shadows under the hedge were somewhat blue and misty. It was only in autumn that you could have seen the mingled green and yellow of the elm foliage, and the fallen leaves that lay about the road, and covered the surface of wayside pools so thickly that the sun was reflected only here and there from little joints and pinholes in that brown coat of proof; or that your ear would have been troubled, as you went forward, by the occasional report of fowling-pieces from all directions and all degrees of distance.

For a long time this dropping fire was the one sign of human activity that came to disturb me as I walked. The lanes were profoundly still. They would have been sad but for the sunshine and the singing of the larks. And as it was, there came over me at times a feeling of isolation that was not disagreeable, and yet was enough to make me quicken my steps eagerly when I saw some one before me on the road. This fellow-voyager proved to be no less a person than the parish constable. It had occurred to me that in a district which was so little populous and so well wooded, a criminal of any intelligence might play hide-and-seek with the authorities for months; and this idea was strengthened by the aspect of the portly constable as he walked by my side with deliberate dignity and turned-out toes. But a few minutes' converse set my heart at rest. These rural criminals are very tame birds, it appeared. If my informant did not immediately lay his hand on an offender, he was content to wait; some evening after nightfall there would come a tap at his door, and the outlaw, weary of outlawry, would give himself quietly up to undergo sentence, and resume his position in the life of the country-side. Married men caused him no disquietude whatever; he had them fast by the foot. Sooner or later they would come back to see their wives, a peeping neighbour would pass the word, and my portly constable would walk quietly over and take the bird sitting. And if there were a few who had no particular ties in the neighbourhood, and preferred to shift into another county when they fell into trouble, their departure moved the placid constable in no degree. He was of Dogberry's opinion; and if a man would not stand in the Prince's name, he took no note of him, but let him go, and thanked God he was rid of a knave. And surely the crime and the law were in admirable keeping; rustic constable was well met with rustic offender. The officer sitting at home over a bit of fire until the criminal came to visit him, and the criminal coming—it was a fair match. One felt as if this must have been the order in that delightful seaboard Bohemia where Florizel and Perdita courted in such sweet accents, and the Puritan sang psalms to hornpipes, and the four-and-twenty shearers danced with nosegays in their bosoms, and chanted their three songs apiece at the old shepherd's festival; and one could not help picturing to oneself what havoc among good people's purses, and tribulation for benignant constables, might be worked here by the arrival, over stile and footpath, of a new Autolycus.

Bidding good-morning to my fellow-traveller, I left the road and struck across country. It was rather a revelation to pass from between the hedgerows and find quite a bustle on the other side, a great coming and going of school-children upon by-paths, and, in every second field, lusty horses and stout country-folk a-ploughing. The way I followed took me through many fields thus occupied, and through many strips of plantation, and then over a little space of smooth turf, very pleasant to the feet, set with tall fir-trees and clamorous with rooks making ready for the winter, and so back again into the quiet road. I was now not far from the end of my day's journey. A few hundred yards farther, and, passing through a gap in the hedge, I began to go down hill through a pretty extensive tract of young beeches. I was soon in shadow myself, but the afternoon sun still coloured the upmost boughs of the wood, and made a fire over my head in the autumnal foliage. A little faint vapour lay among the slim tree-stems in the bottom of the hollow; and from farther up I heard from time to time an outburst of gross laughter, as though clowns were making merry in the bush. There was something about the atmosphere that brought all sights and sounds home to one with a singular purity, so that I felt as if my senses had been washed with water. After I had crossed the little zone of mist, the path began to remount the hill; and just as I, mounting along with it, had got back again, from the head downwards, into the thin golden sunshine, I saw in front of me a donkey tied to a tree. Now, I have a certain liking for donkeys, principally, I believe, because of the delightful things that Sterne has written of them. But this was not after the pattern of the ass at Lyons. He was of a white colour, that seemed to fit him rather for rare festal occasions than for constant drudgery. Besides, he was very small, and of the daintiest proportions you can imagine in a donkey. And so, sure enough, you had only to look at him to see he had never worked. There was something too roguish and wanton in his face, a look too like that of a schoolboy or a street Arab, to have survived much cudgelling. It was plain that these feet had kicked off sportive children oftener than they had plodded with a freight through miry lanes. He was altogether a fine-weather, holiday sort of donkey; and though he was just then somewhat solemnised and rueful, he still gave proof of the levity of his disposition by impudently wagging his ears at me as I drew near. I say he was somewhat solemnised just then; for, with the admirable instinct of all men and animals under restraint, he had so wound and wound the halter about the tree that he could go neither back nor forwards, nor so much as put down his head to browse. There he stood, poor rogue, part puzzled, part angry, part, I believe, amused. He had not given up hope, and dully revolved the problem in his head, giving ever and again another jerk at the few inches of free rope that still remained unwound. A humorous sort of sympathy for the creature took hold upon me. I went up, and, not without some trouble on my part, and much distrust and resistance on the part of Neddy, got him forced backwards until the whole length of the halter was set loose, and he was once more as free a donkey as I dared to make him. I was pleased (as people are) with this friendly action to a fellow-creature in tribulation, and glanced back over my shoulder to see how he was profiting by his freedom. The brute was looking after me; and no sooner did he catch my eye than he put up his long white face into the air, pulled an impudent mouth at me, and began to bray derisively. If ever any one person made a grimace at another, that donkey made a grimace at me. The hardened ingratitude of his behaviour, and the impertinence that inspired his whole face as he curled up his lip, and showed his teeth, and began to bray, so tickled me, and was so much in keeping with what I had imagined to myself about his character, that I could not find it in my heart to be angry, and burst into a peal of hearty laughter. This seemed to strike the ass as a repartee, so he brayed at me again by way of rejoinder; and we went on for a while, braying and laughing, until I began to grow a-weary of it, and, shouting a derisive farewell, turned to pursue my way. In so doing—it was like going suddenly into cold water —I found myself face to face with a prim little old maid. She was all in a flutter, the poor old dear! She had concluded beyond question that this must be a lunatic who stood laughing aloud at a white donkey in the placid beech-woods. I was sure, by her face, that she had already recommended her spirit most religiously to Heaven, and prepared herself for the worst. And so, to reassure her, I uncovered and besought her, after a very staid fashion, to put me on my way to Great Missenden. Her voice trembled a little, to be sure, but I think her mind was set at rest; and she told me, very explicitly, to follow the path until I came to the end of the wood, and then I should see the village below me in the bottom of the valley. And, with mutual courtesies, the little old maid and I went on our respective ways.

Nor had she misled me. Great Missenden was close at hand, as she had said, in the trough of a gentle valley, with many great elms about it. The smoke from its chimneys went up pleasantly in the afternoon sunshine. The sleepy hum of a threshing-machine filled the neighbouring fields and hung about the quaint street corners. A little above, the church sits well back on its haunches against the hill-side—an attitude for a church, you know, that makes it look as if it could be ever so much higher if it liked; and the trees grew about it thickly, so as to make a density of shade in the churchyard. A very quiet place it looks; and yet I saw many boards and posters about threatening dire punishment against those who broke the church windows or defaced the precinct, and offering rewards for the apprehension of those who had done the like already. It was fair-day in Great Missenden. There were three stalls set up, *sub jove*, for the sale of pastry and cheap toys; and a great number of holiday children thronged about the stalls, and noisily invaded every corner of the straggling village. They came round me by coveys, blowing simultaneously upon penny trumpets as though they imagined I should fall to pieces like the battlements of Jericho. I noticed one among them who could make a wheel of himself like a London boy, and seemingly enjoyed a grave pre-eminence upon the strength of the accomplishment. By-and-by, however, the trumpets began to weary me, and I went indoors, leaving the fair, I fancy, at its height.

Night had fallen before I ventured forth again. It was pitch-dark in the village street, and the darkness seemed only the greater for a light here and there in an uncurtained window or from an open door. Into one such window I was rude enough to peep, and saw within a charming *genre* picture. In a room, all white wainscot and crimson wall-paper, a perfect gem of colour after the black, empty darkness in which I had been groping, a pretty girl was telling a story, as well as I could make out, to an attentive child upon her knee, while an old woman sat placidly dozing over the fire. You may be sure I was not behindhand with a story for myself—a good old story after the manner of G. P. R. James and the village melodramas, with a wicked squire, and poachers, and an attorney, and a virtuous young man with a genius for mechanics, who should love, and protect, and ultimately marry the girl in the crimson room. Baudelaire has a few dainty sentences on the fancies that we are inspired with when we look through a window into other people's lives; and I think Dickens has somewhere enlarged on the same text. The subject, at least, is one that I am seldom weary of entertaining. I remember, night after night, at Brussels, watching a good family sup together, make merry, and retire to rest; and night after night I waited to see the candles lit, and the salad made, and the last salutations dutifully exchanged, without any abatement of interest. Night after night I found the scene rivet my attention and keep me awake in bed with all manner of quaint imaginations. Much of the pleasure of the *Arabian Nights* hinges upon this Asmodean interest; and we are not weary of lifting other people's roofs, and going about behind the scenes of life with the Caliph and the serviceable Giaffar. It is a salutary exercise, besides; it is salutary to get out of ourselves and see people living together in perfect unconsciousness of our existence, as they will live when we are gone. If tomorrow the blow falls, and the worst of our ill fears is realised, the girl will none the less tell stories to the child on her lap in the cottage at Great Missenden, nor the good Belgians light their candle, and mix their salad, and go orderly to bed.

The next morning was sunny overhead and damp underfoot, with a thrill in the air like a reminiscence of frost. I went up into the sloping garden behind the inn and smoked a pipe pleasantly enough, to the tune of

my landlady's lamentations over sundry cabbages and
cauliflowers that had been spoiled by caterpillars. She
had been so much pleased in the summer-time, she said,
to see the garden all hovered over by white butterflies.
And now, look at the end of it! She could nowise
reconcile this with her moral sense. And, indeed, unless these butterflies are created with a side-look to the
composition of improving apologues, it is not altogether
easy, even for people who have read Hegel and Dr.
M'Cosh, to decide intelligibly upon the issue raised.
Then I fell into a long and abstruse calculation with my
landlord; having for object to compare the distance
driven by him during eight years' service on the box of
the Wendover coach with the girth of the round world
itself. We tackled the question most conscientiously,
made all necessary allowance for Sundays and leap-
years, and were just coming to a triumphant conclusion
of our labours when we were stayed by a small lacuna
in my information. I did not know the circumference
of the earth. The landlord knew it, to be sure—plainly
he had made the same calculation twice and once before,—but he wanted confidence in his own figures, and
from the moment I showed myself so poor a second
seemed to lose all interest in the result.

Wendover (which was my next stage) lies in the
same valley with Great Missenden, but at the foot of it,
where the hills trend off on either hand like a coast-line,
and a great hemisphere of plain lies, like a sea, before
one. I went up a chalky road, until I had a good outlook over the place. The vale, as it opened out into the
plain, was shallow, and a little bare, perhaps, but full
of graceful convolutions. From the level to which I

have now attained the fields were exposed before me like a map, and I could see all that bustle of autumn field-work which had been hid from me yesterday behind the hedgerows, or shown to me only for a moment as I followed the footpath. Wendover lay well down in the midst, with mountains of foliage about it. The great plain stretched away to the northward, variegated near at hand with the quaint pattern of the fields, but growing ever more and more indistinct, until it became a mere hurly-burly of trees and bright crescents of river, and snatches of slanting road, and finally melted into the ambiguous cloud-land over the horizon. The sky was an opal-grey, touched here and there with blue, and with certain faint russets that looked as if they were reflections of the colour of the autumnal woods below. I could hear the ploughmen shouting to their horses, the uninterrupted carol of larks innumerable overhead, and, from a field where the shepherd was marshalling his flock, a sweet tumultuous tinkle of sheep-bells. All these noises came to me very thin and distinct in the clear air. There was a wonderful sentiment of distance and atmosphere about the day and the place.

I mounted the hill yet farther by a rough staircase of chalky footholds cut in the turf. The hills about Wendover and, as far as I could see, all the hills in Buckinghamshire, wear a sort of hood of beech plantation; but in this particular case the hood had been suffered to extend itself into something more like a cloak, and hung down about the shoulders of the hill in wide folds, instead of lying flatly along the summit. The trees grew so close, and their boughs were so matted together, that the whole wood looked as dense as a bush of heather.

The prevailing colour was a dull, smouldering red, touched here and there with vivid yellow. But the autumn had scarce advanced beyond the outworks; it was still almost summer in the heart of the wood; and as soon as I had scrambled through the hedge, I found myself in a dim green forest atmosphere under eaves of virgin foliage. In places where the wood had itself for a background and the trees were massed together thickly, the colour became intensified and almost gem-like: a perfect fire of green, that seemed none the less green for a few specks of autumn gold. None of the trees were of any considerable age or stature; but they grew well together, I have said; and as the road turned and wound among them, they fell into pleasant groupings and broke the light up pleasantly. Sometimes there would be a colonnade of slim, straight tree-stems with the light running down them as down the shafts of pillars, that looked as if it ought to lead to something, and led only to a corner of sombre and intricate jungle. Sometimes a spray of delicate foliage would be thrown out flat, the light lying flatly along the top of it, so that against a dark background it seemed almost luminous. There was a great hush over the thicket (for, indeed, it was more of a thicket than a wood); and the vague rumours that went among the tree-tops, and the occasional rustling of big birds or hares among the undergrowth, had in them a note of almost treacherous stealthiness, that put the imagination on its guard and made me walk warily on the russet carpeting of last year's leaves. The spirit of the place seemed to be all attention; the wood listened as I went, and held its breath to number my footfalls. One could not help feeling that there ought to be some reason for this still-ness: whether, as the bright old legend goes, Pan lay somewhere near in siesta, or whether, perhaps, the heaven was meditating rain, and the first drops would soon come pattering through the leaves. It was not unpleasant, in such an humour, to catch sight, ever and anon, of large spaces of the open plain. This happened only where the path lay much upon the slope, and there was a flaw in the solid leafy thatch of the wood at some distance below the level at which I chanced my-self to be walking; then, indeed, little scraps of fore-shortened distance, miniature fields, and Lilliputian houses and hedgerow trees would appear for a moment in the aperture, and grow larger and smaller, and change and melt one into another, as I continued to go forward, and so shift my point of view.

For ten minutes, perhaps, I had heard from some-where before me in the wood a strange, continuous noise, as of clucking, cooing, and gobbling, now and again interrupted by a harsh scream. As I advanced towards this noise, it began to grow lighter about me, and I caught sight, through the trees, of sundry gables and enclosure walls, and something like the tops of a rickyard. And sure enough, a rickyard it proved to be, and a neat little farm-steading, with the beech-woods growing almost to the door of it. Just before me, how-ever, as I came up the path, the trees drew back and let in a wide flood of daylight on to a circular lawn. It was here that the noises had their origin. More than a score of peacocks (there are altogether thirty at the farm), a proper contingent of peahens, and a great multitude that I could not number of more ordinary barn-door fowls, were all feeding together on this little open lawn among the beeches. They fed in a dense crowd, which swayed to and fro, and came hither and thither as by a sort of tide, and of which the surface was agitated like the surface of a sea as each bird guzzled his head along the ground after the scattered corn. The clucking, cooing noise that had led me thither was formed by the blending together of countless expressions of individual contentment into one collective expression of contentment, or general grace during meat. Every now and again a big peacock would separate himself from the mob and take a stately turn or two about the lawn, or perhaps mount for a moment upon the rail, and there shrilly publish to the world his satisfaction with himself and what he had to eat. It happened, for my sins, that none of these admirable birds had anything beyond the merest rudiment of a tail. Tails, it seemed, were out of season just then. But they had their necks for all that; and by their necks alone they do as much surpass all the other birds of our grey climate as they fall in quality of song below the blackbird or the lark. Surely the peacock, with its incomparable parade of glorious colour and the scrannel voice of it issuing forth, as in mockery, from its painted throat, must, like my landlady's butterflies at Great Missenden, have been invented by some skilful fabulist for the consolation and support of homely virtue: or rather, perhaps, by a fabulist not quite so skilful, who made points for the moment without having a studious enough eye to the complete effect; for I thought these melting greens and blues so beautiful that afternoon, that I would have given them my vote just then before the sweetest pipe in all the spring woods. For indeed there is no piece of colour of the same extent in nature, that will so flatter and satisfy the lust of a man's eyes; and to come upon so many of them, after these acres of stone-coloured heavens and russet woods, and grey-brown ploughlands and white roads, was like going three whole days' journey to the southward, or a month back into the summer.

I was sorry to leave *Peacock Farm*—for so the place is called, after the name of its splendid pensioners—and go forwards again in the quiet woods. It began to grow both damp and dusk under the beeches; and as the day declined the colour faded out of the foliage; and shadow, without form and void, took the place of all the fine tracery of leaves and delicate gradations of living green that had before accompanied my walk. I had been sorry to leave *Peacock Farm*, but I was not sorry to find myself once more in the open road, under a pale and somewhat troubled-looking evening sky, and put my best foot foremost for the inn at Wendover.

Wendover, in itself, is a straggling, purposeless sort of place. Everybody seems to have had his own opinion as to how the street should go; or rather, every now and then a man seems to have arisen with a new idea on the subject, and led away a little sect of neighbours to join in his heresy. It would have somewhat the look of an abortive watering-place, such as we may now see them here and there along the coast, but for the age of the houses, the comely quiet design of some of them, and the look of long habitation, of a life that is settled and rooted, and makes it worth while to train flowers about the windows, and otherwise shape the dwelling to the humour of the inhabitant. The church, which might perhaps have served as rallying-point for these loose houses, and pulled the township into something like intelligible unity, stands some distance off among great trees; but the inn (to take the public buildings in order of importance) is in what I understand to be the principal street: a pleasant old house, with bay-windows, and three peaked gables, and many swallows' nests plastered about the eaves.

The interior of the inn was answerable to the outside: indeed, I never saw any room much more to be admired than the low wainscoted parlour in which I spent the remainder of the evening. It was a short oblong in shape, save that the fireplace was built across one of the angles so as to cut it partially off, and the opposite angle was similarly truncated by a corner cupboard. The wainscot was white, and there was a Turkey carpet on the floor, so old that it might have been imported by Walter Shandy before he retired, worn almost through in some places, but in others making a good show of blues and oranges, none the less harmonious for being somewhat faded. The corner cupboard was agreeable in design; and there were just the right things upon the shelves—decanters and tumblers, and blue plates, and one red rose in a glass of water. The furniture was old-fashioned and stiff. Everything was in keeping, down to the ponderous leaden inkstand on the round table. And you may fancy how pleasant it looked, all flushed and flickered over by the light of a brisk companionable fire, and seen, in a strange, tilted sort of perspective, in the three compartments of the old mirror above the chimney. As I sat reading in the great armchair, I kept looking round with the tail of my eye at the quaint, bright picture that was about me, and could not help some pleasure and a certain childish pride in forming part of it. The book I read was about Italy in the early Renaissance, the pageantries and the light loves of princes, the passion of men for learning, and poetry, and art; but it was written, by good luck, after a solid, prosaic fashion, that suited the room infinitely more nearly than the matter; and the result was that I thought less, perhaps, of Lippo Lippi, or Lorenzo, or Politian, than of the good Englishman who had written in that volume what he knew of them, and taken so much pleasure in his solemn polysyllables.

I was not left without society. My landlord had a very pretty little daughter, whom we shall call Lizzie. If I had made any notes at the time, I might be able to tell you something definite of her appearance. But faces have a trick of growing more and more spiritualised and abstract in the memory, until nothing remains of them but a look, a haunting expression; just that secret quality in a face that is apt to slip out somehow under the cunningest painter's touch, and leave the portrait dead for the lack of it. And if it is hard to catch with the finest of camel's-hair pencils, you may think how hopeless it must be to pursue after it with clumsy words. If I say, for instance, that this look, which I remember as Lizzie, was something wistful that seemed partly to come of slyness and in part of simplicity, and that I am inclined to imagine it had something to do with the daintiest suspicion of a cast in one of her large eyes, I shall have said all that I can, and the reader will not be much advanced towards comprehension. I had struck up an acquaintance with this little damsel in the morning, and professed much interest in her dolls, and an impatient desire to see the large one which was kept locked away for great occasions. And so I had not been very long in the parlour before the door opened, and in came Miss Lizzie with two dolls tucked clumsily under her arm. She was followed by her brother John, a year or so younger than herself, not simply to play propriety at our interview, but to show his own two whips in emulation of his sister's dolls. I did my best to make myself agreeable to my visitors, showing much admiration for the dolls and dolls' dresses, and, with a very serious demeanour, asking many questions about their age and character. I do not think that Lizzie distrusted my sincerity, but it was evident that she was both bewildered and a little contemptuous. Although she was ready herself to treat her dolls as if they were alive, she seemed to think rather poorly of any grown person who could fall heartily into the spirit of the fiction. Sometimes she would look at me with gravity and a sort of disquietude, as though she really feared I must be out of my wits. Sometimes, as when I inquired too particularly into the question of their names, she laughed at me so long and heartily that I began to feel almost embarrassed. But when, in an evil moment, I asked to be allowed to kiss one of them, she could keep herself no longer to herself. Clambering down from the chair on which she sat perched to show me, Cornelia-like, her jewels, she ran straight out of the room and into the bar—it was just across the passage,—and I could hear her telling her mother in loud tones, but apparently more in sorrow than in merriment, that *the gentleman in the parlour wanted to kiss Dolly*. I fancy she was determined to save me from this humiliating action, even in spite of myself, for she never gave me the desired permission. She reminded me of an old dog I once knew, who would never suffer the master of the house to dance, out of an exaggerated sense of the dignity of that master's place and carriage.

After the young people were gone there was but one more incident ere I went to bed. I heard a party of children go up and down the dark street for a while, singing together sweetly. And the mystery of this little incident was so pleasant to me that I purposely refrained from asking who they were, and wherefore they went singing at so late an hour. One can rarely be in a pleasant place without meeting with some pleasant accident. I have a conviction that these children would not have gone singing before the inn unless the inn-parlour had been the delightful place it was. At least, if I had been in the customary public room of the modern hotel, with all its disproportions and discomforts, my ears would have been dull, and there would have been some ugly temper or other uppermost in my spirit, and so they would have wasted their songs upon an unworthy hearer.

Next morning I went along to visit the church. It is a long-backed red-and-white building, very much restored, and stands in a pleasant graveyard among those great trees of which I have spoken already. The sky was drowned in a mist. Now and again pulses of cold wind went about the enclosure, and set the branches busy overhead, and the dead leaves scurrying into the angles of the church buttresses. Now and again, also, I could hear the dull sudden fall of a chestnut among

the grass—the dog would bark before the rectory door
—or there would come a clinking of pails from the
stable-yard behind. But in spite of these occasional
interruptions—in spite, also, of the continuous autumn
twittering that filled the trees—the chief impression
somehow was one as of utter silence, insomuch that the
little greenish bell that peeped out of a window in the
tower disquieted me with a sense of some possible and
more inharmonious disturbance. The grass was wet,
as if with a hoar-frost that had just been melted. I do
not know that ever I saw a morning more autumnal. As
I went to and fro among the graves, I saw some flowers
set reverently before a recently erected tomb, and drawing near was almost startled to find they lay on the grave
of a man seventy-two years old when he died. We are
accustomed to strew flowers only over the young,
where love has been cut short untimely, and great
possibilities have been restrained by death. We strew
them there in token that these possibilities, in some
deeper sense, shall yet be realised, and the touch of our
dead loves remain with us and guide us to the end.
And yet there was more significance, perhaps, and perhaps a greater consolation, in this little nosegay on the
grave of one who had died old. We are apt to make so
much of the tragedy of death, and think so little of the
enduring tragedy of some men's lives, that we see more
to lament for in a life cut off in the midst of usefulness
and love, than in one that miserably survives all love and
usefulness, and goes about the world the phantom of
itself, without hope, or joy, or any consolation. These
flowers seemed not so much the token of love that survived death, as of something yet more beautiful—of love

that had lived a man's life out to an end with him, and been faithful and companionable, and not weary of loving, throughout all these years.

The morning cleared a little, and the sky was once more the old stone-coloured vault over the sallow meadows and the russet woods, as I set forth on a dog-cart from Wendover to Tring. The road lay for a good distance along the side of the hills, with the great plain below on one hand, and the beech-woods above on the other. The fields were busy with people ploughing and sowing; every here and there a jug of ale stood in the angle of the hedge, and I could see many a team wait smoking in the furrow as ploughman or sower stepped aside for a moment to take a draught. Over all the brown ploughlands, and under all the leafless hedgerows, there was a stout piece of labour abroad, and, as it were, a spirit of picnic. The horses smoked and the men laboured and shouted and drank in the sharp autumn morning; so that one had a strong effect of large, open-air existence. The fellow who drove me was something of a humourist; and his conversation was all in praise of an agricultural labourer's way of life. It was he who called my attention to these jugs of ale by the hedgerow; he could not sufficiently express the liberality of these men's wages; he told me how sharp an appetite was given by breaking up the earth in the morning air, whether with plough or spade, and cordially admired this provision of nature. He sang *O fortunatos agricolas!* indeed, in every possible key, and with many cunning inflections, till I began to wonder what was the use of such people as Mr. Arch, and to sing the same air myself in a more diffident manner.

Tring was reached, and then Tring railway-station; for the two are not very near, the good people of Tring having held the railway, of old days, in extreme apprehension, lest some day it should break loose in the town and work mischief. I had a last walk, among russet beeches as usual, and the air filled, as usual, with the carolling of larks; I heard shots fired in the distance, and saw, as a new sign of the fulfilled autumn, two horsemen exercising a pack of foxhounds. And then the train came and carried me back to London.

VII

A WINTER'S WALK IN CARRICK AND GALLOWAY

(A Fragment: 1876)

AT the famous bridge of Doon, Kyle, the central district of the shire of Ayr, marches with Carrick, the most southerly. On the Carrick side of the river rises a hill of somewhat gentle conformation, cleft with shallow dells, and sown here and there with farms and tufts of wood. Inland, it loses itself, joining, I suppose, the great herd of similar hills that occupies the centre of the Lowlands. Towards the sea, it swells out the coastline into a protuberance, like a bay-window in a plan, and is fortified against the surf behind bold crags. This hill is known as the Brown Hill of Carrick, or, more shortly, Brown Carrick.

It had snowed overnight. The fields were all sheeted up; they were tucked in among the snow, and their shape was modelled through the pliant counterpane, like children tucked in by a fond mother. The wind had made ripples and folds upon the surface, like what the sea, in quiet weather, leaves upon the sand. There was a frosty stifle in the air. An effusion of coppery light on the summit of Brown Carrick showed where the sun was trying to look through; but along the horizon clouds of cold fog had settled down, so that there was no distinction of sky and sea. Over the white shoulders of the headlands, or in the opening of bays, there was nothing but a great vacancy and blackness; and the road as it drew near the edge of the cliff seemed to skirt the shores of creation and void space.

The snow crunched underfoot, and at farms all the dogs broke out barking as they smelt a passer-by upon the road. I met a fine old fellow, who might have sat as the father in "The Cottar's Saturday Night," and who swore most heathenishly at a cow he was driving. And a little after I scraped acquaintance with a poor body tramping out to gather cockles. His face was wrinkled by exposure; it was broken up into flakes and channels, like mud beginning to dry, and weathered in two colours, an incongruous pink and grey. He had a faint air of being surprised—which, God knows, he might well be—that life had gone so ill with him. The shape of his trousers was in itself a jest, so strangely were they bagged and ravelled about his knees; and his coat was all bedaubed with clay as though he had lain in a rain-dub during the New Year's festivity. I will own I was not sorry to think he had had a merry New Year, and been young again for an evening; but I was sorry to see the mark still there. One could not expect such an old gentleman to be much of a dandy, or a great student of respectability in dress; but there might have been a wife at home, who had brushed out similar stains after fifty New Years, now become old, or a round-armed daughter, who would wish to have him neat, were it only out of self-respect and for the ploughman sweetheart when he looks round at night. Plainly, there was nothing of this in his life, and years and loneliness hung heavily on his old arms. He was seventy-six, he told me; and nobody would give a day's work to a man that age: they would think he could n't do it. "And, 'deed," he went on, with a sad little chuckle, "'deed, I doubt if I could." He said good-bye to me at a footpath, and crippled wearily off to his work. It will make your heart ache if you think of his old fingers groping in the snow.

He told me I was to turn down beside the school-house for Dunure. And so, when I found a lone house among the snow, and heard a babble of childish voices from within, I struck off into a steep road leading down-wards to the sea. Dunure lies close under the steep hill: a haven among the rocks, a breakwater in consummate disrepair, much apparatus for drying nets, and a score or so of fishers' houses. Hard by, a few shards of ruined castle overhang the sea, a few vaults, and one tall gable honeycombed with windows. The snow lay on the beach to the tide-mark. It was daubed on to the sills of the ruin; it roosted in the crannies of the rock like white sea-birds; even on outlying reefs there would be a little cock of snow, like a toy lighthouse. Everything was grey and white in a cold and dolorous sort of shepherd's plaid. In the profound silence, broken only by the noise of oars at sea, a horn was sounded twice; and I saw the postman, girt with two bags, pause a moment at the end of the clachan for letters. It is, perhaps, characteristic of Dunure that none were brought him.

The people at the public-house did not seem well pleased to see me, and though I would fain have stayed by the kitchen fire, sent me "ben the hoose" into the guest-room. This guest-room at Dunure was painted in quite æsthetic fashion. There are rooms in the same taste not a hundred miles from London, where persons of an extreme sensibility meet together without embarrassment. It was all in a fine dull bottle-green and black; a grave harmonious piece of colouring, with nothing, so far as coarser folk can judge, to hurt the better feelings of the most exquisite purist. A cherry-red half window-blind kept up an imaginary warmth in the cold room, and threw quite a glow on the floor. Twelve cockle-shells and a halfpenny china figure were ranged solemnly along the mantel-shelf. Even the spittoon was an original note, and instead of sawdust contained sea-shells. And as for the hearth-rug, it would merit an article to itself, and a coloured diagram to help the text. It was patchwork, but the patchwork of the poor: no glowing shreds of old brocade and Chinese silk, shaken together in the kaleidoscope of some tasteful housewife's fancy; but a work of art in its own way, and plainly a labour of love. The patches came exclusively from people's raiment. There was no colour more brilliant than a heather mixture; "My Johnnie's grey breeks," well polished over the oar on the boat's thwart, entered largely into its composition. And the spoils of an old black cloth coat, that had been many a Sunday to church, added something (save the mark!) of preciousness to the material.

While I was at luncheon four carters came in—long-limbed, muscular Ayrshire Scots, with lean, intelligent faces. Four quarts of stout were ordered; they kept filling the tumbler with the other hand as they drank;

and in less time than it takes me to write these words the four quarts were finished—another round was proposed, discussed, and negatived—and they were creaking out of the village with their carts.

The ruins drew you towards them. You never saw any place more desolate from a distance, nor one that less belied its promise near at hand. Some crows and gulls flew away croaking as I scrambled in. The snow had drifted into the vaults. The clachan dabbled with snow, the white hills, the black sky, the sea marked in the coves with faint circular wrinkles, the whole world, as it looked from a loophole in Dunure, was cold, wretched, and out-at-elbows. If you had been a wicked baron and compelled to stay there all the afternoon, you would have had a rare fit of remorse. How you would have heaped up the fire and gnawed your fingers! I think it would have come to homicide before the evening—if it were only for the pleasure of seeing something red! And the masters of Dunure, it is to be noticed, were remarkable of old for inhumanity. One of these vaults where the snow had drifted was that "black voute" where "Mr. Alane Stewart, Commendatour of Crossraguel," endured his fiery trials. On the 1st and 7th of September, 1570 (ill dates for Mr. Alan!), Gilbert, Earl of Cassilis, his chaplain, his baker, his cook, his pantryman, and another servant, bound the poor Commendator "betwix an iron chimlay and a fire," and there cruelly roasted him until he signed away his abbacy. It is one of the ugliest stories of an ugly period, but not, somehow, without such a flavour of the ridiculous as makes it hard to sympathise quite seriously with the victim. And it is consoling to remember that he got away at last, and kept his abbacy, and, over and above, had a pension from the Earl until he died.

Some way beyond Dunure a wide bay, of somewhat less unkindly aspect, opened out. Colzean plantations lay all along the steep shore, and there was a wooded hill towards the centre, where the trees made a sort of shadowy etching over the snow. The road went down and up, and past a blacksmith's cottage that made fine music in the valley. Three compatriots of Burns drove up to me in a cart. They were all drunk, and asked me jeeringly if this was the way to Dunure. I told them it was; and my answer was received with unfeigned merriment. One gentleman was so much tickled he nearly fell out of the cart; indeed, he was only saved by a companion, who either had not so fine a sense of humour or had drunken less.

"The toune of Mayboll," says the inimitable Abercrummie,[1] "stands upon an ascending ground from east to west, and lyes open to the south. It hath one principall street, with houses upon both sides, built of freestone; and it is beautifyed with the situation of two castles, one at each end of this street. That on the east belongs to the Erle of Cassilis. On the west end is a castle, which belonged sometime to the laird of Blairquan, which is now the tolbuith, and is adorned with a pyremide [conical roof], and a row of ballesters round it raised from the top of the staircase, into which they have mounted a fyne clock. There be four lanes which pass from the principall street; one is called the Black

[1] William Abercrombie. See *Fasti Ecclesiæ Scoticanæ*, under "Maybole" (Part iii.).

Vennel, which is steep, declining to the south-west, and leads to a lower street, which is far larger than the high chiefe street, and it runs from the Kirkland to the Well Trees, in which there have been many pretty buildings, belonging to the severall gentry of the countrey, who were wont to resort thither in winter, and divert themselves in converse together at their owne houses. It was once the principall street of the town; but many of these houses of the gentry having been decayed and ruined, it has lost much of its ancient beautie. Just opposite to this vennel, there is another that leads north-west, from the chiefe street to the green, which is a pleasant plott of ground, enclosed round with an earthen wall, wherein they were wont to play football, but now at the Gowff and byasse-bowls. The houses of this towne, on both sides of the street, have their several gardens belonging to them; and in the lower street there be some pretty orchards, that yield store of good fruit." As Patterson says, this description is near enough even to-day, and is mighty nicely written to boot. I am bound to add, of my own experience, that Maybole is tumbledown and dreary. Prosperous enough in reality, it has an air of decay; and though the population has increased, a roofless house every here and there seems to protest the contrary. The women are more than well-favoured, and the men fine tall fellows; but they look slipshod and dissipated. As they slouched at street corners, or stood about gossiping in the snow, it seemed they would have been more at home in the slums of a large city than here in a country place betwixt a village and a town. I heard a great deal about drinking, and a great deal about religious revivals: two things in which the Scottish character is emphatic and most unlovely. In particular, I heard of clergymen who were employing their time in explaining to a delighted audience the physics of the Second Coming. It is not very likely any of us will be asked to help. If we were, it is likely we should receive instructions for the occasion, and that on more reliable authority. And so I can only figure to myself a congregation truly curious in such flights of theological fancy, as one of veteran and accomplished saints, who have fought the good fight to an end and outlived all worldly passion, and are to be regarded rather as a part of the Church Triumphant than the poor, imperfect company on earth. And yet I saw some young fellows about the smoking-room who seemed, in the eyes of one who cannot count himself strait-laced, in need of some more practical sort of teaching. They seemed only eager to get drunk, and to do so speedily. It was not much more than a week after the New Year; and to hear them return on their past bouts with a gusto unspeakable was not altogether pleasing. Here is one snatch of talk, for the accuracy of which I can vouch—

"Ye had a spree here last Tuesday?"

"We had that!"

"I wasna able to be oot o' my bed. Man, I was awful bad on Wednesday."

"Ay, ye were gey bad."

And you should have seen the bright eyes, and heard the sensual accents! They recalled their doings with devout gusto and a sort of rational pride. Schoolboys, after their first drunkenness, are not more boastful; a cock does not plume himself with a more unmingled

141

satisfaction as he paces forth among his harem; and yet these were grown men, and by no means short of wit. It was hard to suppose they were very eager about the Second Coming: it seemed as if some elementary notions of temperance for the men and seemliness for the women would have gone nearer the mark. And yet, as it seemed to me typical of much that is evil in Scotland, Maybole is also typical of much that is best. Some of the factories, which have taken the place of weaving in the town's economy, were originally founded and are still possessed by self-made men of the sterling, stout old breed—fellows who made some little bit of an invention, borrowed some little pocketful of capital, and then, step by step, in courage, thrift, and industry, fought their way upwards to an assured position.

Abercrummie has told you enough of the Tolbooth; but, as a bit of spelling, this inscription on the Tolbooth bell seems too delicious to withhold: "This bell is founded at Maiboll Bi Danel Geli, a Frenchman, the 6th November, 1696, Bi appointment of the heritors of the parish of Maiyboll." The Castle deserves more notice. It is a large and shapely tower, plain from the ground upwards, but with a zone of ornamentation running about the top. In a general way this adornment is perched on the very summit of the chimney-stacks; but there is one corner more elaborate than the rest. A very heavy string-course runs round the upper story, and just above this, facing up the street, the tower carries a small oriel window, fluted and corbelled and carved about with stone heads. It is so ornate it has somewhat the air of a shrine. And it was, indeed, the casket of a very precious jewel, for in the room to which it gives light lay, for long years, the heroine of the sweet old ballad of "Johnnie Faa"—she who, at the call of the gipsies' songs, "came tripping down the stair, and all her maids before her." Some people say the ballad has no basis in fact, and have written, I believe, unanswerable papers to the proof. But in the face of all that, the very look of that high oriel window convinces the imagination, and we enter into all the sorrows of the imprisoned dame. We conceive the burthen of the long, lack-lustre days, when she leaned her sick head against the mullions, and saw the burghers loafing in Maybole High Street, and the children at play, and ruffling gallants riding by from hunt or foray. We conceive the passion of odd moments, when the wind threw up to her some snatch of song, and her heart grew hot within her, and her eyes overflowed at the memory of the past. And even if the tale be not true of this or that lady, or this or that old tower, it is true in the essence of all men and women: for all of us, some time or other, hear the gipsies singing; over all of us is the glamour cast. Some resist and sit resolutely by the fire. Most go and are brought back again, like Lady Cassilis. A few, of the tribe of Waring, go and are seen no more; only now and again, at springtime, when the gipsies' song is afloat in the amethyst evening, we can catch their voices in the glee.

By night it was clearer, and Maybole more visible than during the day. Clouds coursed over the sky in great masses; the full moon battled the other way, and lit up the snow with gleams of flying silver; the town came down the hill in a cascade of brown gables, bestridden by smooth white roofs, and spangled here and there with lighted windows.   At either end the snow stood high up in the darkness, on the peak of the Tolbooth and among the chimneys of the Castle.   As the moon flashed a bull's-eye glitter across the town between the racing clouds, the white roofs leaped into relief over the gables and the chimney-stacks, and their shadows over the white roofs.   In the town itself the lit face of the clock peered down the street; an hour was hammered out on Mr. Geli's bell, and from behind the red curtains of a public-house some one trolled out—a compatriot of Burns, again!—" The saut tear blin's my e'e."

Next morning there was sun and a flapping wind. From the street corners of Maybole I could catch breezy glimpses of green fields.   The road underfoot was wet and heavy—part ice, part snow, part water; and any one I met greeted me, by way of salutation, with " A fine thowe" (thaw).   My way lay among rather bleak hills, and past bleak ponds and dilapidated castles and monasteries, to the Highland-looking village of Kirkoswald.   It has little claim to notice, save that Burns came there to study surveying in the summer of 1777, and there also, in the kirkyard, the original of Tam o' Shanter sleeps his last sleep.   It is worth noticing, however, that this was the first place I thought " Highland-looking."   Over the hill from Kirkoswald a farm-road leads to the coast.   As I came down above Turnberry, the sea view was indeed strangely different from the day before.   The cold fogs were all blown away; and there was Ailsa Craig, like a refraction, magnified and de-formed, of the Bass Rock; and there were the chiselled mountain-tops of Arran, veined and tipped with snow; and behind, and fainter, the low, blue land of Cantyre.

Cottony clouds stood, in a great castle, over the top of Arran, and blew out in long streamers to the south. The sea was bitten all over with white; little ships, tacking up and down the Firth, lay over at different angles in the wind. On Shanter they were ploughing lea; a cart foal, all in a field by himself, capered and whinnied as if the spring were in him.

The road from Turnberry to Girvan lies along the shore, among sand-hills and by wildernesses of tumbled bent. Every here and there a few cottages stood together beside a bridge. They had one odd feature, not easy to describe in words: a triangular porch projected from above the door, supported at the apex by a single upright post; a secondary door was hinged to the post, and could be hasped on either cheek of the real entrance; so, whether the wind was north or south, the cotter could make himself a triangular bight of shelter where to set his chair and finish a pipe with comfort. There is one objection to this device: for, as the post stands in the middle of the fairway, any one precipitately issuing from the cottage must run his chance of a broken head. So far as I am aware, it is peculiar to the little corner of country about Girvan. And that corner is noticeable for more reasons: it is certainly one of the most characteristic districts in Scotland. It has this movable porch by way of architecture; it has, as we shall see, a sort of remnant of provincial costume, and it has the handsomest population in the Lowlands. . . .

VIII

ON THE PLAIN

PERHAPS the reader knows already the aspect of the great levels of the Gâtinais, where they border with the wooded hills of Fontainebleau.   Here and there a few grey rocks creep out of the forest as if to sun themselves.   Here and there a few apple-trees stand together on a knoll.   The quaint, undignified tartan of a myriad small fields dies out into the distance; the strips blend and disappear; and the dead flat lies forth open and empty, with no accident save perhaps a thin line of trees or faint church spire against the sky.   Solemn and vast at all times, in spite of pettiness in the near details, the impression becomes more solemn and vast towards evening.   The sun goes down, a swollen orange, as it were into the sea.   A blue-clad peasant rides home, with a harrow smoking behind him among the dry clods. Another still works with his wife in their little strip. An immense shadow fills the plain; these people stand in it up to their shoulders; and their heads, as they stoop over their work and rise again, are relieved from time to time against the golden sky.

These peasant farmers are well off nowadays, and

146

not by any means overworked; but somehow you
always see in them the historical representative of the
serf of yore, and think not so much of present times,
which may be prosperous enough, as of the old days
when the peasant was taxed beyond possibility of payment, and lived, in Michelet's image, like a hare between
two furrows. These very people now weeding their
patch under the broad sunset, that very man and his
wife, it seems to us, have suffered all the wrongs of
France. It is they who have been their country's scapegoat for long ages; they who, generation after generation, have sowed and not reaped, reaped and another
has garnered; and who have now entered into their
reward, and enjoy their good things in their turn. For
the days are gone by when the Seigneur ruled and profited. "Le Seigneur," says the old formula, "enferme
ses manants comme sous porte et gonds, du ciel à la
terre. Tout est à lui, forêt chenue, oiseau dans l'air,
poisson dans l'eau, bête au buisson, l'onde qui coule,
la cloche dont le son au loin roule." Such was his old
state of sovereignty, a local god rather than a mere king.
And now you may ask yourself where he is, and look
round for vestiges of my late lord, and in all the country-side there is no trace of him but his forlorn and
fallen mansion. At the end of a long avenue, now
sown with grain, in the midst of a close full of cy-
presses and lilacs, ducks and crowing chanticleers and
droning bees, the old château lifts its red chimneys and
peaked roofs and turning vanes into the wind and sun.
There is a glad spring bustle in the air, perhaps, and
the lilacs are all in flower, and the creepers green about
the broken balustrade; but no spring shall revive the

honour of the place. Old women of the people, little children of the people, saunter and gambol in the walled court or feed the ducks in the neglected moat. Plough-horses, mighty of limb, browse in the long stables. The dial-hand on the clock waits for some better hour. Out on the plain, where hot sweat trickles into men's eyes, and the spade goes in deep and comes up slowly, per-haps the peasant may feel a movement of joy at his heart when he thinks that these spacious chimneys are now cold, which have so often blazed and flickered upon gay folk at supper, while he and his hollow-eyed children watched through the night with empty bellies and cold feet. And perhaps, as he raises his head and sees the forest lying like a coast-line of low hills along the sea-like level of the plain, perhaps forest and château hold no unsimilar place in his affections.

If the château was my lord's the forest was my lord the king's; neither of them for this poor Jacques. If he thought to eke out his meagre way of life by some petty theft of wood for the fire, or for a new roof-tree, he found himself face to face with a whole department, from the Grand Master of the Woods and Waters, who was a high-born lord, down to the common sergeant, who was a peasant like himself, and wore stripes or a bandoleer by way of uniform. For the first offence, by the Salic law, there was a fine of fifteen sols; and should a man be taken more than once in fault, or cir-cumstances aggravate the colour of his guilt, he might be whipped, branded, or hanged. There was a hang-man over at Melun, and, I doubt not, a fine tall gibbet hard by the town gate, where Jacques might see his fellows dangle against the sky as he went to market.

And then, if he lived near to a cover, there would be the more hares and rabbits to eat out his harvest, and the more hunters to trample it down. My lord has a new horn from England. He has laid out seven francs in decorating it with silver and gold, and fitting it with a silken leash to hang about his shoulder. The hounds have been on a pilgrimage to the shrine of Saint Mesmer, or Saint Hubert in the Ardennes, or some other holy intercessor who has made a specialty of the health of hunting-dogs. In the grey dawn the game was turned and the branch broken by our best piqueur. A rare day's hunting lies before us. Wind a jolly flourish, sound the *bien-aller* with all your lungs. Jacques must stand by, hat in hand, while the quarry and hound and huntsman sweep across his field, and a year's sparing and labouring is as though it had not been. If he can see the ruin with a good enough grace, who knows but he may fall in favour with my lord; who knows but his son may become the last and least among the servants at his lordship's kennel—one of the two poor varlets who get no wages and sleep at night among the hounds ? [1]

For all that, the forest has been of use to Jacques, not only warming him with fallen wood, but giving him shelter in days of sore trouble, when my lord of the château, with all his troopers and trumpets, had been beaten from field after field into some ultimate fastness, or lay over-seas in an English prison. In these dark days, when the watch on the church steeple

[1] " Deux poures varlez qui n'ont nulz gages et qui gissoient la nuit avec les chiens." See Champollion-Figeac's *Louis et Charles d'Orléans*, i. 63, and for my lord's English horn, *ibid*. 96.

saw the smoke of burning villages on the sky-line, or
a clump of spears and fluttering pennons drawing nigh
across the plain, these good folk gat them up, with all
their household gods, into the wood, whence, from
some high spur, their timid scouts might overlook the
coming and going of the marauders, and see the harvest
ridden down, and church and cottage go up to heaven
all night in flame. It was but an unhomely refuge that
the woods afforded, where they must abide all change of
weather and keep house with wolves and vipers. Often
there was none left alive, when they returned, to show
the old divisions of field from field. And yet, as times
went, when the wolves entered at night into depopu-
lated Paris, and perhaps De Retz was passing by with
a company of demons like himself, even in these caves
and thickets there were glad hearts and grateful prayers.

Once or twice, as I say, in the course of the ages, the
forest may have served the peasant well, but at heart
it is a royal forest, and noble by old association.
These woods have rung to the horns of all the kings of
France, from Philip Augustus downwards. They have
seen Saint Louis exercise the dogs he brought with him
from Egypt; Francis I. go a-hunting with ten thousand
horses in his train; and Peter of Russia following his
first stag. And so they are still haunted for the imagination by royal hunts and progresses, and peopled
with the faces of memorable men of yore. And this
distinction is not only in virtue of the pastime of dead
monarchs. Great events, great revolutions, great cycles
in the affairs of men, have here left their note, here
taken shape in some significant and dramatic situation.
It was hence that Guise and his leaguers led Charles the

Ninth a prisoner to Paris. Here, booted and spurred, and with all his dogs about him, Napoleon met the Pope beside a woodland cross. Here, on his way to Elba not so long after, he kissed the eagle of the Old Guard, and spoke words of passionate farewell to his soldiers. And here, after Waterloo, rather than yield its ensign to the new power, one of his faithful regiments burned that memorial of so much toil and glory on the Grand Master's table, and drank its dust in brandy, as a devout priest consumes the remnants of the Host.

IN THE SEASON

Close into the edge of the forest, so close that the trees of the *bornage* stand pleasantly about the last houses, sits a certain small and very quiet village. There is but one street, and that, not long ago, was a green lane, where the cattle browsed between the door-steps. As you go up this street, drawing ever nearer the beginning of the wood, you will arrive at last before an inn where artists lodge. To the door (for I imagine it to be six o'clock on some fine summer's even), half a dozen, or maybe half a score, of people have brought out chairs, and now sit sunning themselves, and waiting the omnibus from Melun. If you go on into the court you will find as many more, some in the billiard-room over absinthe and a match of corks, some without over a last cigar and a vermouth. The doves coo and flutter from the dovecote; Hortense is drawing water from the well; and as all the rooms open into the court, you can see the white-capped cook over the furnace in the kitchen, and some idle painter, who has stored his canvases and washed his brushes, jangling a waltz on the crazy, tongue-tied piano in the salle-à-manger. "*Edmond, encore un vermouth,*" cries a man in velveteen, adding in a tone of apologetic afterthought, "*un double, s'il vous plaît.*" "Where are you working?" asks one in pure white linen from top to toe. "At the Carrefour de l'Épine," returns the other in corduroy (they are all gaitered, by the way). "I could n't do a thing to it. I ran out of white. Where were you?" "I was n't working, I was looking for motives." Here is an outbreak of jubilation, and a lot of men clustering together about some new-comer with outstretched hands; perhaps the "correspondence" has come in and brought So-and-so from Paris, or perhaps it is only So-and-so who has walked over from Chailly to dinner.

"*À table, Messieurs!*" cries M. Siron, bearing through the court the first tureen of soup. And immediately the company begins to settle down about the long tables in the dining-room, framed all round with sketches of all degrees of merit and demerit. There 's the big picture of the huntsman winding a horn with a dead boar between his legs, and his legs—well, his legs in stockings. And here is the little picture of a raw mutton-chop, in which Such-a-one knocked a hole last summer with no worse a missile than a plum from the dessert. And under all these works of art so much eating goes forward, so much drinking, so much jabbering in French and English, that it would do your heart good merely to peep and listen at the door. One man is telling how they all went last year to the fête at Fleury, and another how well So-and-so would sing of an evening; and here are a third and fourth making plans for the whole future of their lives; and there is a fifth imitating a conjurer and making faces on his clenched fist, surely of all arts the most difficult and admirable! A sixth has eaten his fill, lights a cigarette, and resigns himself to digestion. A seventh has just dropped in, and calls for soup. Number eight, meanwhile, has left the table, and is once more trampling the poor piano under powerful and uncertain fingers.

Dinner over, people drop outside to smoke and chat. Perhaps we go along to visit our friends at the other end of the village, where there is always a good welcome and a good talk, and perhaps some pickled oysters and white wine to close the evening. Or a dance is organised in the dining-room, and the piano exhibits all its paces under manful jockeying, to the light of the three or four candles and a lamp or two, while the waltzers move to and fro upon the wooden floor, and sober men, who are not given to such light pleasures, get up on the table or the sideboard, and sit there looking on approvingly over a pipe and a tumbler of wine. Or sometimes—suppose my lady moon looks forth, and the court from out the half-lit dining-room seems nearly as bright as by day, and the light picks out the window-panes, and makes a clear shadow under every vine-leaf on the wall—sometimes a picnic is proposed, and a basket made ready, and a good procession formed in front of the hotel. The two trumpeters in honour go before; and as we file down the long alley, and up through devious footpaths among rocks and pine-trees, with every here and there a dark passage of shadow, and every here and there a

spacious outlook over moonlit woods, these two precede us and sound many a jolly flourish as they walk.
We gather ferns and dry boughs into the cavern, and
soon a good blaze flutters the shadows of the old
bandits' haunt, and shows shapely beards and comely
faces and toilettes ranged about the wall. The bowl is
lit, and the punch is burnt and sent round in scalding
thimblefuls. So a good hour or two may pass with song
and jest. And then we go home in the moonlight
morning, straggling a good deal among the birch tufts
and the boulders, but ever called together again, as
one of our leaders winds his horn. Perhaps some one
of the party will not heed the summons, but chooses out
some by-way of his own. As he follows the winding
sandy road, he hears the flourishes grow fainter and
fainter in the distance, and die finally out, and still
walks on in the strange coolness and silence and between
the crisp lights and shadows of the moonlit woods,
until suddenly the bell rings out the hour from far-
away Chailly, and he starts to find himself alone. No
surf-bell on forlorn and perilous shores, no passing
knoll over the busy market-place, can speak with a
more heavy and disconsolate tongue to human ears.
Each stroke calls up a host of ghostly reverberations in
his mind. And as he stands rooted, it has grown once
more so utterly silent that it seems to him he might
hear the church bells ring the hour out all the world
over, not at Chailly only, but in Paris, and away in
outlandish cities, and in the village on the river, where
his childhood passed between the sun and flowers.

IDLE HOURS

The woods by night, in all their uncanny effect, are not rightly to be understood until you can compare them with the woods by day. The stillness of the medium, the floor of glittering sand, these trees that go streaming up like monstrous sea-weeds and waver in the moving winds like the weeds in submarine currents, all these set the mind working on the thought of what you may have seen off a foreland or over the side of a boat, and make you feel like a diver, down in the quiet water, fathoms below the tumbling, transitory surface of the sea. And yet in itself, as I say, the strangeness of these nocturnal solitudes is not to be felt fully without the sense of contrast. You must have risen in the morning and seen the woods as they are by day, kindled and coloured in the sun's light; you must have felt the odour of innumerable trees at even, the unsparing heat along the forest roads, and the coolness of the groves.

And on the first morning you will doubtless rise betimes. If you have not been wakened before by the visit of some adventurous pigeon, you will be wakened as soon as the sun can reach your window—for there are no blinds or shutters to keep him out—and the room, with its bare wood floor and bare whitewashed walls, shines all round you in a sort of glory of reflected lights. You may doze awhile longer by snatches, or lie awake to study the charcoal men and dogs and horses with which former occupants have defiled the partitions: Thiers, with wily profile; local celebrities, pipe in hand;

or, maybe, a romantic landscape splashed in oil. Meanwhile artist after artist drops into the salle-à-manger for coffee, and then shoulders easel, sunshade, stool, and paint-box, bound into a fagot, and sets off for what he calls his " motive." And artist after artist, as he goes out of the village, carries with him a little following of dogs. For the dogs, who belong only nominally to any special master, hang about the gate of the forest all day long, and whenever any one goes by who hits their fancy, profit by his escort, and go forth with him to play an hour or two at hunting. They would like to be under the trees all day. But they cannot go alone. They require a pretext. And so they take the passing artist as an excuse to go into the woods, as they might take a walking-stick as an excuse to bathe. With quick ears, long spines, and bandy legs, or perhaps as tall as a greyhound and with a bulldog's head, this company of mongrels will trot by your side all day and come home with you at night, still showing white teeth and wagging stunted tail. Their good humour is not to be exhausted. You may pelt them with stones if you please, and all they will do is to give you a wider berth. If once they come out with you, to you they will remain faithful, and with you return; although if you meet them next morning in the street, it is as like as not they will cut you with a countenance of brass.

The forest—a strange thing for an Englishman—is very destitute of birds. This is no country where every patch of wood among the meadows gives up an incense of song, and every valley wandered through by a streamlet rings and reverberates from side to side with a profusion of clear notes. And this rarity of birds is not to be regretted on its own account only. For the insects prosper in their absence, and become as one of the plagues of Egypt. Ants swarm in the hot sand; mosquitos drone their nasal drone; wherever the sun finds a hole in the roof of the forest, you see a myriad transparent creatures coming and going in the shaft of light; and even between-whiles, even where there is no incursion of sun-rays into the dark arcade of the wood, you are conscious of a continual drift of insects, an ebb and flow of infinitesimal living things between the trees. Nor are insects the only evil creatures that haunt the forest. For you may plump into a cave among the rocks, and find yourself face to face with a wild boar, or see a crooked viper slither across the road.

Perhaps you may set yourself down in the bay between two spreading beech-roots with a book on your lap, and be awakened all of a sudden by a friend: "I say, just keep where you are, will you? You make the jolliest motive." And you reply: "Well, I don't mind, if I may smoke." And thereafter the hours go idly by. Your friend at the easel labours doggedly a little way off, in the wide shadow of the tree; and yet farther, across a strait of glaring sunshine, you see another painter, encamped in the shadow of another tree, and up to his waist in the fern. You cannot watch your own effigy growing out of the white trunk, and the trunk beginning to stand forth from the rest of the wood, and the whole picture getting dappled over with the flecks of sun that slip through the leaves overhead, and, as a wind goes by and sets the trees a-talking, flicker hither and thither like butterflies of light. But you know it is going forward; and, out of emulation with the painter, get ready your own palette, and lay out the colour for a woodland scene in words.

Your tree stands in a hollow paved with fern and heather, set in a basin of low hills, and scattered over with rocks and junipers. All the open is steeped in pitiless sunlight. Everything stands out as though it were cut in cardboard, every colour is strained into its highest key. The boulders are some of them upright and dead like monolithic castles, some of them prone like sleeping cattle. The junipers—looking, in their soiled and ragged mourning, like some funeral procession that has gone seeking the place of sepulchre three hundred years and more in wind and rain—are daubed in forcibly against the glowing ferns and heather. Every tassel of their rusty foliage is defined with pre-Raphaelite minuteness. And a sorry figure they make out there in the sun, like misbegotten yew-trees! The scene is all pitched in a key of colour so peculiar, and lit up with such a discharge of violent sunlight, as a man might live fifty years in England and not see.

Meanwhile at your elbow some one tunes up a song, words of Ronsard to a pathetic tremulous air, of how the poet loved his mistress long ago, and pressed on her the flight of time, and told her how white and quiet the dead lay under the stones, and how the boat dipped and pitched as the shades embarked for the passionless land. Yet a little while, sang the poet, and there shall be no more love; only to sit and remember loves that might have been. There is a falling flourish in the air that remains in the memory and comes back in incongruous places, on the seat of hansoms or in the warm bed at night, with something of a forest savour.

"You can get up now," says the painter; "I 'm at the background."

And so up you get, stretching yourself, and go your way into the wood, the daylight becoming richer and more golden, and the shadows stretching farther into the open. A cool air comes along the highways, and the scents awaken. The fir-trees breathe abroad their ozone. Out of unknown thickets comes forth the soft, secret, aromatic odour of the woods, not like a smell of the free heaven, but as though court ladies, who had known these paths in ages long gone by, still walked in the summer evenings, and shed from their brocades a breath of musk or bergamot upon the woodland winds. One side of the long avenues is still kindled with the sun, the other is plunged in transparent shadow. Over the trees the west begins to burn like a furnace; and the painters gather up their chattels, and go down, by avenue or footpath, to the plain.

A PLEASURE PARTY

As this excursion is a matter of some length, and, moreover, we go in force, we have set aside our usual vehicle, the pony-cart, and ordered a large wagonette from Lejosne's. It has been waiting for near an hour, while one went to pack a knapsack, and t' other hurried over his toilette and coffee; but now it is filled from end to end with merry folk in summer attire, the coachman cracks his whip, and amid much applause from round the inn door off we rattle at a spanking trot. The way lies through the forest, up hill and down dale, and by beech and pine wood, in the cheerful morning sunshine. The English get down at all the ascents and walk on ahead for exercise; the French are mightily entertained at this, and keep coyly underneath the tilt. As we go we carry with us a pleasant noise of laughter and light speech, and some one will be always breaking out into a bar or two of opera bouffe. Before we get to the Route Ronde here comes Desprez, the colourman from Fontainebleau, trudging across on his weekly peddle with a case of merchandise; and it is "Desprez, leave me some malachite green"; "Desprez, leave me so much canvas"; "Desprez, leave me this, or leave me that"; M. Desprez standing the while in the sunlight with grave face and many salutations. The next interruption is more important. For some time back we have had the sound of cannon in our ears; and now, a little past Franchard, we find a mounted trooper holding a led horse, who brings the wagonette to a stand. The artillery is practising in the Quadrilateral, it appears; passage along the Route Ronde formally interdicted for the moment. There is nothing for it but to draw up at the glaring cross-roads, and get down to make fun with the notorious Cocardon, the most ungainly and ill-bred dog of all the ungainly and ill-bred dogs of Barbizon, or clamber about the sandy banks. And meanwhile the Doctor, with sun umbrella, wide Panama, and patriarchal beard, is busy wheedling and (for aught the rest of us know) bribing the too facile sentry. His speech is smooth and dulcet, his manner dignified and insinuating. It is not for nothing that the Doctor has voyaged all the world over, and speaks all languages from French to Patagonian. He has not come home from perilous journeys to be thwarted by a corporal of horse. And so we soon see the soldier's mouth relax, and his shoulders imitate a relenting heart. " *En voiture, Messieurs, Mesdames,*" sings the Doctor; and on we go again at a good round pace, for black care follows hard after us, and discretion prevails not a little over valour in some timorous spirits of the party. At any moment we may meet the sergeant, who will send us back. At any moment we may encounter a flying shell, which will send us somewhere farther off than Grez.

Grez—for that is our destination—has been highly recommended for its beauty. " *Il y a de l'eau,*" people have said, with an emphasis, as if that settled the question, which, for a French mind, I am rather led to think it does. And Grez, when we get there, is indeed a place worthy of some praise. It lies out of the forest, a cluster of houses, with an old bridge, an old castle in ruin, and a quaint old church. The inn garden descends in terraces to the river; stable-yard, kailyard, orchard, and a space of lawn, fringed with rushes and embellished with a green arbour. On the opposite bank there is a reach of English-looking plain, set thickly with willows and poplars. And between the two lies the river, clear and deep, and full of reeds and floating lilies. Water-plants cluster about the starlings of the long low bridge, and stand half-way up upon the piers in green luxuriance. They catch the dipped oar with long antennæ, and chequer the slimy bottom with the shadow of their leaves. And the river wanders hither and thither among the islets, and is smothered and broken up by the reeds, like an old building in the lithe, hardy arms of the climbing ivy. You may watch the box where the good man of the inn keeps fish alive for his kitchen, one oily ripple following another over the top of the yellow deal. And you can hear a splashing and a prattle of voices from the shed under the old kirk, where the village women wash and wash all day among the fish and water-lilies. It seems as if linen washed there should be specially cool and sweet.

We have come here for the river. And no sooner have we all bathed than we board the two shallops and push off gaily, and go gliding under the trees and gathering a great treasure of water-lilies. Some one sings; some trail their hands in the cool water; some lean over the gunwale to see the image of the tall poplars far below, and the shadow of the boat, with the balanced oars and their own head protruded, glide smoothly over the yellow floor of the stream. At last, the day declining—all silent and happy, and up to the knees in the wet lilies—we punt slowly back again to the landing-place beside the bridge. There is a wish for solitude on all. One hides himself in the arbour with a cigarette; another goes a walk in the country with Cocardon; a third inspects the church. And it is not till dinner is on the table, and the inn's best wine goes round from glass to glass, that we begin to throw off the restraint and fuse once more into a jolly fellowship.

Half the party are to return to-night with the wagonette; and some of the others, loath to break up good company, will go with them a bit of the way and drink a stirrup-cup at Marlotte. It is dark in the wagonette

and not so merry as it might have been. The coachman loses the road. So-and-so tries to light fireworks
with the most indifferent success. Some sing, but the
rest are too weary to applaud; and it seems as if the
festival were fairly at an end—

> " Nous avons fait la noce,
> Rentrons à nos foyers! "

And such is the burthen, even after we have come to
Marlotte and taken our places in the court at Mother
Antonine's. There is punch on the long table out in
the open air, where the guests dine in summer weather.
The candles flare in the night wind, and the faces round
the punch are lit up, with shifting emphasis, against a
background of complete and solid darkness. It is all
picturesque enough; but the fact is, we are aweary.
We yawn; we are out of the vein; we have made the
wedding, as the song says, and now, for pleasure's
sake, let 's make an end on 't. When here comes
striding into the court, booted to mid-thigh, spurred
and splashed, in a jacket of green cord, the great,
famous, and redoubtable Blank; and in a moment the
fire kindles again, and the night is witness of our
laughter as he imitates Spaniards, Germans, Englishmen, picture-dealers, all eccentric ways of speaking
and thinking, with a possession, a fury, a strain of
mind and voice, that would rather suggest a nervous
crisis than a desire to please. We are as merry as ever
when the trap sets forth again, and say farewell noisily
to all the good folk going farther. Then, as we are
far enough from thoughts of sleep, we visit Blank in
his quaint house, and sit an hour or so in a great tapes-

tried chamber, laid with furs, littered with sleeping hounds, and lit up, in fantastic shadow and shine, by a wood fire in a mediæval chimney. And then we plod back through the darkness to the inn beside the river.

How quick bright things come to confusion! When we arise next morning, the grey showers fall steadily, the trees hang limp, and the face of the stream is spoiled with dimpling raindrops. Yesterday's lilies encumber the garden walk, or begin, dismally enough, their voyage towards the Seine and the salt sea. A sickly shimmer lies upon the dripping house-roofs, and all the colour is washed out of the green and golden landscape of last night, as though an envious man had taken a water-colour sketch and blotted it together with a sponge. We go out a-walking in the wet roads. But the roads about Grez have a trick of their own. They go on for a while among clumps of willows and patches of vine, and then, suddenly and without any warning, cease and determine in some miry hollow or upon some bald know; and you have a short period of hope, then right-about face, and back the way you came! So we draw about the kitchen fire and play a round game of cards for ha'pence, or go to the billiard-room for a match at corks; and by one consent a messenger is sent over for the wagonette—Grez shall be left to-morrow.

To-morrow dawns so fair that two of the party agree to walk back for exercise, and let their knapsacks follow by the trap. I need hardly say they are neither of them French; for, of all English phrases, the phrase "for exercise" is the least comprehensible across the

Straits of Dover. All goes well for a while with the pedestrians. The wet woods are full of scents in the noontide. At a certain cross, where there is a guard-house, they make a halt, for the forester's wife is the daughter of their good host at Barbizon. And so there they are hospitably received by the comely woman, with one child in her arms and another prattling and tottering at her gown, and drink some syrup of quince in the back parlour, with a map of the forest on the wall, and some prints of love-affairs and the great Napoleon hunting. As they draw near the Quadri-lateral, and hear once more the report of the big guns, they take a by-road to avoid the sentries, and go on awhile somewhat vaguely, with the sound of the cannon in their ears and the rain beginning to fall. The ways grow wider and sandier; here and there there are real sand-hills, as though by the sea-shore; the fir-wood is open and grows in clumps upon the hillocks, and the race of sign-posts is no more. One begins to look at the other doubtfully. "I am sure we should keep more to the right," says one; and the other is just as certain they should hold to the left. And now, suddenly, the heavens open, and the rain falls "sheer and strong and loud," as out of a shower-bath. In a moment they are as wet as shipwrecked sailors. They cannot see out of their eyes for the drift, and the water churns and gurgles in their boots. They leave the track and try across country with a gambler's desperation, for it seems as if it were impossible to make the situation worse; and, for the next hour, go scrambling from boulder to boulder, or plod along paths that are now no more than rivulets, and across waste clearings where the scattered shells and broken fir-trees tell all too plainly of the cannon in the distance. And meantime the cannon grumble out responses to the grumbling thunder. There is such a mixture of melodrama and sheer discomfort about all this, it is at once so grey and so lurid, that it is far more agreeable to read and write about by the chimney-corner than to suffer in the person. At last they chance on the right path, and make Franchard in the early evening, the sorriest pair of wanderers that ever welcomed English ale. Thence, by the Bois d'Hyver, the Ventes-Alexandre, and the Pins Brulés, to the clean hostelry, dry clothes, and dinner.

THE WOODS IN SPRING

I think you will like the forest best in the sharp early springtime, when it is just beginning to reawaken, and innumerable violets peep from among the fallen leaves; when two or three people at most sit down to dinner, and, at table, you will do well to keep a rug about your knees, for the nights are chill, and the salle-à-manger opens on the court. There is less to distract the attention, for one thing, and the forest is more itself. It is not bedotted with artists' sunshades as with unknown mushrooms, nor bestrewn with the remains of English picnics. The hunting still goes on, and at any moment your heart may be brought into your mouth as you hear far-away horns; or you may be told by an agitated peasant that the Vicomte has gone up the avenue, not ten minutes since, " *à fond de train, monsieur, et avec douze piqueurs.*"

If you go up to some coign of vantage in the system

of low hills that permeates the forest, you will see many different tracts of country, each of its own cold and melancholy neutral tint, and all mixed together and mingled the one into the other at the seams. You will see tracts of leafless beeches of a faint yellowish grey, and leafless oaks a little ruddier in the hue. Then zones of pine of a solemn green; and, dotted among the pines, or standing by themselves in rocky clearings, the delicate, snow-white trunks of birches, spreading out into snow-white branches yet more delicate, and crowned and canopied with a purple haze of twigs. And then a long, bare ridge of tumbled boulders, with bright sand-breaks between them, and wavering sandy roads among the bracken and brown heather. It is all rather cold and unhomely. It has not the perfect beauty, nor the gem-like colouring, of the wood in the later year, when it is no more than one vast colonnade of verdant shadow, tremulous with insects, intersected here and there by lanes of sunlight set in purple heather. The loveliness of the woods in March is not, assuredly, of this blowzy rustic type. It is made sharp with a grain of salt, with a touch of ugliness. It has a sting like the sting of bitter ale; you acquire the love of it as men acquire a taste for olives. And the wonderful clear, pure air wells into your lungs the while by voluptuous inhalations, and makes the eyes bright, and sets the heart tinkling to a new tune—or, rather, to an old tune; for you remember in your boyhood something akin to this spirit of adventure, this thirst for exploration, that now takes you masterfully by the hand, plunges you into many a deep grove, and drags you over many a stony crest. It is as if the whole wood were full of friendly voices calling you farther in, and you turn from one side to another, like Buridan's donkey, in a maze of pleasure.

Comely beeches send up their white, straight, clustered branches, barred with green moss, like so many fingers from a half-clenched hand. Mighty oaks stand to the ankles in a fine tracery of underwood; thence the tall shaft climbs upwards, and the great forest of stalwart boughs spreads out into the golden evening sky, where the rooks are flying and calling. On the sward of the Bois d'Hyver the firs stand well asunder with outspread arms, like fencers saluting; and the air smells of resin all around, and the sound of the axe is rarely still. But strangest of all, and in appearance oldest of all, are the dim and wizard upland districts of young wood. The ground is carpeted with fir-tassel, and strewn with fir-apples and flakes of fallen bark. Rocks lie crouching in the thicket, guttered with rain, tufted with lichen, white with years and the rigours of the changeful seasons. Brown and yellow butterflies are sown and carried away again by the light air— like thistledown. The loneliness of these coverts is so excessive, that there are moments when pleasure draws to the verge of fear. You listen and listen for some noise to break the silence, till you grow half mesmerised by the intensity of the strain; your sense of your own identity is troubled; your brain reels, like that of some gymnosophist poring on his own nose in Asiatic jungles; and should you see your own outspread feet, you see them, not as anything of yours, but as a feature of the scene around you.

Still the forest is always, but the stillness is not always unbroken. You can hear the wind pass in the distance over the tree-tops; sometimes briefly, like the noise of a train; sometimes with a long steady rush, like the breaking of waves. And sometimes, close at hand, the branches move, a moan goes through the thicket, and the wood thrills to its heart. Perhaps you may hear a carriage on the road to Fontainebleau, a bird gives a dry continual chirp, the dead leaves rustle underfoot, or you may time your steps to the steady recurrent strokes of the woodman's axe. From time to time, over the low grounds, a flight of rooks goes by; and from time to time the cooing of wild doves falls upon the ear, not sweet and rich and near at hand as in England, but a sort of voice of the woods, thin and far away, as fits these solemn places. Or you hear suddenly the hollow, eager, violent barking of dogs; scared deer flit past you through the fringes of the wood; then a man or two running, in green blouse, with gun and game-bag on a bandoleer; and then, out of the thick of the trees, comes the jar of rifle-shots. Or perhaps the hounds are out, and horns are blown, and scarlet-coated huntsmen flash through the clearings, and the solid noise of horses galloping passes below you, where you sit perched among the rocks and heather. The boar is afoot, and all over the forest, and in all neighbouring villages, there is a vague excitement and a vague hope; for who knows whither the chase may lead? and even to have seen a single piqueur, or spoken to a single sportsman, is to be a man of consequence for the night.

Besides men who shoot and men who ride with the hounds, there are few people in the forest, in the early spring, save wood-cutters plying their axes steadily, and old women and children gathering wood for the fire. You may meet such a party coming home in the twilight: the old woman laden with a fagot of chips, and the little ones hauling a long branch behind them in her wake. That is the worst of what there is to encounter; and if I tell you of what once happened to a friend of mine, it is by no means to tantalise you with false hopes; for the adventure was unique. It was on a very cold, still, sunless morning, with a flat grey sky and a frosty tingle in the air, that this friend (who shall here be nameless) heard the notes of a key-bugle played with much hesitation, and saw the smoke of a fire spread out along the green pine-tops, in a remote uncanny glen, hard by a hill of naked boulders. He drew near warily, and beheld a picnic party seated under a tree in an open. The old father knitted a sock, the mother sat staring at the fire. The eldest son, in the uniform of a private of dragoons, was choosing out notes on a key-bugle. Two or three daughters lay in the neighbourhood picking violets. And the whole party as grave and silent as the woods around them! My friend watched for a long time, he says; but all held their peace; not one spoke or smiled; only the dragoon kept choosing out single notes upon the bugle, and the father knitted away at his work and made strange movements the while with his flexible eyebrows. They took no notice whatever of my friend's presence, which was disquieting in itself, and increased the resemblance of the whole party to mechanical waxworks. Certainly, he affirms, a wax figure might have played the bugle with more spirit than that strange dragoon. And as this hypothesis of his became more certain, the awful insolubility of why they should be left out there in the woods with nobody to wind them up again when they ran down, and a growing disquietude as to what might happen next, became too much for his courage, and he turned tail, and fairly took to his heels. It might have been a singing in his ears, but he fancies he was followed as he ran by a peal of Titanic laughter. Nothing has ever transpired to clear up the mystery; it may be they were automata; or it may be (and this is the theory to which I lean myself) that this is all another chapter of Heine's "Gods in Exile"; that the upright old man with the eyebrows was no other than Father Jove, and the young dragoon with the taste for music either Apollo or Mars.

MORALITY

Strange indeed is the attraction of the forest for the minds of men. Not one or two only, but a great chorus of grateful voices have arisen to spread abroad its fame. Half the famous writers of modern France have had their word to say about Fontainebleau. Chateaubriand, Michelet, Béranger, George Sand, de Senancour, Flaubert, Murger, the brothers Goncourt, Théodore de Banville, each of these has done something to the eternal praise and memory of these woods. Even at the very worst of times, even when the picturesque was anathema in the eyes of all Persons of Taste, the forest still preserved a certain reputation for beauty. It was in 1730 that the Abbé Guilbert published his *Historical Description of the Palace, Town, and Forest of Fontainebleau.* And very droll it is to see him, as he tries to set forth his admiration in terms of what was then permissible. The monstrous rocks, etc., says the Abbé, "sont admirées avec surprise des voyageurs qui s'écrient aussitôt avec Horace: Ut mihi devio rupes et vacuum nemus mirari libet." The good man is not exactly lyrical in his praise; and you see how he sets his back against Horace as against a trusty oak. Horace, at any rate, was classical. For the rest, however, the Abbé likes places where many alleys meet; or which, like the Belle-Étoile, are kept up "by a special gardener," and admires at the Table du Roi the labours of the Grand Master of Woods and Waters, the Sieur de la Falure, "qui a fait faire ce magnifique endroit."

But indeed, it is not so much for its beauty that the forest makes a claim upon men's hearts, as for that subtle something, that quality of the air, that emanation from the old trees, that so wonderfully changes and renews a weary spirit. Disappointed men, sick Francis Firsts and vanquished Grand Monarchs, time out of mind have come here for consolation. Hither perplexed folk have retired out of the press of life, as into a deep bay-window on some night of masquerade, and here found quiet and silence, and rest, the mother of wisdom. It is the great moral spa; this forest without a fountain is itself the great fountain of Juventius. It is the best place in the world to bring an old sorrow that has been a long while your friend and enemy; and if, like Béranger's, your gaiety has run away from home and left open the door for sorrow to come in, of all covers in Europe, it is here you may expect to find the truant hid. With every hour you change. The air penetrates through your clothes, and nestles to your living body. You love exercise and slumber, long fasting and full meals. You forget all your scruples and live awhile in peace and freedom, and for the moment only. For here, all is absent that can stimulate to moral feeling. Such people as you see may be old, or toil-worn, or sorry; but you see them framed in the forest, like figures on a painted canvas; and for you, they are not people in any living and kindly sense. You forget the grim contrariety of interests. You forget the narrow lane where all men jostle together in unchivalrous contention, and the kennel, deep and unclean, that gapes on either hand for the defeated. Life is simple enough, it seems, and the very idea of sacrifice becomes like a mad fancy out of a last night's dream.

Your ideal is not perhaps high, but it is plain and possible. You become enamoured of a life of change and movement and the open air, where the muscles shall be more exercised than the affections. When you have had your will of the forest, you may visit the whole round world. You may buckle on your knapsack and take the road on foot. You may bestride a good nag, and ride forth, with a pair of saddle-bags, into the enchanted East. You may cross the Black Forest, and see Germany wide-spread before you, like a map, dotted with old cities, walled and spired, that dream all day on their own reflections in the Rhine or Danube. You may pass the spinal cord of Europe and go down from Alpine glaciers to where Italy extends her marble moles and glasses her marble palaces in the midland sea. You may sleep in flying trains or wayside taverns. You may be awakened at dawn by the scream of the express or the small pipe of the robin in the

173

hedge. For you the rain should allay the dust of the beaten road; the wind dry your clothes upon you as you walked. Autumn should hang out russet pears and purple grapes along the lane; inn after inn proffer you their cups of raw wine; river by river receive your body in the sultry noon. Wherever you went warm valleys and high trees and pleasant villages should compass you about; and light fellowships should take you by the arm, and walk with you an hour upon your way. You may see from afar off what it will come to in the end—the weather-beaten red-nosed vagabond, consumed by a fever of the feet, cut off from all near touch of human sympathy, a waif, an Ishmael, and an outcast. And yet it will seem well—and yet, in the air of the forest, this will seem the best—to break all the network bound about your feet by birth and old companionship and loyal love, and bear your shovelful of phosphates to and fro, in town and country, until the hour of the great dissolvent.

Or, perhaps, you will keep to the cover. For the forest is by itself, and forest life owns small kinship with life in the dismal land of labour. Men are so far sophisticated that they cannot take the world as it is given to them by the sight of their eyes. Not only what they see and hear, but what they know to be behind, enter into their notion of a place. If the sea, for instance, lie just across the hills, sea-thoughts will come to them at intervals, and the tenor of their dreams from time to time will suffer a sea-change. And so here, in this forest, a knowledge of its greatness is for much in the effect produced. You reckon up the miles that lie between you and intrusion. You may walk before you

174

all day long, and not fear to touch the barrier of your
Eden, or stumble out of fairyland into the land of gin
and steam-hammers.   And there is an old tale enhances
for the imagination the grandeur of the woods of France,
and secures you in the thought of your seclusion.
When Charles VI. hunted in the time of his wild boyhood near Senlis, there was captured an old stag, having a collar of bronze about his neck, and these words
engraved on the collar: " Cæsar mihi hoc donavit."   It
is no wonder if the minds of men were moved at this
occurrence and they stood aghast to find themselves
thus touching hands with forgotten ages, and following an antiquity with hound and horn.   And even for
you, it is scarcely in an idle curiosity that you ponder
how many centuries this stag had carried its free antlers
through the wood, and how many summers and win-
ters had shone and snowed on the imperial badge.   If
the extent of solemn wood could thus safeguard a tall
stag from the hunters' hounds and horses, might not
you also play hide-and-seek, in these groves, with all
the pangs and trepidations of man's life, and elude
Death, the mighty hunter, for more than the span of
human years ?   Here, also, crash his arrows; here, in
the farthest glade, sounds the gallop of the pale horse.
But he does not hunt this cover with all his hounds,
for the game is thin and small: and if you were but
alert and wary, if you lodged ever in the deepest thickets,
you too might live on into later generations and aston-
ish men by your stalwart age and the trophies of an
immemorial success.

For the forest takes away from you all excuse to die.
There is nothing here to cabin or thwart your free de-

sires. Here all the impudencies of the brawling world reach you no more. You may count your hours, like Endymion, by the strokes of the lone wood-cutter, or by the progression of the lights and shadows and the sun wheeling his wide circuit through the naked heavens. Here shall you see no enemies but winter and rough weather. And if a pang comes to you at all, it will be a pang of healthful hunger. All the puling sorrows, all the carking repentance, all this talk of duty that is no duty, in the great peace, in the pure daylight of these woods, fall away from you like a garment. And if perchance you come forth upon an eminence, where the wind blows upon you large and fresh, and the pines knock their long stems together, like an ungainly sort of puppets, and see far away over the plain a factory chimney defined against the pale horizon—it is for you, as for the staid and simple peasant when, with his plough, he upturns old arms and harness from the furrow of the glebe. Ay, sure enough, there was a battle there in the old times; and, sure enough, there is a world out yonder where men strive together with a noise of oaths and weeping and clamorous dispute. So much you apprehend by an athletic act of the imagination. A faint far-off rumour as of Merovingian wars; a legend as of some dead religion.

IX

A MOUNTAIN TOWN IN FRANCE

(A Fragment, 1879: Originally intended to serve as the opening chapter of " Travels with a Donkey in the Cevennes.")

LE MONASTIER is the chief place of a hilly canton in Haute Loire, the ancient Velay. As the name betokens, the town is of monastic origin; and it still contains a towered bulk of monastery and a church of some architectural pretensions, the seat of an archpriest and several vicars. It stands on the side of a hill above the river Gazeille, about fifteen miles from Le Puy, up a steep road where the wolves sometimes pursue the diligence in winter. The road, which is bound for Vivarais, passes through the town from end to end in a single narrow street; there you may see the fountain where women fill their pitchers; there also some old houses with carved doors and pediments and ornamental work in iron. For Monastier, like Maybole in Ayrshire, was a sort of country capital, where the local aristocracy had their town mansions for the winter; and there is a certain baron still alive and, I am told, extremely penitent, who found means to ruin himself by high living in this village on the hills. He certainly has claims to be considered the most remarkable spendthrift on record, How he set about it, in a place where there are no luxuries for sale, and where the board at the best inn comes to little more than a shilling a day, is a problem for the wise. His son, ruined as the family was, went as far as Paris to sow his wild oats; and so the cases of father and son mark an epoch in the history of centralisation in France. Not until the latter had got into the train was the work of Richelieu complete.

It is a people of lace-makers. The women sit in the streets by groups of five or six; and the noise of the bobbins is audible from one group to another. Now and then you will hear one woman clattering off prayers for the edification of the others at their work. They wear gaudy shawls, white caps with a gay ribbon about the head, and sometimes a black felt brigand hat above the cap; and so they give the street colour and brightness and a foreign air. Awhile ago, when England largely supplied herself from this district with the lace called *torchon*, it was not unusual to earn five francs a day; and five francs in Monastier is worth a pound in London. Now, from a change in the market, it takes a clever and industrious workwoman to earn from three to four in the week, or less than an eighth of what she made easily a few years ago. The tide of prosperity came and went, as with our northern pitmen, and left nobody the richer. The women bravely squandered their gains, kept the men in idleness, and gave themselves up, as I was told, to sweethearting and a merry life. From week's end to week's end it was one continuous gala in Monastier; people spent the day in the wine-shops, and the drum or the bagpipes led on the *bourrées* up to ten at night. Now these dancing days are over. "*Il n'y a plus de jeunesse,*" said Victor the garçon. I hear of no great advance in what are thought the essentials of morality; but the *bourrée*, with its rambling, sweet, interminable music, and alert and rustic figures, has fallen into disuse, and is mostly remembered as a custom of the past. Only on the occasion of the fair shall you hear a drum discreetly rattling in a wine-shop or perhaps one of the company singing the measure while the others dance. I am sorry at the change, and marvel once more at the complicated scheme of things upon this earth, and how a turn of fashion in England can silence so much mountain merriment in France. The lace-makers themselves have not entirely forgiven our countrywomen; and I think they take a special pleasure in the legend of the northern quarter of the town, called L'Anglade, because there the English free-lances were arrested and driven back by the potency of a little Virgin Mary on the wall.

From time to time a market is held, and the town has a season of revival; cattle and pigs are stabled in the streets; and pickpockets have been known to come all the way from Lyons for the occasion. Every Sunday the country folk throng in with daylight to buy apples, to attend mass, and to visit one of the wineshops, of which there are no fewer than fifty in this little town. Sunday wear for the men is a green tailcoat of some coarse sort of drugget, and usually a complete suit to match. I have never set eyes on such degrading raiment. Here it clings, there bulges; and the human body, with its agreeable and lively lines, is turned into a mockery and laughing-stock. Another piece of Sunday business with the peasants is to take their ailments to the chemist for advice. It is as much a matter for Sunday as church-going. I have seen a woman who had been unable to speak since the Monday before, wheezing, catching her breath, endlessly and painfully coughing; and yet she had waited upwards of a hundred hours before coming to seek help, and had the week been twice as long, she would have waited still. There was a canonical day for consultation; such was the ancestral habit, to which a respectable lady must study to conform.

Two conveyances go daily to Le Puy, but they rival each other in polite concessions rather than in speed. Each will wait an hour or two hours cheerfully while an old lady does her marketing or a gentleman finishes the papers in a café. The *Courrier* (such is the name of one) should leave Le Puy by two in the afternoon on the return voyage, and arrive at Monastier in good time for a six-o'clock dinner. But the driver dares not disoblige his customers. He will postpone his departure again and again, hour after hour; and I have known the sun to go down on his delay. These purely personal favours, this consideration of men's fancies, rather than the hands of a mechanical clock, as marking the advance of the abstraction, time, makes a more humorous business of stage-coaching than we are used to see it.

As far as the eye can reach, one swelling line of hilltop rises and falls behind another; and if you climb an eminence, it is only to see new and farther ranges behind these. Many little rivers run from all sides in cliffy valleys; and one of them, a few miles from Mo nastier, bears the great name of Loire. The mean level of the country is a little more than three thousand feet above the sea, which makes the atmosphere proportionally brisk and wholesome. There is little timber except pines, and the greater part of the country lies in moorland pasture. The country is wild and tumbled rather than commanding; an upland rather than a mountain district; and the most striking as well as the most agreeable scenery lies low beside the rivers. There, indeed, you will find many corners that take the fancy; such as made the English noble choose his grave by a Swiss streamlet, where nature is at her freshest, and looks as young as on the seventh morning. Such a place is the course of the Gazeille, where it waters the common of Monastier and thence downwards till it joins the Loire; a place to hear birds singing; a place for lovers to frequent. The name of the river was perhaps suggested by the sound of its passage over the stones; for it is a great warbler, and at night, after I was in bed at Monastier, I could hear it go singing down the valley till I fell asleep.

On the whole, this is a Scottish landscape, although not so noble as the best in Scotland; and by an odd coincidence, the population is, in its way, as Scottish as the country. They have abrupt, uncouth, Fifeshire manners, and accost you, as if you were trespassing, with an "*Où'st-ce que vous allez?*" only translatable into the Lowland "Whaur ye gaun?" They keep the Scottish Sabbath. There is no labour done on that day but to drive in and out the various pigs and sheep and cattle that make so pleasant a tinkling in the meadows. The lace-makers have disappeared from the street. Not to attend mass would involve social degradation; and you may find people reading Sunday books, in particular a sort of Catholic *Monthly Visitor* on the doings of Our Lady of Lourdes. I remember one Sunday, when I was walking in the country, that I fell on a hamlet and found all the inhabitants, from the patriarch to the baby, gathered in the shadow of a gable at prayer. One strapping lass stood with her back to the wall and did the solo part, the rest chiming in devoutly. Not far off, a lad lay flat on his face asleep among some straw, to represent the worldly element.

Again, this people is eager to proselytise; and the postmaster's daughter used to argue with me by the half-hour about my heresy, until she grew quite flushed. I have heard the reverse process going on between a Scotswoman and a French girl; and the arguments in the two cases were identical. Each apostle based her claim on the superior virtue and attainments of her clergy, and clenched the business with a threat of hell-fire. "*Pas bong prêtres ici,*" said the Presbyterian, "*bong prêtres en Écosse.*" And the postmaster's daughter, taking up the same weapon, plied me, so to speak, with the butt of it instead of the bayonet. We are a hopeful race, it seems, and easily persuaded for our good. One cheerful circumstance I note in these guerilla missions, that each side relies on hell, and Protestant and Catholic alike address themselves to a supposed misgiving in their adversary's heart. And I call it cheerful, for faith is a more supporting quality than imagination.

Here, as in Scotland, many peasant families boast a son in holy orders. And here also, the young men

have a tendency to emigrate. It is certainly not poverty
that drives them to the great cities or across the seas,
for many peasant families, I was told, have a fortune
of at least 40,000 francs. The lads go forth pricked
with the spirit of adventure and the desire to rise in life,
and leave their homespun elders grumbling and wondering over the event. Once, at a village called Laussonne, I met one of these disappointed parents: a drake
who had fathered a wild swan and seen it take wing
and disappear. The wild swan in question was now
an apothecary in Brazil. He had flown by way of
Bordeaux, and first landed in America, bareheaded and
barefoot, and with a single halfpenny in his pocket.
And now he was an apothecary! Such a wonderful
thing is an adventurous life! I thought he might as
well have stayed at home; but you never can tell
wherein a man's life consists, nor in what he sets his
pleasure: one to drink, another to marry, a third to
write scurrilous articles and be repeatedly caned in
public, and now this fourth, perhaps, to be an apothecary in Brazil. As for his old father, he could conceive
no reason for the lad's behaviour. "I had always bread
for him," he said; "he ran away to annoy me. He
loved to annoy me. He had no gratitude." But at
heart he was swelling with pride over his travelled offspring, and he produced a letter out of his pocket,
where, as he said, it was rotting, a mere lump of paper
rags, and waved it gloriously in the air. "This comes
from America," he cried, "six thousand leagues away!"
And the wine-shop audience looked upon it with a
certain thrill.

I soon became a popular figure, and was known for

miles in the country. *Où'st-ce que vous allez?* was changed for me into *Quoi, vous rentrez au Monastier ce soir?* and in the town itself every urchin seemed to know my name, although no living creature could pronounce it. There was one particular group of lace-makers who brought out a chair for me whenever I went by, and detained me from my walk to gossip. They were filled with curiosity about England, its language, its religion, the dress of the women, and were never weary of seeing the Queen's head on English postage-stamps or seeking for French words in English Journals. The language, in particular, filled them with surprise.

"Do they speak *patois* in England?" I was once asked; and when I told them not, "Ah, then, French?" said they.

"No, no," I said, "not French."

"Then," they concluded, "they speak *patois*."

You must obviously either speak French or *patois*. Talk of the force of logic—here it was in all its weakness. I gave up the point, but proceeding to give illustrations of my native jargon, I was met with a new mortification. Of all *patois* they declared that mine was the most preposterous and the most jocose in sound. At each new word there was a new explosion of laughter, and some of the younger ones were glad to rise from their chairs and stamp about the street in ecstasy; and I looked on upon their mirth in a faint and slightly disagreeable bewilderment. "Bread," which sounds a commonplace, plain-sailing monosyllable in England, was the word that most delighted these good ladies of Monastier; it seemed to them frolicsome and racy, like a page of Pickwick; and they all got it carefully by heart, as a stand-by, I presume, for winter evenings. I have tried it since then with every sort of accent and inflection, but I seem to lack the sense of humour.

They were of all ages: children at their first web of lace, a stripling girl with a bashful but encouraging play of eyes, solid married women, and grandmothers, some on the top of their age and some falling towards decrepitude. One and all were pleasant and natural, ready to laugh and ready with a certain quiet solemnity when that was called for by the subject of our talk. Life, since the fall in wages, had begun to appear to them with a more serious air. The stripling girl would sometimes laugh at me in a provocative and not unadmiring manner, if I judge aright; and one of the grandmothers, who was my great friend of the party, gave me many a sharp word of judgment on my sketches, my heresy, or even my arguments, and gave them with a wry mouth and a humorous twinkle in her eye that were eminently Scottish. But the rest used me with a certain reverence, as something come from afar and not entirely human. Nothing would put them at their ease but the irresistible gaiety of my native tongue. Between the old lady and myself I think there was a real attachment. She was never weary of sitting to me for her portrait, in her best cap and brigand hat, and with all her wrinkles tidily composed, and though she never failed to repudiate the result, she would always insist upon another trial. It was as good as a play to see her sitting in judgment over the last. "No, no," she would say, "that is not

it. I am old, to be sure, but I am better-looking than that. We must try again." When I was about to leave she bade me good-bye for this life in a somewhat touching manner. We should not meet again, she said; it was a long farewell, and she was sorry. But life is so full of crooks, old lady, that who knows? I have said good-bye to people for greater distances and times, and, please God, I mean to see them yet again.

One thing was notable about these women, from the youngest to the oldest, and with hardly an exception. In spite of their piety, they could twang off an oath with Sir Toby Belch in person. There was nothing so high or so low, in heaven or earth or in the human body, but a woman of this neighbourhood would whip out the name of it, fair and square, by way of conversational adornment. My landlady, who was pretty and young, dressed like a lady and avoided *patois* like a weakness, commonly addressed her child in the language of a drunken bully. And of all the swearers that I ever heard, commend me to an old lady in Gondet, a village of the Loire. I was making a sketch, and her curse was not yet ended when I had finished it and took my departure. It is true she had a right to be angry; for here was her son, a hulking fellow, visibly the worse for drink before the day was well begun. But it was strange to hear her unwearying flow of oaths and obscenities, endless like a river, and now and then rising to a passionate shrillness, in the clear and silent air of the morning. In city slums, the thing might have passed unnoticed; but in a country valley, and from a plain and honest countrywoman, this beast-liness of speech surprised the ear.

The *Conductor*, as he is called, *of Roads and Bridges* was my principal companion. He was generally intelligent, and could have spoken more or less falsetto on any of the trite topics; but it was his specialty to have a generous taste in eating. This was what was most indigenous in the man; it was here he was an artist; and I found in his company what I had long suspected, that enthusiasm and special knowledge are the great social qualities, and what they are about, whether white sauce or Shakespeare's plays, an altogether secondary question.

I used to accompany the *Conductor* on his professional rounds, and grew to believe myself an expert in the business. I thought I could make an entry in a stone-breaker's time-book, or order manure off the wayside with any living engineer in France. Gondet was one of the places we visited together; and Laussonne, where I met the apothecary's father, was another. There, at Laussonne, George Sand spent a day while she was gathering materials for the *Marquis de Villemer;* and I have spoken with an old man, who was then a child running about the inn kitchen, and who still remembers her with a sort of reverence. It appears that he spoke French imperfectly; for this reason George Sand chose him for companion, and whenever he let slip a broad and picturesque phrase in *patois*, she would make him repeat it again and again till it was graven in her memory. The word for a frog particularly pleased her fancy; and it would be curious to know if she afterwards employed it in her works. The peasants, who knew nothing of letters and had never so much as heard of local colour, could not explain her chattering with this backward child; and to them she seemed a very homely lady and far from beautiful: the most famous man-killer of the age appealed so little to Velaisian swineherds!

On my first engineering excursion, which lay up by Crouzials towards Mount Mezenc and the borders of Ardèche, I began an improving acquaintance with the foreman road-mender. He was in great glee at having me with him, passed me off among his subalterns as the supervising engineer, and insisted on what he called "the gallantry" of paying for my breakfast in a roadside wine-shop. On the whole, he was a man of great weather-wisdom, some spirits, and a social temper. But I am afraid he was superstitious. When he was nine years old, he had seen one night a company of *bourgeois et dames qui faisaient la manège avec des chaises*, and concluded that he was in the presence of a witches' Sabbath. I suppose, but venture with timidity on the suggestion, that this may have been a romantic and nocturnal picnic party. Again, coming from Pradelles with his brother, they saw a great empty cart drawn by six enormous horses before them on the road. The driver cried aloud and filled the mountains with the cracking of his whip. He never seemed to go faster than a walk, yet it was impossible to overtake him; and at length, at the corner of a hill, the whole equipage disappeared bodily into the night. At the time, people said it was the devil *qui s'amusait à faire ça.*

I suggested there was nothing more likely, as he must have some amusement.

The foreman said it was odd, but there was less of

that sort of thing than formerly. " *C'est difficile*," he added, " *à expliquer*."

When we were well up on the moors and the *Conductor* was trying some road-metal with the gauge—

" Hark! " said the foreman, " do you hear nothing ? "

We listened, and the wind, which was blowing chilly out of the east, brought a faint, tangled jangling to our ears.

" It is the flocks of Vivarais," said he.

For every summer, the flocks out of all Ardèche are brought up to pasture on these grassy plateaux.

Here and there a little private flock was being tended by a girl, one spinning with a distaff, another seated on a wall and intently making lace. This last, when we addressed her, leaped up in a panic and put out her arms, like a person swimming, to keep us at a distance, and it was some seconds before we could persuade her of the honesty of our intentions.

The *Conductor* told me of another herdswoman from whom he had once asked his road while he was yet new to the country, and who fled from him, driving her beasts before her, until he had given up the information in despair. A tale of old lawlessness may yet be read in these uncouth timidities.

The winter in these uplands is a dangerous and melancholy time. Houses are snowed up, and wayfarers lost in a flurry within hail of their own fireside. No man ventures abroad without meat and a bottle of wine, which he replenishes at every wine-shop; and even thus equipped he takes the road with terror. All day the family sits about the fire in a foul and airless hovel, and equally without work or diversion. The father may carve a rude piece of furniture, but that is all that will be done until the spring sets in again, and along with it the labours of the field. It is not for nothing that you find a clock in the meanest of these mountain habitations. A clock and an almanac, you would fancy, were indispensable in such a life. . . .

CRITICISMS

Originally published :
   I. *Fortnightly Review, June, 1874.*
  II. *Academy, April 15, 1876.*
 III. *Magazine of Art, April, 1882.*

CRITICISMS

I

LORD LYTTON'S "FABLES IN SONG"

IT seems as if Lord Lytton, in this new book of his, had found the form most natural to his talent. In some ways, indeed, it may be held inferior to "Chronicles and Characters"; we look in vain for anything like the terrible intensity of the night-scene in "Irene," or for any such passages of massive and memorable writing as appeared, here and there, in the earlier work, and made it not altogether unworthy of its model, Hugo's "Legend of the Ages." But it becomes evident, on the most hasty retrospect, that this earlier work was a step on the way towards the later. It seems as if the author had been feeling about for his definite medium, and was already, in the language of the child's game, growing hot. There are many pieces in "Chronicles and Characters" that might be detached from their original setting, and embodied, as they stand, among the "Fables in Song."

For the term Fable is not very easy to define rigorously. In the most typical form some moral precept is set forth by means of a conception purely fantastic, and usually somewhat trivial into the bargain; there is something playful about it, that will not support a very exacting criticism, and the lesson must be apprehended by the fancy at half a hint. Such is the great mass of the old stories of wise animals or foolish men that have amused our childhood. But we should expect the fable, in company with other and more important literary forms, to be more and more loosely, or at least largely, comprehended as time went on, and so to degenerate in conception from this original type. That depended for much of its piquancy on the very fact that it was fantastic: the point of the thing lay in a sort of humorous inappropriateness; and it is natural enough that pleasantry of this description should become less common, as men learn to suspect some serious analogy underneath. Thus a comical story of an ape touches us quite differently after the proposition of Mr. Darwin's theory. Moreover there lay, perhaps, at the bottom of this primitive sort of fable, a humanity, a tenderness of rough truths; so that at the end of some story, in which vice or folly had met with its destined punishment, the fabulist might be able to assure his auditors, as we have often to assure tearful children on the like occasions, that they may dry their eyes, for none of it was true.

But this benefit of fiction becomes lost with more sophisticated hearers and authors: a man is no longer the dupe of his own artifice, and cannot deal playfully with truths that are a matter of bitter concern to him in his life. And hence, in the progressive centralisation of modern thought, we should expect the old form of fable to fall gradually into desuetude, and be gradually succeeded by another, which is a fable in all points except that it is not altogether fabulous. And this new form, such as we should expect, and such as we do indeed find, still presents the essential character of brevity; as in any other fable also, there is, underlying and animating the brief action, a moral idea; and as in any other fable, the object is to bring this home to the reader through the intellect rather than through the feelings; so that, without being very deeply moved or interested by the characters of the piece, we should recognise vividly the hinges on which the little plot revolves. But the fabulist now seeks analogies where before he merely sought humorous situations. There will be now a logical nexus between the moral expressed and the machinery employed to express it. The machinery, in fact, as this change is developed, becomes less and less fabulous. We find ourselves in presence of quite a serious, if quite a miniature division of creative literature; and sometimes we have the lesson embodied in a sober, every-day narration, as in the parables of the New Testament, and sometimes merely the statement or, at most, the collocation of significant facts in life, the reader being left to resolve for himself the vague, troublesome, and not yet definitely moral sentiment which has been thus created. And step by step with the development of this change, yet another is developed: the moral tends to become more indeterminate and large. It ceases to be possible to append it, in a tag, to the bottom of the piece, as one might write the name below a caricature; and the fable begins to take rank with all other forms of creative literature, as something too ambitious, in spite of its miniature dimensions, to be resumed in any succinct formula without the loss of all that is deepest and most suggestive in it.

Now it is in this widest sense that Lord Lytton understands the term; there are examples in his two pleasant volumes of all the forms already mentioned, and even of another which can only be admitted among fables by the utmost possible leniency of construction. "Composure," "Et Cætera," and several more, are merely similes poetically elaborated. So, too, is the pathetic story of the grandfather and grandchild: the child, having treasured away an icicle and forgotten it for ten minutes, comes back to find it already nearly melted, and no longer beautiful: at the same time, the grandfather has just remembered and taken out a bundle of love-letters, which he too had stored away in years gone by, and then long neglected; and, behold! the letters are as faded and sorrowfully disappointing as the icicle. This is merely a simile poetically worked out; and yet it is in such as these, and some others, to be mentioned further on, that the author seems at his best. Wherever he has really written after the old model, there is something to be deprecated: in spite of all the spirit and freshness, in spite of his happy assumption of that cheerful acceptation of things as they are, which, rightly or wrongly, we come to attribute to the ideal fabulist, there is ever a sense as of something a little out of place. A form of literature so very innocent and primitive looks a little overwritten in Lord Lytton's conscious and highly coloured style. It may be bad taste, but sometimes we should prefer a few sentences of plain prose narration, and a little Bewick by way of tail-piece. So that it is not among those fables that conform most nearly to the old model, but one had nearly said among those that most widely differ from it, that we find the most satisfactory examples of the author's manner.

In the mere matter of ingenuity, the metaphysical fables are the most remarkable; such as that of the windmill who imagined that it was he who raised the wind; or that of the grocer's balance (" Cogito ergo sum ") who considered himself endowed with free-will, reason, and an infallible practical judgment; until, one fine day, the police make a descent upon the shop, and find the weights false and the scales unequal; and the whole thing is broken up for old iron. Capital fables, also, in the same ironical spirit, are " Prometheus Unbound," the tale of the vainglorying of a champagne-cork, and " Teleology," where a nettle justifies the ways of God to nettles while all goes well with it, and, upon a change of luck, promptly changes its divinity.

In all these there is still plenty of the fabulous if you will, although, even here, there may be two opinions possible; but there is another group, of an order of merit perhaps still higher, where we look in vain for any such playful liberties with Nature. Thus we have " Conservation of Force "; where a musician, thinking of a certain picture, improvises in the twilight; a poet, hearing the music, goes home inspired, and writes a poem; and then a painter, under the influence of this poem, paints another picture, thus lineally descended from the first. This is fiction, but not what we have been used to call fable. We miss the incredible element, the point of audacity with which the fabulist was wont to mock at his readers. And still more so is this the case with others. "The Horse and the Fly" states one of the unanswerable problems of life in quite a realistic and straightforward way. A fly startles a cab-horse, the coach is overset; a newly married pair within and the driver, a man with a wife and family, are all killed. The horse continues to gallop off in the loose traces, and ends the tragedy by running over an only child; and there is some little pathetic detail here introduced in the telling, that makes the reader's indignation very white-hot against some one. It remains to be seen who that some one is to be: the fly? Nay, but, on closer inspection, it appears that the fly, actuated by maternal instinct, was only seeking a place for her eggs: is maternal instinct, then, "sole author of these mischiefs all"? "Who's in the Right?" one of the best fables in the book, is somewhat in the same vein. After a battle has been won, a group of officers assemble inside a battery, and debate together who should have the honour of the success: the Prince, the general staff, the cavalry, the engineer who posted the battery in which they then stand talking, are successively named: the sergeant, who pointed the guns, sneers to himself at the mention of the engineer; and, close by, the gunner, who had applied the match, passes away with a smile of triumph, since it was through his hand that the victorious blow had been dealt. Meanwhile, the cannon claims the honour over the gunner; the cannon-ball, who actually goes forth on the dread mission, claims it over the cannon, who remains idly behind; the powder reminds the cannon-ball that, but for him, it would still be lying on the arsenal floor; and the match caps the discussion: powder, cannon-ball, and cannon would be all equally vain and ineffectual without fire. Just then there comes on a shower of rain, which wets the powder and puts out the match, and completes this lesson of dependence, by indicating the negative conditions which are as necessary for any effect, in their absence, as is the presence of this great fraternity of positive conditions, not any one of which can claim priority over any other. But the fable does not end here, as perhaps, in all logical strictness, it should. It wanders off into a discussion as to which is the truer greatness, that of the vanquished fire or that of the victorious rain. And the speech of the rain is charming:

> "Lo, with my little drops I bless again
> And beautify the fields which thou didst blast!
> Rend, wither, waste, and ruin, what thou wilt,
> But call not Greatness what the Gods call Guilt.
> Blossoms and grass from blood in battle spilt,
> And poppied corn, I bring.
> 'Mid mouldering Babels, to oblivion built,
> My violets spring.
> Little by little my small drops have strength
> To deck with green delights the grateful earth."

And so forth, not quite germane (it seems to me) to the matter in hand, but welcome for its own sake.

Best of all are the fables that deal more immediately with the emotions. There is, for instance, that of " The Two Travellers," which is profoundly moving in conception, although by no means as well written as some others. In this, one of the two, fearfully frost-bitten, saves his life out of the snow at the cost of all that was comely in his body; just as, long before, the other, who has now quietly resigned himself to death, had violently freed himself from Love at the cost of all that was finest and fairest in his character. Very graceful and sweet is the fable (if so it should be called) in which the author sings the praises of that "kindly perspective" which lets a wheat-stalk near the eye cover twenty leagues of distant country, and makes the humble circle about a man's hearth more to him than all the possibilities of the external world. The companion fable to this is also excellent. It tells us of a man who had, all his life through, entertained a passion for certain blue hills on the far horizon, and had promised himself to travel thither ere he died, and become familiar with these distant friends. At last, in some political trouble, he is banished to the very place of his dreams. He arrives there overnight, and, when he rises and goes forth in the morning, there sure enough are the blue hills, only now they have changed places with him, and smile across to him, distant as ever, from the old home whence he has come. Such a story might have been very cynically treated; but it is not so done, the whole tone is kindly and consolatory, and the disenchanted man submissively takes the lesson, and understands that things far away are to be loved for their own sake, and that the unattainable is not truly unattainable, when we can make the beauty of it our own. Indeed, throughout all these two volumes, though there is much practical scepticism, and much irony on abstract questions, this kindly and consolatory spirit is never absent. There is much that is cheerful and, after a sedate, fireside fashion, hopeful. No one will be discouraged by reading the book; but the ground of all this hopefulness and cheerfulness remains to the end somewhat vague. It does not seem to arise from any practical belief in the future either of the individual or the race, but rather from the profound personal contentment of the writer. This is, I suppose, all we must look for in the case. It is as much as we can expect, if the fabulist shall prove a shrewd and cheerful fellow-wayfarer, one with whom the world does not seem to have gone much amiss, but who has yet laughingly learned something of its evil. It will depend much, of course, upon our own character and circumstances, whether the encounter will be agreeable and bracing to the spirits, or offend us as an ill-timed mockery. But where, as here, there is a little tincture of bitterness along with the good-nature, where it is plainly not the humour of a man cheerfully ignorant, but of one who looks on, tolerant and superior and smilingly attentive, upon the good and bad of our existence, it will go hardly if we do not catch some reflection of the same spirit to help us on our way. There is here no impertinent and lying proclamation of peace—none of the cheap optimism of the well-to-do; what we find here is a view of life that would be even grievous, were it not enlivened with this abiding cheerfulness, and ever and anon redeemed by a stroke of pathos.

It is natural enough, I suppose, that we should find wanting in this book some of the intenser qualities of the author's work; and their absence is made up for by much happy description after a quieter fashion. The burst of jubilation over the departure of the snow, which forms the prelude to "The Thistle," is full of spirit and of pleasant images. The speech of the forest in "Sans Souci" is inspired by a beautiful sentiment for nature of the modern sort, and pleases us more, I think, as poetry should please us, than anything in "Chronicles and Characters." There are some admirable felicities of expression here and there; as that of the hill, whose summit

> " Did print
> The azure air with pines."

Moreover, I do not recollect in the author's former work any symptom of that sympathetic treatment of still life, which is noticeable now and again in the fables; and perhaps most noticeably, when he sketches the burned letters as they hover along the gusty flue, "Thin, sable veils wherein a restless spark Yet trembled." But the description is at its best when the subjects are unpleasant, or even grisly. There are a few capital lines in this key on the last spasm of the battle before alluded to. Surely nothing could be better, in its own way, than the fish in "The Last Cruise of the Arrogant," "the shadowy, side-faced, silent things," that come butting and staring with lidless eyes at the sunken steam-engine. And although, in yet another, we are told, pleasantly enough, how the water went down into the valleys, where it set itself gaily to saw wood, and on into the plains, where it would soberly carry grain to town; yet the real strength of the fable is when it deals with the shut pool in which certain unfortunate raindrops are imprisoned among slugs and snails, and in the company of an old toad. The sod-

den contentment of the fallen acorn is strangely significant; and it is astonishing how unpleasantly we are
startled by the appearance of her horrible lover, the
maggot.

And now for a last word, about the style. This is
not easy to criticise. It is impossible to deny to it
rapidity, spirit, and a full sound; the lines are never
lame, and the sense is carried forwards with an uninterrupted, impetuous rush. But it is not equal. After
passages of really admirable versification, the author
falls back upon a sort of loose, cavalry manner, not
unlike the style of some of Mr. Browning's minor pieces,
and almost inseparable from wordiness, and an easy
acceptation of somewhat cheap finish. There is nothing here of that compression which is the note of a
really sovereign style. It is unfair, perhaps, to set a
not remarkable passage from Lord Lytton side by side
with one of the signal masterpieces of another, and a
very perfect poet; and yet it is interesting, when we
see how the portraiture of a dog, detailed through thirty-
odd lines, is frittered down and finally almost lost in
the mere laxity of the style, to compare it with the
clear, simple, vigorous delineation that Burns, in four
couplets, has given us of the ploughman's collie. It is
interesting, at first, and then it becomes a little irritating; for when we think of other passages so much
more finished and adroit, we cannot help feeling that
with a little more ardour after perfection of form, criticism would have found nothing left for her to censure.
A similar mark of precipitate work is the number of
adjectives tumultuously heaped together, sometimes to
help out the sense, and sometimes (as one cannot but

suspect) to help out the sound of the verses. I do not believe, for instance, that Lord Lytton himself would defend the lines in which we are told how Laocoön "Revealed to *Roman* crowds, now *Christian* grown, That *Pagan* anguish which, in *Parian* stone, the *Rhodian* artist," and so on. It is not only that this is bad in itself; but that it is unworthy of the company in which it is found; that such verses should not have appeared with the name of a good versifier like Lord Lytton. We must take exception, also, in conclusion, to the excess of alliteration. Alliteration is so liable to be abused that we can scarcely be too sparing of it; and yet it is a trick that seems to grow upon the author with years. It is a pity to see fine verses, such as some in "Demos," absolutely spoiled by the recurrence of one wearisome consonant.

II

SALVINI'S MACBETH

SALVINI closed his short visit to Edinburgh by a performance of *Macbeth*. It was, perhaps, from a sentiment of local colour that he chose to play the Scottish
usurper for the first time before Scotsmen; and the
audience were not insensible of the privilege. Few
things, indeed, can move a stronger interest than to see
a great creation taking shape for the first time. If it is
not purely artistic, the sentiment is surely human. And
the thought that you are before all the world, and have
the start of so many others as eager as yourself, at
least keeps you in a more unbearable suspense before
the curtain rises, if it does not enhance the delight with
which you follow the performance and see the actor
"bend up each corporal agent" to realise a masterpiece
of a few hours' duration. With a player so variable as
Salvini, who trusts to the feeling of the moment for so
much detail, and who, night after night, does the same
thing differently but always well, it can never be safe
to pass judgment after a single hearing. And this is
more particularly true of last week's *Macbeth;* for the
whole third act was marred by a grievously humorous
misadventure. Several minutes too soon the ghost of
Banquo joined the party, and, after having sat help-

less awhile at a table, was ignominiously withdrawn. Twice was this ghostly Jack-in-the-box obtruded on the stage before his time; twice removed again; and yet he showed so little hurry when he was really wanted, that, after an awkward pause, Macbeth had to begin his apostrophe to empty air. The arrival of the belated spectre in the middle, with a jerk that made him nod all over, was the last accident in the chapter, and worthily topped the whole. It may be imagined how lamely matters went throughout these cross-purposes.

In spite of this, and some other hitches, Salvini's Macbeth had an emphatic success. The creation is worthy of a place beside the same artist's Othello and Hamlet. It is the simplest and most unsympathetic of the three; but the absence of the finer lineaments of Hamlet is redeemed by gusto, breadth, and a headlong unity. Salvini sees nothing great in Macbeth beyond the royalty of muscle, and that courage which comes of strong and copious circulation. The moral small-ness of the man is insisted on from the first, in the shudder of uncontrollable jealousy with which he sees Duncan embracing Banquo. He may have some North-ern poetry of speech, but he has not much logical un-derstanding. In his dealings with the supernatural powers he is like a savage with his fetich, trusting them beyond bounds while all goes well, and whenever he is crossed, casting his belief aside and calling "fate into the list." For his wife, he is little more than an agent, a frame of bone and sinew for her fiery spirit to com-mand. The nature of his feeling towards her is ren-dered with a most precise and delicate touch. He always yields to the woman's fascination; and yet his caresses (and we know how much meaning Salvini can give to a caress) are singularly hard and unloving. Sometimes he lays his hand on her as he might take hold of any one who happened to be nearest to him at a moment of excitement. Love has fallen out of this marriage by the way, and left a curious friendship. Only once—at the very moment when she is showing herself so little a woman and so much a high-spirited man— only once is he very deeply stirred towards her; and that finds expression in the strange and horrible transport of admiration, doubly strange and horrible on Salvini's lips—" Bring forth men-children only! "

The murder scene, as was to be expected, pleased the audience best. Macbeth's voice, in the talk with his wife, was a thing not to be forgotten; and when he spoke of his hangman's hands he seemed to have blood in his utterance. Never for a moment, even in the very article of the murder, does he possess his own soul. He is a man on wires. From first to last it is an exhibition of hideous cowardice. For, after all, it is not here, but in broad daylight, with the exhilaration of conflict, where he can assure himself at every blow he has the longest sword and the heaviest hand, that this man's physical bravery can keep him up; he is an unwieldy ship, and needs plenty of way on before he will steer.

In the banquet scene, while the first murderer gives account of what he has done, there comes a flash of truculent joy at the "twenty trenchèd gashes" on Banquo's head. Thus Macbeth makes welcome to his imagination those very details of physical horror which are so soon to turn sour in him. As he runs out to embrace these cruel circumstances, as he seeks to realise to his mind's eye the reassuring spectacle of his dead enemy, he is dressing out the phantom to terrify himself; and his imagination, playing the part of justice, is to "commend to his own lips the ingredients of his poisoned chalice." With the recollection of Hamlet and his father's spirit still fresh upon him, and the holy awe with which that good man encountered things not dreamt of in his philosophy, it was not possible to avoid looking for resemblances between the two apparitions and the two men haunted. But there are none to be found. Macbeth has a purely physical dislike for Banquo's spirit and the "twenty trenchèd gashes." He is afraid of he knows not what. He is abject, and again blustering. In the end he so far forgets himself, his terror, and the nature of what is before him, that he rushes upon it as he would upon a man. When his wife tells him he needs repose, there is something really childish in the way he looks about the room, and, seeing nothing, with an expression of almost sensual relief, plucks up heart enough to go to bed. And what is the upshot of the visitation? It is written in Shakespeare, but should be read with the commentary of Salvini's voice and expression:—"*O! siam nell' opra ancor fanciulli,*"—"We are yet young indeed." Circle below circle. He is looking with horrible satisfaction into the mouth of hell. There may still be a prick to-day; but to-morrow conscience will be dead, and he may move untroubled in this element of blood.

In the fifth act we see this lowest circle reached; and it is Salvini's finest moment throughout the play. From the first he was admirably made up, and looked Macbeth to the full as perfectly as ever he looked Othello. From the first moment he steps upon the stage you can see this character is a creation to the fullest meaning of the phrase; for the man before you is a type you know well already. He arrives with Banquo on the heath, fair and red-bearded, sparing of gesture, full of pride and the sense of animal well-being, and satisfied after the battle like a beast who has eaten his fill. But in the fifth act there is a change. This is still the big, burly, fleshly, handsome-looking Thane; here is still the same face which in the earlier acts could be superficially good-humoured and sometimes royally courteous. But now the atmosphere of blood, which pervades the whole tragedy, has entered into the man and subdued him to its own nature; and an indescribable degradation, a slackness and puffiness, has overtaken his features. He has breathed the air of carnage, and supped full of horrors. Lady Macbeth complains of the smell of blood on her hand: Macbeth makes no complaint— he has ceased to notice it now; but the same smell is in his nostrils. A contained fury and disgust possesses him. He taunts the messenger and the doctor as people would taunt their mortal enemies. And, indeed, as he knows right well, every one is his enemy now, except his wife. About her he questions the doctor with something like a last human anxiety; and, in tones of grisly mystery, asks him if he can "minister to a mind diseased." When the news of her death is brought him, he is staggered and falls into a seat; but somehow it is not anything we can call grief that he displays. There had been two of them against God and man; and now, when there is only one, it makes perhaps less difference than he had expected. And so her death is not only an affliction, but one more disillusion; and he redoubles in bitterness. The speech that follows, given with tragic cynicism in every word, is a dirge, not so much for her as for himself. From that time forth there is nothing human left in him, only "the fiend of Scotland," Macduff's "hell-hound," whom, with a stern glee, we see baited like a bear and hunted down like a wolf. He is inspired and set above fate by a demoniacal energy, a lust of wounds and slaughter. Even after he meets Macduff his courage does not fail; but when he hears the Thane was not born of woman, all virtue goes out of him; and though he speaks sounding words of defiance, the last combat is little better than a suicide.

The whole performance is, as I said, so full of gusto and a headlong unity; the personality of Macbeth is so sharp and powerful; and within these somewhat narrow limits there is so much play and saliency that, so far as concerns Salvini himself, a third great success seems indubitable. Unfortunately, however, a great actor cannot fill more than a very small fraction of the boards; and though Banquo's ghost will probably be more seasonable in his future apparitions, there are some more inherent difficulties in the piece. The company at large did not distinguish themselves. Macduff, to the huge delight of the gallery, out-Macduff'd the average ranter. The lady who filled the principal female part has done better on other occasions, but I fear she has not metal for what she tried last week. Not to succeed in the sleep-walking scene is to make a memorable failure. As it was given, it succeeded in being wrong in art without being true to nature.

And there is yet another difficulty, happily easy to reform, which somewhat interfered with the success of the performance. At the end of the incantation scene the Italian translator has made Macbeth fall insensible upon the stage. This is a change of questionable propriety from a psychological point of view; while in point of view of effect it leaves the stage for some moments empty of all business. To remedy this, a bevy of green ballet-girls came forth and pointed their toes about the prostrate king. A dance of High Church curates, or a hornpipe by Mr. T. P. Cooke, would not be more out of the key; though the gravity of a Scots audience was not to be overcome, and they merely expressed their disapprobation by a round of moderate hisses, a similar irruption of Christmas fairies would most likely convulse a London theatre from pit to gallery with inextinguishable laughter. It is, I am told, the Italian tradition; but it is one more honoured in the breach than the observance. With the total disappearance of these damsels, with a stronger Lady Macbeth, and, if possible, with some compression of those scenes in which Salvini does not appear, and the spectator is left at the mercy of Macduffs and Duncans, the play would go twice as well, and we should be better able to follow and enjoy an admirable work of dramatic art.

III

BAGSTER'S "PILGRIM'S PROGRESS"

I HAVE here before me an edition of the *Pilgrim's Progress*, bound in green, without a date, and described as "illustrated by nearly three hundred engravings, and memoir of Bunyan." On the outside it is lettered "Bagster's Illustrated Edition," and after the author's apology, facing the first page of the tale, a folding pictorial "Plan of the Road" is marked as "drawn by the late Mr. T. Conder," and engraved by J. Basire. No further information is anywhere vouchsafed; perhaps the publishers had judged the work too unimportant; and we are still left ignorant whether or not we owe the woodcuts in the body of the volume to the same hand that drew the plan. It seems, however, more than probable. The literal particularity of mind which, in the map, laid down the flower-plots in the devil's garden, and carefully introduced the court-house in the town of Vanity, is closely paralleled in many of the cuts; and in both, the architecture of the buildings and the disposition of the gardens have a kindred and entirely English air. Whoever he was, the author of these wonderful little pictures may lay claim to be the best illustrator of Bunyan.[1]

[1] The illustrator was, in fact, a lady, Miss Eunice Bagster, eldest daughter of the publisher, Samuel Bagster; except in the case of the cuts depicting

They are not only good illustrations, like so many others; but they are like so few, good illustrations of Bunyan. Their spirit, in defect and quality, is still the same as his own. The designer also has lain down and dreamed a dream, as literal, as quaint, and almost as apposite as Bunyan's; and text and pictures make but the two sides of the same homespun yet impassioned story. To do justice to the designs, it will be necessary to say, for the hundredth time, a word or two about the masterpiece which they adorn.

All allegories have a tendency to escape from the purpose of their creators; and as the characters and incidents become more and more interesting in themselves, the moral, which these were to show forth, falls more and more into neglect. An architect may command a wreath of vine-leaves round the cornice of a monument; but if, as each leaf came from the chisel, it took proper life and fluttered freely on the wall, and if the vine grew, and the building were hidden over with foliage and fruit, the architect would stand in much the same situation as the writer of allegories. The *Faëry Queen* was an allegory, I am willing to believe; but it survives as an imaginative tale in incomparable verse. The case of Bunyan is widely different; and yet in this also Allegory, poor nymph, although never quite forgotten, is sometimes rudely thrust against the wall. Bunyan was fervently in earnest; with "his fingers in his ears, he ran on," straight for his mark. He tells us himself, in

the fight with Apollyon, which were designed by her brother, Mr. Jonathan Bagster. The edition was published in 1845. I am indebted for this information to the kindness of Mr. Robert Bagster, the present managing director of the firm.—[ED.]

the conclusion to the first part, that he did not fear to raise a laugh; indeed, he feared nothing, and said anything; and he was greatly served in this by a certain rustic privilege of his style, which, like the talk of strong uneducated men, when it does not impress by its force, still charms by its simplicity. The mere story and the allegorical design enjoyed perhaps his equal favour. He believed in both with an energy of faith that was capable of moving mountains. And we have to remark in him, not the parts where inspiration fails and is supplied by cold and merely decorative invention, but the parts where faith has grown to be credulity, and his characters become so real to him that he forgets the end of their creation. We can follow him step by step into the trap which he lays for himself by his own entire good faith and triumphant literality of vision, till the trap closes and shuts him in an inconsistency. The allegories of the Interpreter and of the Shepherds of the Delectable Mountains are all actually performed, like stage-plays, before the pilgrims. The son of Mr. Great-grace visibly "tumbles hills about with his words." Adam the First has his condemnation written visibly on his forehead, so that Faithful reads it. At the very instant the net closes round the pilgrims, "the white robe falls from the black man's body." Despair "getteth him a grievous crab-tree cudgel"; it was in "sunshiny weather" that he had his fits; and the birds in the grove about the House Beautiful, "our country birds," only sing their little pious verses "at the spring, when the flowers appear and the sun shines warm." "I often," says Piety, "go out to hear them; we also ofttimes keep them tame on our house." The post between Beulah and the Celestial City sounds his horn, as you may yet hear in country places. Madam Bubble, that "tall, comely dame, something of a swarthy complexion, in very pleasant attire, but old," "gives you a smile at the end of each sentence"—a real woman she; we all know her. Christiana dying "gave Mr. Stand-fast a ring," for no possible reason in the allegory, merely because the touch was human and affecting. Look at Great-heart, with his soldierly ways, garrison ways, as I had almost called them; with his taste in weapons; his delight in any that "he found to be a man of his hands"; his chivalrous point of honour, letting Giant Maul get up again when he was down, a thing fairly flying in the teeth of the moral; above all, with his language in the inimitable tale of Mr. Fearing: "I thought I should have lost my man"—"chicken-hearted"—"at last he came in, and I will say that for my lord, he carried it wonderful lovingly to him." This is no Independent minister; this is a stout, honest, big-busted ancient, adjusting his shoulder-belts, twirling his long moustaches as he speaks. Last and most remarkable, "My sword," says the dying Valiant-for-Truth, he in whom Great-heart delighted, "my sword I give to him that shall succeed me in my pilgrimage, *and my courage and skill to him that can get it.*" And after this boast, more arrogantly unorthodox than was ever dreamed of by the rejected Ignorance, we are told that "all the trumpets sounded for him on the other side."

In every page the book is stamped with the same energy of vision and the same energy of belief. The quality is equally and indifferently displayed in the spirit

of the fighting, the tenderness of the pathos, the startling vigour and strangeness of the incidents, the natural
strain of the conversations, and the humanity and charm
of the characters. Trivial talk over a meal, the dying
words of heroes, the delights of Beulah or the Celestial
City, Apollyon and my Lord Hate-good, Great-heart,
and Mr. Worldly Wiseman, all have been imagined with
the same clearness, all written of with equal gusto and
precision, all created in the same mixed element, of
simplicity that is almost comical, and art that, for its
purpose, is faultless.

It was in much the same spirit that our artist sat down
to his drawings. He is by nature a Bunyan of the
pencil. He, too, will draw anything, from a butcher at
work on a dead sheep, up to the courts of Heaven.
"A Lamb for Supper" is the name of one of his designs,
"Their Glorious Entry" of another. He has the same
disregard for the ridiculous, and enjoys somewhat of
the same privilege of style, so that we are pleased even
when we laugh the most. He is literal to the verge of
folly. If dust is to be raised from the unswept parlour,
you may be sure it will "fly abundantly" in the picture.
If Faithful is to lie "as dead" before Moses, dead he
shall lie with a warrant—dead and stiff like granite; nay
(and here the artist must enhance upon the symbolism
of the author), it is with the identical stone tables of the
law that Moses fells the sinner. Good and bad people,
whom we at once distinguish in the text by their names,
Hopeful, Honest, and Valiant-for-Truth on the one hand,
as against By-ends, Sir Having Greedy, and the Lord
Old-man on the other, are in these drawings as simply
distinguished by their costume. Good people, when

216

not armed *cap-à-pie*, wear a speckled tunic girt about the waist, and low hats, apparently of straw. Bad people swagger in tail-coats and chimney-pots, a few with knee-breeches, but the large majority in trousers, and for all the world like guests at a garden-party. Worldly Wiseman alone, by some inexplicable quirk, stands before Christian in laced hat, embroidered waist-coat, and trunk-hose. But above all examples of this artist's intrepidity, commend me to the print entitled "Christian Finds it Deep." "A great darkness and horror," says the text, have fallen on the pilgrim; it is the comfortless death-bed with which Bunyan so strikingly concludes the sorrows and conflicts of his hero. How to represent this worthily the artist knew not; and yet he was determined to represent it somehow. This was how he did: Hopeful is still shown to his neck above the water of death; but Christian has bodily disappeared, and a blot of solid blackness indicates his place.

As you continue to look at these pictures, about an inch square for the most part, sometimes printed three or more to the page, and each having a printed legend of its own, however trivial the event recorded, you will soon become aware of two things: first, that the man can draw, and, second, that he possesses the gift of an imagination. "Obstinate reviles," says the legend; and you should see Obstinate reviling. "He warily retraces his steps"; and there is Christian, posting through the plain, terror and speed in every muscle. "Mercy yearns to go" shows you a plain interior with packing going forward, and, right in the middle, Mercy yearning to go—every line of the girl's figure yearning.

In "The Chamber called Peace" we see a simple English room, bed with white curtains, window valance and door, as may be found in many thousand unpretentious houses; but far off, through the open window, we behold the sun uprising out of a great plain, and Christian hails it with his hand:

"Where am I now ! is this the love and care
Of Jesus, for the men that pilgrims are !
Thus to provide ! That I should be forgiven !
And dwell already the next door to heaven ! "

A page or two further, from the top of the House Beautiful, the damsels point his gaze towards the Delectable Mountains: "The Prospect," so the cut is ticketed—and I shall be surprised, if on less than a square of paper you can show me one so wide and fair. Down a cross-road on an English plain, a cathedral city outlined on the horizon, a hazel shaw upon the left, comes Madam Wanton dancing with her fair enchanted cup, and Faithful, book in hand, half pauses. The cut is perfect as a symbol: the giddy movement of the sorceress, the uncertain poise of the man struck to the heart by a temptation, the contrast of that even plain of life whereon he journeys with the bold, ideal bearing of the wanton—the artist who invented and portrayed this had not merely read Bunyan, he had also thoughtfully lived. The Delectable Mountains—I continue skimming the first part—are not on the whole happily rendered. Once, and once only, the note is struck, when Christian and Hopeful are seen coming, shoulder-high, through a thicket of green shrubs—box, perhaps, or perfumed nutmeg; while behind them, domed or

218

pointed, the hills stand ranged against the sky. A little further, and we come to that masterpiece of Bunyan's insight into life, the Enchanted Ground; where, in a few traits, he has set down the latter end of such a number of the would-be good; where his allegory goes so deep that, to people looking seriously on life, it cuts like satire. The true significance of this invention lies, of course, far out of the way of drawing; only one feature, the great tedium of the land, the growing weariness in well-doing, may be somewhat represented in a symbol. The pilgrims are near the end: "Two Miles Yet," says the legend. The road goes ploughing up and down over a rolling heath; the wayfarers, with outstretched arms, are already sunk to the knees over the brow of the nearest hill; they have just passed a milestone with the cipher two; from overhead a great, piled, summer cumulus, as of a slumberous summer afternoon, beshadows them: two miles! it might be hundreds. In dealing with the Land of Beulah the artist lags, in both parts, miserably behind the text, but in the distant prospect of the Celestial City more than regains his own. You will remember when Christian and Hopeful "with desire fell sick." "Effect of the Sunbeams" is the artist's title. Against the sky, upon a cliffy mountain, the radiant temple beams upon them over deep, subjacent woods; they, behind a mound, as if seeking shelter from the splendour—one prostrate on his face, one kneeling, and with hands ecstatically lifted—yearn with passion after that immortal city. Turn the page, and we behold them walking by the very shores of death; Heaven, from this nigher view, has risen half-way to the zenith, and sheds a wider glory; and the two pilgrims, dark against that brightness, walk and sing out of the fulness of their hearts. No cut more thoroughly illustrates at once the merit and the weakness of the artist. Each pilgrim sings with a book in his grasp—a family Bible at the least for bigness; tomes so recklessly enormous that our second impulse is to laughter. And yet that is not the first thought, nor perhaps the last. Something in the attitude of the mani-kins—faces they have none, they are too small for that—something in the way they swing these monstrous volumes to their singing, something perhaps borrowed from the text, some subtle dif-ferentiation from the cut that went before and the cut that follows after—something, at least, speaks clearly of a fearful joy, of Heaven seen from the death-bed, of the horror of the last pas-sage no less than of the glorious coming home. There is that in the action of one of them which always reminds me, with a difference, of that haunting last glimpse of Thomas Idle, travelling to Tyburn in the cart. Next come the Shining Ones, wooden and trivial enough; the pilgrims pass into the river; the blot already mentioned settles over and obliterates Christian. In two more cuts we be-hold them drawing nearer to the other shore; and then, between two radiant angels, one of whom points upwards, we see them mounting in new weeds, their former lendings left behind them on the inky river. More angels meet them; Heaven is displayed, and if no better, certainly no worse, than it has been shown by others—a place, at least, infinitely populous and glorious with light—a place that haunts solemnly the hearts of children. And then this symbolic draughtsman once more strikes into his proper vein. Three cuts conclude the first part. In the first the gates close, black against the glory struggling from within. The second shows us Ignorance—alas! poor Arminian!—hailing, in a sad twilight, the ferryman Vain-Hope; and in the third we behold him, bound hand and foot, and black already with the hue of his eternal fate, carried high over the mountain-tops of the world by two angels of the anger of the Lord. "Carried to Another Place," the artist enigmatically names his plate—a terrible design.

Wherever he touches on the black side of the supernatural his pencil grows more daring and incisive. He has many true inventions in the perilous and diabolic; he has many startling nightmares realised. It is not easy to select the best; some may like one and some another; the nude, depilated devil bounding and casting darts against the Wicket Gate; the scroll of flying horrors that hang over Christian by the Mouth of Hell; the horned shade that comes behind him whispering blasphemies; the daylight breaking through that rent cave-mouth of the mountains and falling chill adown the haunted tunnel; Christian's further progress along the causeway, between the two black pools, where, at every yard or two, a gin, a pitfall, or a snare awaits the passer-by—loathsome white devilkins harbouring close under the bank to work the springes, Christian himself pausing and pricking with his sword's point at the nearest noose, and pale discomfortable mountains rising on the farther side; or yet again, the two ill-favoured ones that beset the first of Christian's journey, with the frog-like structure of the skull, the frog-like limberness of limbs—crafty, slippery, lustful-looking devils, drawn always in outline as though possessed of a dim, infernal luminosity. Horrid fellows are they, one and all; horrid fellows and horrific scenes. In another spirit that Good-Conscience "to whom Mr. Honest had spoken in his lifetime," a cowled, grey, awful figure, one hand pointing to the heavenly shore, realises, I will not say all, but some at least of the strange impressiveness of Bunyan's words. It is no easy nor pleasant thing to speak in one's lifetime with Good-Conscience; he is an austere, unearthly friend, whom maybe Torquemada knew; and the folds of his raiment are not merely claustral, but have something of the horror of the pall. Be not afraid, however; with the hand of that appearance Mr. Honest will get safe across.

Yet perhaps it is in sequences that this artist best displays himself. He loves to look at either side of a thing: as, for instance, when he shows us both sides of the wall—" Grace Inextinguishable " on the one side, with the devil vainly pouring buckets on the flame, and "The Oil of Grace " on the other, where the Holy Spirit, vessel in hand, still secretly supplies the fire. He loves, also, to show us the same event twice over, and to repeat his instantaneous photographs at the interval of but a moment. So we have, first, the whole troop of Pilgrims coming up to Valiant, and Greatheart to the front, spear in hand and parleying; and next, the same cross-roads, from a more distant view, the convoy now scattered and looking safely and curiously on, and Valiant handing over for inspection his "right Jerusalem blade." It is true that this designer has no great care after consistency: Apollyon's spear is laid by, his quiver of darts will disappear, whenever they might hinder the designer's freedom; and the fiend's tail is blobbed or forked at his good pleasure. But this is not unsuitable to the illustration of the fervent Bunyan, breathing hurry and momentary inspiration. He, with his hot purpose, hunting sinners with a lasso, shall himself forget the things that he has written yesterday. He shall first slay Heedless in the Valley of the Shadow, and then take leave of him talking in his sleep, as if nothing had happened, in an arbour on the Enchanted Ground. And again, in his rhymed prologue, he shall assign some of the glory of the siege of Doubting Castle to his favourite Valiant-for-Truth, who did not meet with the besiegers till long after, at that dangerous corner by Deadman's Lane. And, with all inconsistencies and freedoms, there is a power shown in these sequences of cuts: a power of joining on one action or one humour to another; a power of following out the moods, even of the dismal subterhuman fiends engendered by the artist's fancy; a power of sustained continuous realisation, step by step, in nature's order, that can tell a story, in all its ins and outs, its pauses and surprises, fully and figuratively, like the art of words.

One such sequence is the fight of Christian and Apollyon—six cuts, weird and fiery, like the text. The pilgrim is throughout a pale and stockish figure; but the devil covers a multitude of defects. There is no better devil of the conventional order than our artist's Apollyon, with his mane, his wings, his bestial legs, his changing and terrifying expression, his infernal energy to slay. In cut the first you see him afar off, still obscure in form, but already formidable in suggestion. Cut the second, "The Fiend in Discourse," represents him, not reasoning, railing rather, shaking his spear at the pilgrim, his shoulder advanced, his tail writhing in the air, his foot ready for a spring, while Christian stands back a little, timidly defensive. The third illustrates these magnificent words: "Then Apollyon straddled quite over the whole breadth of the way, and said, I am void of fear in this matter: prepare thyself to die; for I swear by my infernal den that thou shalt go no farther: here will I spill thy soul! And with that he threw a flaming dart at his breast." In the cut he throws a dart with either hand, belching pointed flames out of his mouth, spreading his broad vans, and straddling the while across the path, as only a fiend can straddle who has just sworn by his infernal den. The defence will not be long against such vice, such flames, such red-hot nether energy. And in the fourth cut, to be sure, he has leaped bodily upon his victim, sped by foot and pinion, and roaring as he leaps. The fifth shows the climacteric of the battle; Christian has reached nimbly out and got his sword, and dealt that deadly home-thrust, the fiend still stretched upon him, but "giving back, as one that had received his mortal wound." The raised head, the bellowing mouth, the paw clapped upon the sword, the one wing relaxed in agony, all realise vividly these words of the text. In the sixth and last, the trivial armed figure of the pilgrim is seen kneeling with clasped hands on the betrodden scene of contest and among the shivers of the darts; while just at the margin the hinder quarters and the tail of Apollyon are whisking off, indignant and discomfited.

In one point only do these pictures seem to be unworthy of the text, and that point is one rather of the difference of arts than the difference of artists. Throughout his best and worst, in his highest and most divine imaginations as in the narrowest sallies of his sectarianism, the human-hearted piety of Bunyan touches and ennobles, convinces, accuses the reader. Through no art besides the art of words can the kindness of a man's affections be expressed. In the cuts you shall find faithfully parodied the quaintness and the power, the triviality and the surprising freshness of the author's fancy; there you shall find him outstripped in ready symbolism and the art of bringing things essentially invisible before the eyes: but to feel the contact of essential goodness, to be made in love with piety, the book must be read and not the prints examined.

Farewell should not be taken with a grudge; nor can I dismiss in any other words than those of gratitude a series of pictures which have, to one at least, been the visible embodiment of Bunyan from childhood up, and shown him, through all his years, Great-heart lungeing at Giant Maul, and Apollyon breathing fire at Christian, and every turn and town along the road to the Celestial City, and that bright place itself, seen as to a stave of music, shining afar off upon the hill-top, the candle of the world.

LETTER TO THE CLERGY
OF THE CHURCH OF SCOTLAND

Originally published as a pamphlet by W. Blackwood and Sons, Edinburgh and London, 1875

AN APPEAL TO THE CLERGY
OF THE CHURCH OF SCOTLAND
WITH A NOTE FOR THE LAITY

"Had I a strong voice, as it is the weakest alive, yea, could I lift it up as a trumpet, I would sound a retreat from our unnatural contentions, and irreligious strivings for religion."—ARCHBISHOP LEIGHTON, 1669.

GENTLEMEN,—The position of the Church of Scotland is now one of considerable difficulty; not only the credit of the Church, not only the credit of Christianity, but to some extent also that of the national character, is at stake. You have just gained a great victory, in spite of an opposition neither very logical nor very generous; you have succeeded in effecting, by quiet constitutional processes, a great reform, which brings your Church somewhat nearer in character to what is required by your Dissenting brethren. It remains to be seen whether you can prove yourselves as generous as you have been wise and patient. And the position, as I say, is one of difficulty. Many, doubtless, left the Church for a reason which is now removed; many have joined other sects who would rather have joined themselves with you, had you been then as you now are; and for these you are bound to render as easy as may be the way of reconciliation, and show, by some notable action, the reality of your own desire for Peace. But i am not unaware that there are others, and those possibly a majority, who hold very different opinions—who regard the old quarrel as still competent, or have found some new reason for dissent; and from these the Church, if she makes such an advance as she ought to make, in all loyalty and charity, may chance to meet that most sensible of insults—ridicule, in return for an honest offer of reconciliation. I am not unaware, also, that there is yet another ground of difficulty; and that those even who would be most ready to hold the cause of offence as now removed will find it hard to forget the past—will continue to think themselves unjustly used—will not be willing to come back, as though they were repentant offenders, among those who delayed the reform and quietly enjoyed their benefices, while they bore the heat and burthen of the day in a voluntary exile for the Truth's sake.

In view of so many elements of difficulty, no intelligent person can be free from apprehension for the result; and you, gentlemen, may be perhaps more ready now to receive advice, to hear and weigh the opinion of one who is free, because he writes without name, than you would be at any juncture less critical. There is now a hope, at least, that some term may be put to our more clamorous dissensions. Those who are at all open to a feeling of national disgrace look eagerly forward to such a possibility; they have been witnesses already too long to the strife that has divided this small corner of Christendom; and they cannot remember without shame that there has been as much noise, as much recrimination, as much severance of friends, about mere logical abstractions in our remote island, as would have sufficed for the great dogmatic battles of the Continent. It would be difficult to exaggerate the pity that fills the heart at such a reflection; at the thought of how this neck of barren hills between two inclement seaways has echoed for three centuries with the uproar of sectarian battle; of how the east wind has carried out the sound of our shrill disputations into the desolate Atlantic, and the west wind has borne it over the German Ocean, as though it would make all Europe privy to how well we Scottish brethren abide together in unity. It is not a bright page in the annals of a small country: it is not a pleasant commentary on the Christianity that we profess; there is something in it pitiful, as I have said, for the pitiful man, but bitterly humorous for others. How much time we have lost, how much of the precious energy and patience of good men we have exhausted, on these trivial quarrels, it would be nauseous to consider; we know too much already when we know the facts in block; we know enough to make us hide our heads for shame, and grasp gladly at any present humiliation, if it would ensure a little more quiet, a little more charity, a little more brotherly love in the distant future.

And it is with this before your eyes that, as I feel certain, you are now addressing yourselves to the consideration of this important crisis. It is with a sense of the blackness of this discredit upon the national character and national Christianity that not you alone but many of other Churches are now setting themselves to square their future course with the exigencies of the new position of sects; and it is with you that the responsibility remains. The obligation lies ever on the victor; and just so surely as you have succeeded in the face of captious opposition in carrying forth the substance of a reform of which others had despaired, just as surely does it lie upon you as a duty to take such steps as shall make that reform available, not to you only, but to all your brethren who will consent to profit by it; not only to all the clergy, but to the cause of decency and peace, throughout your native land. It is earnestly hoped that you may show yourselves worthy of a great opportunity, and do more for the public minds by the example of one act of generosity and humility than you could do by an infinite series of sermons.

Without doubt, it is your intention, on the earliest public opportunity, to make some advance. Without doubt, it is your purpose to improve the advantage you have gained, and to press upon those who quitted your communion some thirty years ago your great desire to be once more united to them. This, at least, will find a place in the most unfriendly programme you can entertain; and if there are any in the Free Church (as I doubt not there are some) who seceded, not so much from any dislike to the just supremacy of the law, as from a belief that the law in these ecclesiastical matters was applied unjustly, I know well that you will be most eager to receive them back again; I know well that you will not let any petty vanity, any scruple of worldly dignity, stand between them and their honourable return. If, therefore, there were no more to be done than to display to these voluntary exiles the deep sense of your respect for their position, this appeal would be unnecessary, and you might be left to the guidance of your own good feeling.

But it seems to me that there is need of something more; it seems to me, and I think that it will seem so to you also, that you must go even further if you would be equal to the importance of the situation. If there are any among the Dissenters whose consciences are so far satisfied with the provisions of the recent Act that they could now return to your communion, to such, it must not be forgotten, you stand in a position of great delicacy. The conduct of these men you have so far justified; you have tacitly admitted that there was some ground for dissatisfaction with the former condition of the Church; and though you may still judge those to have been over-scrupulous who were moved by this imperfection to secede, instead of waiting patiently with you until it could be remedied by peaceful means, you must not forget that it is the strong stomach, according to Saint Paul, that is to consider the weak, and should come forward to meet these brethren with something better than compliments upon your lips. Observe, I speak only of those who would now see their way back to your communion with a clear conscience; it is their conduct, and their conduct alone, that you have justified, and therefore it is only for them that your special generosity is here solicited. But towards them, if there are any such, your countrymen would desire to see you behave with all consideration. I do not pretend to lay before you any definite scheme of action; I wish only to let you understand what thoughts are busy in the heads of some outside your councils, so that you may take this also into consideration when you come to decide. And this, roughly, is how it appears to these: These good men have exposed themselves to the chance of hardship for the sake of their scruples, whilst you, being of a stronger stomach, continued to enjoy the security of national endowments. Some of you occupy the very livings which they resigned for conscience' sake. To others preferment has fallen which would have fallen to them had they been still eligible. If, then, any of them are now content to return, you are bound, if not in justice, then in honour, to do all that you can to testify your respect for brave conviction, and to repair to them such losses as they may have suffered, whether for their first secession or their second. You owe a special duty, not only to the courage that left the Church, but to the wisdom and moderation that now returns to it. And your sense of this duty will find a vent not only in word but in action. You will facilitate their return not only by considerate and brotherly language, but by pecuniary aid; you will seek, by some new endowment scheme, to preserve for them their ecclesiastical status. That they have no claim will be their strongest claim on your consideration. Many of you, if not all, will set apart some share out of your slender livings for their assistance and support; you will give them what you can afford; and you will say to them, as you do so, what I dare say to you, that what you give is theirs—not only in honour but in justice.

For you know that the justice which should rule the

dealings of Christians, how much more of Christian ministers, is not as the justice of courts of law or equity; and those who profess the morality of Jesus Christ have abjured, in that profession, all that can be urged by policy or worldly prudence. From them we can accept no half-hearted and calculating generosity; they must make haste to be liberal; they must catch with eagerness at all opportunities of service, and the mere whisper of an obligation should be to them more potent than the decree of a court to others who make profession of a less stringent code. And remember that it lies with you to show to the world that Christianity is something more than a verbal system. In the lapse of generations men grow weary of unsupported precept. They may wait long, and keep long in memory the bright doings of former days, but they will weary at the last; they will begin to trouble you for your credentials; if you cannot give them miracles, they will demand virtue; if you cannot heal the sick, they will call upon you for some practice of the Christian ethics. Thus people will knock often at a door if only it be opened to them now and again; but if the door remains closed too long, they will judge the house uninhabited and go elsewhere. And thus it is that a season of persecution, constantly endured, revives the fainting confidence of the people, and some centuries of prosperity may prepare a Church for ruin. You have here at your hand an opportunity to do more for the credit of your Christianity than ever you could do by visions, miracles, or prophecies. A sacrifice such as this would be better worth, as I said before, than many sermons; and there is a disposition in mankind

235

that would ennoble it beyond much that is more ostentatious; for men, whether lay or clerical, suffer better the flame of the stake than a daily inconvenience or a pointed sneer, and will not readily be martyred without some external circumstance and a concourse looking on. And you need not fear that your virtue will be thrown away; the people of Scotland will be quick to understand, in default of visible fire and halter, that you have done a brave action for Christianity and the national weal; and if they are spared in the future any of the present ignoble jealousy of sect against sect, they will not forget that to that end you gave of your household comfort and stinted your children. Even if you fail—ay, and even if there were not found one to profit by your invitation—your virtue would still have its own reward. Your predecessors gave their lives for ends not always the most Christian; they were tempted, and slain with the sword; they wandered in deserts and in mountains, in caves and in dens of the earth. But your action will not be less illustrious; what you may have to suffer may be a small thing if the world will, but it will have been suffered for the cause of peace and brotherly love.

I have said that the people of Scotland will be quick to appreciate what you do. You know well that they will be quick also to follow your example. But the sign should come from you. It is more seemly that you should lead than follow in this matter. Your predecessors gave the word from their free pulpits which was to brace men for sectarian strife: it would be a pleasant sequel if the word came from you that was to bid them bury all jealousy, and forget the ugly and contentious past in a good hope of peace to come.

What is said in these few pages may be objected to as vague; it is no more vague than the position seemed to me to demand. Each man must judge for himself what it behoves him to do at this juncture, and the whole Church for herself. All that is intended in this appeal is to begin, in a tone of dignity and disinterestedness, the consideration of the question; for when such matters are much pulled about in public prints, and have been often discussed from many different, and not always from very high, points of view, there is ever a tendency that the decision of the parties may contract some taint of meanness from the spirit of their critics. All that is desired is to press upon you, as ministers of the Church of Scotland, some sense of the high expectation with which your country looks to you at this time; and how many reasons there are that you should show an example of signal disinterestedness and zeal in the encouragement that you give to returning brethren. For, first, it lies with you to clear the Church from the discredit of our miserable contentions; and surely you can never have a fairer opportunity to improve her claim to the style of a peacemaker. Again, it lies with you, as I have said, to take the first step, and prove your own true ardour for an honourable union; and how else are you to prove it? It lies with you, moreover, to justify in the eyes of the world the time you have been enjoying your benefices, while these others have voluntarily shut themselves out from all participation in their convenience; and how else are you to convince the world that there was not something of selfishness in your motives ? It lies with you, lastly, to keep your example unspotted before your congregations; and I do not know how better you are to do that.

It is never a thankful office to offer advice; and advice is the more unpalatable, not only from the difficulty of the service recommended, but often from its very obviousness. We are fired with anger against those who make themselves the spokesmen of plain obligations; for they seem to insult us as they advise. In the present case I should have feared to waken some such feeling, had it not been that I was addressing myself to a body of special men on a very special occasion. I know too much of the history of ideas to imagine that the sentiments advocated in this appeal are peculiar to me and a few others. I am confident that your own minds are already busy with similar reflections. But I know at the same time how difficult it is for one man to speak to another in such a matter; how he is withheld by all manner of personal considerations, and dare not propose what he has nearest his heart, because the other has a larger family or a smaller stipend, or is older, more venerable, and more conscientious than himself; and it is in view of this that I have determined to profit by the freedom of an anonymous writer, and give utterance to what many of you would have uttered already, had they been (as I am) apart from the battle. It is easy to be virtuous when one's own convenience is not affected; and it is no shame to any man to follow the advice of an outsider who owns that, while he sees which is the better part, he might not have the courage to profit himself by this opinion.

[*Note for the Laity*]

The foregoing pages have been in type since the beginning of last September. I have been advised to give them to the public; and it is only necessary to add that nothing of all that has taken place since they were written has made me modify an opinion or so much as change a word. The question is not one that can be altered by circumstances.

I need not tell the laity that with them this matter ultimately rests. Whether we regard it as a question of mere expense or as a question of good feeling against ill feeling, the solution must come from the Church members. The lay purse is the long one; and if the lay opinion does not speak from so high a place, it speaks all the week through and with innumerable voices. Trumpets and captains are all very well in their way; but if the trumpets were ever so clear, and the captains as bold as lions, it is still the army that must take the fort.

The laymen of the Church have here a question before them, on the answering of which, as I still think, many others attend. If the Established Church could throw off its lethargy, and give the Dissenters some speaking token of its zeal for union, I still think that union, to some extent, would be the result. There is a motion tabled (as I suppose all know) for the next meeting of the General Assembly; but something more than motions must be tabled, and something more must be given than votes. It lies practically with the laymen, by a new endowment scheme, to put the

Church right with the world in two ways, so that those who left it more than thirty years ago, and who may now be willing to return, shall lose neither in money nor in ecclesiastical status. At the outside, what will they have to do? They will have to do for (say) ten years what the laymen of the Free Church have done cheerfully ever since 1843.

February 12, 1875.

LITERARY PAPERS

LITERARY PAPERS

I

ON SOME TECHNICAL ELEMENTS OF STYLE IN LITERATURE[1]

THERE is nothing more disenchanting to man than to be shown the springs and mechanism of any art. All our arts and occupations lie wholly on the surface; it is on the surface that we perceive their beauty, fitness, and significance; and to pry below is to be appalled by their emptiness and shocked by the coarseness of the strings and pulleys. In a similar way, psychology itself, when pushed to any nicety, discovers an abhorrent baldness, but rather from the fault of our analysis than from any poverty native to the mind. And perhaps in æsthetics the reason is the same: those disclosures which seem fatal to the dignity of art seem so perhaps only in the proportion of our ignorance; and those conscious and unconscious artifices which it seems unworthy of the serious artist to employ were yet, if we had the power to trace them to their springs, indications of a delicacy of the sense finer than we conceive, and hints of ancient harmonies

[1] First published in the *Contemporary Review*, April, 1885.

243

in nature. This ignorance at least is largely irremedi‑
able. We shall never learn the affinities of beauty, for
they lie too deep in nature and too far back in the mys‑
terious history of man. The amateur, in consequence,
will always grudgingly receive details of method, which
can be stated but never can wholly be explained;
nay, on the principle laid down in "Hudibras," that

> "Still the less they understand,
> The more they admire the sleight-of-hand,"

many are conscious at each new disclosure of a diminu‑
tion in the ardour of their pleasure. I must therefore
warn that well-known character, the general reader, that
I am here embarked upon a most distasteful business:
taking down the picture from the wall and looking on
the back; and, like the inquiring child, pulling the mu‑
sical cart to pieces.

1. *Choice of Words.*—The art of literature stands
apart from among its sisters, because the material in
which the literary artist works is the dialect of life;
hence, on the one hand, a strange freshness and im‑
mediacy of address to the public mind, which is ready
prepared to understand it; but hence, on the other, a
singular limitation. The sister arts enjoy the use of a
plastic and ductile material, like the modeller's clay;
literature alone is condemned to work in mosaic with
finite and quite rigid words. You have seen these
blocks, dear to the nursery: this one a pillar, that a
pediment, a third a window or a vase. It is with
blocks of just such arbitrary size and figure that the
literary architect is condemned to design the palace
of his art. Nor is this all; for since these blocks, or

words, are the acknowledged currency of our daily affairs, there are here possible none of those suppressions by which other arts obtain relief, continuity, and vigour: no hieroglyphic touch, no smoothed impasto, no inscrutable shadow, as in painting; no blank wall, as in architecture; but every word, phrase, sentence, and paragraph must move in a logical progression, and convey a definite conventional import.

Now the first merit which attracts in the pages of a good writer, or the talk of a brilliant conversationalist, is the apt choice and contrast of the words employed. It is, indeed, a strange art to take these blocks, rudely conceived for the purpose of the market or the bar, and by tact of application touch them to the finest meanings and distinctions, restore to them their primal energy, wittily shift them to another issue, or make of them a drum to rouse the passions. But though this form of merit is without doubt the most sensible and seizing, it is far from being equally present in all writers. The effect of words in Shakespeare, their singular justice, significance, and poetic charm, is different, indeed, from the effect of words in Addison or Fielding. Or, to take an example nearer home, the words in Carlyle seem electrified into an energy of lineament, like the faces of men furiously moved; whilst the words in Macaulay, apt enough to convey his meaning, harmonious enough in sound, yet glide from the memory like undistinguished elements in a general effect. But the first class of writers have no monopoly of literary merit. There is a sense in which Addison is superior to Carlyle; a sense in which Cicero is better than Tacitus, in which Voltaire excels Montaigne: it certainly lies not in the choice of words; it lies not in the interest or value of the matter; it lies not in force of intellect, of poetry, or of humour. The three first are but infants to the three second; and yet each, in a particular point of literary art, excels his superior in the whole. What is that point?

2. *The Web.*—Literature, although it stands apart by reason of the great destiny and general use of its medium in the affairs of men, is yet an art like other arts. Of these we may distinguish two great classes: those arts, like sculpture, painting, acting, which are representative, or, as used to be said very clumsily, imitative; and those, like architecture, music, and the dance, which are self-sufficient, and merely presentative. Each class, in right of this distinction, obeys principles apart; yet both may claim a common ground of existence, and it may be said with sufficient justice that the motive and end of any art whatever is to make a pattern; a pattern, it may be, of colours, of sounds, of changing attitudes, geometrical figures, or imitative lines; but still a pattern. That is the plane on which these sisters meet; it is by this that they are arts; and if it be well they should at times forget their childish origin, addressing their intelligence to virile tasks, and performing unconsciously that necessary function of their life, to make a pattern, it is still imperative that the pattern shall be made.

Music and literature, the two temporal arts, contrive their pattern of sounds in time; or, in other words, of sounds and pauses. Communication may be made in broken words, the business of life be carried on with substantives alone; but that is not what we call literature; and the true business of the literary artist is to plait or weave his meaning, involving it around itself; so that each sentence, by successive phrases, shall first come into a kind of knot, and then, after a moment of suspended meaning, solve and clear itself. In every properly constructed sentence there should be observed this knot or hitch; so that (however delicately) we are led to foresee, to expect, and then to welcome the successive phrases. The pleasure may be heightened by an element of surprise, as, very grossly, in the common figure of the antithesis, or, with much greater subtlety, where an antithesis is first suggested and then deftly evaded. Each phrase, besides, is to be comely in itself; and between the implication and the evolution of the sentence there should be a satisfying equipoise of sound; for nothing more often disappoints the ear than a sentence solemnly and sonorously prepared, and hastily and weakly finished. Nor should the balance be too striking and exact, for the one rule is to be infinitely various; to interest, to disappoint, to surprise, and yet still to gratify; to be ever changing, as it were, the stitch, and yet still to give the effect of an ingenious neatness.

The conjurer juggles with two oranges, and our pleasure in beholding him springs from this, that neither is for an instant overlooked or sacrificed. So with the writer. His pattern, which is to please the supersensual ear, is yet addressed, throughout and first of all, to the demands of logic. Whatever be the obscurities, whatever the intricacies of the argument, the neatness of the fabric must not suffer, or the artist has been proved unequal to his design. And, on the other hand, no form of words must be selected, no knot must be tied among the phrases, unless knot and word be precisely what is wanted to forward and illuminate the argument; for to fail in this is to swindle in the game. The genius of prose rejects the *cheville* no less emphatically than the laws of verse; and the *cheville*, I should perhaps explain to some of my readers, is any meaningless or very watered phrase employed to strike a balance in the sound. Pattern and argument live in each other; and it is by the brevity, clearness, charm, or emphasis of the second, that we judge the strength and fitness of the first.

Style is synthetic; and the artist, seeking, so to speak, a peg to plait about, takes up at once two or more elements or two or more views of the subject in hand; combines, implicates, and contrasts them; and while, in one sense, he was merely seeking an occasion for the necessary knot, he will be found, in the other, to have greatly enriched the meaning, or to have transacted the work of two sentences in the space of one. In the change from the successive shallow statements of the old chronicler to the dense and luminous flow of highly synthetic narrative, there is implied a vast amount of both philosophy and wit. The philosophy we clearly see, recognising in the synthetic writer a far more deep and stimulating view of life, and a far keener sense of the generation and affinity of events. The wit we might imagine to be lost, but it is not so, for it is just that wit, these perpetual nice contrivances, these difficulties overcome, this double purpose attained, these two oranges kept simultaneously dancing in the air, that, consciously or not, afford the reader his delight. Nay, and this wit, so little recognised, is the necessary organ of that philosophy which we so much admire. That style is therefore the most perfect, not, as fools say, which is the most natural, for the most natural is the disjointed babble of the chronicler; but which attains the highest degree of elegant and pregnant implication unobtrusively; or if obtrusively, then with the greatest gain to sense and vigour. Even the derangement of the phrases from their (so-called) natural order is luminous for the mind; and it is by the means of such designed reversal that the elements of a judgment may be most pertinently marshalled, or the stages of a complicated action most perspicuously bound into one.

The web, then, or the pattern: a web at once sensuous and logical, an elegant and pregnant texture: that is style, that is the foundation of the art of literature. Books indeed continue to be read, for the interest of the fact or fable, in which this quality is poorly represented, but still it will be there. And, on the other hand, how many do we continue to peruse and reperuse with pleasure whose only merit is the elegance of texture? I am tempted to mention Cicero; and since Mr. Anthony Trollope is dead, I will. It is a poor diet for the mind, a very colourless and toothless "criticism of life"; but we enjoy the pleasure of a most intricate and dexterous pattern, every stitch a model at once of elegance and of good sense; and the two oranges, even if one of them be rotten, kept dancing with inimitable grace.

Up to this moment I have had my eye mainly upon prose; for though in verse also the implication of the logical texture is a crowning beauty, yet in verse it may be dispensed with. You would think that here was a death-blow to all I have been saying; and far from that, it is but a new illustration of the principle involved. For if the versifier is not bound to weave a pattern of his own, it is because another pattern has been formally imposed upon him by the laws of verse. For that is the essence of a prosody. Verse may be rhythmical; it may be merely alliterative; it may, like the French, depend wholly on the (quasi) regular recurrence of the rhyme; or, like the Hebrew, it may consist in the strangely fanciful device of repeating the same idea. It does not matter on what principle the law is based, so it be a law. It may be pure convention; it may have no inherent beauty; all that we have a right to ask of any prosody is, that it shall lay down a pattern for the writer, and that what it lays down shall be neither too easy nor too hard. Hence it comes that it is much easier for men of equal facility to write fairly pleasing verse than reasonably interesting prose; for in prose the pattern itself has to be invented, and the difficulties first created before they can be solved. Hence, again, there follows the peculiar greatness of the true versifier: such as Shakespeare, Milton, and Victor Hugo, whom I place beside them as versifier merely, not as poet. These not only knit and knot the logical texture of the style with all the dexterity and strength of prose; they not only fill up the pattern of the verse with infinite variety and sober wit; but they give us, besides, a rare and special pleasure, by the art, comparable to that of counterpoint, with which they follow at the same time, and now contrast, and now combine, the double pattern of the texture and the verse. Here the sounding line concludes; a little further on, the well-knit sentence; and yet a little further, and both will reach their solution on the same ringing syllable. The best that can be offered by the best writer of prose is to show us the development of the idea and the stylistic pattern proceed hand in hand, sometimes by an obvious and triumphant effort, sometimes with a great air of ease and nature. The writer of verse, by virtue of conquering another difficulty, delights us with a new series of triumphs. He follows three purposes where his rival followed only two; and the change is of precisely the same nature as that from melody to harmony. Or if you prefer to return to the juggler, behold him now, to the vastly increased enthusiasm of the spectators, juggling with three oranges instead of two. Thus it is: added difficulty, added beauty; and the pattern, with every fresh element, becoming more interesting in itself.

Yet it must not be thought that verse is simply an addition; something is lost as well as something gained; and there remains plainly traceable, in comparing the best prose with the best verse, a certain broad distinction of method in the web. Tight as the versifier may draw the knot of logic, yet for the ear he still leaves the tissue of the sentence floating somewhat loose. In prose, the sentence turns upon a pivot, nicely balanced, and fits into itself with an obtrusive neatness like a puzzle. The ear remarks and is singly gratified by this return and balance; while in verse it is all diverted to the measure. To find comparable passages is hard; for either the versifier is hugely the superior of the rival, or, if he be not, and still persist in his more delicate enterprise, he fails to be as widely his inferior. But let us select them from the pages of the same writer, one who was ambidexter; let us take, for instance, Rumour's Prologue to the Second Part of *Henry IV.*, a fine flourish of eloquence in Shakespeare's second manner, and set it side by side with Falstaff's praise of sherris, act iv. scene i.; or let us compare the beautiful prose spoken throughout by Rosalind and Orlando; compare, for example, the first speech of all, Orlando's speech to Adam, with what passage it shall please you to select—the Seven Ages from the same play, or even such a stave of nobility as Othello's farewell to war; and still you will be able to perceive, if you have an ear for that class of music, a certain superior degree of organisation in the prose; a compacter fitting of the parts; a balance in the swing and the return as of a throbbing pendulum. We must not, in things temporal, take from those who have little, the little that they have; the merits of prose are inferior, but they are not the same; it is a little kingdom, but an independent.

3. Rhythm of the Phrase.—Some way back, I used a word which still awaits an application. Each phrase, I said, was to be comely; but what is a comely phrase? In all ideal and material points, literature, being a representative art, must look for analogies to painting and the like; but in what is technical and executive, being a temporal art, it must seek for them in music. Each phrase of each sentence, like an air or a recitative in music, should be so artfully compounded out of long and short, out of accented and unaccented, as to gratify the sensual ear. And of this the ear is the sole judge.

It is impossible to lay down laws. Even in our accentual and rhythmic language no analysis can find the secret of the beauty of a verse; how much less, then, of those phrases, such as prose is built of, which obey no law but to be lawless and yet to please? The little that we know of verse (and for my part I owe it all to my friend Professor Fleeming Jenkin) is, however, particularly interesting in the present connection. We have been accustomed to describe the heroic line as five iambic feet, and to be filled with pain and confusion whenever, as by the conscientious schoolboy, we have heard our own description put in practice.

"All nìght | the dreàd | less àn | gel ùn | pursùed," [1]

goes the schoolboy; but though we close our ears, we cling to our definition, in spite of its proved and naked insufficiency. Mr. Jenkin was not so easily pleased, and readily discovered that the heroic line consists of four groups, or, if you prefer the phrase, contains four pauses:

"All night | the dreadless | angel | unpursued."

Four groups, each practically uttered as one word: the first, in this case, an iamb; the second, an amphibrachys; the third, a trochee; and the fourth, an amphimacer; and yet our schoolboy, with no other liberty but that of inflicting pain, had triumphantly scanned it as five iambs. Perceive, now, this fresh richness of intricacy in the web; this fourth orange, hitherto unremarked, but still kept flying with the others. What had seemed to be one thing it now appears is two;

[1] Milton.

and, like some puzzle in arithmetic, the verse is made at the same time to read in fives and to read in fours.

But again, four is not necessary. We do not, indeed, find verses in six groups, because there is not room for six in the ten syllables; and we do not find verses of two, because one of the main distinctions of verse from prose resides in the comparative shortness of the group; but it is even common to find verses of three. Five is the one forbidden number; because five is the number of the feet; and if five were chosen, the two patterns would coincide, and that opposition which is the life of verse would instantly be lost. We have here a clue to the effect of polysyllables, above all in Latin, where they are so common and make so brave an architecture in the verse; for the polysyllable is a group of Nature's making. If but some Roman would return from Hades (Martial, for choice), and tell me by what conduct of the voice these thundering verses should be uttered—" *Aut Lacedæmonium Tarentum*," for a case in point—I feel as if I should enter at last into the full enjoyment of the best of human verses.

But, again, the five feet are all iambic, or supposed to be; by the mere count of syllables the four groups cannot be all iambic; as a question of elegance, I doubt if any one of them requires to be so; and I am certain that for choice no two of them should scan the same. The singular beauty of the verse analysed above is due, so far as analysis can carry us, part, indeed, to the clever repetition of L, D, and N, but part to this variety of scansion in the groups. The groups which, like the bar in music, break up the verse for utterance, fall uniambically; and in declaiming a so-called iambic verse, it may so happen that we never utter one iambic foot. And yet to this neglect of the original beat there is a limit.

"Athens, the eye of Greece, mother of arts,"[1]

is, with all its eccentricities, a good heroic line; for though it scarcely can be said to indicate the beat of the iamb, it certainly suggests no other measure to the ear. But begin

"Mother Athens, eye of Greece,"

or merely "Mother Athens," and the game is up, for the trochaic beat has been suggested. The eccentric scansion of the groups is an adornment; but as soon as the original beat has been forgotten, they cease implicitly to be eccentric. Variety is what is sought; but if we destroy the original mould, one of the terms of this variety is lost, and we fall back on sameness. Thus, both as to the arithmetical measure of the verse, and the degree of regularity in scansion, we see the laws of prosody to have one common purpose: to keep alive the opposition of two schemes simultaneously followed; to keep them notably apart, though still coincident; and to balance them with such judicial nicety before the reader, that neither shall be unperceived and neither signally prevail.

The rule of rhythm in prose is not so intricate. Here, too, we write in groups, or phrases, as I prefer to call them, for the prose phrase is greatly longer and is much more nonchalantly uttered than the group in verse; so

[1] Milton.

that not only is there a greater interval of continuous sound between the pauses, but, for that very reason, word is linked more readily to word by a more summary enunciation. Still, the phrase is the strict analogue of the group, and successive phrases, like successive groups, must differ openly in length and rhythm. The rule of scansion in verse is to suggest no measure but the one in hand; in prose, to suggest no measure at all. Prose must be rhythmical, and it may be as much so as you will; but it must not be metrical. It may be anything, but it must not be verse. A single heroic line may very well pass and not disturb the somewhat larger stride of the prose style; but one following another will produce an instant impression of poverty, flatness, and disenchantment. The same lines delivered with the measured utterance of verse would perhaps seem rich in variety. By the more summary enunciation proper to prose, as to a more distant vision, these niceties of difference are lost. A whole verse is uttered as one phrase; and the ear is soon wearied by a succession of groups identical in length. The prose writer, in fact, since he is allowed to be so much less harmonious, is condemned to a perpetually fresh variety of movement on a larger scale, and must never disappoint the ear by the trot of an accepted metre. And this obligation is the third orange with which he has to juggle, the third quality which the prose writer must work into his pattern of words. It may be thought perhaps that this is a quality of ease rather than a fresh difficulty; but such is the inherently rhythmical strain of the English language, that the bad writer—and must I take for example that admired friend of my boyhood,

Captain Reid?—the inexperienced writer, as Dickens in his earlier attempts to be impressive, and the jaded writer, as any one may see for himself, all tend to fall at once into the production of bad blank verse. And here it may be pertinently asked, Why bad? And I suppose it might be enough to answer that no man ever made good verse by accident, and that no verse can ever sound otherwise than trivial when uttered with the delivery of prose. But we can go beyond such answers. The weak side of verse is the regularity of the beat, which in itself is decidedly less impressive than the movement of the nobler prose; and it is just into this weak side, and this alone, that our careless writer falls. A peculiar density and mass, consequent on the nearness of the pauses, is one of the chief good qualities of verse; but this our accidental versifier, still following after the swift gait and large gestures of prose, does not so much as aspire to imitate. Lastly, since he remains unconscious that he is making verse at all, it can never occur to him to extract those effects of counterpoint and opposition which I have referred to as the final grace and justification of verse, and, I may add, of blank verse in particular.

4. *Contents of the Phrase.*—Here is a great deal of talk about rhythm—and naturally; for in our canorous language rhythm is always at the door. But it must not be forgotten that in some languages this element is almost, if not quite, extinct, and that in our own it is probably decaying. The even speech of many educated Americans sounds the note of danger. I should see it go with something as bitter as despair, but I should not

be desperate. As in verse no element, not even rhythm, is necessary, so, in prose also, other sorts of beauty will arise and take the place and play the part of those that we outlive. The beauty of the expected beat in verse, the beauty in prose of its larger and more lawless melody, patent as they are to English hearing, are already silent in the ears of our next neighbours; for in France the oratorical accent and the pattern of the web have almost or altogether succeeded to their places; and the French prose writer would be astounded at the labours of his brother across the Channel, and how a good quarter of his toil, above all *invita Minerva*, is to avoid writing verse. So wonderfully far apart have races wandered in spirit, and so hard it is to understand the literature next door!

Yet French prose is distinctly better than English; and French verse, above all while Hugo lives, it will not do to place upon one side. What is more to our purpose, a phrase or a verse in French is easily distinguishable as comely or uncomely. There is then another element of comeliness hitherto overlooked in this analysis: the contents of the phrase. Each phrase in literature is built of sounds, as each phrase in music consists of notes. One sound suggests, echoes, demands, and harmonises with another; and the art of rightly using these concordances is the final art in literature. It used to be a piece of good advice to all young writers to avoid alliteration; and the advice was sound, in so far as it prevented daubing. None the less for that, was it abominable nonsense, and the mere raving of those blindest of the blind who will not see. The beauty of the contents of a phrase, or of a sentence, depends implicitly upon alliteration and upon assonance. The vowel demands to be repeated; the consonant demands to be repeated; and both cry aloud to be perpetually varied. You may follow the adventures of a letter through any passage that has particularly pleased you; find it, perhaps, denied awhile, to tantalise the ear; find it fired again at you in a whole broadside; or find it pass into congenerous sounds, one liquid or labial melting away into another. And you will find another and much stranger circumstance. Literature is written by and for two senses: a sort of internal ear, quick to perceive "unheard melodies"; and the eye, which directs the pen and deciphers the printed phrase. Well, even as there are rhymes for the eye, so you will find that there are assonances and alliterations; that where an author is running the open A, deceived by the eye and our strange English spelling, he will often show a tenderness for the flat A; and that where he is running a particular consonant, he will not improbably rejoice to write it down even when it is mute or bears a different value.

Here, then, we have a fresh pattern—a pattern, to speak grossly, of letters—which makes the fourth preoccupation of the prose writer, and the fifth of the versifier. At times it is very delicate and hard to perceive, and then perhaps most excellent and winning (I say perhaps); but at times again the elements of this literal melody stand more boldly forward and usurp the ear. It becomes, therefore, somewhat a matter of conscience to select examples; and as I cannot very well ask the reader to help me, I shall do the next best by giving him the reason or the history of each selection.

The two first, one in prose, one in verse, I chose without previous analysis, simply as engaging passages that had long re-echoed in my ear.

"I cannot praise a fugitive and cloistered virtue, unexercised and unbreathed, that never sallies out and sees her adversary, but slinks out of the race where that immortal garland is to be run for, not without dust and heat."[1] Down to "virtue," the current S and R are both announced and repeated unobtrusively, and by way of a grace-note that almost inseparable group PVF is given entire.[2] The next phrase is a period of repose, almost ugly in itself, both S and R still audible, and B given as the last fulfilment of PVF. In the next four phrases, from "that never" down to "run for," the mask is thrown off, and, but for a slight repetition of the F and V, the whole matter turns, almost too obtrusively, on S and R; first S coming to the front, and then R. In the concluding phrase all these favourite letters, and even the flat A, a timid preference for which is just perceptible, are discarded at a blow and in a bundle; and to make the break more obvious, every word ends with a dental, and all but one with T, for which we have been cautiously prepared since the beginning. The singular dignity of the first clause, and this hammer-stroke of the last, go far to make the charm of this exquisite sentence. But it is fair to own that S and R are used a little coarsely.

[1] Milton.

[2] As PVF will continue to haunt us through our English examples, take, by way of comparison, this Latin verse, of which it forms a chief adornment, and do not hold me answerable for the all too Roman freedom of the sense: "Hanc volo, quæ facilis, quæ palliolata vagatur."

" In Xanadv did Kubla Khan	(KĂNDL)
A stately pleasure dome decree,	(KDLSR)
Where Alph the sacred river ran,	(KĂNDLSR)
Through caverns measureless to man,	(KĂNLSR)
Down to a sunless sea." [1]	(NDLS)

Here I have put the analysis of the main group along-side the lines; and the more it is looked at, the more interesting it will seem. But there are further niceties. In lines two and four, the current S is most delicately varied with Z. In line three, the current flat A is twice varied with the open A, already suggested in line two, and both times ("where" and "sacred") in· conjunc-tion with the current R. In the same line F and V (a harmony in themselves, even when shorn of their comrade P) are admirably contrasted. And in line four there is a marked subsidiary M, which again was announced in line two. I stop from weariness, for more might yet be said.

My next example was recently quoted from Shake-speare as an example of the poet's colour sense. Now, I do not think literature has anything to do with colour, or poets anyway the better of such a sense; and I in-stantly attacked this passage, since "purple" was the word that had so pleased the writer of the article, to see if there might not be some literary reason for its use. It will be seen that I succeeded amply; and I am bound to say I think the passage exceptional in Shake-speare—exceptional, indeed, in literature; but it was not I who chose it.

> " The BaRge she sat iN, like a BURNished throNe
> BURNt oN the water : the POOP was BeateN gold,

[1] Coleridge.

261

PURPle the sails and so PUR * Fumèd that   * per
The wiNds were love-sick with them." [1]

It may be asked why I have put the F of " perfumèd "
in capitals; and I reply, because this change from P to
F is the completion of that from B to P, already so
adroitly carried out. Indeed, the whole passage is a
monument of curious ingenuity; and it seems scarce
worth while to indicate the subsidiary S, L, and W. In
the same article, a second passage from Shakespeare was
quoted, once again as an example of his colour sense:

> " A mole cinque-spotted like the crimson drops
> I' the bottom of a cowslip." [2]

It is very curious, very artificial, and not worth while
to analyse at length: I leave it to the reader. But before
I turn my back on Shakespeare, I should like to quote a
passage, for my own pleasure, and for a very model of
every technical art:

> " But in the wind and tempest of her frown,   W. P. V.[3] F. (st) (ow)
> Distinction with a loud and powerful fan,   W. P. F. (st) (ow) L
> Puffing at all, winnows the light away;   W. P. F. L
> And what hath mass and matter by itself   W. F. L. M. Ă.
> Lies rich in virtue and unmingled." [4]   V. L. M.

From these delicate and choice writers I turned with
some curiosity to a player of the big drum—Macaulay. I
had in hand the two-volume edition, and I opened at the
beginning of the second volume. Here was what I read:

" The violence of revolutions is generally proportioned to the degree
of the maladministration which has produced them. It is therefore not

---

[1] *Antony and Cleopatra.*   [2] *Cymbeline.*
[3] The V is in " of."   [4] *Troilus and Cressida.*

strange that the government of Scotland, having been during many years greatly more corrupt than the government of England, should have fallen with a far heavier ruin. The movement against the last king of the house of Stuart was in England conservative, in Scotland destructive. The English complained not of the law, but of the violation of the law."

This was plain-sailing enough; it was our old friend PVF, floated by the liquids in a body; but as I read on, and turned the page, and still found PVF with his attendant liquids, I confess my mind misgave me utterly. This could be no trick of Macaulay's; it must be the nature of the English tongue. In a kind of despair, I turned half-way through the volume; and coming upon his lordship dealing with General Cannon, and fresh from Claverhouse and Killiecrankie, here, with elucidative spelling, was my reward:

" Meanwhile the disorders of Kannon's Kamp went on inKreasing. He Kalled a Kouncil of war to Konsider what Kourse it would be advisable to taKe. But as soon as the Kouncil had met, a preliminary Kuestion was raised. The army was almost eKsKlusively a Highland army. The recent viKtory had been won eKsKlusively by Highland warriors. Great chiefs who had brought siKs or Seven hundred fighting men into the field did not think it fair that they should be outvoted by gentlemen from Ireland, and from the Low Kountries, who bore indeed King James's Kommission, and were Kalled Kolonels and Kaptains, but who were Kolonels without regiments and Kaptains without Kompanies."

A moment of FV in all this world of K's! It was not the English language, then, that was an instrument of one string, but Macaulay that was an incomparable dauber.

It was probably from this barbaric love of repeating the same sound, rather than from any design of clearness, that he acquired his irritating habit of repeating words; I say the one rather than the other, because such a trick of the ear is deeper-seated and more original in man than any logical consideration. Few writers, indeed, are probably conscious of the length to which they push this melody of letters. One, writing very diligently, and only concerned about the meaning of his words and the rhythm of his phrases, was struck into amazement by the eager triumph with which he cancelled one expression to substitute another. Neither changed the sense; both being monosyllables, neither could affect the scansion; and it was only by looking back on what he had already written that the mystery was solved: the second word contained an open A, and for nearly half a page he had been riding that vowel to the death.

In practice, I should add, the ear is not always so exacting; and ordinary writers, in ordinary moments, content themselves with avoiding what is harsh, and here and there, upon a rare occasion, buttressing a phrase, or linking two together, with a patch of assonance or a momentary jingle of alliteration. To understand how constant is this preoccupation of good writers, even where its results are least obtrusive, it is only necessary to turn to the bad. There, indeed, you will find cacophony supreme, the rattle of incongruous consonants only relieved by the jaw-breaking hiatus, and whole phrases not to be articulated by the powers of man.

Conclusion.—We may now briefly enumerate the elements of style. We have, peculiar to the prose writer, the task of keeping his phrases large, rhythmical, and pleasing to the ear, without ever allowing them to fall into the strictly metrical: peculiar to the versifier, the task of combining and contrasting his double, treble, and quadruple pattern, feet and groups, logic and metre —harmonious in diversity: common to both, the task of artfully combining the prime elements of language into phrases that shall be musical in the mouth; the task of weaving their argument into a texture of committed phrases and of rounded periods—but this particularly binding in the case of prose: and, again common to both, the task of choosing apt, explicit, and communicative words. We begin to see now what an intricate affair is any perfect passage; how many faculties, whether of taste or pure reason, must be held upon the stretch to make it; and why, when it is made, it should afford us so complete a pleasure. From the arrangement of according letters, which is altogether arabesque and sensual, up to the architecture of the elegant and pregnant sentence, which is a vigorous act of the pure intellect, there is scarce a faculty in man but has been exercised. We need not wonder, then, if perfect sentences are rare, and perfect pages rarer.

II

A NOTE ON REALISM [1]

STYLE is the invariable mark of any master; and for the student who does not aspire so high as to be numbered with the giants, it is still the one quality in which he may improve himself at will. Passion, wisdom, creative force, the power of mystery or colour, are allotted in the hour of birth, and can be neither learned nor simulated. But the just and dexterous use of what qualities we have, the proportion of one part to another and to the whole, the elision of the useless, the accentuation of the important, and the preservation of a uniform character from end to end—these, which taken together constitute technical perfection, are to some degree within the reach of industry and intellectual courage. What to put in and what to leave out; whether some particular fact be organically necessary or purely ornamental; whether, if it be purely ornamental, it may not weaken or obscure the general design; and finally, whether, if we decide to use it, we should do so grossly and notably, or in some conventional disguise: are questions of plastic style continually rearising. And the sphinx that patrols the highways

[1] First published in the *Magazine of Art* in 1883.

of executive art has no more unanswerable riddle to propound.

In literature (from which I must draw my instances) the great change of the past century has been effected by the admission of detail. It was inaugurated by the romantic Scott; and at length, by the semi-romantic Balzac and his more or less wholly unromantic followers, bound like a duty on the novelist. For some time it signified and expressed a more ample contemplation of the conditions of man's life; but it has recently (at least in France) fallen into a merely technical and decorative stage, which it is, perhaps, still too harsh to call survival. With a movement of alarm, the wiser or more timid begin to fall a little back from these extremities; they begin to aspire after a more naked, narrative articulation; after the succinct, the dignified, and the poetic; and as a means to this, after a general lightening of this baggage of detail. After Scott we beheld the starveling story—once, in the hands of Voltaire, as abstract as a parable—begin to be pampered upon facts. The introduction of these details developed a particular ability of hand; and that ability, childishly indulged, has led to the works that now amaze us on a railway journey. A man of the unquestionable force of M. Zola spends himself on technical successes. To afford a popular flavour and attract the mob, he adds a steady current of what I may be allowed to call the rancid. That is exciting to the moralist; but what more particularly interests the artist is this tendency of the extreme of detail, when followed as a principle, to degenerate into mere *feux-de-joie* of literary tricking. The other day even

M. Daudet was to be heard babbling of audible colours and visible sounds.

This odd suicide of one branch of the realists may serve to remind us of the fact which underlies a very dusty conflict of the critics. All representative art, which can be said to live, is both realistic and ideal; and the realism about which we quarrel is a matter purely of externals. It is no especial cultus of nature and veracity, but a mere whim of veering fashion, that has made us turn our back upon the larger, more various, and more romantic art of yore. A photographic exactitude in dialogue is now the exclusive fashion; but even in the ablest hands it tells us no more—I think it even tells us less—than Molière, wielding his artificial medium, has told to us and to all time of Alceste or Orgon, Dorine or Chrysale. The historical novel is forgotten. Yet truth to the conditions of man's nature and the conditions of man's life, the truth of literary art, is free of the ages. It may be told us in a carpet comedy, in a novel of adventure, or a fairy tale. The scene may be pitched in London, on the sea-coast of Bohemia, or away on the mountains of Beulah. And by an odd and luminous accident, if there is any page of literature calculated to awake the envy of M. Zola, it must be that *Troilus and Cressida* which Shakespeare, in a spasm of unmanly anger with the world, grafted on the heroic story of the siege of Troy.

This question of realism, let it then be clearly understood, regards not in the least degree the fundamental truth, but only the technical method, of a work of art. Be as ideal or as abstract as you please, you will be none the less veracious; but if you be weak, you run the risk of being tedious and inexpressive; and if you be very strong and honest, you may chance upon a masterpiece.

A work of art is first cloudily conceived in the mind; during the period of gestation it stands more clearly forward from these swaddling mists, puts on expressive lineaments, and becomes at length that most faultless, but also, alas! that incommunicable product of the human mind, a perfected design. On the approach to execution all is changed. The artist must now step down, don his working clothes, and become the artisan. He now resolutely commits his airy conception, his delicate Ariel, to the touch of matter; he must decide, almost in a breath, the scale, the style, the spirit, and the particularity of execution of his whole design.

The engendering idea of some works is stylistic; a technical preoccupation stands them instead of some robuster principle of life. And with these the execution is but play; for the stylistic problem is resolved beforehand, and all large originality of treatment wilfully foregone. Such are the verses, intricately designed, which we have learnt to admire, with a certain smiling admiration, at the hands of Mr. Lang and Mr. Dobson; such, too, are those canvases where dexterity or even breadth of plastic style takes the place of pictorial nobility of design. So, it may be remarked, it was easier to begin to write *Esmond* than *Vanity Fair*, since, in the first, the style was dictated by the nature of the plan; and Thackeray, a man probably of some indolence of mind, enjoyed and got good profit of this economy of effort. But the case is exceptional. Usually in all works of art that have been conceived from

within outwards, and generously nourished from the
author's mind, the moment in which he begins to exe-
cute is one of extreme perplexity and strain. Artists
of indifferent energy and an imperfect devotion to their
own ideal make this ungrateful effort once for all; and,
having formed a style, adhere to it through life. But
those of a higher order cannot rest content with a process which, as they continue to employ it, must in-
fallibly degenerate towards the academic and the
cut-and-dried. Every fresh work in which they em-
bark is the signal for a fresh engagement of the whole
forces of their mind; and the changing views which
accompany the growth of their experience are marked
by still more sweeping alterations in the manner of
their art. So that criticism loves to dwell upon and
distinguish the varying periods of a Raphael, a Shakespeare, or a Beethoven.

It is, then, first of all, at this initial and decisive
moment when execution is begun, and thenceforth
only in a less degree, that the ideal and the real do
indeed, like good and evil angels, contend for the direction of the work. Marble, paint, and language, the
pen, the needle, and the brush, all have their gross-
nesses, their ineffable impotences, their hours, if I may
so express myself, of insubordination. It is the work
and it is a great part of the delight of any artist to contend with these unruly tools, and now by brute energy,
now by witty expedient, to drive and coax them to effect
his will. Given these means, so laughably inadequate,
and given the interest, the intensity, and the multiplicity of the actual sensation whose effect he is to
render with their aid, the artist has one main and neces-

sary resource which he must, in every case and upon any theory, employ. He must, that is, suppress much and omit more. He must omit what is tedious or irrelevant, and suppress what is tedious and necessary. But such facts as, in regard to the main design, subserve a variety of purposes, he will perforce and eagerly retain. And it is the mark of the very highest order of creative art to be woven exclusively of such. There, any fact that is registered is contrived a double or a treble debt to pay, and is at once an ornament in its place, and a pillar in the main design. Nothing would find room in such a picture that did not serve, at once, to complete the composition, to accentuate the scheme of colour, to distinguish the planes of distance, and to strike the note of the selected sentiment; nothing would be allowed in such a story that did not, at the same time, expedite the progress of the fable, build up the characters, and strike home the moral or the philosophical design. But this is unattainable. As a rule, so far from building the fabric of our works exclusively with these, we are thrown into a rapture if we think we can muster a dozen or a score of them, to be the plums of our confection. And hence, in order that the canvas may be filled or the story proceed from point to point, other details must be admitted. They must be admitted, alas! upon a doubtful title; many without marriage robes. Thus any work of art, as it proceeds towards completion, too often—I had almost written always— loses in force and poignancy of main design. Our little air is swamped and dwarfed among hardly relevant orchestration; our little passionate story drowns in a deep sea of descriptive eloquence or slipshod talk.

271

But again, we are rather more tempted to admit those particulars which we know we can describe; and hence those most of all which, having been described very often, have grown to be conventionally treated in the practice of our art. These we choose, as the mason chooses the acanthus to adorn his capital, because they come naturally to the accustomed hand. The old stock incidents and accessories, tricks of workmanship and schemes of composition (all being admirably good, or they would long have been forgotten) haunt and tempt our fancy, offer us ready-made but not perfectly appropriate solutions for any problem that arises, and wean us from the study of nature and the uncompromising practice of art. To struggle, to face nature, to find fresh solutions, and give expression to facts which have not yet been adequately or not yet elegantly expressed, is to run a little upon the danger of extreme self-love. Difficulty sets a high price upon achievement; and the artist may easily fall into the error of the French naturalists, and consider any fact as welcome to admission if it be the ground of brilliant handiwork; or, again, into the error of the modern landscape-painter, who is apt to think that difficulty overcome and science well displayed can take the place of what is, after all, the one excuse and breath of art—charm. A little further, and he will regard charm in the light of an unworthy sacrifice to prettiness, and the omission of a tedious passage as an infidelity to art.

We have now the matter of this difference before us. The idealist, his eye singly fixed upon the greater outlines, loves rather to fill up the interval with detail of the conventional order, briefly touched, soberly sup pressed in tone, courting neglect. But the realist, with a fine intemperance, will not suffer the presence of anything so dead as a convention; he shall have all fiery, all hot-pressed from nature, all charactered and notable, seizing the eye. The style that befits either of these extremes, once chosen, brings with it its necessary disabilities and dangers. The immediate danger of the realist is to sacrifice the beauty and significance of the whole to local dexterity, or, in the insane pursuit of completion, to immolate his readers under facts; but he comes in the last resort, and as his energy declines, to discard all design, abjure all choice, and, with scientific thoroughness, steadily to communicate matter which is not worth learning. The danger of the idealist is, of course, to become merely null and lose all grip of fact, particularity, or passion.

We talk of bad and good. Everything, indeed, is good which is conceived with honesty and executed with communicative ardour. But though on neither side is dogmatism fitting, and though in every case the artist must decide for himself, and decide afresh and yet afresh for each succeeding work and new creation; yet one thing may be generally said, that we of the last quarter of the nineteenth century, breathing as we do the intellectual atmosphere of our age, are more apt to err upon the side of realism than to sin in quest of the ideal. Upon that theory it may be well to watch and correct our own decisions, always holding back the hand from the least appearance of irrelevant dexterity, and resolutely fixed to begin no work that is not philosophical, passionate, dignified, happily mirthful, or, at the last and least, romantic in design.

III

THE MORALITY OF THE PROFESSION OF LETTERS [1]

THE profession of letters has been lately debated in the public prints; and it has been debated, to put the matter mildly, from a point of view that was calculated to surprise high-minded men, and bring a general contempt on books and reading. Some time ago, in particular, a lively, pleasant, popular writer [2] devoted an essay, lively and pleasant like himself, to a very encouraging view of the profession. We may be glad that his experience is so cheering, and we may hope that all others, who deserve it, shall be as handsomely rewarded; but I do not think we need be at all glad to have this question, so important to the public and ourselves, debated solely on the ground of money. The salary in any business under heaven is not the only, nor indeed the first, question. That you should continue to exist is a matter for your own consideration; but that your business should be first honest, and second useful, are points in which honour and morality are concerned. If the writer to whom I refer succeeds in persuading a number of young persons to adopt this

---

[1] First published in the *Fortnightly Review*, April, 1881.
[2] Mr. James Payn.

way of life with an eye set singly on the livelihood, we must expect them in their works to follow profit only, and we must expect in consequence, if he will pardon me the epithets, a slovenly, base, untrue, and empty literature. Of that writer himself I am not speaking: he is diligent, clean, and pleasing; we all owe him periods of entertainment, and he has achieved an amiable popularity which he has adequately deserved. But the truth is, he does not, or did not when he first embraced it, regard his profession from this purely mercenary side. He went into it, I shall venture to say, if not with any noble design, at least in the ardour of a first love; and he enjoyed its practice long before he paused to calculate the wage. The other day an author was complimented on a piece of work, good in itself and exceptionally good for him, and replied, in terms unworthy of a commercial traveller, that as the book was not briskly selling he did not give a copper farthing for its merit. It must not be supposed that the person to whom this answer was addressed received it as a profession of faith; he knew, on the other hand, that it was only a whiff of irritation; just as we know, when a respectable writer talks of literature as a way of life, like shoemaking, but not so useful, that he is only debating one aspect of a question, and is still clearly conscious of a dozen others more important in themselves and more central to the matter in hand. But while those who treat literature in this penny-wise and virtue-foolish spirit are themselves truly in possession of a better light, it does not follow that the treatment is decent or improving, whether for themselves or others. To treat all subjects in the highest, the most honourable, and the pluckiest spirit, consistent with the fact, is the first duty of a writer. If he be well paid, as I am glad to hear he is, this duty becomes the more urgent, the neglect of it the more disgraceful. And perhaps there is no subject on which a man should speak so gravely as that industry, whatever it may be, which is the occupation or delight of his life; which is his tool to earn or serve with; and which, if it be unworthy, stamps himself as a mere incubus of dumb and greedy bowels on the shoulders of labouring humanity. On that subject alone even to force the note might lean to virtue's side. It is to be hoped that a numerous and enterprising generation of writers will follow and surpass the present one; but it would be better if the stream were stayed, and the roll of our old, honest English books were closed, than that esurient book-makers should continue and debase a brave tradition, and lower, in their own eyes, a famous race. Better that our serene temples were deserted than filled with trafficking and juggling priests.

There are two just reasons for the choice of any way of life: the first is inbred taste in the chooser; the second some high utility in the industry selected. Literature, like any other art, is singularly interesting to the artist; and, in a degree peculiar to itself among the arts, it is useful to mankind. These are the sufficient justifications for any young man or woman who adopts it as the business of his life. I shall not say much about the wages. A writer can live by his writing. If not so luxuriously as by other trades, then less luxuriously. The nature of the work he does all day will more affect his happiness than the quality of his dinner at night.

Whatever be your calling, and however much it brings you in the year, you could still, you know, get more by cheating. We all suffer ourselves to be too much concerned about a little poverty; but such considerations should not move us in the choice of that which is to be the business and justification of so great a portion of our lives; and like the missionary, the patriot, or the philosopher, we should all choose that poor and brave career in which we can do the most and best for mankind. Now nature, faithfully followed, proves herself a careful mother. A lad, for some liking to the jingle of words, betakes himself to letters for his life; by-and-by, when he learns more gravity, he finds that he has chosen better than he knew; that if he earns little, he is earning it amply; that if he receives a small wage, he is in a position to do considerable services; that it is in his power, in some small measure, to protect the oppressed and to defend the truth. So kindly is the world arranged, such great profit may arise from a small degree of human reliance on oneself, and such, in particular, is the happy star of this trade of writing, that it should combine pleasure and profit to both parties, and be at once agreeable, like fiddling, and useful, like good preaching.

This is to speak of literature at its highest; and with the four great elders who are still spared to our respect and admiration, with Carlyle, Ruskin, Browning, and Tennyson before us, it would be cowardly to consider it at first in any lesser aspect. But while we cannot follow these athletes, while we may none of us, perhaps, be very vigorous, very original, or very wise, I still contend that, in the humblest sort of literary work, we have it in our power either to do great harm or great good. We may seek merely to please; we may seek, having no higher gift, merely to gratify the idle nine days' curiosity of our contemporaries; or we may essay, however feebly, to instruct. In each of these we shall have to deal with that remarkable art of words which, because it is the dialect of life, comes home so easily and powerfully to the minds of men; and since that is so, we contribute, in each of these branches, to build up the sum of sentiments and appreciations which goes by the name of Public Opinion or Public Feeling. The total of a nation's reading, in these days of daily papers, greatly modifies the total of the nation's speech; and the speech and reading, taken together, form the efficient educational medium of youth. A good man or woman may keep a youth some little while in clearer air; but the contemporary atmosphere is all-powerful in the end on the average of mediocre characters. The copious Corinthian baseness of the American reporter or the Parisian *chroniquer*, both so lightly readable, must exercise an incalculable influence for ill; they touch upon all subjects, and on all with the same ungenerous hand; they begin the consideration of all, in young and unprepared minds, in an unworthy spirit; on all, they supply some pungency for dull people to quote. The mere body of this ugly matter overwhelms the rare utterances of good men; the sneering, the selfish, and the cowardly are scattered in broad sheets on every table, while the antidote, in small volumes, lies unread upon the shelf. I have spoken of the American and the French, not because they are so much baser, but so much more readable, than the English; their evil is done more effectively, in America for the masses, in French for the few that care to read; but with us as with them, the duties of literature are daily neglected, truth daily perverted and suppressed, and grave subjects daily degraded in the treatment. The journalist is not reckoned an important officer; yet judge of the good he might do, the harm he does; judge of it by one instance only: that when we find two journals on the reverse sides of politics each, on the same day. openly garbling a piece of news for the interest of its own party, we smile at the discovery (no discovery now!) as over a good joke and pardonable stratagem. Lying so open is scarce lying, it is true; but one of the things that we profess to teach our young is a respect for truth; and I cannot think this piece of education will be crowned with any great success, so long as some of us practise and the rest openly approve of public falsehood.

There are two duties incumbent upon any man who enters on the business of writing: truth to the fact and a good spirit in the treatment. In every department of literature, though so low as hardly to deserve the name, truth to the fact is of importance to the education and comfort of mankind, and so hard to preserve, that the faithful trying to do so will lend some dignity to the man who tries it. Our judgments are based upon two things: first, upon the original preferences of our soul; but, second, upon the mass of testimony to the nature of God, man, and the universe which reaches us, in divers manners, from without. For the most part these divers manners are reducible to one, all that we learn of past times and much that we learn of our own reaching us through the medium of books or papers, and even he who cannot read learning from the same source at second-hand and by the report of him who can. Thus the sum of the contemporary knowledge or ignorance of good and evil is, in large measure, the handiwork of those who write. Those who write have to see that each man's knowledge is, as near as they can make it, answerable to the facts of life; that he shall not suppose himself an angel or a monster; nor take this world for a hell; nor be suffered to imagine that all rights are concentred in his own caste or country, or all veracities in his own parochial creed. Each man should learn what is within him, that he may strive to mend; he must be taught what is without him, that he may be kind to others. It can never be wrong to tell him the truth; for, in his disputable state, weaving as he goes his theory of life, steering himself, cheering or reproving others, all facts are of the first importance to his conduct; and even if a fact shall discourage or corrupt him, it is still best that he should know it; for it is in this world as it is, and not in a world made easy by educational suppressions, that he must win his way to shame or glory. In one word, it must always be foul to tell what is false; and it can never be safe to suppress what is true. The very fact that you omit may be the fact which somebody was wanting, for one man's meat is another man's poison, and I have known a person who was cheered by the perusal of *Candide*. Every fact is a part of that great puzzle we must set together; and none that comes directly in a writer's path but has some nice relations, unperceivable by him, to the totality and bearing of the subject under hand. Yet there are certain classes of fact eternally more necessary than others, and it is with these that literature must first bestir itself. They are not hard to distinguish, nature once more easily leading us; for the necessary, because the efficacious, facts are those which are most interesting to the natural mind of man. Those which are coloured, picturesque, human, and rooted in morality, and those, on the other hand, which are clear, indisputable, and a part of science, are alone vital in importance, seizing by their interest, or useful to communicate. So far as the writer merely narrates, he should principally tell of these. He should tell of the kind and wholesome and beautiful elements of our life; he should tell unsparingly of the evil and sorrow of the present, to move us with instances; he should tell of wise and good people in the past, to excite us by example; and of these he should tell soberly and truthfully, not glossing faults, that we may neither grow discouraged with ourselves nor exacting to our neighbours. So the body of contemporary literature, ephemeral and feeble in itself, touches in the minds of men the springs of thought and kindness, and supports them (for those who will go at all are easily supported) on their way to what is true and right. And if, in any degree, it does so now, how much more might it do so if the writers chose! There is not a life in all the records of the past but, properly studied, might lend a hint and a help to some contemporary. There is not a juncture in to-day's affairs but some useful word may yet be said of it. Even the reporter has an office, and, with clear eyes and honest language, may unveil injustices and point the way to progress. And for a last word: in all narration there is only one way to be clever, and that is to be exact.   To be vivid is a secondary quality which must presuppose the first; for vividly to convey a wrong impression is only to make failure conspicuous.

But a fact may be viewed on many sides; it may be chronicled with rage, tears, laughter, indifference, or admiration, and by each of these the story will be transformed to something else.   The newspapers that told of the return of our representatives from Berlin, even if they had not differed as to the facts, would have sufficiently differed by their spirits; so that the one description would have been a second ovation, and the other a prolonged insult.   The subject makes but a trifling part of any piece of literature, and the view of the writer is itself a fact more important because less disputable than the others.   Now this spirit in which a subject is regarded, important in all kinds of literary work, becomes all-important in works of fiction, meditation, or rhapsody; for there it not only colours but itself chooses the facts; not only modifies but shapes the work.   And hence, over the far larger proportion of the field of literature, the health or disease of the writer's mind or momentary humour forms not only the leading feature of his work, but is, at bottom, the only thing he can communicate to others.   In all works of art, widely speaking, it is first of all the author's attitude that is narrated, though in the attitude there be implied a whole experience and a theory of life.   An author who has begged the question and reposes in some narrow faith cannot, if he would, express the whole or even many of the sides of this various existence; for, his own life being maim, some of them are not admitted in his theory, and were only dimly and unwillingly

to do anything else is to do a far more perilous thing than to risk being immoral: it is to be sure of being untrue. To ape a sentiment, even a good one, is to travesty a sentiment; that will not be helpful. To conceal a sentiment, if you are sure you hold it, is to take a liberty with truth. There is probably no point of view possible to a sane man but contains some truth and, in the true connection, might be profitable to the race. I am not afraid of the truth, if any one could tell it me, but I am afraid of parts of it impertinently uttered. There is a time to dance and a time to mourn; to be harsh as well as to be sentimental; to be ascetic as well as to glorify the appetites; and if a man were to combine all these extremes into his work, each in its place and proportion, that work would be the world's masterpiece of morality as well as of art. Partiality is immorality; for any book is wrong that gives a misleading picture of the world and life. The trouble is that the weakling must be partial; the work of one proving dank and depressing; of another, cheap and vulgar; of a third, epileptically sensual; of a fourth, sourly ascetic. In literature as in conduct, you can never hope to do exactly right. All you can do is to make as sure as possible; and for that there is but one rule. Nothing should be done in a hurry that can be done slowly. It is no use to write a book and put it by for nine or even ninety years; for in the writing you will have partly convinced yourself; the delay must precede any beginning; and if you meditate a work of art, you should first long roll the subject under the tongue to make sure you like the flavour, before you brew a volume that shall taste of it from end to end;

or if you propose to enter on the field of controversy, you should first have thought upon the question under all conditions, in health as well as in sickness, in sorrow as well as in joy. It is this nearness of examination necessary for any true and kind writing, that makes the practice of the art a prolonged and noble education for the writer.

There is plenty to do, plenty to say, or to say over again, in the meantime. Any literary work which conveys faithful facts or pleasing impressions is a service to the public. It is even a service to be thankfully proud of having rendered. The slightest novels are a blessing to those in distress, not chloroform itself a greater. Our fine old sea-captain's life was justified when Carlyle soothed his mind with *The King's Own* or *Newton Forster*. To please is to serve; and so far from its being difficult to instruct while you amuse, it is difficult to do the one thoroughly without the other. Some part of the writer or his life will crop out in even a vapid book; and to read a novel that was conceived with any force is to multiply experience and to exercise the sympathies. Every article, every piece of verse, every essay, every *entre-filet*, is destined to pass, however swiftly, through the minds of some portion of the public, and to colour, however transiently, their thoughts. When any subject falls to be discussed, some scribbler on a paper has the invaluable opportunity of beginning its discussion in a dignified and human spirit; and if there were enough who did so in our public press, neither the public nor the Parliament would find it in their minds to drop to meaner thoughts. The writer has the chance to stumble, by the way, on something pleasing, something interesting, something encouraging, were it only to a single reader. He will be unfortunate, indeed, if he suit no one. He has the chance, besides, to stumble on something that a dull person shall be able to comprehend; and for a dull person to have read anything and, for that once, comprehended it, makes a marking epoch in his education.

Here, then, is work worth doing and worth trying to do well. And so, if I were minded to welcome any great accession to our trade, it should not be from any reason of a higher wage, but because it was a trade which was useful in a very great and in a very high degree; which every honest tradesman could make more serviceable to mankind in his single strength; which was difficult to do well and possible to do better every year; which called for scrupulous thought on the part of all who practised it, and hence became a perpetual education to their nobler natures; and which, pay it as you please, in the large majority of the best cases will still be underpaid. For surely, at this time of day in the nineteenth century, there is nothing that an honest man should fear more timorously than getting and spending more than he deserves.

IV

THE DAY AFTER TO-MORROW [1]

HISTORY is much decried; it is a tissue of errors, we are told, no doubt correctly; and rival historians expose each other's blunders with gratification. Yet the worst historian has a clearer view of the period he studies than the best of us can hope to form of that in which we live. The obscurest epoch is to-day; and that for a thousand reasons of inchoate tendency, conflicting report, and sheer mass and multiplicity of experience; but chiefly, perhaps, by reason of an insidious shifting of landmarks. Parties and ideas continually move, but not by measurable marches on a stable course; the political soil itself steals forth by imperceptible degrees, like a travelling glacier, carrying on its bosom not only political parties but their flag-posts and cantonments; so that what appears to be an eternal city founded on hills is but a flying island of Laputa. It is for this reason in particular that we are all becoming Socialists without knowing it; by which I would not in the least refer to the acute case of Mr. Hyndman and his horn-blowing supporters, sounding their trumps of a Sunday within the walls of our individualist Jericho, but to

[1] First published in the *Contemporary Review*, April, 1887.

the stealthy change that has come over the spirit of
Englishmen and English legislation. A little while ago,
and we were still for liberty; "Crowd a few more
thousands on the bench of Government," we seemed
to cry; "keep her head direct on liberty, and we cannot
help but come to port." This is over; *laisser-faire* declines in favour; our legislation grows authoritative,
grows philanthropical, bristles with new duties and
new penalties, and casts a spawn of inspectors, who
now begin, note-book in hand, to darken the face of
England. It may be right or wrong, we are not trying
that; but one thing it is beyond doubt: it is Socialism
in action, and the strange thing is that we scarcely
know it.

Liberty has served us a long while, and it may be
time to seek new altars. Like all other principles, she
has been proved to be self-exclusive in the long run.
She has taken wages besides (like all other virtues) and
dutifully served Mammon; so that many things we
were accustomed to admire as the benefits of freedom
and common to all were truly benefits of wealth, and
took their value from our neighbours' poverty. A few
shocks of logic, a few disclosures (in the journalistic
phrase) of what the freedom of manufacturers, land-
lords, or ship-owners may imply for operatives, tenants,
or seamen, and we not unnaturally begin to turn to
that other pole of hope, beneficent tyranny. Freedom,
to be desirable, involves kindness, wisdom, and all the
virtues of the free; but the free man as we have seen
him in action has been, as of yore, only the master of
many helots; and the slaves are still ill fed, ill clad, ill
taught, ill housed, insolently treated, and driven to their

mines and workshops by the lash of famine. So much, in other men's affairs, we have begun to see clearly; we have begun to despair of virtue in these other men, and from our seat in Parliament begin to discharge upon them, thick as arrows, the host of our inspectors. The landlord has long shaken his head over the manufacturer; those who do business on land have lost all trust in the virtues of the ship-owner; the professions look askance upon the retail traders and have even started their co-operative stores to ruin them; and from out the smoke-wreaths of Birmingham a finger has begun to write upon the wall the condemnation of the landlord. Thus, piece by piece, do we condemn each other, and yet not perceive the conclusion, that our whole estate is somewhat damnable. Thus, piece by piece, each acting against his neighbour, each sawing away the branch on which some other interest is seated, do we apply in detail our Socialistic remedies, and yet not perceive that we are all labouring together to bring in Socialism at large. A tendency so stupid and so selfish is like to prove invincible; and if Socialism be at all a practicable rule of life, there is every chance that our grandchildren will see the day and taste the pleasures of existence in something far liker an ant-heap than any previous human polity. And this not in the least because of the voice of Mr. Hyndman or the horns of his followers; but by the mere glacier movement of the political soil, bearing forward on its bosom, apparently undisturbed, the proud camps of Whig and Tory. If Mr. Hyndman were a man of keen humour, which is far from my conception of his character, he might rest from his troubling and look on: the walls of Jericho begin already to crumble and dissolve. That great servile war, the Armageddon of money and numbers, to which we looked forward when young, becomes more and more unlikely; and we may rather look to see a peaceable and blindfold evolution, the work of dull men immersed in political tactics and dead to political results.

The principal scene of this comedy lies, of course, in the House of Commons; it is there, besides, that the details of this new evolution (if it proceed) will fall to be decided; so that the state of Parliament is not only diagnostic of the present but fatefully prophetic of the future. Well, we all know what Parliament is, and we are all ashamed of it. We may pardon it some faults, indeed, on the ground of Irish obstruction—a bitter trial, which it supports with notable good-humour. But the excuse is merely local; it cannot apply to similar bodies in America and France; and what are we to say of these? President Cleveland's letter may serve as a picture of the one; a glance at almost any paper will convince us of the weakness of the other. Decay appears to have seized on the organ of popular government in every land; and this just at the moment when we begin to bring to it, as to an oracle of justice, the whole skein of our private affairs to be unravelled, and ask it, like a new Messiah, to take upon itself our frailties and play for us the part that should be played by our own virtues. For that, in few words, is the case. We cannot trust ourselves to behave with decency; we cannot trust our consciences; and the remedy proposed is to elect a round number of our neighbours, pretty much at random, and say to these: "Be ye our conscience; make laws so wise, and continue from year to year to administer them so wisely, that they shall save us from ourselves and make us righteous and happy, world without end. Amen." And who can look twice at the British Parliament and then seriously bring it such a task? I am not advancing this as an argument against Socialism: once again, nothing is further from my mind. There are great truths in Socialism, or no one, not even Mr. Hyndman, would be found to hold it; and if it came, and did one-tenth part of what it offers, I for one should make it welcome. But if it is to come, we may as well have some notion of what it will be like; and the first thing to grasp is that our new polity will be designed and administered (to put it courteously) with something short of inspiration. It will be made, or will grow, in a human parliament; and the one thing that will not very hugely change is human nature. The Anarchists think otherwise, from which it is only plain that they have not carried to the study of history the lamp of human sympathy.

Given, then, our new polity, with its new wagonload of laws, what head-marks must we look for in the life? We chafe a good deal at that excellent thing, the income tax, because it brings into our affairs the prying fingers, and exposes us to the tart words, of the official. The official, in all degrees, is already something of a terror to many of us. I would not willingly have to do with even a police constable in any other spirit than that of kindness. I still remember in my dreams the eye-glass of a certain *attaché* at a certain embassy—an eye-glass that was a standing indignity to all on whom it looked; and my next most disagreeable remembrance is of a bracing, Republican postman in the city of San Francisco. I lived in that city among working-folk, and what my neighbours accepted at the postman's hands—nay, what I took from him myself—it is still distasteful to recall. The bourgeois, residing in the upper parts of society, has but few opportunities of tasting this peculiar bowl; but about the income tax, as I have said, or perhaps about a patent, or in the halls of an embassy at the hands of my friend of the eye-glass, he occasionally sets his lips to it; and he may thus imagine (if he has that faculty of imagination, without which most faculties are void) how it tastes to his poorer neighbours, who must drain it to the dregs. In every contact with authority, with their employer, with the police, with the School Board officer, in the hospital, or in the workhouse, they have equally the occasion to appreciate the light-hearted civility of the man in office; and as an experimentalist in several out-of-the-way provinces of life, I may say it has but to be felt to be appreciated. Well, this golden age of which we are speaking will be the golden age of officials. In all our concerns it will be their beloved duty to meddle, with what tact, with what obliging words, analogy will aid us to imagine. It is likely these gentlemen will be periodically elected; they will therefore have their turn of being underneath, which does not always sweeten men's conditions. The laws they will have to administer will be no clearer than those we know to-day, and the body which is to regulate their administration no wiser than the British Parliament. So that upon all hands we may look for a form of servitude

293

most galling to the blood—servitude to many and changing masters—and for all the slights that accompany the rule of Jack in office. And if the Socialistic programme be carried out with the least fulness, we shall have lost a thing in most respects not much to be regretted, but, as a moderator of oppression, a thing nearly invaluable—the newspaper. For the independent journal is a creature of capital and competition; it stands and falls with millionaires and railway-bonds and all the abuses and glories of to-day; and as soon as the State has fairly taken its bent to authority and philanthropy, and laid the least touch on private property, the days of the independent journal are numbered. State railways may be good things, and so may State bakeries; but a State newspaper will never be a very trenchant critic of the State officials.

But again, these officials would have no sinecure. Crime would perhaps be less, for some of the notives of crime we may suppose would pass away. But if Socialism were carried out with any fulness, there would be more contraventions. We see already new sins springing up like mustard—School Board sins, factory sins, Merchant Shipping Act sins—none of which I would be thought to except against in particular, but all of which, taken together, show us that Socialism can be a hard master even in the beginning. If it go on to such heights as we hear proposed and lauded, if it come actually to its ideal of the ant-heap, ruled with iron justice, the number of new contraventions will be out of all proportion multiplied. Take the case of work alone. Man is an idle animal. He is at least as intelligent as the ant; but generations of ad-

visers have in vain recommended him the ant's example.
Of those who are found truly indefatigable in business,
some are misers; some are the practisers of delightful
industries, like gardening; some are students, artists,
inventors, or discoverers, men lured forward by successive hopes; and the rest are those who live by
games of skill or hazard—financiers, billiard-players,
gamblers, and the like. But in unloved toils, even
under the prick of necessity, no man is continually
sedulous. Once eliminate the fear of starvation, once
eliminate or bound the hope of riches, and we shall see
plenty of skulking and malingering. Society will then
be something not wholly unlike a cotton plantation in
the old days; with cheerful, careless, demoralised slaves,
with elected overseers, and, instead of the planter, a
chaotic popular assembly. If the blood be purposeful
and the soil strong, such a plantation may succeed, and
be, indeed, a busy ant-heap, with full granaries and
long hours of leisure. But even then I think the whip
will be in the overseer's hand, and not in vain. For,
when it comes to be a question of each man doing his
own share or the rest doing more, prettiness of sentiment will be forgotten. To dock the skulker's food is
not enough; many will rather eat haws and starve on
petty pilferings than put their shoulder to the wheel
for one hour daily. For such as these, then, the whip
will be in the overseer's hand; and his own sense of
justice and the superintendence of a chaotic popular
assembly will be the only checks on its employment.
Now, you may be an industrious man and a good citizen, and yet not love, nor yet be loved by, Dr. Fell the
inspector. It is admitted by private soldiers that the

disfavour of a sergeant is an evil not to be combated; offend the sergeant, they say, and in a brief while you will either be disgraced or have deserted. And the sergeant can no longer appeal to the lash. But if these things go on, we shall see, or our sons shall see, what it is to have offended an inspector.

This for the unfortunate. But with the fortunate also, even those whom the inspector loves, it may not be altogether well. It is concluded that in such a state of society, supposing it to be financially sound, the level of comfort will be high. It does not follow: there are strange depths of idleness in man, a too-easily-got sufficiency, as in the case of the sago-eaters, often quenching the desire for all besides; and it is possible that the men of the richest ant-heaps may sink even into squalor. But suppose they do not; suppose our tricksy instrument of human nature, when we play upon it this new tune, should respond kindly; suppose no one to be damped and none exasperated by the new conditions, the whole enterprise to be financially sound—a vaulting supposition—and all the inhabitants to dwell together in a golden mean of comfort: we have yet to ask ourselves if this be what man desire, or if it be what man will even deign to accept for a continuance. It is certain that man loves to eat; it is not certain that he loves that only or that best. He is supposed to love comfort; it is not a love, at least, that he is faithful to. He is supposed to love happiness; it is my contention that he rather loves excitement. Danger, enterprise, hope, the novel, the aleatory, are dearer to man than regular meals. He does not think so when he is hungry, but he thinks so again as soon as he is fed; and on the hypothesis of a successful ant-heap, he would never go hungry. It would be always after dinner in that society, as, in the land of the Lotus-eaters, it was always afternoon; and food, which, when we have it not, seems all-important, drops in our esteem, as soon as we have it, to a mere prerequisite of living.

That for which man lives is not the same thing for all individuals nor in all ages; yet it has a common base; what he seeks and what he must have is that which will seize and hold his attention. Regular meals and weather-proof lodgings will not do this long. Play in its wide sense, as the artificial induction of sensation, including all games and all arts, will, indeed, go far to keep him conscious of himself; but in the end he wearies for realities. Study or experiment, to some rare natures, is the unbroken pastime of a life. These are enviable natures; people shut in the house by sickness often bitterly envy them; but the commoner man cannot continue to exist upon such altitudes: his feet itch for physical adventure; his blood boils for physical dangers, pleasures, and triumphs; his fancy, the looker after new things, cannot continue to look for them in books and crucibles, but must seek them on the breathing stage of life. Pinches, buffets, the glow of hope, the shock of disappointment, furious contention with obstacles: these are the true elixir for all vital spirits, these are what they seek alike in their romantic enterprises and their unromantic dissipations. When they are taken in some pinch closer than the common, they cry, "Catch me here again!" and sure enough you catch them there again—perhaps before the week is out. It is as old as *Robinson Crusoe;* as old as man.

Our race has not been strained for all these ages through that sieve of dangers that we call Natural Selection, to sit down with patience in the tedium of safety; the voices of its fathers call it forth. Already in our society as it exists, the bourgeois is too much cottoned about for any zest in living; he sits in his parlour out of reach of any danger, often out of reach of any vicissitudes but one of health; and there he yawns. If the people in the next villa took pot-shots at him, he might be killed indeed, but so long as he escaped he would find his blood oxygenated and his views of the world brighter. If Mr. Mallock, on his way to the publishers, should have his skirts pinned to the wall by a javelin, it would not occur to him—at least for several hours— to ask if life were worth living; and if such peril were a daily matter, he would ask it nevermore; he would have other things to think about, he would be living indeed—not lying in a box with cotton, safe, but immeasurably dull. The aleatory, whether it touch life, or fortune, or renown—whether we explore Africa or only toss for halfpence—that is what I conceive men to love best, and that is what we are seeking to exclude from men's existences. Of all forms of the aleatory, that which most commonly attends our working-men —the danger of misery from want of work—is the least inspiriting: it does not whip the blood, it does not evoke the glory of contest; it is tragic, but it is passive; and yet, in so far as it is aleatory, and a peril sensibly touching them, it does truly season the men's lives. Of those who fail, I do not speak—despair should be sacred; but to those who even modestly succeed, the changes of their life bring interest: a job found, a shilling saved,

a dainty earned, all these are wells of pleasure springing afresh for the successful poor; and it is not from
these but from the villa-dweller that we hear complaints
of the unworthiness of life.   Much, then, as the average
of the proletariat would gain in this new state of life,
they would also lose a certain something, which would
not be missed in the beginning, but would be missed
progressively, and progressively lamented.   Soon there
would be a looking back: there would be tales of the
old world humming in young men's ears, tales of the
tramp and the pedlar, and the hopeful emigrant.   And
in the stall-fed life of the successful ant-heap—with its
regular meals, regular duties, regular pleasures, an even
course of life, and fear excluded—the vicissitudes, delights, and havens of to-day will seem of epic breadth.
This may seem a shallow observation; but the springs
by which men are moved lie much on the surface.
Bread, I believe, has always been considered first, but
the circus comes close upon its heels.   Bread we suppose to be given amply; the cry for circuses will be
the louder, and if the life of our descendants be such
as we have conceived, there are two beloved pleasures
on which they will be likely to fall back: the pleasures
of intrigue and of sedition.

In all this I have supposed the ant-heap to be financially sound.   I am no economist, only a writer of
fiction; but even as such, I know one thing that bears
on the economic question—I know the imperfection of
man's faculty for business.   The Anarchists, who count
some rugged elements of common-sense among what
seem to me their tragic errors, have said upon this
matter all that I could wish to say, and condemned be-

forehand great economical polities.   So far it is obvious
that they are right; they may be right also in predicting
a period of communal independence, and they may
even be right in thinking that desirable.   But the rise
of communes is none the less the end of economic
equality, just when we were told it was beginning.
Communes will not be all equal in extent, nor in quality
of soil, nor in growth of population; nor will the surplus produce of all be equally marketable.   It will be
the old story of competing interests, only with a new
unit; and, as it appears to me, a new, inevitable danger.
For the merchant and the manufacturer, in this new
world, will be a sovereign commune; it is a sovereign
power that will see its crops undersold, and its manu-
factures worsted in the market.   And all the more
dangerous that the sovereign power should be small.
Great powers are slow to stir; national affronts, even
with the aid of newspapers, filter slowly into popular
consciousness; national losses are so unequally shared
that one part of the population will be counting its gains
while another sits by a cold hearth.   But in the sovereign commune all will be centralised and sensitive.
When jealousy springs up, when (let us say) the
commune of Poole has overreached the commune of
Dorchester, irritation will run like quicksilver throughout
the body politic; each man in Dorchester will have to
suffer directly in his diet and his dress; even the secretary, who drafts the official correspondence, will sit
down to his task embittered, as a man who has dined
ill and may expect to dine worse; and thus a business
difference between communes will take on much the
same colour as a dispute between diggers in the lawless

West, and will lead as directly to the arbitrament of blows. So that the establishment of the communal system will not only reintroduce all the injustices and heartburnings of economic inequality, but will, in all human likelihood, inaugurate a world of hedgerow warfare. Dorchester will march on Poole, Sherborne on Dorchester, Wimborne on both; the wagons will be fired on as they follow the highway, the trains wrecked on the lines, the ploughman will go armed into the field of tillage; and if we have not a return of ballad literature, the local press at least will celebrate in a high vein the victory of Cerne Abbas or the reverse of Toller Porcorum. At least this will not be dull; when I was younger, I could have welcomed such a world with relief; but it is the New-Old with a vengeance, and irresistibly suggests the growth of military powers and the foundation of new empires.

V

BOOKS WHICH HAVE INFLUENCED ME [1]

THE Editor [2] has somewhat insidiously laid a trap for his correspondents, the question put appearing at first so innocent, truly cutting so deep. It is not, indeed, until after some reconnaissance and review that the writer awakes to find himself engaged upon something in the nature of autobiography, or, perhaps worse, upon a chapter in the life of that little, beautiful brother whom we once all had, and whom we have all lost and mourned, the man we ought to have been, the man we hoped to be. But when word has been passed (even to an editor), it should, if possible, be kept; and if sometimes I am wise and say too little, and sometimes weak and say too much, the blame must lie at the door of the person who entrapped me.

The most influential books, and the truest in their influence, are works of fiction. They do not pin the reader to a dogma, which he must afterwards discover to be inexact; they do not teach him a lesson, which he must afterwards unlearn. They repeat, they rearrange, they clarify the lessons of life; they disengage

---

[1] First published in the *British Weekly*, May 13, 1887.
[2] Of the *British Weekly*.

us from ourselves, they constrain us to the acquaintance of others; and they show us the web of experience, not as we can see it for ourselves, but with a singular change—that monstrous, consuming *ego* of ours being, for the nonce, struck out. To be so, they must be reasonably true to the human comedy; and any work that is so serves the turn of instruction. But the course of our education is answered best by those poems and romances where we breathe a magnanimous atmosphere of thought and meet generous and pious characters. Shakespeare has served me best. Few living friends have had upon me an influence so strong for good as Hamlet or Rosalind. The last character, already well beloved in the reading, I had the good fortune to see, I must think, in an impressionable hour, played by Mrs. Scott Siddons. Nothing has ever more moved, more delighted, more refreshed me; nor has the influence quite passed away. Kent's brief speech over the dying Lear had a great effect upon my mind, and was the burthen of my reflections for long, so profoundly, so touchingly generous did it appear in sense, so overpowering in expression. Perhaps my dearest and best friend outside of Shakespeare is D'Artagnan—the elderly D'Artagnan of the *Vicomte de Bragelonne*. I know not a more human soul, nor, in his way, a finer; I shall be very sorry for the man who is so much of a pedant in morals that he cannot learn from the Captain of Musketeers. Lastly, I must name the *Pilgrim's Progress*, a book that breathes of every beautiful and valuable emotion.

But of works of art little can be said; their influence is profound and silent, like the influence of nature; they mould by contact; we drink them up like water, and are bettered, yet know not how. It is in books more specifically didactic that we can follow out the effect, and distinguish and weigh and compare. A book which has been very influential upon me fell early into my hands, and so may stand first, though I think its influence was only sensible later on, and perhaps still keeps growing, for it is a book not easily outlived: the *Essais* of Montaigne. That temperate and genial picture of life is a great gift to place in the hands of persons of to-day; they will find in these smiling pages a magazine of heroism and wisdom, all of an antique strain; they will have their "linen decencies" and excited orthodoxies fluttered, and will (if they have any gift of reading) perceive that these have not been fluttered without some excuse and ground of reason; and (again if they have any gift of reading) they will end by seeing that this old gentleman was in a dozen ways a finer fellow, and held in a dozen ways a nobler view of life, than they or their contemporaries.

The next book, in order of time, to influence me, was the New Testament, and in particular the Gospel according to St. Matthew. I believe it would startle and move any one if they could make a certain effort of imagination and read it freshly like a book, not droningly and dully like a portion of the Bible. Any one would then be able to see in it those truths which we are all courteously supposed to know and all modestly refrain from applying. But upon this subject it is perhaps better to be silent.

I come next to Whitman's *Leaves of Grass*, a book of singular service, a book which tumbled the world

upside down for me, blew into space a thousand cob-
webs of genteel and ethical illusion, and, having thus
shaken my tabernacle of lies, set me back again upon
a strong foundation of all the original and manly virtues. But it is, once more, only a book for those who
have the gift of reading. I will be very frank—I believe
it is so with all good books except, perhaps, fiction.
The average man lives, and must live, so wholly in
convention, that gunpowder charges of the truth are
more apt to discompose than to invigorate his creed.
Either he cries out upon blasphemy and indecency, and
crouches the closer round that little idol of part-truths
and part-conveniences which is the contemporary deity,
or he is convinced by what is new, forgets what is old,
and becomes truly blasphemous and indecent himself.
New truth is only useful to supplement the old; rough
truth is only wanted to expand, not to destroy, our
civil and often elegant conventions. He who cannot
judge had better stick to fiction and the daily papers.
There he will get little harm, and, in the first at least,
some good.

Close upon the back of my discovery of Whitman,
I came under the influence of Herbert Spencer. No
more persuasive rabbi exists, and few better. How
much of his vast structure will bear the touch of time,
how much is clay and how much brass, it were too
curious to inquire. But his words, if dry, are always
manly and honest; there dwells in his pages a spirit of
highly abstract joy, plucked naked like an algebraic
symbol but still joyful; and the reader will find there a
caput mortuum of piety, with little indeed of its loveliness, but with most of its essentials; and these two

qualities make him a wholesome, as his intellectual vigour makes him a bracing, writer. I should be much of a hound if I lost my gratitude to Herbert Spencer.

Goethe's Life, by Lewes, had a great importance for me when it first fell into my hands—a strange instance of the partiality of man's good and man's evil. I know no one whom I less admire than Goethe; he seems a very epitome of the sins of genius, breaking open the doors of private life, and wantonly wounding friends, in that crowning offence of *Werther*, and in his own character a mere pen-and-ink Napoleon, conscious of the rights and duties of superior talents as a Spanish inquisitor was conscious of the rights and duties of his office. And yet in his fine devotion to his art, in his honest and serviceable friendship for Schiller, what lessons are contained! Biography, usually so false to its office, does here for once perform for us some of the work of fiction, reminding us, that is, of the truly mingled tissue of man's nature, and how huge faults and shining virtues cohabit and persevere in the same character. History serves us well to this effect, but in the originals, not in the pages of the popular epitomiser, who is bound, by the very nature of his task, to make us feel the difference of epochs instead of the essential identity of man, and even in the originals only to those who can recognise their own human virtues and defects in strange forms, often inverted and under strange names, often interchanged. Martial is a poet of no good repute, and it gives a man new thoughts to read his works dispassionately, and find in this unseemly jester's serious passages the image of a kind, wise, and self-respecting gentleman. It is customary, I suppose, in reading Martial, to leave out these pleasant verses; I never heard of them, at least, until I found them for myself; and this partiality is one among a thousand things that help to build up our distorted and hysterical conception of the great Roman Empire.

This brings us by a natural transition to a very noble book—the *Meditations* of Marcus Aurelius. The dispassionate gravity, the noble forgetfulness of self, the tenderness of others, that are there expressed and were practised on so great a scale in the life of its writer, make this book a book quite by itself. No one can read it and not be moved. Yet it scarcely or rarely appeals to the feelings—those very mobile, those not very trusty parts of man. Its address lies further back: its lesson comes more deeply home; when you have read, you carry away with you a memory of the man himself; it is as though you had touched a loyal hand, looked into brave eyes, and made a noble friend; there is another bond on you thenceforward, binding you to life and to the love of virtue.

Wordsworth should perhaps come next. Every one has been influenced by Wordsworth, and it is hard to tell precisely how. A certain innocence, a rugged austerity of joy, a sight of the stars, "the silence that is in the lonely hills," something of the cold thrill of dawn, cling to his work and give it a particular address to what is best in us. I do not know that you learn a lesson; you need not—Mill did not—agree with any one of his beliefs; and yet the spell is cast. Such are the best teachers: a dogma learned is only a new error —the old one was perhaps as good; but a spirit communicated is a perpetual possession. These best

teacners climb beyond teaching to the plane of art; it
is themselves, and what is best in themselves, that
they communicate.

I should never forgive myself if I forgot *The Egoist*.
It is art, if you like, but it belongs purely to didactic
art, and from all the novels I have read (and I have read
thousands) stands in a place by itself. Here is a Nathan
for the modern David; here is a book to send the blood
into men's faces. Satire, the angry picture of human
faults, is not great art; we can all be angry with our
neighbour; what we want is to be shown, not his defects, of which we are too conscious, but his merits,
to which we are too blind. And *The Egoist* is a satire;
so much must be allowed; but it is a satire of a singular
quality, which tells you nothing of that obvious mote,
which is engaged from first to last with that invisible
beam. It is yourself that is hunted down; these are
your own faults that are dragged into the day and
numbered, with lingering relish, with cruel cunning
and precision. A young friend of Mr. Meredith's (as I
have the story) came to him in an agony. "This is
too bad of you," he cried. "Willoughby is me!"
"No, my dear fellow," said the author; "he is all of
us." I have read *The Egoist* five or six times myself,
and I mean to read it again; for I am like the young
friend of the anecdote—I think Willoughby an unmanly
but a very serviceable exposure of myself.

I suppose, when I am done, I shall find that I have
forgotten much that was most influential, as I see
already I have forgotten Thoreau, and Hazlitt, whose
paper "On the Spirit of Obligations" was a turning-
point in my life, and Penn, whose little book of apho-

risms had a brief but strong effect on me, and Mitford's *Tales of Old Japan*, wherein I learned for the first time the proper attitude of any rational man to his country's laws—a secret found, and kept, in the Asiatic islands. That I should commemorate all is more than I can hope or the Editor could ask. It will be more to the point, after having said so much upon improving books, to say a word or two about the improvable reader. The gift of reading, as I have called it, is not very common, nor very generally understood. It consists, first of all, in a vast intellectual endowment—a free grace, I find I must call it—by which a man rises to understand that he is not punctually right, nor those from whom he differs absolutely wrong. He may hold dogmas; he may hold them passionately; and he may know that others hold them but coldly, or hold them differently, or hold them not at all. Well, if he has the gift of reading, these others will be full of meat for him. They will see the other side of propositions and the other side of virtues. He need not change his dogma for that, but he may change his reading of that dogma, and he must supplement and correct his deductions from it. A human truth, which is always very much a lie, hides as much of life as it displays. It is men who hold another truth, or, as it seems to us, perhaps, a dangerous lie, who can extend our restricted field of knowledge, and rouse our drowsy consciences. Something that seems quite new, or that seems insolently false or very dangerous, is the test of a reader. If he tries to see what it means, what truth excuses it, he has the gift, and let him read. If he is merely hurt, or offended, or exclaims upon his author's folly he had better take to the daily papers; he will never be a reader.

And here, with the aptest illustrative force, after I have laid down my part-truth, I must step in with its opposite. For, after all, we are vessels of a very limited content. Not all men can read all books; it is only in a chosen few that any man will find his appointed food; and the fittest lessons are the most palatable, and make themselves welcome to the mind. A writer learns this early, and it is his chief support; he goes on unafraid, laying down the law; and he is sure at heart that most of what he says is demonstrably false, and much of a mingled strain, and some hurtful, and very little good for service; but he is sure besides that when his words fall into the hands of any genuine reader, they will be weighed and winnowed, and only that which suits will be assimilated; and when they fall into the hands of one who cannot intelligently read, they come there quite silent and inarticulate, falling upon deaf ears, and his secret is kept as if he had not written.

THE GREAT NORTH ROAD

Posthumously published, Illustrated London News,
Christmas, 1895

CONTENTS

THE GREAT NORTH ROAD

I

NANCE AT THE GREEN DRAGON

NANCE HOLDAWAY was on her knees before the fire, blowing the green wood that voluminously smoked upon the dogs, and only now and then shot forth a smothered flame; her knees already ached and her eyes smarted, for she had been some while at this ungrateful task, but her mind was gone far away to meet the coming stranger. Now she met him in the wood, now at the castle gate, now in the kitchen by candle-light; each fresh presentment eclipsed the one before; a form so elegant, manners so sedate, a countenance so brave and comely, a voice so winning and resolute—sure such a man was never seen! The thick-coming fancies poured and brightened in her head like the smoke and flames upon the hearth.

Presently the heavy foot of her Uncle Jonathan was heard upon the stair, and as he entered the room she bent the closer to her work. He glanced at the green fagots with a sneer, and looked askance at the bed and the white sheets, at the strip of carpet laid, like an island, on the great expanse of the stone floor, and at the broken glazing of the casement clumsily repaired with paper.

"Leave that fire a-be," he cried. "What, have I toiled all my life to turn innkeeper at the hind end? Leave it a-be, I say."

"La, uncle, it does n't burn a bit; it only smokes," said Nance, looking up from her position.

"You are come of decent people on both sides," returned the old man. "Who are you to blow the coals for any Robin-run-agate? Get up, get on your hood, make yourself useful, and be off to the Green Dragon."

"I thought you was to go yourself," Nance faltered.

"So did I," quoth Jonathan; "but it appears I was mistook."

The very excess of her eagerness alarmed her, and she began to hang back. "I think I would rather not, dear uncle," she said. "Night is at hand, and I think, dear, I would rather not."

"Now you look here," replied Jonathan; "I have my Lord's orders, have I not? Little he gives me, but it 's all my livelihood. And do you fancy, if I disobey my Lord, I 'm likely to turn round for a lass like you? No; I 've that hell-fire of pain in my old knee, I would n't walk a mile, not for King George upon his bended knees." And he walked to the window and looked down the steep scarp to where the river foamed in the bottom of the dell.

Nance stayed for no more bidding. In her own room, by the glimmer of the twilight, she washed her hands and pulled on her Sunday mittens; adjusted her black hood, and tied a dozen times its cherry ribbons; and in less than ten minutes, with a fluttering heart and ex-

cellently bright eyes, she passed forth under the arch
and over the bridge, into the thickening shadows of
the groves. A well-marked wheel-track conducted
her. The wood, which upon both sides of the river
dell was a mere scrambling thicket of hazel, hawthorn,
and holly, boasted on the level of more considerable
timber. Beeches came to a good growth, with here
and there an oak; and the track now passed under a
high arcade of branches, and now ran under the open
sky in glades. As the girl proceeded these glades became more frequent, the trees began again to decline in
size, and the wood to degenerate into furzy coverts.
Last of all there was a fringe of elders; and beyond
that the track came forth upon an open, rolling moorland, dotted with wind-bowed and scanty bushes, and
all golden-brown with the winter, like a grouse. Right
over against the girl the last red embers of the sunset
burned under horizontal clouds; the night fell clear and
still and frosty, and the track in low and marshy passages began to crackle underfoot with ice.

Some half a mile beyond the borders of the wood the
lights of the Green Dragon hove in sight, and running
close beside them, very faint in the dying dusk, the
pale ribbon of the Great North Road. It was the back
of the post-house that was presented to Nance Holdaway; and as she continued to draw near and the night
to fall more completely, she became aware of an unusual
brightness and bustle. A post-chaise stood in the yard,
its lamps already lighted: light shone hospitably in the
windows and from the open door; moving lights and
shadows testified to the activity of servants bearing
lanterns. The clank of pails, the stamping of hoofs on

the firm causeway, the jingle of harness, and, last of all, the energetic hissing of a groom, began to fall upon her ear. By the stir you would have thought the mail was at the door, but it was still too early in the night. The down mail was not due at the Green Dragon for hard upon an hour; the up mail from Scotland not before two in the black morning.

Nance entered the yard somewhat dazzled. Sam, the tall hostler, was polishing the curb-chain with sand; the lantern at his feet letting up spouts of candle-light through the holes with which its conical roof was peppered.

" Hey, miss," said he, jocularly, " you won't look at me any more, now you have gentry at the castle."

Her cheeks burned with anger.

" That 's my Lord's chay," the man continued, nodding at the chaise; " Lord Windermoor's. Came all in a fluster—dinner, bowl of punch, and put the horses to. For all the world like a runaway match, my dear —bar the bride. He brought Mr. Archer in the chay with him."

" Is that Holdaway? " cried the landlord from the lighted entry, where he stood shading his eyes.

" Only me, sir," answered Nance.

" O, you, Miss Nance," he said. " Well, come in quick, my pretty. My Lord is waiting for your uncle."

And he ushered Nance into a room cased with yellow wainscot and lighted by tall candles, where two gentlemen sat at a table finishing a bowl of punch. One of these was stout, elderly, and irascible, with a face like a full moon, well dyed with liquor, thick tremulous lips, a short purple hand, in which he brandished a

long pipe, and an abrupt and gobbling utterance. This
was my Lord Windermóor. In his companion, Nance
beheld a younger man, tall, quiet, grave, demurely
dressed, and wearing his own hair. Her glance but
lighted on him, and she flushed, for in that second she
made sure that she had twice betrayed herself—betrayed
by the involuntary flash of her black eyes her secret
impatience to behold this new companion, and, what
was far worse, betrayed her disappointment in the
realisation of her dreams. He, meanwhile, as if unconscious, continued to regard her with unmoved decorum.

"O, a man of wood," thought Nance.

"What—what?" said his Lordship. "Who is this?"

"If you please, my Lord, I am Holdaway's niece,"
replied Nance, with a courtesy.

"Should have been here himself," observed his Lordship. "Well, you tell Holdaway that I 'm aground;
not a stiver—not a stiver. I 'm running from the
beagles—going abroad, tell Holdaway. And he need
look for no more wages: glad of 'em myself, if I could
get 'em. He can live in the castle if he likes, or go to
the devil. O, and here is Mr. Archer; and I recommend
him to take him in—a friend of mine—and Mr. Archer
will pay, as I wrote. And I regard that in the light of
a precious good thing for Holdaway, let me tell you,
and a set-off against the wages."

"But O, my Lord!" cried Nance, "we live upon the
wages, and what are we to do without?"

"What am I to do?—what am I to do?" replied Lord
Windermoor, with some exasperation. "I have no
wages. And there is Mr. Archer. And if Holdaway

does n't like it, he can go to the devil, and you with him!—and you with him!"

"And yet, my Lord," said Mr. Archer, "these good people will have as keen a sense of loss as you or I; keener, perhaps, since they have done nothing to deserve it."

"Deserve it?" cried the peer. "What? What? If a rascally highwayman comes up to me with a confounded pistol, do you say that I 've deserved it? How often am I to tell you, sir, that I was cheated—that I was cheated?"

"You are happy in the belief," returned Mr. Archer, gravely.

"Archer, you would be the death of me!" exclaimed his Lordship. "You know you 're drunk; you know it, sir; and yet you can't get up a spark of animation."

"I have drunk fair, my Lord," replied the younger man; "but I own I am conscious of no exhilaration."

"If you had as black a look-out as me, sir," cried the peer, "you would be very glad of a little innocent exhilaration, let me tell you. I am glad of it—glad of it, and I only wish I was drunker. For let me tell you it 's a cruel hard thing upon a man of my time of life and my position, to be brought down to beggary because the world is full of thieves and rascals—thieves and rascals. What? For all I know, you may be a thief and a rascal yourself; and I would fight you for a pinch of snuff—a pinch of snuff," exclaimed his Lordship.

Here Mr. Archer turned to Nance Holdaway with a pleasant smile, so full of sweetness, kindness, and composure that, at one bound, her dreams returned to her.

"My good Miss Holdaway," said he, "if you are

willing to show me the road, I am eager to be gone.
As for his Lordship and myself, compose yourself;
there is no fear; this is his Lordship's way."

"What? What?" cried his Lordship. "My way?
Ish no such a thing, my way."

"Come, my Lord," cried Archer; "you and I very
thoroughly understand each other; and let me suggest,
it is time that both of us were gone. The mail will
soon be due. Here, then, my Lord, I take my leave
of you, with the most earnest assurance of my gratitude
for the past, and a sincere offer of any services I may
be able to render in the future."

"Archer," exclaimed Lord Windermoor, "I love you
like a son. Le' 's have another bowl."

"My Lord, for both our sakes, you will excuse me,"
replied Mr. Archer. "We both require caution; we
must both, for some while at least, avoid the chance of
a pursuit."

"Archer," quoth his Lordship, "this is a rank ingratis-
hood. What? I 'm to go firing away in the dark in
the cold po'-chaise, and not so much as a game of écarté
possible, unless I stop and play with the postilion—the
postilion; and the whole country swarming with
thieves and rascals and highwaymen."

"I beg your Lordship's pardon," put in the landlord,
who now appeared in the doorway to announce the
chaise. "but this part of the North Road is known for
safety. There has not been a robbery, to call a robbery,
this five years' time. Farther south, of course, it 's nearer
London, and another story," he added.

"Well, then, if that 's so," concluded my Lord, "le' 's
have t' other bowl and a pack of cards."

"My Lord, you forget," said Archer, "I might still gain, but it is hardly possible for me to lose."

"Think I 'm a sharper ?" inquired the peer. "Gen'le-man's parole 's all I ask."

But Mr. Archer was proof against these blandishments, and said farewell gravely enough to Lord Windermoor, shaking his hand and at the same time bowing very low. "You will never know," said he, "the service you have done me." And with that, and before my Lord had finally taken up his meaning, he had slipped about the table, touched Nance lightly but imperiously on the arm, and left the room. In face of the outbreak of his Lordship's lamentations, she made haste to follow the truant.

II

IN WHICH MR. ARCHER IS INSTALLED

THE chaise had been driven around to the front door; the courtyard lay all deserted, and only lit by a lantern set upon a window-sill. Through this Nance rapidly led the way, and began to ascend the swellings of the moor with a heart that somewhat fluttered in her bosom. She was not afraid, but in the course of these last passages with Lord Windermoor Mr. Archer had ascended to that pedestal on which her fancy waited to install him. The reality, she felt, excelled her dreams, and this cold night walk was the first romantic incident in her experience.

It was the rule in those days to see gentlemen unsteady after dinner, yet Nance was both surprised and amused when her companion, who had spoken so soberly, began to stumble and waver by her side with the most airy divagations. Sometimes he would get so close to her that she must edge away; and at others lurch clear out of the track and plough among deep heather. His courtesy and gravity meanwhile remained unaltered. He asked her how far they had to go; whether the way lay all upon the moorland, and when he learned they had to pass a wood expressed his pleasure. "For," said he, "I am passionately fond of trees.

Trees and fair lawns, if you consider of it rightly, are the ornaments of nature, as palaces and fine approaches—" And here he stumbled into a patch of slough and nearly fell. The girl had hard work not to laugh, but at heart she was lost in admiration for one who talked so elegantly.

They had got to about a quarter of a mile from the Green Dragon, and were near the summit of the rise, when a sudden rush of wheels arrested them. Turning and looking back, they saw the post-house, now much declined in brightness; and speeding away northward the two tremulous bright dots of my Lord Windermoor's chaise-lamps. Mr. Archer followed these yellow and unsteady stars until they dwindled into points and disappeared.

"There goes my only friend," he said. "Death has cut off those that loved me, and change of fortune estranged my flatterers; and but for you, poor bankrupt, my life is as lonely as this moor."

The tone of his voice affected both of them. They stood there on the side of the moor, and became thrillingly conscious of the void waste of the night, without a feature for the eye, and except for the fainting whisper of the carriage-wheels without a murmur for the ear. And instantly, like a mockery, there broke out, very far away, but clear and jolly, the note of the mail-guard's horn. "Over the hills," was his air. It rose to the two watchers on the moor with the most cheerful sentiment of human company and travel, and at the same time in and around the Green Dragon it woke up a great bustle of lights running to and fro and clattering hoofs. Presently after, out of the darkness to southward, the mail drew near with a growing rumble. Its lamps were very large and bright, and threw their radiance forward in overlapping cones; the four cantering horses swarmed and steamed; the body of the coach followed like a great shadow; and this lit picture slid with a sort of ineffectual swiftness over the black field of night, and was eclipsed by the buildings of the Green Dragon.

Mr. Archer turned abruptly and resumed his former walk; only that he was now more steady, kept better alongside his young conductor, and had fallen into a silence broken by sighs. Nance waxed very pitiful over his fate, contrasting an imaginary past of courts and great society, and perhaps the King himself, with the tumbledown ruin in a wood to which she was now conducting him.

"You must try, sir, to keep your spirits up," said she. "To be sure, this is a great change for one like you; but who knows the future?"

Mr. Archer turned towards her in the darkness, and she could clearly perceive that he smiled upon her very kindly. "There spoke a sweet nature," said he, "and I must thank you for these words. But I would not have you fancy that I regret the past for any happiness found in it, or that I fear the simplicity and hardship of the country. I am a man that has been much tossed about in life; now up, now down; and do you think that I shall not be able to support what you support—you who are kind, and therefore know how to feel pain; who are beautiful, and therefore hope; who are young, and therefore (or am I the more mistaken?) discontented?"

"Nay, sir, not that at least," said Nance; "not discontented. If I were to be discontented, how should I look those that have real sorrows in the face? I have faults enough, but not that fault; and I have my merits too, for I have a good opinion of myself. But for beauty, I am not so simple but that I can tell a banter from a compliment."

"Nay, nay," said Mr. Archer, "I had half forgotten; grief is selfish, and I was thinking of myself and not of you, or I had never blurted out so bold a piece of praise. 'T is the best proof of my sincerity. But come, now, I would lay a wager you are no coward?"

"Indeed, sir, I am not more afraid than another," said Nance. "None of my blood are given to fear."

"And you are honest?" he returned.

"I will answer for that," said she.

"Well, then, to be brave, to be honest, to be kind, and to be contented, since you say you are so—is not that to fill up a great part of virtue?"

"I fear you are but a flatterer," said Nance, but she did not say it clearly, for what with bewilderment and satisfaction, her heart was quite oppressed.

There could be no harm, certainly, in these grave compliments; but yet they charmed and frightened her, and to find favour, for reasons however obscure, in the eyes of this elegant, serious, and most unfortunate young gentleman, was a giddy elevation, was almost an apotheosis, for a country maid.

But she was to be no more exercised; for Mr. Archer, disclaiming any thought of flattery, turned off to other subjects, and held her all through the wood in conversation, addressing her with an air of perfect sincerity.

and listening to her answers with every mark of interest.
Had open flattery continued, Nance would have soon
found refuge in good sense; but the more subtle lure
she could not suspect, much less avoid. It was the
first time she had ever taken part in a conversation
illuminated by any ideas. All was then true that she
had heard and dreamed of gentlemen; they were a race
apart, like deities knowing good and evil. And then
there burst upon her soul a divine thought, hope's
glorious sunrise: since she could understand, since it
seemed that she too, even she, could interest this sorrowful Apollo, might she not learn? Or was she not
learning? Would not her soul awake and put forth
wings? Was she not, in fact, an enchanted princess,
waiting but a touch to become royal? She saw herself transformed, radiantly attired, but in the most exquisite taste: her face grown longer and more refined;
her tint etherealised; and she heard herself with delighted wonder talking like a book.

Meanwhile they had arrived at where the track comes
out above the river dell, and saw in front of them the
castle, faintly shadowed on the night, covering with
its broken battlements a bold projection of the bank,
and showing at the extreme end, where were the habitable tower and wing, some crevices of candle-light.
Hence she called loudly upon her uncle, and he was
seen to issue, lantern in hand, from the tower door,
and, where the ruins did not intervene, to pick his way
over the swarded courtyard, avoiding treacherous cellars
and winding among blocks of fallen masonry. The
arch of the great gate was still entire, flanked by two
tottering bastions, and it was here that Jonathan met

them, standing at the edge of the bridge, bent some·
what forward, and blinking at them through the glow
of his own lantern. Mr. Archer greeted him with civility; but the old man was in no humour of compliance.
He guided the new-comer across the courtyard, looking
sharply and quickly in his face, and grumbling all the
time about the cold, and the discomfort and dilapida-
tion of the castle.

He was sure he hoped that Mr. Archer would like it;
but in truth he could not think what brought him there.
Doubtless he had a good reason—this with a look of
cunning scrutiny—but, indeed, the place was quite unfit
for any person of repute; he himself was eaten up with
the rheumatics. It was the most rheumaticky place in
England, and, some fine day, the whole habitable part
(to call it habitable) would fetch away bodily and go
down the slope into the river. He had seen the cracks
widening; there was a plaguy issue in the bank below;
he thought a spring was mining it; it might be to-morrow, it might be next day; but they were all sure of a
come-down sooner or later. " And that is a poor death,"
said he, " for any one, let alone a gentleman, to have a
whole old ruin dumped upon his belly. Have a care to
your left there: these cellar vaults have all broke down,
and the grass and the hemlock hide 'em. Well, sir,
here is welcome to you, such as it is, and wishing you
well away."

And with that Jonathan ushered his guest through
the tower door, and down three steps on the left hand
into the kitchen or common room of the castle. It
was a huge, low room, as large as a meadow, occu-
pying the whole width of the habitable wing, with six

barred windows looking on the court, and two into the
river valley. A dresser, a table, and a few chairs stood
dotted here and there upon the uneven flags. Under
the great chimney a good fire burned in an iron fire-
basket; a high old settee, rudely carved with figures
and Gothic lettering, flanked it on either side; there were
a hinge table and a stone bench in the chimney corner,
and above the arch hung guns, axes, lanterns, and great
sheaves of rusty keys.

Jonathan looked about him, holding up the lantern,
and shrugged his shoulders with a pitying grimace.
"Here it is," he said. "See the damp on the floor, look
at the moss; where there 's moss you may be sure that
it 's rheumaticky. Try and get near that fire for to
warm yourself; it 'll blow the coat off your back. And
with a young gentleman with a face like yours, as pale
as a tallow candle, I 'd be afeard of a churchyard cough
and a galloping decline," said Jonathan, naming the
maladies with gloomy gusto, "or the cold might strike
and turn your blood," he added.

Mr. Archer fairly laughed. "My good Mr. Holdaway," said he, "I was born with that same tallow-
candle face, and the only fear that you inspire me with
is the fear that I intrude unwelcomely upon your private
hours. But I think I can promise you that I am very
little troublesome, and I am inclined to hope that the
terms which I can offer may still pay you the derangement."

"Yes, the terms," said Jonathan, "I was thinking of
that. As you say, they are very small," and he shook
his head.

"Unhappily, I can afford no more," said Mr. Archer.

329

"But this we have arranged already," he added with a certain stiffness; "and as I am aware that Miss Holdaway has matter to communicate, I will, if you permit, retire at once. To-night I must bivouac; to-morrow my trunk is to follow from the Dragon. So, if you will show me to my room I shall wish you a good slumber and a better awakening."

Jonathan silently gave the lantern to Nance, and she, turning and courtesying in the doorway, proceeded to conduct their guest up the broad winding staircase of the tower. He followed with a very brooding face.

"Alas!" cried Nance, as she entered the room, "your fire is black out," and setting down the lantern she clapped upon her knees before the chimney and began to rearrange the charred and still smouldering remains. Mr. Archer looked about the gaunt apartment with a sort of shudder. The great height, the bare stone, the shattered windows, the aspect of the uncurtained bed, with one of its four fluted columns broken short, all struck a chill upon his fancy. From this dismal survey his eyes turned to Nance crouching before the fire, the candle in one hand and artfully puffing at the embers; the flames as they broke forth played upon the soft outline of her cheek—she was alive and young, coloured with the bright hues of life, and a woman. He looked upon her, softening; and then sat down and continued to admire the picture.

"There, sir," said she, getting upon her feet, "your fire is doing bravely now. Good-night."

He rose and held out his hand. "Come," said he, "you are my only friend in these parts, and you must shake hands."

She brushed her hand upon her skirt, and offered it, blushing.

"God bless you, my dear," said he.

And then, when he was alone, he opened one of the windows, and stared down into the dark valley. A gentle wimpling of the river among stones ascended to his ear; the trees upon the other bank stood very black against the sky; farther away an owl was hooting. It was dreary and cold, and as he turned back to the hearth and the fine glow of fire, "Heavens!" said he to himself, "what an unfortunate destiny is mine!"

He went to bed, but sleep only visited his pillow in uneasy snatches. Outbreaks of loud speech came up the staircase; he heard the old stones of the castle crack in the frosty night with sharp reverberations, and the bed complained under his tossings. Lastly, far on into the morning, he awakened from a doze to hear, very far off, in the extreme and breathless quiet, a wailing flourish on the horn. The down mail was drawing near to the Green Dragon. He sat up in bed; the sound was tragical by distance, and the modulation appealed to his ear like human speech. It seemed to call upon him with a dreary insistence—to call him far away, to address him personally, and to have a meaning that he failed to seize. It was thus, at least, in this nodding castle, in a cold, miry woodland, and so far from men and society, that the traffic on the Great North Road spoke to him in the intervals of slumber.

III

JONATHAN HOLDAWAY

Nance descended the tower-stair, pausing at every step. She was in no hurry to confront her uncle with bad news, and she must dwell a little longer on the rich note of Mr. Archer's voice, the charm of his kind words, and the beauty of his manner and person. But, once at the stair-foot, she threw aside the spell and recovered her sensible and workaday self.

Jonathan was seated in the middle of the settle, a mug of ale beside him, in the attitude of one prepared for trouble; but he did not speak, and suffered her to fetch her supper and eat of it, with a very excellent appetite, in silence. When she had done, she, too, drew a tankard of home-brewed, and came and planted herself in front of him upon the settle.

"Well?" said Jonathan.

"My Lord has run away," said Nance.

"What?" cried the old man.

"Abroad," she continued. "Run away from creditors. He said he had not a stiver, but he was drunk enough. He said you might live on in the castle, and Mr. Archer would pay you; but you was to look for no more wages, since he would be glad of them himself."

332

Jonathan's face contracted; the flush of a black, bilious anger mounted to the roots of his hair; he gave an inarticulate cry, leapt upon his feet, and began rapidly pacing the stone floor. At first he kept his hands behind his back in a tight knot; then he began to gesticulate as he turned.

"This man—this Lord," he shouted, "who is he? He was born with a gold spoon in his mouth, and I with a dirty straw. He rolled in his coach when he was a baby. I have dug and toiled and laboured since I was that high—that high." And he shouted again. "I'm bent and broke, and full of pains. D' ye think I don't know the taste of sweat? Many 's the gallon I 've drunk of it—ay, in the midwinter, toiling like a slave. All through, what has my life been? Bend, bend, bend my old creaking back till it would ache like breaking; wade about in the foul mire, never a dry stitch; empty belly, sore hands, hat off to my Lord Redface; kicks and ha'pence; and now, here, at the hind end, when I 'm worn to my poor bones, a kick and done with it." He walked a little while in silence, and then, extending his hand, "Now, you Nance Holdaway," said he, "you come of my blood, and you 're a good girl. When that man was a boy, I used to carry his gun for him. I carried the gun all day on my two feet, and many a stitch I had, and chewed a bullet for. He rode upon a horse, with feathers in his hat, but it was him that had the shots and took the game home. Did I complain? Not I. I knew my station. What did I ask, but just the chance to live and die honest? Nance Holdaway, don't let them deny it to me—don't let them do it. I 've been poor as Job, and honest as the day,

but now, my girl, you mark these words of mine, I 'm
getting tired of it."

"I would n't say such words, at least," said Nance.

"You would n't?" said the old man, grimly. "Well,
and did I when I was your age? Wait till your back 's
broke, and your hands tremble, and your eyes fail, and
you 're weary of the battle, and ask no more but to lie
down in your bed and give the ghost up like an honest
man; and then let there up and come some insolent,
ungodly fellow—ah! if I had him in these hands!
'Where 's my money that you gambled?' I should
say. 'Where 's my money that you drank and
diced? Thief!' is what I would say; thief!" he
roared, "thief!"

"Mr. Archer will hear you, if you don't take care,"
said Nance; "and I would be ashamed, for one, that he
should hear a brave, old, honest, hard-working man
like Jonathan Holdaway talk nonsense like a boy."

"D' ye think I mind for Mr. Archer?" he cried shrilly,
with a clack of laughter; and then he came close up to
her, stooped down with his two palms upon his knees,
and looked her in the eyes, with a strange hard expression, something like a smile. "Do I mind for God,
my girl?" he said, "that 's what it 's come to be now,
do I mind for God?"

"Uncle Jonathan," she said, getting up and taking
him by the arm; "you sit down again, where you were
sitting. There, sit still; I 'll have no more of this;
you 'll do yourself a mischief. Come, take a drink of
this good ale, and I 'll warm a tankard for you. La,
well; we 'll pull through, you 'll see. I 'm young, as
you say, and it 's my turn to carry the bundle; and don't

you worry your bile, or we 'll have sickness, too, as well as sorrow."

"D' ye think that I 'd forgotten you?" said Jonathan, with something like a groan; and thereupon his teeth clicked to, and he sat silent with the tankard in his hand and staring straight before him.

"Why," says Nance, setting on the ale to mull, "men are always children, they say, however old; and if ever I heard a thing like this, to set to and make yourself sick, just when the money 's failing! Keep a good heart up; you have n't kept a good heart these seventy years, nigh hand, to break down about a pound or two. Here 's this Mr. Archer come to lodge, that you disliked so much. Well, now you see it was a clear Providence. Come, let 's think upon our mercies. And here is the ale mulling lovely; smell of it; I 'll take a drop myself, it smells so sweet. And, Uncle Jonathan, you let me say one word. You 've lost more than money before now; you lost my aunt, and bore it like a man. Bear this."

His face once more contracted; his fist doubled, and shot forth into the air, and trembled. "Let them look out!" he shouted. "Here, I warn all men; I 've done with this foul kennel of knaves. Let them look out."

"Hush, hush! for pity's sake," cried Nance.

And then all of a sudden he dropped his face into his hands, and broke out with a great hiccoughing dry sob that was horrible to hear. "O," he cried, "my God, if my son had n't left me, if my Dick was here!" and the sobs shook him; Nance sitting still and watching him, with distress. "O, if he were here to help his

335

father!" he went on again. "If I had a son like other fathers, he would save me now, when all is breaking down; O, he would save me! Ay, but where is he? Raking taverns, a thief perhaps. My curse be on him!" he added, rising again into wrath.

"Hush!" cried Nance, springing to her feet: "your boy, your dead wife's boy—Aunt Susan's baby, that she loved—would you curse him? O, God forbid!"

The energy of her address surprised him from his mood. He looked upon her, tearless and confused. "Let me go to my bed," he said at last, and he rose and, shaking as with ague, but quite silent, lighted his candle, and left the kitchen.

Poor Nance! the pleasant current of her dreams was all diverted. She beheld a golden city, where she aspired to dwell; she had spoken with a deity, and had told herself that she might rise to be his equal; and now the earthly ligaments that bound her down had been straitened. She was like a tree looking skyward, her roots were in the ground. It seemed to her a thing so coarse, so rustic, to be thus concerned about a loss in money; when Mr. Archer, fallen from the sky-level of counts and nobles, faced his changed destiny with so immovable a courage. To weary of honesty; that, at least, no one could do, but even to name it was already a disgrace; and she beheld in fancy her uncle, and the young lad, all laced and feathered, hand upon hip, bestriding his small horse. The opposition seemed to perpetuate itself from generation to generation; one side still doomed to the clumsy and servile, the other born to beauty.

She thought of the golden zones in which gentlemen were bred, and figured with so excellent a grace; zones in which wisdom and smooth words, white linen and slim hands, were the mark of the desired inhabitants; where low temptations were unknown, and honesty no virtue, but a thing as natural as breathing.

MINGLING THREADS

IT was nearly seven before Mr. Archer left his apartment. On the landing he found another door beside his own, opening on a roofless corridor, and presently he was walking on the top of the ruins. On one hand he could look down a good depth into the green courtyard; on the other, his eye roved along the downward course of the river, the wet woods all smoking, the shadows long and blue, the mists golden and rosy in the sun, here and there the water flashing across an obstacle. His heart expanded and softened to a grateful melancholy, and with his eye fixed upon the distance, and no thought of present danger, he continued to stroll along the elevated and treacherous promenade.

A terror-stricken cry rose to him from the courtyard. He looked down, and saw in a glimpse Nance standing below with hands clasped in horror and his own foot trembling on the margin of a gulf. He recoiled and leant against a pillar, quaking from head to foot, and covering his face with his hands; and Nance had time to run round by the stair and rejoin him where he stood before he had changed a line of his position.

"Ah!" he cried, and clutched her wrist; "don't leave me. The place rocks; I have no head for altitudes."

"Sit down against that pillar," said Nance. "Don't you be afraid; I won't leave you; and don't look up or down: look straight at me. How white you are!"

"The gulf," he said, and closed his eyes again and shuddered.

"Why," said Nance, "what a poor climber you must be! That was where my cousin Dick used to get out of the castle after Uncle Jonathan had shut the gate. I 've been down there myself with him helping me. I would n't try with you," she said, and laughed merrily.

The sound of her laughter was sincere and musical, and perhaps its beauty barbed the offence to Mr. Archer. The blood came into his face with a quick jet, and then left it paler than before. "It is a physical weakness," he said harshly, "and very droll, no doubt, but one that I can conquer on necessity. See, I am still shaking. Well, I advance to the battlements and look down. Show me your cousin's path."

"He would go sure-foot along that little ledge," said Nance, pointing as she spoke; "then out through the breach and down by yonder buttress. It is easier coming back, of course, because you see where you are going. From the buttress-foot a sheep-walk goes along the scarp—see, you can follow it from here in the dry grass. And now, sir," she added, with a touch of womanly pity, "I would come away from here if I were you, for indeed you are not fit."

Sure enough, Mr. Archer's pallor and agitation had continued to increase; his cheeks were deathly, his clenched fingers trembled pitifully. "The weakness is physical," he sighed, and had nearly fallen. Nance led him from the spot, and he was no sooner back in the tower-stair, than he fell heavily against the wall and put his arm across his eyes. A cup of brandy had to be brought him before he could descend to breakfast; and the perfection of Nance's dream was for the first time troubled.

Jonathan was waiting for them at table, with yellow, blood-shot eyes and a peculiar dusky complexion. He hardly waited till they found their seats, before, raising one hand, and stooping with his mouth above his plate, he put up a prayer for a blessing on the food and a spirit of gratitude in the eaters, and thereupon, and without more civility, fell to. But it was notable that he was no less speedily satisfied than he had been greedy to begin. He pushed his plate away and drummed upon the table.

"These are silly prayers," said he, "that they teach us. Eat and be thankful, that 's no such wonder. Speak to me of starving—there 's the touch. You 're a man, they tell me, Mr. Archer, that has met with some reverses ? "

"I have met with many," replied Mr. Archer.

"Ha!" said Jonathan, "none reckons but the last. Now, see; I tried to make this girl here understand me."

"Uncle," said Nance, "what should Mr. Archer care for your concerns ? He hath troubles of his own, and came to be at peace, I think."

"I tried to make her understand me," repeated Jonathan, doggedly; "and now I 'll try you. Do you think this world is fair ? "

"Fair and false! " quoth Mr. Archer.

The old man laughed immoderately. "Good," said

he; "very good. But what I mean is this: do you know what it is to get up early and go to bed late, and never take so much as a holiday but four; and one of these your own marriage day, and the other three the funerals of folk you loved, and all that, to have a quiet old age in shelter, and bread for your old belly, and a bed to lay your crazy bones upon, with a clear conscience?"

"Sir," said Mr. Archer, with an inclination of his head, "you portray a very brave existence."

"Well," continued Jonathan, "and in the end thieves deceive you, thieves rob and rook you, thieves turn you out in your grey old age and send you begging. What have you got for all your honesty? A fine return! You that might have stole scores of pounds, there you are out in the rain with your rheumatics!"

Mr. Archer had forgotten to eat; with his hand upon his chin he was studying the old man's countenance. "And you conclude?" he asked.

"Conclude!" cried Jonathan. "I conclude I 'll be upsides with them."

"Ay," said the other, "we are all tempted to revenge."

"You have lost money?" asked Jonathan.

"A great estate," said Archer, quietly.

"See now!" says Jonathan, "and where is it?"

"Nay, I sometimes think that every one has had his share of it but me," was the reply. "All England hath paid his taxes with my patrimony: I was a sheep that left my wool on every brier."

"And you sit down under that?" cried the old man. "Come now, Mr. Archer, you and me belong to different stations? and I know mine—no man better—but since we have both been rooked, and are both sore

341

with it, why, here 's my hand with a very good heart, and I ask for yours, and no offence, I hope."

"There is surely no offence, my friend," returned Mr. Archer, as they shook hands across the table; "for, believe me, my sympathies are quite acquired to you. This life is an arena where we fight with beasts; and, indeed," he added, sighing, "I sometimes marvel why we go down to it unarmed."

In the meanwhile, a creaking of ungreased axles had been heard descending through the wood; and presently after the door opened, and the tall hostler entered the kitchen carrying one end of Mr. Archer's trunks. The other was carried by an aged beggarman of that district, known and welcome for some twenty miles about under the name of Old Cumberland. Each was soon perched upon a settle, with a cup of ale; and the hostler, who valued himself upon his affability, began to entertain the company, still with half an eye on Nance, to whom in gallant terms he expressly dedicated every sip of ale. First he told of the trouble they had to get his Lordship started in the chaise; and how he had dropped a rouleau of gold on the threshold, and the passage and door-step had been strewn with guinea-pieces. At this old Jonathan looked at Mr. Archer. Next the visitor turned to news of a more thrilling character: how the down mail had been stopped again near Grantham by three men on horseback—a white and two bays; how they had handkerchiefs on their faces; how Tom the guard's blunderbuss missed fire, but he swore he had winged one of them with a pistol; and how they had got clean away with seventy pounds in money, some valuable papers, and a watch or two.

"Brave, brave!" cried Jonathan, in ecstasy. "Seventy pounds! O, it's brave!"

"Well, I don't see the great bravery," observed the hostler, misapprehending him. "Three men, and you may call that three to one. I 'll call it brave when some one stops the mail single-handed; that 's a risk."

"And why should they hesitate?" inquired Mr. Archer. "The poor souls who are fallen to such a way of life, pray, what have they to lose? If they get the money, well; but if a ball should put them from their troubles, why, so better."

"Well, sir," said the hostler, "I believe you 'll find they won't agree with you. They count on a good fling, you see; or who would risk it?—And here 's my best respects to you, Miss Nance."

"And I forgot the part of cowardice," resumed Mr. Archer. "All men fear."

"O, surely not!" cried Nance.

"All men," reiterated Mr. Archer.

"Ay, that 's a true word," observed Old Cumberland, "and a thief, anyway, for it 's a coward's trade."

"But these fellows, now," said Jonathan, with a curious, appealing manner—"these fellows with their seventy pounds! Perhaps, Mr. Archer, they were no true thieves after all, but just people who had been robbed and tried to get their own again. What was that you said, about all England and the taxes? One takes, another gives; why, that 's almost fair. If I 've been rooked and robbed, and the coat taken off my back, I call it almost fair to take another's."

"Ask Old Cumberland," observed the hostler, "you

ask Old Cumberland, Miss Nance!" and he bestowed a wink upon his favoured fair one.

"Why that?" asked Jonathan.

"He had his coat taken, ay, and his shirt too," returned the hostler.

"Is that so?" cried Jonathan, eagerly. "Was you robbed too?"

"That was I," replied Cumberland, "with a warrant! I was a well-to-do man when I was young."

"Ay! See that!" says Jonathan. "And you don't long for a revenge?"

"Eh! Not me!" answered the beggar. "It's too long ago. But if you'll give me another mug of your good ale, my pretty lady, I won't say no to that."

"And shalt have! And shalt have!" cried Jonathan; "or brandy even, if you like it better."

And as Cumberland did like it better, and the hostler chimed in, the party pledged each other in a dram of brandy before separating.

As for Nance, she slipped forth into the ruins, partly to avoid the hostler's gallantries, partly to lament over the defects of Mr. Archer. Plainly, he was no hero. She pitied him; she began to feel a protecting interest mingle with and almost supersede her admiration, and was at the same time disappointed and yet drawn to him. She was, indeed, conscious of such unshaken fortitude in her own heart, that she was almost tempted by an occasion to be bold for two. She saw herself, in a brave attitude, shielding her imperfect hero from the world; and she saw, like a piece of Heaven, his gratitude for her protection.

V

LIFE IN THE CASTLE

From that day forth the life of these three persons in the ruins ran very smoothly. Mr. Archer now sat by the fire with a book, and now passed whole days abroad, returning late, dead weary. His manner was a mask; but it was half transparent; through the even tenor of his gravity and courtesy profound revolutions of feeling were betrayed, seasons of numb despair, of restlessness, of aching temper. For days he would say nothing beyond his usual courtesies and solemn compliments; and then, all of a sudden, some fine evening beside the kitchen fire, he would fall into a vein of elegant gossip, tell of strange and interesting events, the secrets of families, brave deeds of war, the miraculous discovery of crime, the visitations of the dead. Nance and her uncle would sit till the small hours with eyes wide open: Jonathan applauding the unexpected incidents with many a slap of his big hand; Nance, perhaps, more pleased with the narrator's eloquence and wise reflections. And then, again, days would follow of abstraction, of listless humming, of frequent apologies and long hours of silence. Once only, and then after a week of unrelieved melancholy, he went over to the Green Dragon, spent the afternoon with the landlord and a bowl of punch, and returned as on the first night, devious in step, but courteous and unperturbed of speech.

If he seemed more natural and more at his ease, it was when he found Nance alone; and laying by some of his reserve, talked before her rather than to her of his destiny, character, and hopes. To Nance these interviews were but a doubtful privilege. At times he would seem to take a pleasure in her presence, to consult her gravely, to hear and discuss her counsels; at times even, but these were rare and brief, he would talk of herself, praise the qualities that she possessed, touch indulgently on her defects, and lend her books to read and even examine her upon her reading; but far more often he would fall into a half-unconsciousness, put her a question and then answer it himself, drop into the veiled tone of voice of one soliloquising, and leave her at last as though he had forgotten her existence. It was odd, too, that in all this random converse not a fact of his past life, and scarce a name, should ever cross his lips. A profound reserve kept watch upon his most unguarded moments. He spoke continually of himself, indeed, but still in enigmas; the veiled prophet of egoism.

The base of Nance's feelings for Mr. Archer was admiration as for a superior being; and with this, his treatment, consciously or not, accorded happily. When he forgot her, she took the blame upon herself. His formal politeness was so exquisite that this essential brutality stood excused. His compliments, besides, were always grave and rational; he would offer reason for his praise, convict her of merit, and thus disarm

346

suspicion. Nay, and the very hours when he forgot and remembered her alternately could by the ardent fallacies of youth be read in the light of an attention. She might be far from his confidence; but still she was nearer it than any one. He might ignore her presence, but yet he sought it.

Moreover, she, upon her side, was conscious of one point of superiority. Beside this rather dismal, rather effeminate man, who recoiled from a worm, who grew giddy on the castle wall, who bore so helplessly the weight of his misfortunes, she felt herself a head and shoulders taller in cheerful and sterling courage. She could walk, head in air, along the most precarious rafter; her hand feared neither the grossness nor the harshness of life's web, but was thrust cheerfully, if need were, into the brier bush, and could take hold of any crawling horror. Ruin was mining the walls of her cottage, as already it had mined and subverted Mr. Archer's palace. Well, she faced it with a bright countenance and a busy hand. She had got some washing, some rough seamstress work from the Green Dragon, and from another neighbour ten miles across the moor. At this she cheerfully laboured, and from that height she could afford to pity the useless talents and poor attitude of Mr. Archer. It did not change her admiration, but it made it bearable. He was above her in all ways; but she was above him in one. She kept it to herself, and hugged it. When, like all young creatures, she made long stories to justify, to nourish, and to forecast the course of her affection, it was this private superiority that made all rosy, that cut the knot, and that, at last, in some great situation, fetched to her knees the dazzling but imperfect hero. With this pretty exercise she beguiled the hours of labour, and consoled herself for Mr. Archer's bearing. Pity was her weapon and her weakness. To accept the loved one's faults, although it has an air of freedom, is to kiss the chain, and this pity it was which, lying nearer to her heart, lent the one element of true emotion to a fanciful and merely brainsick love.

Thus it fell out one day that she had gone to the Green Dragon and brought back thence a letter to Mr. Archer. He, upon seeing it, winced like a man under the knife: pain, shame, sorrow, and the most trenchant edge of mortification cut into his heart and wrung the steady composure of his face.

"Dear heart! have you bad news?" she cried.

But he only replied by a gesture and fled to his room, and when, later on, she ventured to refer to it, he stopped her on the threshold, as if with words prepared beforehand. "There are some pains," said he, "too acute for consolation, or I would bring them to my kind consoler. Let the memory of that letter, if you please, be buried." And then as she continued to gaze at him, being, in spite of herself, pained by his elaborate phrase, doubtfully sincere in word and matter: "Let it be enough," he added haughtily, "that if this matter wring my heart, it doth not touch my conscience. I am a man, I would have you to know, who suffers undeservedly."

He had never spoken so directly: never with so convincing an emotion; and her heart thrilled for him. She could have taken his pains and died of them with joy.

348

Meanwhile she was left without support. Jonathan now swore by his lodger, and lived for him. He was a fine talker. He knew the finest sight of stories; he was a man and a gentleman, take him for all in all, and a perfect credit to Old England. Such were the old man's declared sentiments, and sure enough he clung to Mr. Archer's side, hung upon his utterance when he spoke, and watched him with unwearying interest when he was silent. And yet his feeling was not clear; in the partial wreck of his mind, which was leaning to decay, some afterthought was strongly present. As he gazed in Mr. Archer's face a sudden brightness would kindle in his rheumy eyes, his eyebrows would lift as with a sudden thought, his mouth would open as though to speak, and close again in silence. Once or twice he even called Mr. Archer mysteriously forth into the dark courtyard, took him by the button, and laid a demonstrative finger on his chest; but there his ideas or his courage failed him; he would shufflingly excuse himself and return to his position by the fire without a word of explanation. "The good man was growing old," said Mr. Archer, with a suspicion of a shrug. But the good man had his idea, and even when he was alone the name of Mr. Archer fell from his lips continually in the course of mumbled and gesticulative conversation.

VI

THE BAD HALF-CROWN

HOWEVER early Nance arose, and she was no sluggard, the old man, who had begun to outlive the earthly habit of slumber, would usually have been up long before, the fire would be burning brightly, and she would see him wandering among the ruins, lantern in hand, and talking assiduously to himself. One day, however, after he had returned late from the market-town, she found that she had stolen a march upon that indefatigable early riser. The kitchen was all blackness. She crossed the castle yard to the wood-cellar, her steps printing the thick hoar-frost. A scathing breeze blew out of the north-east and slowly carried a regiment of black and tattered clouds over the face of Heaven, which was already kindled with the wild light of morning, but where she walked, in shelter of the ruins, the flame of her candle burned steady. The extreme cold smote upon her conscience. She could not bear to think this bitter business fell usually to the lot of one so old as Jonathan, and made desperate resolutions to be earlier in the future.

The fire was a good blaze before he entered, limping dismally into the kitchen. "Nance," said he, "I be all knotted up with the rheumatics; will you rub me a bit?" She came and rubbed him where and how he bade her. "This is a cruel thing that old age should be rheumaticky," said he. "When I was young I stood my turn of the teethache like a man! for why? because it could n't last for ever; but these rheumatics come to live and die with you. Your aunt was took before the time came; never had an ache to mention. Now I lie all night in my single bed and the blood never warms in me; this knee of mine it seems like lighted up with the rheumatics; it seems as though you could see to sew by it; and all the strings of my old body ache, as if devils was pulling 'em. Thank you kindly; that 's someways easier now, but an old man, my dear, has little to look for; it 's pain, pain, pain to the end of the business, and I 'll never be rightly warm again till I get under the sod," he said, and looked down at her with a face so aged and weary that she had nearly wept.

"I lay awake all night," he continued; "I do so mostly, and a long walk kills me. Eh, deary me, to think that life should run to such a puddle! And I remember long syne when I was strong, and the blood all hot and good about me, and I loved to run, too— deary me, to run! Well, that 's all by. You 'd better pray to be took early, Nance, and not live on till you get to be like me, and are robbed in your grey old age, your cold, shivering, dark old age, that 's like a winter's morning"; and he bitterly shuddered, spreading his hands before the fire.

"Come now," said Nance, "the more you say the less you 'll like it, Uncle Jonathan; but if I were you I would be proud for to have lived all your days honest and beloved, and come near the end with your good

351

name: is n't that a fine thing to be proud of? Mr. Archer was telling me in some strange land they used to run races each with a lighted candle, and the art was to keep the candle burning. Well, now, I thought that was like life: a man's good conscience is the flame he gets to carry, and if he comes to the winning-post with that still burning, why, take it how you will, the man 's a hero—even if he was low-born like you and me."

"Did Mr. Archer tell you that?" asked Jonathan.

"No, dear," said she, "that 's my own thought about it. He told me of the race. But see, now," she continued, putting on the porridge, "you say old age is a hard season, but so is youth. You 're half out of the battle, I would say; you loved my aunt and got her, and buried her, and some of these days soon you 'll go to meet her; and take her my love and tell her I tried to take good care of you; for so I do, Uncle Jonathan."

Jonathan struck with his fist upon the settle. "D' ye think I want to die, ye vixen!" he shouted. "I want to live ten hundred years."

This was a mystery beyond Nance's penetration, and she stared in wonder as she made the porridge.

"I want to live," he continued, "I want to live and to grow rich. I want to drive my carriage and to dice in hells and see the ring, I do. Is this a life that I lived? I want to be a rake, d' ye understand? I want to know what things are like. I don't want to die like a blind kitten, and me seventy-six."

"O fie!" said Nance.

The old man thrust out his jaw at her, with the grimace of an irreverent schoolboy. Upon that aged face it seemed a blasphemy. Then he took out of his bosom a long leather purse, and emptying its contents on the settle, began to count and recount the pieces, ringing and examining each, and suddenly he leapt like a young man. "What!" he screamed. "Bad? O Lord! I'm robbed again!" And falling on his knees before the settle he began to pour forth the most dreadful curses on the head of his deceiver. His eyes were shut, for to him this vile solemnity was prayer. He held up the bad half-crown in his right hand, as though he were displaying it to Heaven, and what increased the horror of the scene, the curses he invoked were those whose efficacy he had tasted—old age and poverty, rheumatism and an ungrateful son. Nance listened appalled; then she sprang forward and dragged down his arm and laid her hand upon his mouth.

"Whist!" she cried. "Whist ye, for God's sake! O my man, whist ye! If Heaven were to hear; if poor Aunt Susan were to hear! Think, she may be listening." And with the histrionism of strong emotion she pointed to a corner of the kitchen.

His eyes followed her finger. He looked there for a little, thinking, blinking; then he got stiffly to his feet and resumed his place upon the settle, the bad piece still in his hand. So he sat for some time, looking upon the half-crown, and now wondering to himself on the injustice and partiality of the law, now computing again and again the nature of his loss. So he was still sitting when Mr. Archer entered the kitchen. At this a light came into his face, and after some seconds of rumination he despatched Nance upon an errand.

"Mr. Archer," said he, as soon as they were alone

together, "would you give me a guinea-piece for silver ? "

"Why, sir, I believe I can," said Mr. Archer.

And the exchange was just effected when Nance re-entered the apartment. The blood shot into her face. "What's to do here ? " she asked rudely.

"Nothing, my deary," said old Jonathan, with a touch of whine.

"What's to do ? " she said again.

"Your uncle was but changing me a piece of gold," returned Mr. Archer.

"Let me see what he hath given you, Mr. Archer," replied the girl. "I had a bad piece, and I fear it is mixed up among the good."

"Well, well," replied Mr. Archer, smiling, "I must take the merchant's risk of it. The money is now mixed."

"I know my piece," quoth Nance. "Come, let me see your silver, Mr. Archer. If I have to get it by a theft I'll see that money," she cried.

"Nay, child, if you put as much passion to be honest as the world to steal, I must give way, though I betray myself," said Mr. Archer. "There it is as I received it."

Nance quickly found the bad half-crown. "Give him another," she said, looking Jonathan in the face; and when that had been done, she walked over to the chimney and flung the guilty piece into the reddest of the fire. Its base constituents began immediately to run; even as she watched it the disc crumpled, and the lineaments of the King became confused. Jonathan, who had followed close behind, beheld these changes from over her shoulder, and his face darkened sorely.

"Now," said she, "come back to table, and to-day it is I that shall say grace, as I used to do in the old times, day about with Dick"; and covering her eyes with one hand, "O Lord," said she, with deep emotion, "make us thankful; and, O Lord, deliver us from evil! For the love of the poor souls that watch for us in Heaven, O deliver us from evil!"

VII

THE year moved on to March; and March, though **it** blew bitter keen from the North Sea, yet blinked kindly betweenwhiles on the river dell. The mire dried up in the closest covert; life ran in the bare branches, and the air of the afternoon would be suddenly sweet with the fragrance of new grass.

Above and below the castle the river crooked like the letter "S." The lower loop was to the left, and embraced the high and steep projection which was crowned by the ruins; the upper loop enclosed a lawny promontory, fringed by thorn and willow. It was easy to reach it from the castle side, for the river ran in this part very quietly among innumerable boulders and over dam-like walls of rock. The place was all enclosed, the wind a stranger, the turf smooth and solid; so it was chosen by Nance to be her bleaching-green.

One day she brought a bucketful of linen, and had but begun to wring and lay them out when Mr. Archer stepped from the thicket on the far side, drew very deliberately near, and sat down in silence on the grass. Nance looked up to greet him with a smile, but finding her smile was not returned, she fell into embarrassment and stuck the more busily to her employment. Man or woman, the whole world looks well at any work to which they are accustomed; but the girl was ashamed of what she did. She was ashamed, besides, of the sun-bonnet that so well became her, and ashamed of her bare arms, which were her greatest beauty.

"Nausicaä," said Mr. Archer, at last, "I find you like Nausicaä."

"And who was she?" asked Nance, and laughed in spite of herself, an empty and embarrassed laugh, that sounded in Mr. Archer's ears, indeed, like music, but to her own like the last grossness of rusticity.

"She was a princess of the Grecian islands," he replied. "A king, being shipwrecked, found her washing by the shore. Certainly I, too, was shipwrecked," he continued, plucking at the grass. "There was never a more desperate castaway—to fall from polite life, fortune, a shrine of honour, a grateful conscience, duties willingly taken up and faithfully discharged; and to fall to this—idleness, poverty, inutility, remorse." He seemed to have forgotten her presence, but here he remembered her again. "Nance," said he, "would you have a man sit down and suffer or rise up and strive?"

"Nay," she said. "I would always rather see him doing."

"Ha!" said Mr. Archer, "but yet you speak from an imperfect knowledge. Conceive a man damned to a choice of only evil—misconduct upon either side, not a fault behind him, and yet naught before him but this choice of sins. How would you say then?"

"I would say that he was much deceived, Mr. Archer," returned Nance. "I would say there was a third choice, and that the right one."

"I tell you," said Mr. Archer, "the man I have in view hath two ways open, and no more. One to wait, like a poor mewling baby, till Fate save or ruin him; the other to take his troubles in his hand, and to perish or be saved at once. It is no point of morals; both are wrong. Either way this step-child of Providence must fall; which shall he choose, by doing, or not doing?"

"Fall, then, is what I would say," replied Nance. "Fall where you will, but do it! For O, Mr. Archer," she continued, stooping to her work, "you that are good and kind, and so wise, it doth sometimes go against my heart to see you live on here like a sheep in a turnip-field! If you were braver—" and here she paused, conscience-smitten.

"Do I, indeed, lack courage?" inquired Mr. Archer of himself. "Courage, the footstool of the virtues, upon which they stand? Courage, that a poor private carrying a musket has to spare of; that does not fail a weasel or a rat; that is a brutish faculty? I to fail there, I wonder? But what is courage, then? The constancy to endure oneself or to see others suffer? The itch of ill-advised activity—mere shuttle-wittedness —or to be still and patient? To inquire of the significance of words is to rob ourselves of what we seem to know, and yet, of all things, certainly to stand still is the least heroic. Nance," he said, "did you ever hear of *Hamlet?*"

"Never," said Nance.

"'T is an old play," returned Mr. Archer, "and frequently enacted. This while I have been talking Hamlet. You must know this Hamlet was a Prince among the Danes," and he told her the play in a very good
358

style, here and there quoting a verse or two with solemn emphasis.

"It is strange," said Nance; "he was then a very poor creature?"

"That was what he could not tell," said Mr. Archer. "Look at me; am I as poor a creature?"

She looked, and what she saw was the familiar thought of all her hours; the tall figure very plainly habited in black, the spotless ruffles, the slim hands; the long, well-shapen, serious, shaven face, the wide and somewhat thin-lipped mouth, the dark eyes that were so full of depth and change and colour. He was gazing at her with his brows a little knit, his chin upon one hand and that elbow resting on his knee.

"Ye look a man!" she cried, "ay, and should be a great one! The more shame to you to lie here idle like a dog before the fire."

"My fair Holdaway," quoth Mr. Archer, "you are much set on action. I cannot dig, to beg I am ashamed." He continued, looking at her with a half-absent fixity: "'T is a strange thing, certainly, that in my years of fortune I should never taste happiness, and now when I am broke, enjoy so much of it, for was I ever happier than to-day? Was the grass softer, the stream pleasanter in sound, the air milder, the heart more at peace? Why should I not sink? To dig—why, after all, it should be easy. To take a mate, too? Love is of all grades since Jupiter; love fails to none; and children—" but here he passed his hand suddenly over his eyes. "O fool and coward, fool and coward!" he said bitterly; "can you forget your fetters? You did not know that I was fettered, Nance?" he asked, again addressing her.

But Nance was somewhat sore. "I know you keep talking," she said, and, turning half away from him, began to wring out a sheet across her shoulder. "I wonder you are not wearied of your voice. When the hands lie abed the tongue takes a walk."

Mr. Archer laughed unpleasantly, rose and moved to the water's edge. In this part the body of the river poured across a little narrow fell, ran some ten feet very smoothly over a bed of pebbles, then getting wind, as it were, of another shelf of rock which barred the channel, began, by imperceptible degrees, to separate towards either shore in dancing currents, and to leave the middle clear and stagnant. The set towards either side was nearly equal: about one half of the whole water plunged on the side of the castle, through a narrow gullet; about one half ran lipping past the margin of the green and slipped across a babbling rapid.

"Here," said Mr. Archer, after he had looked for some time at the fine and shifting demarcation of these currents, "come here and see me try my fortune."

"I am not like a man," said Nance; "I have no time to waste."

"Come here," he said again. "I ask you seriously, Nance. We are not always childish when we seem so."

She drew a little nearer.

"Now," said he, "you see these two channels— choose one."

"I 'll choose the nearest, to save time," said Nance.

"Well, that shall be for action," returned Mr. Archer. "And since I wish to have the odds against me, not only the other channel but yon stagnant water in the midst shall be for lying still. You see this?" he continued, pulling up a withered rush, "I break it in three. I shall put each separately at the top of the upper fall, and according as they go by your way or by the other I shall guide my life."

"This is very silly," said Nance, with a movement of her shoulders.

"I do not think it so," said Mr. Archer.

"And then," she resumed, "if you are to try your fortune, why not evenly?"

"Nay," returned Mr. Archer, with a smile, "no man can put complete reliance in blind Fate; he must still cog the dice."

By this time he had got upon the rock beside the upper fall, and, bidding her look out, dropped a piece of rush into the middle of the intake. The rusty fragment was sucked at once over the fall, came up again far on the right hand, leaned ever more and more in the same direction, and disappeared under the hanging grasses on the castle side.

"One," said Mr. Archer, "one for standing still."

But the next launch had a different fate, and after hanging for a while about the edge of the stagnant water, steadily approached the bleaching-green and danced down the rapid under Nance's eyes.

"One for me," she cried with some exultation; and then she observed that Mr. Archer had grown pale, and was kneeling on the rock, with his hand raised like a person petrified. "Why," said she, "you do not mind it, do you?"

"Does a man not mind a throw of dice by which a fortune hangs?" said Mr. Archer, rather hoarsely. "And this is more than fortune. Nance, if you have

361

any kindness for my fate, put up a prayer before I launch the next one."

"A prayer," she cried, "about a game like this? I would not be so heathen."

"Well," said he, "then without," and he closed his eyes and dropped the piece of rush. This time there was no doubt. It went for the rapid as straight as any arrow.

"Action then!" said Mr. Archer, getting to his feet; "and then God forgive us," he added, almost to himself.

"God forgive us, indeed," cried Nance, "for wasting the good daylight! But come, Mr. Archer, if I see you look so serious I shall begin to think you was in earnest."

"Nay," he said, turning upon her suddenly, with a full smile; "but is not this good advice? I have consulted God and demigod; the nymph of the river, and what I far more admire and trust, my blue-eyed Minerva. Both have said the same. My own heart was telling it already. Action, then, be mine; and into the deep sea with all this paralysing casuistry. I am happy to-day for the first time."

VIII

THE MAIL-GUARD

SOMEWHERE about two in the morning a squall had burst upon the castle, a clap of screaming wind that made the towers rock, and a copious drift of rain that streamed from the windows. The wind soon blew itself out, but the day broke cloudy and dripping, and when the little party assembled at breakfast, their humours appeared to have changed with the change of weather. Nance had been brooding on the scene at the river-side, applying it in various ways to her particular aspirations, and the result, which was hardly to her mind, had taken the colour out of her cheeks. Mr. Archer, too, was somewhat absent; his thoughts were of a mingled strain; and even upon his usually impassive countenance there were betrayed successive depths of depression and starts of exultation, which the girl translated in terms of her own hopes and fears. But Jonathan was the most altered: he was strangely silent, hardly passing a word, and watched Mr. Archer with an eager and furtive eye. It seemed as if the idea that had so long hovered before him had now taken a more solid shape, and, while it still attracted, somewhat alarmed his imagination.

At this rate, conversation languished into a silence

which was only broken by the gentle and ghostly noises of the rain on the stone roof and about all that field of ruins; and they were all relieved when the note of a man whistling and the sound of approaching footsteps in the grassy court announced a visitor. It was the hostler from the Green Dragon bringing a letter for Mr. Archer. Nance saw her hero's face contract and then relax again at the sight of it; and she thought that she knew why, for the sprawling, gross black characters of the address were easily distinguishable from the fine writing on the former letter that had so much disturbed him. He opened it and began to read; while the hostler sat down to table with a pot of ale, and proceeded to make himself agreeable after his fashion.

"Fine doings down our way, Miss Nance," said he. "I have n't been abed this blessed night."

Nance expressed a polite interest, but her eye was on Mr. Archer, who was reading his letter with a face of such extreme indifference that she was tempted to suspect him of assumption.

"Yes," continued the hostler, "not been the like of it this fifteen years: the North Mail stopped at the three stones."

Jonathan's cup was at his lip, but at this moment he choked with a great splutter; and Mr. Archer, as if startled by the noise, made so sudden a movement that one corner of the sheet tore off and stayed between his finger and thumb. It was some little time before the old man was sufficiently recovered to beg the hostler to go on, and he still kept coughing and crying and rubbing his eyes. Mr. Archer, on his side, laid the

letter down, and putting his hands in his pocket, listened gravely to the tale.

"Yes," resumed Sam, "the North Mail was stopped
by a single horseman; dash my wig, but I admire him!
There were four insides and two out, and poor Tom
Oglethorpe, the guard. Tom showed himself a man;
let fly his blunderbuss at him; had him covered, too,
and could swear to that; but the Captain never let on,
up with a pistol and fetched poor Tom a bullet through
the body. Tom, he squelched upon the seat, all over
blood. Up comes the Captain to the window. 'Oblige
me,' says he, 'with what you have.' Would you believe it? not a man says cheep!—not them! 'Thy
hands over thy head.' Four watches, rings, snuff-boxes,
seven-and-forty pounds overhead in gold. One Dicksee, a grazier, tries it on: gives him a guinea. 'Beg
your pardon,' says the Captain, 'I think too highly of
you to take it at your hand. I will not take less than
ten from such a gentleman.' This Dicksee had his
money in his stocking, but there was the pistol at his
eye. Down he goes, offs with his stocking, and there
was thirty golden guineas. 'Now,' says the Captain,
'you 've tried it on with me, but I scorns the advantage.
Ten, I said,' he says, 'and ten I take.' So, dash my
buttons, I call that man a man!" cried Sam, in cordial
admiration.

"Well, and then?" says Mr. Archer.

"Then," resumed Sam, "that old fat fagot Engleton,
him as held the ribbons and drew up like a lamb when
he was told to, picks up his cattle, and drives off again.
Down they came to the Dragon, all singing like as if
they was scalded, and poor Tom saying nothing. You

would 'a' thought they had all lost the King's crown
to hear them. Down gets this Dicksee. 'Postmaster,'
he says, taking him by the arm, 'this is a most abominable thing,' he says. Down gets a Major Clayton, and
gets the old man by the other arm. 'We 've been
robbed,' he cries, 'robbed!' Down gets the others,
and all round the old man telling their story, and what
they had lost, and how they was all as good as ruined;
till at last old Engleton says, says he, 'How about
Oglethorpe?' says he. 'Ay,' says the others, 'how
about the guard?' Well, with that we bousted him
down, as white as a rag and all blooded like a sop. I
thought he was dead. Well, he ain't dead; but he 's
dying, I fancy."

"Did you say four watches?" said Jonathan.

"Four, I think. I wish it had been forty," cried Sam.
"Such a party of soured herrings I never did see—not
a man among them bar poor Tom. But us that are the
servants on the road have all the risk and none of the
profit."

"And this brave fellow," asked Mr. Archer, very
quietly, "this Oglethorpe—how is he now?"

"Well, sir, with my respects, I take it he has a hole
bang through him," said Sam. "The doctor has n't
been yet. He 'd 'a' been bright and early if it had been
a passenger. But, doctor or no, I 'll make a good guess
that Tom won't see to-morrow. He 'll die on a Sunday, will poor Tom; and they do say that 's fortunate."

"Did Tom see him that did it?" asked Jonathan.

"Well, he saw him," replied Sam, "but not to swear
by. Said he was a very tall man, and very big, and
had a 'andkerchief about his face, and a very quick

366

shot, and sat his horse like a thorough gentleman, as
he is."

"A gentleman!" cried Nance. "The dirty knave!"

"Well, I calls a man like that a gentleman," returned
the hostler; "that's what I mean by a gentleman."

"You don't know much of them, then," said Nance.
"A gentleman would scorn to stoop to such a thing.
I call my uncle a better gentleman than any thief."

"And you would be right," said Mr. Archer.

"How many snuff-boxes did he get?" asked Jonathan.

"O, dang me, if I know," said Sam; "I didn't take
an inventory."

"I will go back with you, if you please," said Mr.
Archer. "I should like to see poor Oglethorpe. He
has behaved well."

"At your service, sir," said Sam, jumping to his feet.
"I dare to say a gentleman like you would not forget a
poor fellow like Tom—no, nor a plain man like me, sir,
that went without his sleep to nurse him. And excuse
me, sir," added Sam, "you won't forget about the
letter, neither?"

"Surely not," said Mr. Archer.

Oglethorpe lay in a low bed, one of several in a long
garret of the inn. The rain soaked in places through
the roof and fell in minute drops; there was but one
small window; the beds were occupied by servants,
the air of the garret was both close and chilly. Mr.
Archer's heart sank at the threshold to see a man lying
perhaps mortally hurt in so poor a sick-room, and as he
drew near the low bed he took his hat off. The guard
was a big, blowzy, innocent-looking soul with a thick

lip and a broad nose, comically turned up; his cheeks were crimson, and when Mr. Archer laid a finger on his brow he found him burning with fever.

"I fear you suffer much," he said, with a catch in his voice, as he sat down on the bedside.

"I suppose I do, sir," returned Oglethorpe; "it is main sore."

"I am used to wounds and wounded men," returned the visitor. "I have been in the wars and nursed brave fellows before now; and, if you will suffer me, I propose to stay beside you till the doctor comes."

"It is very good of you, sir, I am sure," said Oglethorpe. "The trouble is they won't none of them let me drink."

"If you will not tell the doctor," said Mr. Archer, "I will give you some water. They say it is bad for a green wound, but in the Low Countries we all drank water when we found the chance, and I could never perceive we were the worse for it."

"Been wounded yourself, sir, perhaps?" called Oglethorpe.

"Twice," said Mr. Archer, "and was as proud of these hurts as any lady of her bracelets. 'T is a fine thing to smart for one's duty; even in the pangs of it there is contentment."

"Ah, well!" replied the guard, "if you've been shot yourself, that explains. But as for contentment, why, sir, you see, it smarts, as you say. And then, I have a good wife, you see, and a bit of a brat—a little thing, so high."

"Don't move," said Mr. Archer.

"No, sir, I will not, and thank you kindly," said

368

Oglethorpe. " At York they are. A very good lass is my wife—far too good for me. And the little rascal— well, I don't know how to say it, but he sort of comes around you. If I were to go, sir, it would be hard on my poor girl—main hard on her!"

" Ay, you must feel bitter hardly to the rogue that laid you here," said Mr. Archer.

" Why, no, sir, more against Engleton and the passengers," replied the guard. " He played his hand, if you come to look at it; and I wish he had shot worse, or me better. And yet I 'll go to my grave but what I covered him," he cried. " It looks like witchcraft. I 'll go to my grave but what he was drove full of slugs like a pepper-box."

" Quietly," said Mr. Archer, " you must not excite yourself. These deceptions are very usual in war; the eye, in a moment of alert, is hardly to be trusted, and when the smoke blows away you see the man you fired at, taking aim, it may be, at yourself. You should observe, too, that you were in the dark night, and somewhat dazzled by the lamps, and that the sudden stopping of the mail had jolted you. In such circumstances a man may miss, ay, even with a blunderbuss, and no blame attach to his marksmanship." . . .

EDITORIAL NOTE

THE Editor is unable to furnish any information as to the intended plot of the story which breaks off thus abruptly. From very early days Mr. Stevenson had purposed to write (since circumstances did not allow him to enact) a romance of the highway. The purpose seems to have ripened after his recovery from the acute attack of illness which interrupted his work from about Christmas, 1883, to September, 1884. The chapters above printed were written at Bournemouth soon after the latter date; but neither Mr. Henley nor I, though we remember many conversations with the writer on highway themes in general, can recall the origin or intended course of this particular story. Its plot can hardly be forecast from these opening chapters; nor do the writer's own words, in a letter written at the time to Mr. Henley, take us much further, except in so far as they show that it was growing under his hands to be a more serious effort than he first contemplated. "*The Great North Road,*" he writes, "which I thought to rattle off, like *Treasure Island,* for coin, has turned into my most ambitious design, and will take piles of writing and thinking; so that is what my highwayman has turned to! The ways of Providence are inscrutable. Mr. Archer and Jonathan Holdaway are both grand premier parts of unusual difficulty, and Nance and the Sergeant—the first very delicate, and the second demanding great geniality. I quail before the gale, but so help me, it shall be done. It is highly picturesque, most dramatic, and if it can be made, as human as man. Besides, it is a true *story,* and not, like *Otto,* one half story and one half play." Soon after the date of this letter the author laid aside the tale in order to finish for press the second half of *More New Arabian Nights—The Dynamiter,* and never took it up again.

THE YOUNG CHEVALIER

A FRAGMENT

Now printed for the first time

CONTENTS

THE YOUNG CHEVALIER

PROLOGUE

THE WINE-SELLER'S WIFE

T HERE was a wine-seller's shop, as you went down
to the river in the city of the Antipopes. There
a man was served with good wine of the country and
plain country fare; and the place being clean and quiet,
with a prospect on the river, certain gentlemen who
dwelt in that city in attendance on a great personage
made it a practice (when they had any silver in their
purses) to come and eat there and be private.

They called the wine-seller Paradou. He was built
more like a bullock than a man, huge in bone and
brawn, high in colour, and with a hand like a baby for
size. Marie-Madeleine was the name of his wife; she
was of Marseilles, a city of entrancing women, nor
was any fairer than herself. She was tall, being almost
of a height with Paradou; full-girdled, point-device in
every form, with an exquisite delicacy in the face; her
nose and nostrils a delight to look at from the fineness
of the sculpture, her eyes inclined a hair's-breadth in-
ward, her colour between dark and fair, and laid on

even like a flower's. A faint rose dwelt in it, as though she had been found unawares bathing, and had blushed from head to foot. She was of a grave countenance, rarely smiling; yet it seemed to be written upon every part of her that she rejoiced in life. Her husband loved the heels of her feet and the knuckles of her fingers; he loved her like a glutton and a brute; his love hung about her like an atmosphere; one that came by chance into the wine-shop was aware of that passion; and it might be said that by the strength of it the woman had been drugged or spell-bound. She knew not if she loved or loathed him; he was always in her eyes like something monstrous—monstrous in his love, monstrous in his person, horrific but imposing in his violence; and her sentiment swung back and forward from desire to sickness. But the mean, where it dwelt chiefly, was an apathetic fascination, partly of horror; as of Europa in mid-ocean with her bull.

On the 10th November, 1749, there sat two of the foreign gentlemen in the wine-seller's shop. They were both handsome men of a good presence, richly dressed. The first was swarthy and long and lean, with an alert, black look, and a mole upon his cheek. The other was more fair. He seemed very easy and sedate, and a little melancholy for so young a man, but his smile was charming. In his grey eyes there was much abstraction, as of one recalling fondly that which was past and lost. Yet there was strength and swiftness in his limbs; and his mouth set straight across his face, the under lip a thought upon side, like that of a man accustomed to resolve. These two talked together in a rude outlandish speech that no frequenter of that wine-shop understood. The swarthy man answered to the name of *Ballantrae;* he of the dreamy eyes was sometimes called *Balmile,* and sometimes *my Lord,* or *my Lord Gladsmuir;* but when the title was given him, he seemed to put it by as if in jesting, not without bitterness.

The mistral blew in the city. The first day of that wind, they say in the countries where its voice is heard, it blows away all the dust, the second all the stones, and the third it blows back others from the mountains. It was now come to the third day; outside the pebbles flew like hail, and the face of the river was puckered, and the very building-stones in the walls of houses seemed to be curdled, with the savage cold and fury of that continuous blast. It could be heard to hoot in all the chimneys of the city; it swept about the wine-shop, filling the room with eddies; the chill and gritty touch of it passed between the nearest clothes and the bare flesh; and the two gentlemen at the far table kept their mantles loose about their shoulders. The roughness of these outer hulls, for they were plain travellers' cloaks that had seen service, set the greater mark of richness on what showed below of their laced clothes; for the one was in scarlet and the other in violet and white, like men come from a scene of ceremony; as indeed they were.

It chanced that these fine clothes were not without their influence on the scene which followed, and which makes the prologue of our tale. For a long time Balmile was in the habit to come to the wine-shop and eat a meal or drink a measure of wine; sometimes with a comrade; more often alone, when he would sit and

377

dream and drum upon the table, and the thoughts would show in the man's face in little glooms and lightenings, like the sun and the clouds upon a water. For a long time Marie-Madeleine had observed him apart. His sadness, the beauty of his smile when by any chance he remembered her existence and addressed her, the changes of his mind signalled forth by an abstruse play of feature, the mere fact that he was foreign and a thing detached from the local and the accustomed, insensibly attracted and affected her. Kindness was ready in her mind; it but lacked the touch of an occasion to effervesce and crystallise. Now Balmile had come hitherto in a very poor plain habit; and this day of the mistral, when his mantle was just open, and she saw beneath it the glancing of the violet and the velvet and the silver, and the clustering fineness of the lace, it seemed to set the man in a new light, with which he shone resplendent to her fancy.

The high inhuman note of the wind, the violence and continuity of its outpouring, and the fierce touch of it upon man's whole periphery, accelerated the functions of the mind. It set thoughts whirling, as it whirled the trees of the forest; it stirred them up in flights, as it stirred up the dust in chambers. As brief as sparks, the fancies glittered and succeeded each other in the mind of Marie-Madeleine; and the grave man with the smile, and the bright clothes under the plain mantle, haunted her with incongruous explanations. She considered him, the unknown, the speaker of an unknown tongue, the hero (as she placed him) of an unknown romance, the dweller upon unknown memories. She recalled him sitting there alone, so immersed, so stupe-

fied; yet she was sure he was not stupid. She recalled
one day when he had remained a long time motionless,
with parted lips, like one in the act of starting up, his
eyes fixed on vacancy. Any one else must have looked
foolish; but not he. She tried to conceive what manner
of memory had thus entranced him; she forged for him
a past; she showed him to herself in every light of
heroism and greatness and misfortune; she brooded
with petulant intensity on all she knew and guessed of
him. Yet, though she was already gone so deep, she
was still unashamed, still unalarmed; her thoughts
were still disinterested; she had still to reach the stage
at which—beside the image of that other whom we
love to contemplate and to adorn—we place the image
of ourself and behold them together with delight.

She stood within the counter, her hands clasped behind her back, her shoulders pressed against the wall,
her feet braced out. Her face was bright with the wind
and her own thoughts; as a fire in a similar day of
tempest glows and brightens on a hearth, so she seemed
to glow, standing there, and to breathe out energy. It
was the first time Ballantrae had visited that wine-
seller's, the first time he had seen the wife; and his
eyes were true to her.

"I perceive your reason for carrying me to this very
draughty tavern," he said at last.

"I believe it is propinquity," returned Balmile.

"You play dark," said Ballantrae, "but have a care!
Be more frank with me, or I will cut you out. I go
through no form of qualifying my threat, which would
be commonplace and not conscientious. There is only
one point in these campaigns: that is the degree of

admiration offered by the man; and to our hostess I am in a posture to make victorious love."

"If you think you have the time, or the game worth the candle," replied the other, with a shrug.

"One would suppose you were never at the pains to observe her," said Ballantrae.

"I am not very observant," said Balmile. "She seems comely."

"You very dear and dull dog!" cried Ballantrae; "chastity is the most besotting of the virtues. Why, she has a look in her face beyond singing! I believe, if you were to push me hard, I might trace it home to a trifle of a squint. What matters? The height of beauty is in the touch that's wrong, that's the modulation in a tune. 'T is the devil we all love; I owe many a conquest to my mole"—he touched it as he spoke with a smile, and his eyes glittered; "we are all hunchbacks, and beauty is only that kind of deformity that I happen to admire. But come! Because you are chaste, for which I am sure I pay you my respects, that is no reason why you should be blind. Look at her, look at the delicious nose of her, look at her cheek, look at her ear, look at her hand and wrist—look at the whole baggage from heels to crown, and tell me if she would n't melt on a man's tongue."

As Ballantrae spoke, half jesting, half enthusiastic, Balmile was constrained to do as he was bidden. He looked at the woman, admired her excellences, and was at the same time ashamed for himself and his companion. So it befell that when Marie-Madeleine raised her eyes, she met those of the subject of her contemplations fixed directly on herself with a look that is unmistakable, the look of a person measuring and valuing another,—and, to clench the false impression, that his glance was instantly and guiltily withdrawn. The blood beat back upon her heart and leaped again; her obscure thoughts flashed clear before her; she flew in fancy straight to his arms like a wanton, and fled again on the instant like a nymph. And at that moment there chanced an interruption, which not only spared her embarrassment, but set the last consecration on her now articulate love.

Into the wine-shop there came a French gentleman, arrayed in the last refinement of the fashion, though a little tumbled by his passage in the wind. It was to be judged he had come from the same formal gathering at which the others had preceded him; and perhaps that he had gone there in the hope to meet with them, for he came up to Ballantrae with unceremonious eagerness.

"At last, here you are!" he cried in French. "I thought I was to miss you altogether."

The Scotsmen rose, and Ballantrae, after the first greetings, laid his hand on his companion's shoulder.

"My Lord," said he, "allow me to present to you one of my best friends and one of our best soldiers, the Lord Viscount Gladsmuir."

The two bowed with the elaborate elegance of the period.

"*Monseigneur,*" said Balmile, "*je n'ai pas la prétention de m'affubler d'un titre que la mauvaise fortune de mon roi ne me permet pas de porter comme il sied. Je m'appelle, pour vous servir, Blair de Balmile tout court.*"

("My Lord, I have not the effrontery to cumber myself

with a title which the ill fortunes of my king will not suffer me to bear the way it should be. I call myself, at your service, plain Blair of Balmile.")

" *Monsieur le Vicomte ou Monsieur Blèr' de Balmaïl,*" replied the new-comer, " *le nom n'y fait rien, et l'on connait vos beaux faits.*" (" The name matters nothing; your gallant actions are known.")

A few more ceremonies, and these three, sitting down together to the table, called for wine. It was the happiness of Marie-Madeleine to wait unobserved upon the prince of her desires. She poured the wine, he drank of it; and that link between them seemed to her, for the moment, close as a caress. Though they lowered their tones, she surprised great names passing in their conversation, names of kings, the names of De Gesvre and Belle-Isle; and the man who dealt in these high matters, and she who was now coupled with him in her own thoughts, seemed to swim in mid-air in a transfiguration. Love is a crude core, but it has singular and far-reaching fringes; in that passionate attraction for the stranger that now swayed and mastered her, his harsh incomprehensible language, and these names of grandees in his talk, were each an element.

The Frenchman stayed not long, but it was plain he left behind him matter of much interest to his companions; they spoke together earnestly, their heads down, the woman of the wine-shop totally forgotten; and they were still so occupied when Paradou returned.

This man's love was unsleeping. The even bluster of the mistral, with which he had been combating some hours, had not suspended, though it had embittered, that predominant passion. His first look was for his wife, a look of hope and suspicion, menace and humility and love, that made the over-blooming brute appear for the moment almost beautiful. She returned his glance, at first as though she knew him not, then with a swiftly waxing coldness of intent; and at last, without changing their direction, she had closed her eyes.

There passed across her mind during that period much that Paradou could not have understood had it been told to him in words: chiefly the sense of an enlightening contrast betwixt the man who talked of kings and the man who kept a wine-shop, betwixt the love she yearned for and that to which she had been long exposed like a victim bound upon the altar. There swelled upon her, swifter than the Rhone, a tide of abhorrence and disgust. She had succumbed to the monster, humbling herself below animals; and now she loved a hero, aspiring to the semi-divine. It was in the pang of that humiliating thought that she had closed her eyes.

Paradou—quick, as beasts are quick, to translate silence—felt the insult through his blood; his inarticulate soul bellowed within him for revenge. He glanced about the shop. He saw the two indifferent gentlemen deep in talk, and passed them over: his fancy flying not so high. There was but one other present, a country lout who stood swallowing his wine, equally unobserved by all and unobserving; to him he dealt a glance of murderous suspicion, and turned direct upon his wife. The wine-shop had lain hitherto, a space of shelter, the scene of a few ceremonial passages and some whispered conversation, in the howling river of the wind; the clock had not yet ticked a score of times since Paradou's appearance; and now, as he suddenly

383

gave tongue, it seemed as though the mistral had entered at his heels.

"What ails you, woman?" he cried, smiting on the counter.

"Nothing ails me," she replied. It was strange; but she spoke and stood at that moment like a lady of degree, drawn upward by her aspirations.

"You speak to me, by God, as though you scorned me!" cried the husband.

The man's passion was always formidable; she had often looked on upon its violence with a thrill—it had been one ingredient in her fascination; and she was now surprised to behold him, as from afar off, gesticulating but impotent. His fury might be dangerous like a torrent or a gust of wind, but it was inhuman; it might be feared or braved, it should never be respected. And with that there came in her a sudden glow of courage and that readiness to die which attends so closely upon all strong passions.

"I do scorn you," she said.

"What is that?" he cried.

"I scorn you," she repeated, smiling.

"You love another man!" said he.

"With all my soul," was her reply.

The wine-seller roared aloud so that the house rang and shook with it.

"Is this the——?" he cried, using a foul word, common in the South; and he seized the young countryman and dashed him to the ground. There he lay for the least interval of time insensible; thence fled from the house, the most terrified person in the county. The heavy measure had escaped from his hands, splashing

384

the wine high upon the wall. Paradou caught it.
" And you ? " he roared to his wife, giving her the same
name in the feminine, and he aimed at her the deadly
missile. She expected it, motionless, with radiant
eyes.

But before it sped, Paradou was met by another adversary, and the unconscious rivals stood confronted.
It was hard to say at that moment which appeared the
more formidable. In Paradou, the whole muddy and
truculent depths of the half-man were stirred to frenzy;
the lust of destruction raged in him; there was not a
feature in his face but it talked murder. Balmile had
dropped his cloak: he shone out at once in his finery,
and stood to his full stature; girt in mind and body;
all his resources, all his temper, perfectly in command;
in his face the light of battle. Neither spoke; there
was no blow nor threat of one; it was war reduced to
its last element, the spiritual; and the huge wine-seller
slowly lowered his weapon. Balmile was a noble, he
a commoner; Balmile exulted in an honourable cause.
Paradou already perhaps began to be ashamed of his
violence. Of a sudden, at least, the tortured brute
turned and fled from the shop, in the footsteps of his
former victim, to whose continued flight his reappear-
ance added wings.

So soon as Balmile appeared between her husband
and herself, Marie-Madeleine transferred to him her
eyes. It might be her last moment, and she fed upon
that face; reading there inimitable courage and illimit-
able valour to protect. And when the momentary
peril was gone by, and the champion turned a little
awkwardly towards her whom he had rescued, it was

to meet, and quail before, a gaze of admiration more distinct than words. He bowed, he stammered, his words failed him; he who had crossed the floor a moment ago, like a young god, to smite, returned like one discomfited: got somehow to his place by the table, muffled himself again in his discarded cloak, and for a last touch of the ridiculous, seeking for anything to restore his countenance, drank of the wine before him, deep as a porter after a heavy lift. It was little wonder if Ballantrae, reading the scene with malevolent eyes, laughed out loud and brief, and drank with raised glass, " To the champion of the Fair."

Marie-Madeleine stood in her old place within the counter; she disdained the mocking laughter; it fell on her ears, but it did not reach her spirit. For her, the world of living persons was all resumed again into one pair, as in the days of Eden; there was but the one end in life, the one hope before her, the one thing needful, the one thing possible,—to be his.

THE PRINCE

THAT same night there was in the city of Avignon a young man in distress of mind. Now he sat, now walked in a high apartment, full of draughts and shadows. A single candle made the darkness visible; and the light scarce sufficed to show upon the wall, where they had been recently and rudely nailed, a few miniatures and a copper medal of the young man's head. The same was being sold that year in London to admiring thousands. The original was fair; he had beautiful brown eyes, a beautiful bright open face; a little feminine, a little hard, a little weak; still full of the light of youth, but already beginning to be vulgarised; a sordid bloom come upon it, the lines coarsened with a touch of puffiness. He was dressed, as for a gala, in peach-colour and silver; his breast sparkled with stars and was bright with ribbons; for he had held a levee in the afternoon and received a distinguished personage incognito. Now he sat with a bowed head, now walked precipitately to and fro, now went and gazed from the uncurtained window, where the wind was still blowing, and the lights winked in the darkness.

The bells of Avignon rose into song as he was gazing;

387

and the high notes and the deep tossed and drowned. boomed suddenly near or were suddenly swallowed up, in the current of the mistral. Tears sprang in the pale blue eyes; the expression of his face was changed to that of a more active misery; it seemed as if the voices of the bells reached, and touched and pained him, in a waste of vacancy where even pain was welcome. Outside in the night they continued to sound on, swelling and fainting; and the listener heard in his memory, as it were their harmonies, joy-bells clashing in a Northern city, and the acclamations of a multitude, the cries of battle, the gross voices of cannon, the stridor of an animated life. And then all died away, and he stood face to face with himself in the waste of vacancy, and a horror came upon his mind, and a faintness on his brain, such as seizes men upon the brink of cliffs.

On the table, by the side of the candle, stood a tray of glasses, a bottle, and a silver bell. He went thither swiftly, then his hand lowered first above the bell, then settled on the bottle. Slowly he filled a glass, slowly drank it out; and, as a tide of animal warmth recomforted the recesses of his nature, stood there smiling at himself. He remembered he was young; the funeral curtains rose, and he saw his life shine and broaden and flow out majestically, like a river sunward. The smile still on his lips, he lit a second candle, and a third; a fire stood ready built in a chimney, he lit that also; and the fir-cones and the gnarled olive billets were swift to break in flame and to crackle on the hearth, and the room brightened and enlarged about him like his hopes. To and fro, to and fro, he went, his hands lightly clasped, his breath deeply and pleasurably taken.

Victory walked with him; he marched to crowns and empires among shouting followers; glory was his dress. And presently again the shadows closed upon the solitary. Under the gilt of flame and candle-light, the stone walls of the apartment showed down bare and cold; behind the depicted triumph loomed up the actual failure: defeat, the long distress of the flight, exile, despair, broken followers, mourning faces, empty pockets, friends estranged. The memory of his father rose in his mind: he, too, estranged and defied; despair sharpened into wrath. There was one who had led armies in the field, who had staked his life upon the family enterprise, a man of action and experience, of the open air, the camp, the court, the council-room; and he was to accept direction from an old, pompous gentleman in a home in Italy, and buzzed about by priests? A pretty king, if he had not a martial son to lean upon! A king at all?

"There was a weaver (of all people) joined me at St. Ninians; he was more of a man than my papa!" he thought. "I saw him lie doubled in his blood and a grenadier below him—and he died for my papa! All died for him, or risked the dying, and I lay for him all those months in the rain and skulked in heather like a fox; and now he writes me his advice! calls me Carluccio—me, the man of the house, the only king in that king's race!" He ground his teeth. "The only king in Europe! Who else? Who has done and suffered except me? who has lain and run and hidden with his faithful subjects, like a second Bruce? Not my accursed cousin, Louis of France, at least, the lewd effeminate traitor!" And filling the glass to the brim, he drank a king's damnation.   Ah, if he had the power of Louis, what a king were here!

The minutes followed each other into the past, and still he persevered in this debilitating cycle of emotions, still fed the fire of his excitement with driblets of Rhine wine; a boy at odds with life, a boy with a spark of the heroic, which he was now burning out and drowning in futile reverie and solitary excess.

From two rooms beyond, the sudden sound of a raised voice attracted him.

"By . . .

EDITORIAL NOTE

THE first suggestion for the story of which the above is the opening was received by the author from Mr. Andrew Lang. It is mentioned in *Vailima Letters* (p. 113 of this edition) under date January 3, 1892. Writing of the subject again on March 25 of the same year (p. 133), Mr. Stevenson speculates on the title to be chosen and the turn the plot is to take; and later again (towards the end of May, pp. 150,151) announces that he has written the first "prologuial episode," that, namely, which the reader has now before him. "There are only four characters," he observes: "Francis Blair of Balmile (Jacobite Lord Gladsmuir), my hero; the Master of Ballantrae; Paradou, a wine-seller of Avignon; Marie-Madeleine, his wife. These last two I am now done with, and I think they are successful, and I hope I have Balmile on his feet; and the style seems to be found. It is a little charged and violent; sins on the side of violence; but I think will carry the tale. I think it is a good idea so to introduce my hero, being made love to by an episodic woman." If the reader will turn to the passage, he will find more about the intended developments of the story, which was to hinge on the rescue by the Prince of a young lady from a fire at an inn, and to bring back upon the scene not only the Master of Ballantrae, but one of the author's and his readers' favourite characters, Alan Breck. Mr. Lang has been good enough to furnish the following interesting notes as to its origin:

"The novel of *The Young Chevalier*," writes Mr. Lang, " of which only the fragment here given exists, was based on a suggestion of my own. But it is plain that Mr. Stevenson's purpose differed widely from my crude idea. In reading the curious *Tales of the Century* (1847), by 'John Sobieski Holberg Stuart and Charles Edward Stuart,' I had been struck by a long essay on Prince Charles's mysterious incognito. Expelled from France after the treaty of Aix-la-Chapelle, His Royal Highness, in December, 1748, sought refuge in the papal city of Avignon, whence, annoyed by English remonstrances with the Vatican, he vanished in the last days of February, 1749. The Jacobite account of his secret adventures is given in a little romance, purporting to be a 'Letter from Henry Goring,' his equerry, brother of Sir Charles Goring. I had a transcript made from this rather scarce old pamphlet, and sent it to Mr. Stevenson, in Samoa. According to the pamphlet (which is perfectly untrustworthy), a mysterious stranger, probably meant for the Earl Marischal, came to Avignon. There came, too, an equally mysterious Scottish exile. Charles eloped in company with Henry Goring (which is true), joined the stranger, travelled to a place near Lyons, and thence to Strasbourg, which is probable. Here he rescued from a fire a lovely girl, travelling alone, and disdained to profit by her sudden passion for 'le Comte d'Espoir,' his travelling-name. Moving into Germany, he was attacked by assassins, headed by the second mysterious stranger, a Scottish spy; he performs prodigies of valour. He then visits foreign courts, Berlin being indicated, and wins the heart of a lady, probably the Princess Radziwill, whom he is to marry when his prospects improve. All or much of this is false. Charles really visited Paris, by way of Dijon, and Mme. de Talmont; thence he went to Venice. But the stories about Berlin and the Polish marriage were current at the time among bewildered diplomatists.[1]

"My idea was to make the narrator a young Scottish Jacobite at Avignon. He was to be sent by Charles to seek an actual hidden treasure—the fatal gold of the hoard buried at Loch Arkaig a few days after Culloden. He was to be a lover of Miss Clementina Walkinshaw, who later played the part of Beatrix Esmond to the Prince.

"Mr. Stevenson liked something in the notion, to which he refers in his *Vailima Letters*. He told me that Alan Breck and the Master of Ballantrae were to appear in the tale. I sent him such books about Avignon as I could collect, and he also made inquiries about Mandrin, the famous French brigand. Shortly before his death I sent him transcripts of the unpublished letters of his old friend, James More Macgregor, and of Pickle the Spy, from the Pelham MSS. in the British Museum. But these, I think, arrived too late for his perusal. In Pickle he would have found some one not very unlike his Ballantrae. The fragment, as it stands, looks as if the Scottish assassin and the other mysterious stranger were not to appear, or not so early as one had supposed. The beautiful woman of the inn and her surly husband (Mandrin?) were inventions of his own. Other

[1] The real facts, as far as known, are given in *Pickle the Spy*.—[A. L.]

projects superseded his interest in this tale, and deprived us of a fresh view of Alan Breck. His dates, as indicated in the fragment, are not exact; and there is no reason to believe that Charles's house at Avignon (that of the De Rochefort family) was dismantled and comfortless, as here represented.

" Mr. Stevenson made, as was his habit, a list of chapter headings, which I unluckily did not keep. One, I remember, was 'Ballantrae to the Rescue,' of whom or of what did not appear. It is impossible to guess how the story would have finally shaped itself in his fancy. One naturally regrets what we have lost, however great the compensation in the works which took the place of the sketch. Our Prince Charles of romance must remain the Prince of *Waverley* and the King of *Redgauntlet*. No other hand now can paint him in the adventurous and mysterious years of 1749–59. Often, since Mr. Stevenson's death, in reading Jacobite MSS. unknown to me or to any one when the story was planned, I have thought, 'He could have done something with this,' or 'This would have interested him.' Eheu! "

HEATHERCAT

A FRAGMENT

Now published for the first time

CONTENTS

PART I

THE KILLING-TIME

HEATHERCAT

PART I: THE KILLING-TIME

I

TRAQUAIRS OF MONTROYMONT

THE period of this tale is in the heat of the *killing-time ;* the scene laid for the most part in solitary hills and morasses, haunted only by the so-called Mountain Wanderers, the dragoons that came in chase of them, the women that wept on their dead bodies, and the wild birds of the moorland that have cried there since the beginning. It is a land of many rain-clouds; a land of much mute history, written there in prehistoric symbols. Strange green raths are to be seen commonly in the country, above all by the kirkyards; barrows of the dead, standing stones; beside these, the faint, durable footprints and handmarks of the Roman; and an antiquity older perhaps than any, and still living and active—a complete Celtic nomenclature and a scarce-mingled Celtic population. These rugged and grey hills were once included in the boundaries of the Caledonian Forest. Merlin sat here below his apple-tree and lamented Gwendolen; here spoke with Kentigern; here fell into his enchanted trance. And the legend of his slumber seems to body forth the story of that Celtic race, deprived for so many centuries of their authentic speech, surviving with their ancestral inheritance of melancholy perversity and patient, unfortunate courage.

The Traquairs of Montroymont (*Mons Romanus*, as the erudite expound it) had long held their seat about the head waters of the Dule and in the back parts of the moorland parish of Balweary. For two hundred years they had enjoyed in these upland quarters a certain decency (almost to be named distinction) of repute; and the annals of their house, or what is remembered of them, were obscure and bloody. Ninian Traquair was "cruallie slochtered" by the Crozers at the kirk-door of Balweary, anno 1482. Francis killed Simon Ruthven of Drumshoreland, anno 1540; bought letters of slayers at the widow and heir, and, by a barbarous form of compounding, married (without tocher) Simon's daughter Grizzel, which is the way the Traquairs and Ruthvens came first to an intermarriage. About the last Traquair and Ruthven marriage, it is the business of this book, among many other things, to tell.

The Traquairs were always strong for the Covenant; for the King also, but the Covenant first; and it began to be ill days for Montroymont when the Bishops came in and the dragoons at the heels of them. Ninian (then laird) was an anxious husband of himself and the property, as the times required, and it may be said of him that he lost both. He was heavily suspected of the Pentland Hills rebellion. When it came the length of

Bothwell Brig, he stood his trial before the Secret
Council, and was convicted of talking to some insur-
gents by the wayside, the subject of the conversation
not very clearly appearing, and of the reset and main-
tenance of one Gale, a gardener-man, who was seen
before Bothwell with a musket, and afterwards, for a
continuance of months, delved the garden at Montroymont. Matters went very ill with Ninian at the Council; some of the lords were clear for treason; and even
the boot was talked of. But he was spared that tor-
ture; and at last, having pretty good friendship among
great men, he came off with a fine of seven thousand
marks, that caused the estate to groan. In this case,
as in so many others, it was the wife that made the
trouble. She was a great keeper of conventicles;
would ride ten miles to one, and when she was fined,
rejoiced greatly to suffer for the Kirk; but it was rather
her husband that suffered. She had their only son,
Francis, baptised privately by the hands of Mr. Kidd;
there was that much the more to pay for! She could
neither be driven nor wiled into the parish kirk; as for
taking the sacrament at the hands of any Episcopalian
curate, and tenfold more at those of Curate Haddo,
there was nothing further from her purposes; and
Montroymont had to put his hand in his pocket month
by month and year by year. Once, indeed, the little
lady was cast in prison, and the laird, worthy, heavy,
uninterested man, had to ride up and take her place;
from which he was not discharged under nine months
and a sharp fine. It scarce seemed she had any gratitude to him; she came out of jail herself, and plunged
immediately deeper in conventicles, resetting recusants,

and all her old, expensive folly, only with greater vigour
and openness, because Montroymont was safe in the
Tolbooth and she had no witness to consider.   When
he was liberated and came back, with his fingers singed,
in December, 1680, and late in the black night, my lady
was from home.   He came into the house at his alight-
ing, with a riding-rod yet in his hand; and, on the ser-
vant-maid telling him, caught her by the scruff of the
neck, beat her violently, flung her down in the passageway, and went up-stairs to his bed fasting and without a light.   It was three in the morning when my lady
returned from that conventicle, and, hearing of the
assault (because the maid had sat up for her, weeping),
went to their common chamber with a lantern in hand
and stamping with her shoes so as to wake the dead;
it was supposed, by those that heard her, from a design to have it out with the goodman at once.   The
house-servants gathered on the stair, because it was a
main interest with them to know which of these two
was the better horse; and for the space of two hours
they were heard to go at the matter, hammer and tongs.
Montroymont alleged he was at the end of his possibilities; it was no longer within his power to pay the
annual rents; she had served him basely by keeping
conventicles while he lay in prison for her sake; his
friends were weary, and there was nothing else before
him but the entire loss of the family lands, and to begin
life again by the wayside as a common beggar.   She
took him up very sharp and high: called upon him, if
he were a Christian? and which he most considered,
the loss of a few dirty, miry glebes, or of his soul?
Presently he was heard to weep, and my lady's voice

to go on continually like a running burn, only the words
indistinguishable; whereupon it was supposed a victory
for her ladyship, and the domestics took themselves to
bed. The next day Traquair appeared like a man who
had gone under the harrows; and his lady wife thenceforward continued in her old course without the least
deflection.

Thenceforward Ninian went on his way without
complaint, and suffered his wife to go on hers without
remonstrance. He still minded his estate, of which, it
might be said, he took daily a fresh farewell, and
counted it already lost; looking ruefully on the acres
and the graves of his fathers, on the moorlands where
the wild-fowl consorted, the low, gurgling pool of the
trout, and the high, windy place of the calling curlews
—things that were yet his for the day and would be
another's to-morrow; coming back again, and sitting
ciphering till the dusk at his approaching ruin, which
no device of arithmetic could postpone beyond a year
or two. He was essentially the simple ancient man,
the farmer and landholder; he would have been content
to watch the seasons come and go, and his cattle increase, until the limit of age; he would have been content at any time to die, if he could have left the estates
undiminished to an heir male of his ancestors, that duty
standing first in his instinctive calendar. And now he
saw everywhere the image of the new proprietor come
to meet him, and go sowing and reaping, or fowling
for his pleasure on the red moors, or eating the very
gooseberries in the Place garden; and saw always, on
the other hand, the figure of Francis go forth, a beggar,
into the broad world.

It was in vain the poor gentleman sought to moderate; took every test and took advantage of every indulgence; went and drank with the dragoons in Balweary; attended the communion and came regularly to the church to Curate Haddo, with his son beside him. The mad, raging, Presbyterian zealot of a wife at home made all of no avail; and indeed the house must have fallen years before if it had not been for the secret indulgence of the curate, who had a great sympathy with the laird, and winked hard at the doings in Montroymont. This curate was a man very ill reputed in the country-side, and indeed in all Scotland. "Infamous Haddo" is Shield's expression. But Patrick Walker is more copious. "Curate Hall Haddo," says he, *sub voce* Peden, "or *Hell* Haddo as he was more justly to be called, a pokeful of old condemned errors and the filthy lusts of the flesh, a published whoremonger, a common gross drunkard, continually and godlessly scraping and skirling on a fiddle, continually breathing flames against the remnant of Israel. But the Lord put an end to his piping, and all these offences were composed into one bloody grave." No doubt this was written to excuse his slaughter; and I have never heard it claimed for Walker that he was either a just witness or an indulgent judge. At least, in a merely human character, Haddo comes off not wholly amiss in the matter of these Traquairs: not that he showed any graces of the Christian, but had a sort of pagan decency, which might almost tempt one to be concerned about his sudden, violent, and unprepared fate.

II

FRANCIE

FRANCIE was eleven years old, shy, secret, and rather childish of his age, though not backward in schooling, which had been pushed on far by a private governor, one M'Brair, a forfeited minister harboured in that capacity at Montroymont. The boy, already much employed in secret by his mother, was the most apt hand conceivable to run upon a message, to carry food to lurking fugitives, or to stand sentry on the sky-line above a conventicle. It seemed no place on the moorlands was so naked but what he would find cover there; and as he knew every hag, boulder, and heatherbush in a circuit of seven miles about Montroymont, there was scarce any spot but what he could leave or approach it unseen. This dexterity had won him a reputation in that part of the country; and among the many children employed in these dangerous affairs, he passed under the by-name of Heathercat.

How much his father knew of this employment might be doubted. He took much forethought for the boy's future, seeing he was like to be left so poorly, and would sometimes assist at his lessons, sighing heavily, yawning deep, and now and again patting Francie on the shoulder if he seemed to be doing ill, by way of a private, kind encouragement. But a great part of the day was passed in aimless wanderings with his eyes sealed, or in his cabinet sitting bemused over the particulars of the coming bankruptcy; and the boy would be absent a dozen times for once that his father would observe it.

On the 2nd of July, 1682, the boy had an errand from his mother, which must be kept private from all, the father included in the first of them. Crossing the braes, he hears the clatter of a horse's shoes, and claps down incontinent in a hag by the wayside. And presently he spied his father come riding from one direction, and Curate Haddo walking from another; and Montroymont leaning down from the saddle, and Haddo getting on his toes (for he was a little, ruddy, bald-pated man, more like a dwarf), they greeted kindly, and came to a halt within two fathoms of the child.

"Montroymont," the curate said, "the de'il 's in 't but I 'll have to denunciate your leddy again."

"De'il 's in 't indeed!" says the laird.

"Man! can ye no induce her to come to the kirk? " pursues Haddo; "or to a communion at the least of it. For the conventicles, let be! and the same for yon solemn fule, M'Brair: I can blink at them. But she 's got to come to the kirk, Montroymont."

"Dinna speak of it," says the laird. "I can do nothing with her."

"Could n't ye try the stick to her? It works wonders whiles," suggested Haddo. "No? I 'm wae to hear it. And I suppose ye ken where you 're going? "

"Fine! " said Montroymont. "Fine do I ken where: Bankrup'cy and the Bass Rock! "

" Praise to my bones that I never married! " cried the curate. " Well, it 's a grievous thing to me to see an auld house dung down that was here before Flodden Field. But naebody can say it was with my wish."

"No more they can, Haddo! " says the laird. " A good friend ye 've been to me, first and last. I can give you that character with a clear conscience."

Whereupon they separated, and Montroymont rode briskly down into the Dule Valley. But of the curate Francie was not to be quit so easily. He went on with his little, brisk steps to the corner of a dyke, and stopped and whistled and waved upon a lassie that was herding cattle there. This Janet M‘Clour was a big lass, being taller than the curate; and what made her look the more so, she was kilted very high. It seemed for a while she would not come, and Francie heard her calling Haddo a ' daft auld fule," and saw her running and dodging him among the whins and hags till he was fairly blown. But at the last he gets a bottle from his plaid-neuk and holds it up to her; whereupon she came at once into a composition, and the pair sat, drinking of the bottle, and daffing and laughing together, on a mound of heather. The boy had scarce heard of these vanities, or he might have been minded of a nymph and satyr, if anybody could have taken long-leggit Janet for a nymph. But they seemed to be huge friends, he thought; and was the more surprised, when the curate had taken his leave, to see the lassie fling stones after him with screeches of laughter, and Haddo turn about and caper, and shake his staff at her, and laugh louder than herself. A wonderful merry pair, they seemed; and when Francie crawled out of the hag, he had a great deal to consider in his mind. It was possible they were all fallen in error about Mr. Haddo, he reflected, —having seen him so tender with Montroymont, and so kind and playful with the lass Janet; and he had a temptation to go out of his road and question her herself upon the matter. But he had a strong spirit of duty on him; and plodded on instead over the braes till he came near the House of Cairngorm. There, in a hollow place by the burn-side that was shaded by some birks, he was aware of a barefoot boy, perhaps a matter of three years older than himself. The two approached with the precautions of a pair of strange dogs, looking at each other queerly.

"It 's ill weather on the hills," said the stranger, giving the watchword.

"For a season," said Francie, "but the Lord will appear."

"Richt," said the barefoot boy. "Wha' 're ye frae?"

"The Leddy Montroymont," says Francie.

"Ha'e then!" says the stranger, and handed him a folded paper, and they stood and looked at each other again. "It 's unco het," said the boy.

"Dooms het," says Francie.

"What do they ca' ye?" says the other.

"Francie," says he. "I 'm young Montroymont. They ca' me Heathercat."

"I 'm Jock Crozer," said the boy. And there was another pause, while each rolled a stone under his foot.

"Cast your jaiket and I 'll fecht ye for a bawbee," cried the elder boy, with sudden violence, and dramatically throwing back his jacket.

"Na, I have nae time the now," said Francie, with a

sharp thrill of alarm, because Crozer was much the heavier boy.

"Ye 're feard. Heathercat indeed!" said Crozer, for among this infantile army of spies and messengers the fame of Crozer had gone forth and was resented by his rivals. And with that they separated.

On his way home Francie was a good deal occupied with the recollection of this untoward incident. The challenge had been fairly offered and basely refused: the tale would be carried all over the country, and the lustre of the name of Heathercat be dimmed. But the scene between Curate Haddo and Janet M'Clour had also given him much to think of; and he was still puzzling over the case of the curate, and why such ill words were said of him, and why, if he were so merry-spirited, he should yet preach so dry, when, coming over a know, whom should he see but Janet, sitting with her back to him, minding her cattle! He was always a great child for secret, stealthy ways, having been employed by his mother on errands when the same was necessary; and he came behind the lass without her hearing.

"Jennet," says he.

"Keep me!" cries Janet, springing up. "O, it 's you, Maister Francie! Save us, what a fricht ye gied me!"

"Ay, it 's me," said Francie. "I 've been thinking, Jennet; I saw you and the curate awhile back—"

"Brat!" cried Janet, and coloured up crimson; and the one moment made as if she would have stricken him with a ragged stick she had to chase her bestial with, and the next was begging and praying that he would mention it to none. It was "naebody's business, whatever," she said; "it would just start a clash in the country"; and there would be nothing left for her but to drown herself in Dule Water.

"Why?" says Francie.

The girl looked at him and grew scarlet again.

"And it isna that, anyway," continued Francie. "It was just that he seemed so good to ye—like our Father in Heaven, I thought; and I thought that mebbe, perhaps, we had all been wrong about him from the first. But I 'll have to tell Mr. M'Brair; I 'm under a kind of a bargain to him to tell him all."

"Tell it to the divil if ye like for me!" cried the lass. "I 've naething to be ashamed of. Tell M'Brair to mind his ain affairs," she cried again; "they 'll be hot eneugh for him, if Haddie likes!" And so strode off, shoving her beasts before her, and ever and again looking back and crying angry words to the boy, where he stood mystified.

By the time he had got home his mind was made up that he would say nothing to his mother. My Lady Montroymont was in the keeping-room, reading a godly book; she was a wonderful frail little wife to make so much noise in the world and be able to steer about that patient sheep her husband; her eyes were like sloes, the fingers of her hands were like tobacco-pipe shanks, her mouth shut tight like a trap; and even when she was the most serious, and still more when she was angry, there hung about her face the terrifying semblance of a smile.

"Have ye gotten the billet, Francie?" said she; and when he had handed it over, and she had read and burned it, "Did you see anybody?" she asked.

"I saw the laird," said Francie.

"He dinna see you, though?" asked his mother.

"De'il a fear," from Francie.

"Francie!" she cried. "What's that I hear? an aith? The Lord forgive me, have I broughten forth a brand for the burning, a fagot for hell-fire?"

"I'm very sorry, ma'am," said Francie. "I humbly beg the Lord's pardon, and yours, for my wickedness."

"H'm," grunted the lady. "Did ye see nobody else?"

"No, ma'am," said Francie, with the face of an angel, "except Jock Crozer, that gied me the billet."

"Jock Crozer!" cried the lady. "I'll Crozer them! Crozers indeed! What next? Are we to repose the lives of a suffering remnant in Crozers? The whole clan of them wants hanging, and if I had my way of it, they wouldna want it long. Are you aware, sir, that these Crozers killed your forebear at the kirk-door?"

"You see, he was bigger 'n me," said Francie.

"Jock Crozer," continued the lady. "That 'll be Clement's son, the biggest thief and reiver in the country-side. To trust a note to him! But I 'll give the benefit of my opinions to Lady Whitecross when we two forgather. Let her look to herself! I have no patience with half-hearted carlines, that complies on the Lord's-day morning with the kirk, and comes tai-gling the same night to the conventicle. The one or the other! is what I say: Hell or Heaven—Haddie's abomi-nations or the pure word of God dreeping from the lips of Mr. Arnot,

> "'Like honey from the honeycomb
> That dreepeth, sweeter far.'"

My lady was now fairly launched, and that upon two congenial subjects: the deficiencies of the Lady Whitecross, and the turpitudes of the whole Crozer race—which, indeed, had never been conspicuous for respectability. She pursued the pair of them for twenty minutes on the clock with wonderful animation and detail, something of the pulpit manner, and the spirit of one possessed. "O hellish compliance!" she exclaimed. "I would not suffer a complier to break bread with Christian folk. Of all the sins of this day there is not one so God-defying, so Christ-humiliating, as damnable compliance"; the boy standing before her meanwhile, and brokenly pursuing other thoughts, mainly of Haddo and Janet, and Jock Crozer stripping off his jacket. And yet, with all his distraction, it might be argued that he heard too much; his father and himself being "compliers"—that is to say, attending the church of the parish as the law required.

Presently, the lady's passion beginning to decline, or her flux of ill words to be exhausted, she dismissed her audience. Francie bowed low, left the room, closed the door behind him; and then turned him about in the passageway, and with a low voice, but a prodigious deal of sentiment, repeated the name of the evil one twenty times over, to the end of which, for the greater efficacy, he tacked on "damnable" and "hellish." *Fas est ab hoste doceri*—disrespect is made more pungent by quotation; and there is no doubt but he felt relieved, and went up-stairs into his tutor's chamber with a quiet mind. M'Brair sat by the cheek of the peat-fire and shivered, for he had a quartan ague, and this was his day. The great nightcap and plaid, the dark unshaven

cheeks of the man, and the white, thin hands that held
the plaid about his chittering body, made a sorrowful
picture. But Francie knew and loved him; came
straight in, nestled close to the refugee, and told his
story. M'Brair had been at the College with Haddo;
the Presbytery had licensed both on the same day; and
at this tale, told with so much innocency by the boy,
the heart of the tutor was commoved.

"Woe upon him! Woe upon that man!" he cried.
"O the unfaithful shepherd! O the hireling and apos-
tate minister! Make my matters hot for me? quo' she!
the shameless limmer! And true it is that he could
repose me in that nasty, stinking hole, the Canongate
Tolbooth, from which your mother drew me out—the
Lord reward her for it!—or to that cold, unbieldy,
marine place of the Bass Rock, which, with my delicate
kist, would be fair ruin to me. But I will be valiant in
my Master's service. I have a duty here: a duty to
my God, to myself, and to Haddo: in His strength, I
will perform it."

Then he straightly discharged Francie to repeat the
tale, and bade him in the future to avert his very eyes
from the doings of the curate. "You must go to his
place of idolatry; look upon him there!" says he, "but
nowhere else. Avert your eyes, close your ears, pass
him by like a three days' corp'. He is like that damnable
monster Basiliscus, which defiles—yea, poisons!—by
the sight." All which was hardly claratory to the boy's
mind.

Presently Montroymont came home, and called up
the stairs to Francie. Traquair was a good shot and
swordsman; and it was his pleasure to walk with his

son over the braes of the moor-fowl, or to teach him arms in the back court, when they made a mighty comely pair, the child being so lean and light and active, and the laird himself a man of a manly, pretty stature, his hair (the periwig being laid aside) showing already white with many anxieties, and his face of an even, flaccid red. But this day Francie's heart was not in the fencing.

"Sir," says he, suddenly lowering his point, "will ye tell me a thing if I was to ask it?"

"Ask away," says the father.

"Well, it's this," said Francie: "Why do you and me comply if it's so wicked?"

"Ay, ye have the cant of it too!" cries Montroymont. "But I'll tell ye for all that. It's to try and see if we can keep the rigging on this house, Francie. If she had her way, we would be beggar-folk, and hold our hands out by the wayside. When ye hear her—when ye hear folk," he corrected himself briskly, "call me a coward, and one that betrayed the Lord, and I kenna what else, just mind it was to keep a bed to ye to sleep in and a bite for ye to eat.—On guard!" he cried, and the lesson proceeded again till they were called to supper.

"There's another thing yet," said Francie, stopping his father. "There's another thing that I am not sure I am very caring for. She—she sends me errands."

"Obey her, then, as is your bounden duty," said Traquair.

"Ay, but wait till I tell ye," says the boy. "If I was to see you I was to hide."

Montroymont sighed. "Well, and that's good of her too," said he. "The less that I ken of thir doings

414

the better for me; and the best thing you can do is just to obey her, and see and be a good son to her, the same as ye are to me, Francie."

At the tenderness of this expression the heart of Francie swelled within his bosom, and his remorse was poured out. "Faither!" he cried, "I said 'de'il' to-day; many 's the time I said it, and 'damnable' too, and 'hellitsh.' I ken they 're all right; they 're beeblical. But I didna say them beeblically; I said them for sweir-words—that 's the truth of it."

"Hout, ye silly bairn!" said the father; "dinna do it nae mair, and come in by to your supper." And he took the boy, and drew him close to him a moment, as they went through the door, with something very fond and secret, like a caress between a pair of lovers.

The next day M'Brair was abroad in the afternoon, and had a long advising with Janet on the braes where she herded cattle. What passed was never wholly known; but the lass wept bitterly, and fell on her knees to him among the whins. The same night, as soon as it was dark, he took the road again for Balweary. In the Kirkton, where the dragoons quartered, he saw many lights, and heard the noise of a ranting song and people laughing grossly, which was highly offensive to his mind. He gave it the wider berth, keeping among the fields; and came down at last by the water-side, where the manse stands solitary between the river and the road. He tapped at the back door, and the old woman called upon him to come in, and guided him through the house to the study, as they still called it, though there was little enough study there in Haddo's days, and more song-books than theology.

"Here 's yin to speak wi' ye, Mr. Haddie!" cries the old wife.

And M'Brair, opening the door and entering, found the little, round, red man seated in one chair and his feet upon another. A clear fire and a tallow dip lighted him barely. He was taking tobacco in a pipe, and smiling to himself; and a brandy-bottle and glass, and his fiddle and bow, were beside him on the table.

"Hech, Patey M'Brair, is this you?" said he, a trifle tipsily. "Step in by, man, and have a drop brandy: for the stomach's sake! Even the de'il can quote Scripture—eh, Patey?"

"I will neither eat nor drink with you," replied M'Brair. "I am come upon my Master's errand: woe be upon me if I should anyways mince the same. Hall Haddo, I summon you to quit this kirk which you encumber."

"Muckle obleeged!" says Haddo, winking.

"You and me have been to kirk and market together," pursued M'Brair: "we have had blessed seasons in the kirk, we have sat in the same teaching-rooms and read in the same book; and I know you still retain for me some carnal kindness. It would be my shame if I denied it; I live here at your mercy and by your favour, and glory to acknowledge it. You have pity on my wretched body, which is but grass, and must soon be trodden under; but O, Haddo! how much greater is the yearning with which I yearn after and pity your immortal soul! Come now, let us reason together! I drop all points of controversy, weighty though these be; I take your defaced and damnified kirk on your own terms; and I ask you, Are you a worthy minister?

The communion season approaches; how can you pronounce thir solemn words, ' The elders will now bring forrit the elements,' and not quail? A parishioner may be summoned to-night; you may have to rise from your miserable orgies; and I ask you, Haddo, what does your conscience tell you? Are you fit? Are you fit to smooth the pillow of a parting Christian? And if the summons should be for yourself, how then?"

Haddo was startled out of all composure and the better part of his temper. "What's this of it?" he cried. "I'm no waur than my neebours. I never set up to be speeritual; I never did. I'm a plain, canty creature; godliness is cheerfulness, says I; give me my fiddle and a dram, and I wouldna hairm a flee."

"And I repeat my question," said M'Brair: "Are you fit—fit for this great charge? Fit to carry and save souls?"

"Fit? Blethers! As fit's yoursel'," cried Haddo.

"Are you so great a self-deceiver?" said M'Brair. "Wretched man, trampler upon God's covenants, crucifier of your Lord afresh! I will ding you to the earth with one word: How about the young woman, Janet M'Clour?"

"Well, what about her? what do I ken?" cries Haddo. "M'Brair, ye daft auld wife, I tell ye as true's truth, I never meddled her. It was just daffing, I tell ye: daffing, and nae mair: a piece of fun, like! I'm no denying but what I'm fond of fun, sma' blame to me! But for onything sarious—hout, man, it might come to a deposeetion! I'll sweir it to ye. Where's a Bible, till you hear me sweir?"

"There is nae Bible in your study," said M'Brair, severely.

And Haddo, after a few distracted turns, was constrained to accept the fact.

"Weel, and suppose there isna?" he cried, stamping. "What mair can ye say of us, but just that I'm fond of my joke, and so's she? I declare to God, by what I ken, she might be the Virgin Mary—if she would just keep clear of the dragoons. But me! na, de'il haet o' me!"

"She is penitent at least," says M'Brair.

"Do you mean to actually up and tell me to my face that she accused me?" cried the curate.

"I canna just say that," replied M'Brair. "But I rebuked her in the name of God, and she repented before me on her bended knees."

"Weel, I daur say she's been ower far wi' the dragoons," said Haddo. "I never denied that. I ken naething by it."

"Man, you but show your nakedness the more plainly," said M'Brair. "Poor, blind, besotted creature —and I see you stoitering on the brink of dissolution: your light out, and your hours numbered. Awake, man!" he shouted with a formidable voice, "awake, or it be ower late."

"Be damned if I stand this!" exclaimed Haddo, casting his tobacco-pipe violently on the table, where it was smashed in pieces. "Out of my house with ye, or I'll call for the dragoons."

"The speerit of the Lord is upon me," said M'Brair, with solemn ecstasy. "I sist you to compear before the Great White Throne, and I warn you the summons shall be bloody and sudden."

And at this, with more agility than could have been expected, he got clear of the room and slammed the door behind him in the face of the pursuing curate. The next Lord's day the curate was ill, and the kirk closed, but for all his ill words, Mr. M'Brair abode unmolested in the house of Montroymont.

III

THIS was a bit of a steep broken hill that overlooked upon the west a moorish valley, full of ink-black pools. These presently drained into a burn that made off, with little noise and no celerity of pace, about the corner of the hill. On the far side the ground swelled into a bare heath, black with junipers, and spotted with the presence of the standing stones for which the place was famous. They were many in that part, shapeless, white with lichen—you would have said with age; and had made their abode there for untold centuries, since first the heathens shouted for their installation. The ancients had hallowed them to some ill religion, and their neighbourhood had long been avoided by the prudent before the fall of day; but of late, on the up-springing of new requirements, these lonely stones on the moor had again become a place of assembly. A watchful picket on the Hill-end commanded all the northern and eastern approaches; and such was the disposition of the ground, that by certain cunningly posted sentries the west also could be made secure against surprise: there was no place in the country where a conventicle could meet with more quiet of mind or a more certain retreat open, in the case of

interference from the dragoons. The minister spoke
from a know close to the edge of the Ring, and poured
out the words God gave him on the very threshold of
the devils of yore. When they pitched a tent (which
was often in wet weather, upon a communion occasion) it was rigged over the huge isolated pillar that
has the name of Anes-Errand, none knew why. And
the congregation sat partly clustered on the slope below,
and partly among the idolatrous monoliths and on the
turfy soil of the Ring itself. In truth the situation was
well qualified to give a zest to Christian doctrines, had
there been any wanted. But these congregations assembled under conditions at once so formidable and
romantic as made a zealot of the most cold. They
were the last of the faithful; God, who had averted His
face from all other countries of the world, still leaned
from Heaven to observe, with swelling sympathy, the
doings of His moorland remnant; Christ was by them
with His eternal wounds, with dropping tears; the Holy
Ghost (never perfectly realised nor firmly adopted by
Protestant imaginations) was dimly supposed to be in
the heart of each and on the lips of the minister. And
over against them was the army of the hierarchies, from
the men Charles and James Stuart, on to King Lewie
and the Emperor; and the scarlet Pope, and the muckle
black devil himself, peering out the red mouth of hell
in an ecstasy of hate and hope. "One pull more!" he
seemed to cry; "one pull more, and it's done. There's
only Clydesdale and the Stewartry, and the three Bailie-
ries of Ayr, left for God." And with such an august
assistance of powers and principalities looking on
at the last conflict of good and evil, it was scarce pos-

sible to spare a thought to those old, infirm, debile, *ab agendo* devils whose holy place they were now violating.

There might have been three hundred to four hundred present. At least there were three hundred horse tethered for the most part in the Ring; though some of the hearers on the outskirts of the crowd stood with their bridles in their hand, ready to mount at the first signal. The circle of faces was strangely characteristic; long, serious, strongly marked, the tackle standing out in the lean brown cheeks, the mouth set and the eyes shining with a fierce enthusiasm; the shepherd, the labouring man, and the rarer laird, stood there in their broad blue bonnets or laced hats, and presenting an essential identity of type. From time to time a long-drawn groan of adhesion rose in this audience, and was propagated like a wave to the outskirts, and died away among the keepers of the horses. It had a name; it was called "a holy groan."

A squall came up; a great volley of flying mist went out before it and whelmed the scene; the wind stormed with a sudden fierceness that carried away the minister's voice and twitched his tails and made him stagger, and turned the congregation for a moment into a mere pother of blowing plaid-ends and prancing horses; and the rain followed and was dashed straight into their faces. Men and women panted aloud in the shock of that violent shower-bath; the teeth were bared along all the line in an involuntary grimace; plaids, mantles, and riding-coats were proved vain, and the worshippers felt the water stream on their naked flesh. The minister, reinforcing his great and shrill voice, continued to contend against and triumph over the rising of the squall and the dashing of the rain.

"In that day ye may go thirty mile and not hear a crawing cock," he said; "and fifty mile and not get a light to your pipe; and an hundred mile and not see a smoking house. For there 'll be naething in all Scotland but deid men's banes and blackness, and the living anger of the Lord. O, where to find a bield—O sirs, where to find a bield from the wind of the Lord's anger? Do ye call *this* a wind? Be thankit! Sirs, this is but a temporary dispensation; this is but a puff of wind, this is but a spit of rain and by with it. Already there 's a blue bow in the west, and the sun will take the crown of the causeway again, and your things 'll be dried upon ye, and your flesh will be warm upon your bones. But O, sirs, sirs! for the day of the Lord's anger!"

His rhetoric was set forth with an ear-piercing elocution, and a voice that sometimes crashed like cannon. Such as it was, it was the gift of all hill-preachers, to a singular degree of likeness or identity. Their images scarce ranged beyond the red horizon of the moor and the rainy hill-top, the shepherd and his sheep, a fowling-piece, a spade, a pipe, a dunghill, a crowing cock, the shining and the withdrawal of the sun. An occasional pathos of simple humanity, and frequent patches of big biblical words, relieved the homely tissue. It was a poetry apart; bleak, austere, but genuine, and redolent of the soil.

A little before the coming of the squall there was a different scene enacting at the outposts. For the most part the sentinels were faithful to their important duty; the Hill-end of Drumlowe was known to be a safe meeting-place; and the out-pickets on this particular day had been somewhat lax from the beginning, and grew laxer during the inordinate length of the discourse. Francie lay there in his appointed hiding-hole, looking abroad between two whin-bushes. His view was across the course of the burn, then over a piece of plain moorland, to a gap between two hills; nothing moved but grouse, and some cattle who slowly traversed his field of view, heading northward: he heard the psalms, and sang words of his own to the savage and melancholy music; for he had his own design in hand, and terror and cowardice prevailed in his bosom alternately, like the hot and the cold fit of an ague. Courage was uppermost during the singing, which he accompanied through all its length with this impromptu strain:

> " And I will ding Jock Crozer down
> No later than the day."

Presently the voice of the preacher came to him in wafts, at the wind's will, as by the opening and shutting of a door; wild spasms of screaming, as of some undiscerned gigantic hill-bird stirred with inordinate passion, succeeded to intervals of silence; and Francie heard them with a critical ear. "Ay," he thought at last, " he 'll do; he has the bit in his mou' fairly."

He had observed that his friend, or rather his enemy, Jock Crozer, had been established at a very critical part of the line of outposts; namely, where the burn issues by an abrupt gorge from the semicircle of high moors. If anything was calculated to nerve him to battle it was this. The post was important; next to the Hill-end itself, it might be called the key to the position; and it was where the cover was bad, and in which it was most natural to place a child. It should have been Heathercat's; why had it been given to Crozer? An exquisite fear of what should be the answer passed through his marrow every time he faced the question. Was it possible that Crozer could have boasted? that there were rumours abroad to his—Heathercat's—discredit? that his honour was publicly sullied? All the world went dark about him at the thought; he sank without a struggle into the midnight pool of despair; and every time he so sank, he brought back with him—not drowned heroism indeed, but half-drowned courage by the locks. His heart beat very slowly as he deserted his station, and began to crawl towards that of Crozer. Something pulled him back, and it was not the sense of duty, but a remembrance of Crozer's build and hateful readiness of fist. Duty, as he conceived it, pointed him forward on the rueful path that he was travelling. Duty bade him redeem his name if he were able, at the risk of broken bones; and his bones and every tooth in his head ached by anticipation. An awful subsidiary fear whispered him that if he were hurt, he should disgrace himself by weeping. He consoled himself, boy-like, with the consideration that he was not yet committed; he could easily steal over unseen to Crozer's post, and he had a continuous private idea that he would very probably steal back again. His course took him so near the minister that he could hear some of his words: "What news, minister, of Claver'se? He's going round like a roaring, rampaging lion . . .

425

EDITORIAL NOTE

THE story, which opens with these scenes of covenanting life and char-acter in Scotland, was intended to shift presently across the Atlantic, first to the Carolina plantations, and next to the ill-fated Scotch settlement in Darien. Practically all that we know of it is contained in one or two passages of letters from the author to Mr. Charles Baxter and Mr. S. R. Crockett. To Mr. Baxter he writes as follows:

"6 Decr., 1893.

"'Oct. 25, 1685, at Privy Council, George Murray, Lieutenant of the King's Guard, and others, did, on the 21 of September last, obtain a clandestine order of Privy Council to apprehend the person of Janet Pringle, daughter to the late Clifton, and she having retired out of the way upon information, he got an order against Andrew Pringle, her uncle, to produce her. . . . But she having married Andrew Pringle, her uncle's son (to disappoint all their designs of selling her), a boy of 13 years old'—but my boy is 14, so I extract no further (*Fountainhall*, i. 320). May 6, 1685, Wappus Pringle of Clifton was still alive after all,[1] and in prison for debt, and transacts with Lieutenant Murray, giving security for 7000 marks (i. 320).

"My dear Charles, the above is my story, and I wonder if any light can be thrown on it. I prefer the girl's father dead; and the question is how in that case could Lieutenant George Murray get his order to apprehend and his power to sell her in marriage? Or . . . might Lieutenant G. be her tutor, and the fugitive to the Pringles, and on the discovery of her whereabouts hastily married? A good legal note on these points is very ardently desired by me; it will be the corner-stone of my novel.

"This is for—I am quite wrong to tell you, for you will tell others, and nothing will teach you that all my schemes are in the air, and vanish and reappear again like shapes in the clouds—it is for *Heathercat;* whereof

[1] No; it seems to have been *her* brother who had succeeded.

the first volume will be called *The Killing Time;* and I believe I have authorities ample for that. But the second volume is to be called (I believe) *Darien,* and for that I want, I fear, a good deal of truck.

> Darien papers,
> Carstairs papers,
> Marchmont papers,
> Jerviswood correspondence—

I hope may do me; some sort of general history of the Darien affair (if there is a decent one, which I misdoubt) it would also be well to have; the one with most details, if possible. It is singular how obscure to me this decade of Scots History remains, 1690–1700: a deuce of a want of light and grouping to it. However, I believe I shall be mostly out of Scotland in my tale; first in Carolina and next in Darien."

The place of Andrew Pringle, in the historical extract above quoted, was evidently to be taken in Stevenson's story by Ninian Traquair of Montroymont. In a rough draft of chapter headings, chap. vi. bears the title, "The Ward Comes Home"; another chapter shows that her name was to have been Jean Ruthven; plainly Francie Traquair was to be the boy-husband to whom this Jean was to be united in order to frustrate the designs of those who hoped to control her person and traffic in her marriage.

The references in the author's letters to Mr. Crockett date from June 30, 1893, and afterwards. His correspondent was about this time engaged in preparing a covenanting romance of his own—*The Men of the Moss-Hags.* On the first-named date Stevenson writes: "It may interest you to know that *Weir of Hermiston,* or *The Hanging Judge,* or whatever the mischief the thing is to be called, centres about the grave of the Praying Weaver of Balweary. And when *Heathercat* is written, if it ever is, O, then there will be another chance for the Societies" (i.e., the United Societies, generally known in history as the Cameronians). A little later Stevenson received from the same correspondent, at his own request, materials for his work in the shape of extracts collected from the Earlston papers by the Rev. John Anderson, Assistant Curator of the Historical Department, Register House, Edinburgh; the minutes of the Societies, edited by the Rev. John Howie of Lochgoin, entitled "Faithful Contendings," etc., etc. Later, he sends a humorous sketch of a trespassing board and gallows, with R. L. S. in the act of hanging S. R. C., and on the board the words: "Notice—The Cameronians are the proppaty of me, R. L. S.—trespassers and Raiders will be hung." In the letter accompanying this he says: "I have made many notes for *Heathercat*, but do not get much forrader. For one thing, I am not inside these people yet. Wait three years and *I'll race you*. For another thing, I am not a keen partisan, and to write a good book you must be. The Society men were brave, dour-headed, strong-hearted men fighting a hard battle and fighting it hardly. That is about all the use I have for them." Finally, in a letter written shortly before his death, he mentions having laid the story on the shelf, whether permanently or only for a while he does not know.

ESSAYS AND FRAGMENTS
WRITTEN AT VAILIMA

These papers were draughted in 1893 or 1894 towards a projected new series of essays for "Scribner's Magazine," and are here printed for the first time.

ESSAYS AND FRAGMENTS

WRITTEN AT VAILIMA

I

THE GENESIS OF " THE MASTER OF BALLANTRAE "

I WAS walking one night in the verandah of a small
house in which I lived, outside the hamlet of Sara-
nac. It was winter; the night was very dark; the air
extraordinary clear and cold, and sweet with the purity
of forests. From a good way below, the river was to
be heard contending with ice and boulders: a few lights
appeared, scattered unevenly among the darkness, but
so far away as not to lessen the sense of isolation. For
the making of a story here were fine conditions. I was
besides moved with the spirit of emulation, for I had
just finished my third or fourth perusal of *The Phantom
Ship*. "Come," said I to my engine, "let us make a
tale, a story of many years and countries, of the sea
and the land, savagery and civilisation; a story that
shall have the same large features and may be treated
in the same summary elliptic method as the book you
have been reading and admiring." I was here brought
up with a reflection exceedingly just in itself, but which,
as the sequel shows, I failed to profit by. I saw that

Marryat, not less than Homer, Milton, and Virgil, profited by the choice of a familiar and legendary subject; so that he prepared his readers on the very title-page; and this set me cudgelling my brains, if by any chance I could hit upon some similar belief to be the centrepiece of my own meditated fiction. In the course of this vain search there cropped up in my memory a singular case of a buried and resuscitated fakir, which I had been often told by an uncle of mine, then lately dead, Inspector-General John Balfour.

On such a fine frosty night, with no wind and the thermometer below zero, the brain works with much vivacity; and the next moment I had seen the circumstance transplanted from India and the tropics to the Adirondack wilderness and the stringent cold of the Canadian border. Here then, almost before I had begun my story, I had two countries, two of the ends of the earth involved: and thus though the notion of the resuscitated man failed entirely on the score of general acceptation, or even (as I have since found) acceptability, it fitted at once with my design of a tale of many lands; and this decided me to consider further of its possibilities. The man who should thus be buried was the first question: a good man, whose return to life would be hailed by the reader and the other characters with gladness? This trenched upon the Christian picture and was dismissed. If the idea, then, was to be of any use at all for me, I had to create a kind of evil genius to his friends and family, take him through many disappearances, and make this final restoration from the pit of death, in the icy American wilderness, the last and grimmest of the series. I need not tell my brothers of

the craft that I was now in the most interesting moment of an author's life; the hours that followed that
night upon the balcony, and the following nights and
days, whether walking abroad or lying wakeful in my
bed, were hours of unadulterated joy. My mother,
who was then living with me alone, perhaps had less
enjoyment; for, in the absence of my wife, who is my
usual helper in these times of parturition, I must spur
her up at all seasons to hear me relate and try to clarify
my unformed fancies.

And while I was groping for the fable and the characters required, behold, I found them lying ready and
nine years old in my memory. Pease porridge hot, pease
porridge cold, pease porridge in the pot, nine years old.
Was there ever a more complete justification of the rule
of Horace ? Here, thinking of quite other things, I had
stumbled on the solution, or perhaps I should rather say
(in stagewright phrase) the Curtain or final Tableau of a
story conceived long before on the moors between
Pitlochry and Strathardle, conceived in the Highland
rain, in the blend of the smell of heather and bog-plants,
and with a mind full of the Athole correspondence and
the memories of the dumlicide Justice. So long ago,
so far away it was, that I had first evoked the faces and
the mutual tragic situation of the men of Durisdeer.

My story was now world-wide enough: Scotland,
India, and America being all obligatory scenes. But of
these India was strange to me except in books; I had
never known any living Indian save a Parsee, a member
of my club in London, equally civilised and (to all
seeing) equally occidental with myself. It was plain,
thus far, that I should have to get into India and out of

it again upon a foot of fairy lightness; and I believe this first suggested to me the idea of the Chevalier Burke for a narrator. It was at first intended that he should be Scottish, and I was then filled with fears that he might prove only the degraded shadow of my own Alan Breck. Presently, however, it began to occur to me it would be like my Master to curry favour with the Prince's Irishmen; and that an Irish refugee would have a particular reason to find himself in India with his countryman, the unfortunate Lally. Irish, therefore, I decided he should be, and then, all of a sudden, I was aware of a tall shadow across my path, the shadow of Barry Lyndon. No man (in Lord Foppington's phrase) of a nice morality could go very deep with my Master: in the original idea of this story conceived in Scotland, this companion had been besides intended to be worse than the bad elder son with whom (as it was then meant) he was to visit Scotland; if I took an Irishman, and a very bad Irishman, in the midst of the eighteenth century, how was I to evade Barry Lyndon? The wretch besieged me, offering his services; he gave me excellent references; he proved that he was highly fitted for the work I had to do; he, or my own evil heart, suggested it was easy to disguise his ancient livery with a little lace and a few frogs and buttons, so that Thackeray himself should hardly recognise him. And then of a sudden there came to me memories of a young Irishman, with whom I was once intimate, and had spent long nights walking and talking with, upon a very desolate coast in a bleak autumn: I recalled him as a youth of an extraordinary moral simplicity—almost vacancy; plastic to any influence, the creature of his admirations: and putting such a youth in fancy into the career of a soldier of fortune, it occurred to me that he would serve my turn as well as Mr. Lyndon, and in place of entering into competition with the Master, would afford a slight though a distinct relief. I know not if I have done him well, though his moral dissertations always highly entertained me: but I own I have been surprised to find that he reminded some critics of Barry Lyndon after all. . . .

II

RANDOM MEMORIES: "ROSA QUO LOCORUM"

i

THROUGH what little channels, by what hints and premonitions, the consciousness of the man's art dawns first upon the child, it should be not only interesting but instructive to inquire. A matter of curiosity to-day, it will become the ground of science to-morrow. From the mind of childhood there is more history and more philosophy to be fished up than from all the printed volumes in a library. The child is conscious of an interest, not in literature, but in life. A taste for the precise, the adroit, or the comely in the use of words, comes late; but long before that he has enjoyed in books a delightful dress-rehearsal of experience. He is first conscious of this material—I had almost said this practical—preoccupation; it does not follow that it really came the first. I have some old fogged negatives in my collection that would seem to imply a prior stage. "The Lord is gone up with a shout, and God with the sound of a trumpet"—memorial version, I know not where to find the text—rings still in my ear from my first childhood, and perhaps with something of my nurse's accent. There was possibly some sort of image written in my mind by these loud words, but I believe the words themselves were what I cherished. I had about the same time, and under the same influence—that of my dear nurse—a favourite author: it is possible the reader has not heard of him—the Rev. Robert Murray M'Cheyne. My nurse and I admired his name exceedingly, so that I must have been taught the love of beautiful sounds before I was breeched; and I remember two specimens of his muse until this day:

> " Behind the hills of Naphtali
>   The sun went slowly down,
>   Leaving on mountain, tower, and tree,
>   A tinge of golden brown."

There is imagery here, and I set it on one side. The other—it is but a verse—not only contains no image, but is quite unintelligible even to my comparatively instructed mind, and I know not even how to spell the outlandish vocable that charmed me in my childhood:

> " Jehovah Tschidkenu is nothing to her "; [1]

I may say, without flippancy, that He was nothing to me either, since I had no ray of a guess of what He was about; yet the verse, from then to now, a longer interval than the life of a generation, has continued to haunt me.

I have said that I should set a passage distinguished by obvious and pleasing imagery, however faint; for the child thinks much in images, words are very live

---

[1] " Jehovah Tsidkenu," translated in the Authorised Version as " The Lord our Righteousness " (Jeremiah xxiii. 6 and xxxiii.16).

to him, phrases that imply a picture eloquent beyond their value. Rummaging in the dusty pigeonholes of memory, I came once upon a graphic version of the famous psalm, "The Lord is my shepherd": and from the places employed in its illustration, which are all in the immediate neighbourhood of a house then occupied by my father, I am able to date it before the seventh year of my age, although it was probably earlier in fact. The "pastures green" were represented by a certain suburban stubble-field, where I had once walked with my nurse, under an autumnal sunset, on the banks of the Water of Leith: the place is long ago built up; no pastures now, no stubble-fields; only a maze of little streets and smoking chimneys and shrill children. Here, in the fleecy person of a sheep, I seemed to myself to follow something unseen, unrealised, and yet benignant; and close by the sheep in which I was incarnated —as if for greater security—rustled the skirts of my nurse. "Death's dark vale" was a certain archway in the Warriston Cemetery: a formidable yet beloved spot, for children love to be afraid,—in measure as they love all experience of vitality. Here I beheld myself some paces ahead (seeing myself, I mean, from behind), utterly alone in that uncanny passage: on the one side of me a rude, knobby shepherd's staff, such as cheers the heart of the cockney tourist, on the other a rod like a billiard-cue appeared to accompany my progress: the staff sturdily upright, the billiard-cue inclined confidentially, like one whispering, towards my ear. I was aware—I will never tell you how—that the presence of these articles afforded me encouragement. The third and last of my pictures illustrated the words:

> " My table Thou hast furnishèd
>   In presence of my foes:
> My head Thou dost with oil anoint,
>   And my cup overflows ":

and this was perhaps the most interesting of the series. I saw myself seated in a kind of open stone summer-house at table; over my shoulder a hairy, bearded, and robed presence anointed me from an authentic shoe-horn; the summer-house was part of the green court of a ruin, and from the far side of the court black and white imps discharged against me ineffectual arrows. The picture appears arbitrary, but I can trace every detail to its source, as Mr. Brock analysed the dream of Alan Armadale. The summer-house and court were muddled together out of Billings' *Antiquities of Scotland;* the imps conveyed from Bagster's *Pilgrim's Progress;* the bearded and robed figure from any one of a thousand Bible pictures; and the shoe-horn was plagiarised from an old illustrated Bible, where it figured in the hand of Samuel anointing Saul, and had been pointed out to me as a jest by my father. It was shown me for a jest, remark; but the serious spirit of infancy adopted it in earnest. Children are all classics; a bottle would have seemed an intermediary too trivial —that divine refreshment of whose meaning I had no guess; and I seized on the idea of that mystic shoe-horn with delight, even as, a little later, I should have written flagon, chalice, hanaper, beaker, or any word that might have appealed to me at the moment as least contaminate with mean associations. In this string of pictures I believe the gist of the psalm to have consisted; I believe it had no more to say to me; and the result was consolatory. I would go to sleep dwelling with restfulness upon these images; they passed before me, besides, to an appropriate music; for I had already singled out from that rude psalm the one lovely verse which dwells in the minds of all, not growing old, not disgraced by its association with long Sunday tasks, a scarce conscious joy in childhood, in age a companion thought:

> "In pastures green Thou leadest me,
> The quiet waters by."

The remainder of my childish recollections are all of the matter of what was read to me, and not of any manner in the words. If these pleased me, it was unconsciously; I listened for news of the great vacant world upon whose edge I stood; I listened for delightful plots that I might re-enact in play, and romantic scenes and circumstances that I might call up before me, with closed eyes, when I was tired of Scotland, and home, and that weary prison of the sick-chamber in which I lay so long in durance. *Robinson Crusoe;* some of the books of that cheerful, ingenious, romantic soul, Mayne Reid; and a work (rather gruesome and bloody for a child, but very picturesque) called *Paul Blake;* these are the three strongest impressions I remember: *The Swiss Family Robinson* came next, *longo intervallo.* At these I played, conjured up their scenes, and delighted to hear them rehearsed unto seventy times seven. I am not sure but what *Paul Blake* came after I could read. It seems connected with a visit to the country, and an experience unforgetable. The day had been warm; H—— and I had played together charmingly all day in a sandy wilderness across the road; then came the evening with a great flash of colour and a heavenly sweetness in the air. Somehow my playmate had vanished, or is out of the story, as the sagas say, but I was sent into the village on an errand; and, taking a book of fairy tales, went down alone through a fir-wood, reading as I walked. How often since then it has befallen me to be happy even so; but that was the first time: the shock of that pleasure I have never since forgot, and if my mind serves me to the last, I never shall; for it was then that I knew I loved reading.

II

To pass from hearing literature to reading it is to take a great and dangerous step. With not a few, I think a large proportion of their pleasure then comes to an end; "the malady of not marking" overtakes them; they read thenceforward by the eye alone and hear never again the chime of fair words or the march of the stately period. *Non ragioniam* of these. But to all the step is dangerous; it involves coming of age; it is even a kind of second weaning. In the past all was at the choice of others; they chose, they digested, they read aloud for us and sang to their own tune the books of childhood. In the future we are to approach the silent, inexpressive type alone, like pioneers; and the choice of what we are to read is in our own hands thenceforward. For instance, in the passages already adduced, I detect and applaud the ear of my old nurse; they were of her choice, and she imposed them on my infancy, reading the works of others as a poet would scarce dare to read his own; gloating on the rhythm, dwelling with delight on assonances and alliterations. I know very well my mother must have been all the while trying to educate my taste upon more secular authors; but the vigour and the continual opportunities of my nurse triumphed, and after a long search, I can find in these earliest volumes of my autobiography no mention of anything but nursery rhymes, the Bible, and Mr. M'Cheyne.

I suppose all children agree in looking back with delight on their school Readers. We might not now find so much pathos in " Bingen on the Rhine," " A soldier of the Legion lay dying in Algiers," or in " The Soldier's Funeral," in the declaration of which I was held to have surpassed myself. " Robert's voice," said the master on this memorable occasion, " is not strong, but impressive ": an opinion which I was fool enough to carry home to my father; who roasted me for years in consequence. I am sure one should not be so deliciously tickled by the humorous pieces:

> "What, crusty? cries Will, in a taking,
>   Who would not be crusty with half a year's baking?"

I think this quip would leave us cold. The " Isles of Greece " seem rather tawdry too; but on the " Address to the Ocean," or on " The Dying Gladiator," " time has writ no wrinkle."

> "'T is the morn, but dim and dark;
>   Whither flies the silent lark?"—

does the reader recall the moment when his eye first fell upon these lines in the Fourth Reader; and " surprised with joy, impatient as the wind," he plunged into the sequel? And there was another piece, this time in prose, which none can have forgotten; many like me must have searched Dickens with zeal to find it again, and in its proper context, and have perhaps been conscious of some inconsiderable measure of disappointment, that it was only Tom Pinch who drove, in such a pomp of poetry, to London.

But in the Reader we are still under guides. What a boy turns out for himself, as he rummages the bookshelves, is the real test and pleasure. My father's library was a spot of some austerity: the proceedings of learned societies, some Latin divinity, cyclopædias, physical science, and, above all, optics, held the chief place upon the shelves, and it was only in holes and corners that anything really legible existed as by accident. The *Parent's Assistant, Rob Roy, Waverley*, and *Guy Mannering*, the *Voyages of Captain Woods Rogers*, Fuller's and Bunyan's *Holy Wars, The Reflections of Robinson Crusoe, The Female Bluebeard*, G. Sand's *Mare au Diable* (how came it in that grave assembly!), Ainsworth's *Tower of London*, and four old volumes of *Punch*—these were the chief exceptions. In these latter, which made for years the chief of my diet, I very early fell in love (almost as soon as I could spell) with the Snob Papers. I knew them almost by heart, particularly the visit to the Pontos; and I remember my surprise when I found, long afterwards, that they were famous, and signed with a famous name; to me, as I read and admired them, they were the works of Mr. Punch. Time and again I tried to read *Rob Roy*, with whom of course I was acquainted from the *Tales of a*

Grandfather ; time and again the early part, with Rash-
leigh and (think of it!) the adorable Diana, choked me
off; and I shall never forget the pleasure and surprise
with which, lying on the floor one summer evening, I
struck of a sudden into the first scene with Andrew
Fairservice. "The worthy Dr. Lightfoot"—"mistrysted
with a bogle "—" a wheen green trash "—"Jenny, lass,
I think I ha'e her": from that day to this the phrases
have been unforgotten. I read on, I need scarce say;
I came to Glasgow, I bided tryst on Glasgow Bridge,
I met Rob Roy and the Bailie in the Tolbooth, all with
transporting pleasure; and then the clouds gathered
once more about my path; and I dozed and skipped
until I stumbled half-asleep into the clachan of Aber-
foyle, and the voices of Iverach and Galbraith recalled
me to myself. With that scene and the defeat of Captain Thornton the book concluded; Helen and her sons
shocked even the little schoolboy of nine or ten with
their unreality; I read no more, or I did not grasp what
I was reading; and years elapsed before I consciously
met Diana and her father among the hills, or saw Rash-
leigh dying in the chair. When I think of that novel
and that evening, I am impatient with all others; they
seem but shadows and impostors; they cannot satisfy
the appetite which this awakened; and I dare be known
to think it the best of Sir Walter's by nearly as much
as Sir Walter is the best of novelists. Perhaps Mr. Lang
is right, and our first friends in the land of fiction are
always the most real. And yet I had read before this
Guy Mannering, and some of *Waverley*, with no such
delighted sense of truth and humour, and I read immediately after the greater part of the Waverley Novels,

and was never moved again in the same way or to the same degree. One circumstance is suspicious: my critical estimate of the Waverley Novels has scarce changed at all since I was ten. *Rob Roy, Guy Mannering,* and *Redgauntlet* first; then, a little lower, *The Fortunes of Nigel ;* then, after a huge gulf, *Ivanhoe* and *Anne of Geierstein :* the rest nowhere; such was the verdict of the boy. Since then *The Antiquary, St. Ronan's Well, Kenilworth,* and *The Heart of Midlothian* have gone up in the scale; perhaps *Ivanhoe* and *Anne of Geierstein* have gone a trifle down; Diana Vernon has been added to my admirations in that enchanted world of *Rob Roy ;* I think more of the letters in *Redgauntlet,* and Peter Peebles, that dreadful piece of realism, I can now read about with equanimity, interest, and I had almost said pleasure, while to the childish critic he often caused unmixed distress. But the rest is the same; I could not finish *The Pirate* when I was a child, I have never finished it yet; *Peveril of the Peak* dropped half-way through from my schoolboy hands, and though I have since waded to an end in a kind of wager with myself, the exercise was quite without enjoyment. There is something disquieting in these considerations. I still think the visit to Ponto's the best part of the *Book of Snobs :* does that mean that I was right when I was a child, or does it mean that I have never grown since then, that the child is not the man's father, but the man ? and that I came into the world with all my faculties complete, and have only learned sinsyne to be more tolerant of boredom ? . . .

LETTERS FROM SAMOA

LETTERS FROM SAMOA

THE two collections which here follow both consist of letters written from Samoa and referring to Samoan matters. In other respects they are quite unlike. The first is a reprint of correspondence which appeared in London newspapers at intervals from 1889 to 1895, and of which the object was to call the attention of the English public to political events in the islands: first to the proceedings of the representatives of the German Empire before the Treaty of Berlin; next to the administration of the two chief officials appointed by the three Powers under that treaty; and lastly, after those officials had been withdrawn and succeeded by others, to the part played by the three Consuls in the government. Mr. Stevenson may have been right or wrong—or, as is more probable, partly right and partly wrong—in his outspoken criticism of the various authorities engaged in administering the embroiled affairs of the islands where he had fixed his home, and for whose population he felt so warm a sympathy. But at all events he believed himself to be working in the interests of justice and of peace; he was entirely devoid of personal animus and personal motive; and as to one main part of his contention, though not the rest, the action of the three Powers practically confirmed his views. As these matters filled so large a part of his time and thoughts, it seemed proper (following a suggestion of his own made in correspondence) to give, as supplementing his *Footnote to History*, the letters referring to the same subjects which he contributed to the public press both before and after the appearance of that volume.

The letters in the second group are of a wholly different character. They were written playfully in order to convey impressions of life at Vailima to boys and girls. The first three are addressed, through a lady who had been a friend and correspondent of the writer's in Bournemouth days, to some children in a convalescent home in Kilburn which she helped to manage; the remainder to a member of his own household, his wife's grandson Austin Strong, at times when he was away in California or New Zealand. This correspondence might seem more properly to belong to the collection of general letters which will accompany the Life of the author now in preparation; but as it has already been published in *St. Nicholas* (December, 1895; January and February, 1896), it has been thought well to reprint it here. — [S. C.]

LETTERS TO THE "TIMES," "PALL MALL GAZETTE," ETC.

I

TO THE EDITOR OF THE "TIMES"

Yacht "Casco," Hawaiian Islands, February 10, 1889.

SIR,—News from Polynesia is apt to come piecemeal, and thus fail of its effect, the first step being forgotten before the second comes to hand. For this reason I should like to be allowed to recapitulate a little of the past before I go on to illustrate the present extraordinary state of affairs in the Samoan Islands.

It is quite true that this group was largely opened up by German enterprise, and that the port of Apia is much the creation of the Godeffroys. So far the German case extends; no further. Apia was governed till lately by a tripartite municipality, the American, English, and German Consuls, and one other representative of each of the three nations making up the body. To both America and Germany a harbour had been ceded. England, I believe, had no harbour, but that her position was quite equal to that of her neighbours one fact eloquently displays. Malietoa—then King of Samoa, now a prisoner on the Marshall Islands—offered to accept the supremacy of England. Unhappily for himself, his offer was refused, Her Majesty's Government declaring, I am told, that they would prefer to see him independent. As he now wanders the territory of his island prison, under the guns of an Imperial war-ship, his independence (if it still exists) must be confined entirely to his bosom.

Such was the former equal and pacific state of the three nations at Apia. It would be curious to tell at length by what steps of encroachment on the one side and weakness on the other the present reign of terror has been brought about; but my time before the mail departs is very short, your space is limited, and in such a history much must be only matter of conjecture. Briefly and roughly, then, there came a sudden change in the attitude of Germany. Another treaty was proposed to Malietoa and refused; the cause of the rebel Tamasese was invented or espoused; Malietoa was seized and deported, Tamasese installed, the tripartite municipality dissolved, the German Consul seated autocratically in its place, and the Hawaiian Embassy (sent by a Power of the same race to moderate among Samoans) dismissed with threats and insults. In the course of these events villages have been shelled, the German flag has been at least once substituted for the English, and the Stars and Stripes (only the other day) were burned at Matafatatele. On the day of the chase after Malietoa the houses of both English and Americans were violently entered by the Germans. Since the dissolution of the municipality English and Americans have paid their taxes into the hands of their own Consuls, where they accumulate, and the German representative, unrecognised and unsupported, rules single in Apia. I have had through my hands a file of Consular proclamations, the most singular reading—a state of war declared, all other authority but that of the German representative suspended, punishment (and the punishment of death in particular) liberally threatened. It is enough to make a man rub his eyes when he reads Colonel de Coetlogon's protest and the high-handed rejoinder posted alongside of it the next day by Dr. Knappe. Who is Dr. Knappe, thus to make peace and war, deal in life and death, and close with a buffet the mouth of English Consuls? By what process known to diplomacy has he risen from his one-sixth part of municipal authority to be the Bismarck of a Polynesian island? And what spell has been cast on the Cabinets of Washington and St. James's, that Mr. Blacklock should have been so long left unsupported, and that Colonel de Coetlogon must bow his head under a public buffet?

I have not said much of the Samoans. I despair, in so short a space, to interest English readers in their wrongs; with the mass of people at home they will pass for some sort of cannibal islanders, with whom faith were superfluous, upon whom kindness might be partly thrown away. And, indeed, I recognise with gladness that (except as regards the captivity of Malietoa) the Samoans have had throughout the honours of the game. Tamasese, the German puppet, has had everywhere the under hand; almost none, except those of his own clan, have ever supported his cause, and even these begin now to desert him. "This is no Samoan war," said one of them, as he transferred his followers and services to the new Malietoa—Mataafa; "this is a German war." Mataafa, if he be cut off from Apia and the sea, lies inexpugnable in the foot-hills immediately behind with five thousand warriors at his back. And beyond titles to a great deal of land, which they extorted in exchange for rifles and ammunition from the partisans of Tamasese, of all this bloodshed and bullying the Germans behold no profit. I have it by last advices that Dr. Knappe has approached the King privately with fair speeches, assuring him that the state of war, bombardments, and other evils of the day, are not at all directed at Samoans, but against the English and Americans; and that, when these are extruded, peace shall again smile on a German island. It can never be proved, but is highly possible he may have said so; and, whether he said it or not, there is a sense in which the thing is true. Violence has not been found to succeed with the Samoans; with the two Anglo-Saxon Powers it has been found to work like a charm. I conclude with two instances, one American, one English:

First. Mr. Klein, an American journalist, was on the beach with Malietoa's men on the night of the recent German defeat. Seeing the boats approach in the darkness, Mr. Klein hailed them and warned them of the Samoan ambush, and, by this innocent and humane step, made public the fact of his presence. Where much else is contested so much appears to be admitted (and, indeed, claimed) upon both sides. Mr. Klein is now accused of firing on the Germans and of advising the Samoans to fire, both of which he denies. He is accused, after the fight, of succouring only the wounded of Malietoa's party; he himself declares that he helped both; and, at any rate, the offence appears a novel one, and the accusation threatens to introduce fresh dangers into Red Cross work. He was on the beach that night in the exercise of his profession. If he was with Malietoa's men, which is the real gist of his offence, we who are not Germans may surely ask, Why not? On what grounds is Malietoa a rebel? The Germans have not conquered Samoa that I ever heard of; they are there on treaty like their neighbours, and Dr. Knappe himself (in the eyes of justice) is no more than one-sixth part of the town council of Apia. Lastly, Mr. Klein's innocence stands very clearly proven by the openness with which he declared his presence. For all that, this gentleman lay for a considerable time, watched day and night by German sailors, a prisoner in the American Consulate; even after he had succeeded in running the gantlet of the German guards, and making his escape in a canoe to the American war-ship *Nipsic*, he was imperiously redemanded from under his own flag, and it is probable his extradition is being already called for at Washington.

Secondly. An English artist had gone into the bush sketching. I believe he had been to Malietoa's camp, so that his guilt stands on somewhat the same ground as Mr. Klein's. He was forcibly seized on board the British packet *Richmond*, carried half-dressed on board the *Adler*, and detained there, in spite of all protest, until an English war-ship had been cleared for action. This is of notoriety, and only one case (although a strong one) of many. Is it what the English people understand by the sovereignty of the seas?—I am, etc.,

ROBERT LOUIS STEVENSON.

II

TO THE EDITOR OF THE "TIMES"

Vailima, Upolu, Samoa, October 12, 1891.

SIR,—I beg leave to lay before your readers a copy of a correspondence, or (should that have reached you by another channel) to offer a few words of narrative and comment.

On Saturday, September 5, Mr. Cedercrantz, the Chief Justice of Samoa, sailed on a visit to Fiji, leaving behind him certain prisoners in jail, and Baron Senfft von Pilsach, President of the Municipal Council, master of the field. The prisoners were five chiefs of Manono who had surrendered of their own accord, or at the desire of Mataafa, had been tried by a native magistrate, and received sentence of six months' confinement under "gentlemanly" (*sic*) conditions. As they were marched to prison, certain of their country-folk of Manono ran beside and offered an immediate rescue; but Lieutenant Ulfsparre ordered the men of the escort to load, and the disturbance blew by. How little weight was attached to this incident by the Chief Justice is sufficiently indicated by the fact of his departure. It was unhappily otherwise with those whom he left behind. Panic seems to have marked them for her own; they despaired at once of all lawful defence; and on Sunday, the day after the Chief Justice's departure, Apia was in consequence startled with strange news. Dynamite brought from the wrecker ship, an electrical machine and a mechanic hired, the prison mined, and a letter despatched to the people of Manono advising them of the fact, and announcing that if any rescue were attempted prison and prisoners should be blown up—such were the voices of rumour; and the design appearing equally feeble, reckless, and wicked, considerable agitation was aroused. Perhaps it had some effect. Our Government at least, which had rushed so hastily to one extreme, now dashed with the same speed into another. Sunday was the day of dynamite, Tuesday dawned the day of deportation. A cutter was hurriedly prepared for sea, and the prisoners, whom the Chief Justice had left three days before under a sentence of " gentlemanly " detention, found themselves under way to exile in the Tokelaus.

A Government of this agility escapes criticism : by multiplying surprises it obliterates the very memory of past mistakes. Some, perhaps, forgot the dynamite; some, hearing no more of it, set it down to be a trick of rumour such as we are all well used to in the islands. But others were not so sure. Others considered that the rumour (even if unfounded) was of an ill example, might bear deplorable fruit, and, from all points of view of morality and policy, required a public contradiction. Eleven of these last entered accordingly into the annexed correspondence with the President. It will be seen in the crevice of what quibble that gentleman sought refuge and sits inexpugnable. In a question affecting his humanity, his honour, and the well-being of the kingdom which he serves, he has preferred to maintain what I can only call a voluble silence. The public must judge of the result; but there is one point to which I may be allowed to draw attention—that passage in the fourth of the appended documents in which he confesses that he was already acquainted with the rumours in question, and that he has been present (and apparently not protesting) when the scandal was discussed and the proposed enormity commended.

The correspondence was still passing when the President surprised Apia with a fresh gambado. He has been a long while in trouble as to his disposition of the funds. His intention to build a house for himself—to all appearances with native money—his sending the taxes out of the islands and locking them up in deposits, and his noisy squabbles with the King and native Parliament as to the currency, had all aroused unfavourable comment. On Saturday, the 3rd of October, a correspondence on the last point appeared in the local paper. By this it appeared that our not too resolute King and Parliament had at last and in one particular defied his advice and maintained their own opinion. If vengeance were to be the order of the day, it might have been expected to fall on the King and Parliament; but this would have been too direct a course, and the blow was turned instead against an innocent municipal council. On the 7th the President appeared before that body, informed them that his authority was lessened by the publication, that he had applied to the King for a month's leave of (theatrical) absence, and must now refuse to fulfil his duties. With this he retired to his own house, which is under the same roof, leaving the councillors and the municipality to do what they pleased and drift where they could without him. It is reported he has since declared his life to be in danger, and even applied to his Consul for protection. This seems to pass the bounds of credibility; but the movements of Baron Senfft von Pilsach have been throughout so agitated and so unexpected that we know not what to look for; and the signatories of the annexed addresses, if they were accused to-morrow of a design on the man's days, would scarce have spirit left to be surprised.

It must be clearly pointed out that this is no quarrel of German and anti-German. The German officials, consular and naval, have behaved with perfect loyalty. A German wrote the letter to the paper which unchained this thunderbolt; and it was a German who took the chair which the President had just vacated at the table of the municipal board. And though the Baron is himself of German race, his conduct presents no appearance of design, how much less of conspiracy! Doubtless certain journals will so attempt to twist it, but to the candid it will seem no more than the distracted evolutions of a weak man in a series of panics.

Such is the rough outline of the events to which I would fain direct the attention of the public at home, in the States, and still more in Germany. It has for me but one essential point. Budgets have been called in question, and officials publicly taken the pet before now. But the dynamite scandal is unique.

If it be unfounded, our complaint is already grave. It was the President's duty, as a man and as a responsible official, to have given it instant and direct denial: and since he neither did so of his own motion, nor consented to do so on our repeated instances, he has shown that he neither understands nor yet is willing to be taught the condition of this country. From what I have been able to collect, Samoans are indignant because the thing was decided between the King and President without consultation with the native Parliament. The thing itself, it does not enter in their thoughts to call in question; they receive gratefully a fresh lesson in civilised methods and civilised justice; a day may come when they shall put that lesson in practice for themselves; and if they are then decried for their barbarity—as they will surely be—and punished for it, as is highly probable, I will ask candid people what they are to think? "How?" they will say. "Your own white people intended to do this, and you said nothing. We do it, and you call us treacherous savages!"

This is to suppose the story false. Suppose it true, however; still more, suppose the plan had been carried out. Suppose these chiefs to have surrendered to the white man's justice, administered or not by a brown judge; suppose them tried, condemned, confined in that snare of a jail, and some fine night their mangled limbs cast in the faces of their countrymen: I leave others to predict the consequences of such an object-lesson in the arts of peace and the administration of the law. The Samoans are a mild race, but their patience is in some points limited. Under Captain Brandeis a single skirmish and the death of a few youths sufficed to kindle an enduring war and bring on the ruin of the Government. The residents have no desire for war, and they deprecate altogether a war embittered from the beginning by atrocities. Nor can they think the stakes at all equal between themselves and Baron Senfft. He has nothing to lose but a situation; he is here in what he stands in; he can swarm to-morrow on board a war-ship and be off. But the residents have some of them sunk capital on these shores; some of them are involved in extended affairs; they are tied to the stake, and they protest against being plunged into war by the violence, and having that war rendered more implacable by the preliminary cruelties, of a white official.

I leave entirely upon one side all questions of morality; but there is still one point of expediency on which I must touch. The old native Government (which was at least cheap) failed to enforce the law, and fell, in consequence, into the manifold troubles which have made the name of Samoa famous. The enforcement of the law—that was what was required, that was the salvation looked for. And here we have a Government at a high figure, and it cannot defend its own jail, and can find no better remedy than to assassinate its prisoners. What we have bought at this enormous increase of expenditure is the change from King Log to King Stork—from the man who failed to punish petty theft to the man who plots the destruction of his own jail and the death of his own prisoners.

On the return of the Chief Justice, the matter will be brought to his attention; but the cure of our troubles must come from home; it is from the Great Powers that we look for deliverance. They sent us the President. Let them either remove the man, or see that he is stringently instructed—instructed to respect public decency, so we be no longer menaced with doings worthy of a revolutionary committee; and instructed to respect the administration of the law, so if I be fined a dollar to-morrow for fast riding in Apia street, I may not awake next morning to find my sentence increased to one of banishment or death by dynamite.—I am, Sir, your obedient servant,   ROBERT LOUIS STEVENSON.

P. S., October 14.—I little expected fresh developments before the mail left. But the unresting President still mars the quiet of his neighbours. Even while I was writing the above lines, Apia was looking on in mere amazement on the continuation of his gambols. A white man had written to the King, and the King had answered the letter—crimes against Baron Senfft von Pilsach and (his private reading of) the Berlin Treaty. He offered to resign—I was about to say "accordingly," for the unexpected is here the normal—from the presidency of the municipal board, and to retain his position as the King's adviser. He was instructed that he must resign both, or neither; resigned both; fell out with the Consuls on details; and is now, as we are advised, seeking to resile from his resignations. Such an official I never remember to have read of, though I have seen the like, from across the footlights and the orchestra, evolving in similar figures to the strains of Offenbach.   R. L. S.

COPIES OF A CORRESPONDENCE BETWEEN CERTAIN RESIDENTS OF APIA AND BARON SENFFT VON PILSACH

I

September 28, 1891.

BARON SENFFT VON PILSACH.

SIR,—We are requested to lay the enclosed appeal before you, and to express the desire of the signatories to meet your views as to the manner of the answer.

Should you prefer to reply by word of mouth, a deputation will be ready to wait upon you on Thursday, at any hour you may please to appoint.

Should you prefer to reply in writing, we are asked only to impress upon you the extreme desire of the signatories that no time should be unnecessarily lost.

Should you condescend in either of the ways suggested to set at rest our anxiety, we need scarce assure you that the step will be received with gratitude.—We have the honour to be, Sir, your obedient servants,

ROBERT LOUIS STEVENSON.
E. W. GURR.

II

(Enclosed in No. 1.)

The attention of the President of the Municipal Council is respectfully directed to the following rumours:

1. That at his suggestion, or with his authority, dynamite was purchased, or efforts were made to procure dynamite, and the use of an electrical machine was secured, or attempted to be obtained.

2. That this was for the purpose of undermining, or pretending to undermine, the jail in which the Manono prisoners were confined.

3. That notification of this design was sent to the friends of the prisoners.

4. That a threat of blowing up the jail and the prisoners, in the event of an attempted rescue, was made.

Upon all and upon each of these points severally the white residents anxiously expect and respectfully beg information.

It is suggested for the President's consideration that rumours uncorrected or unexplained acquire almost the force of admitted truth.

That any want of confidence between the governed and the Government must be fruitful in loss to both.

That the rumours in their present form tend to damage the white races in the native mind, and to influence for the worse the manners of the Samoans.

And that the President alone is in a position to deny, to explain, or to correct these rumours.

Upon these grounds the undersigned ask to be excused for any informality in their address, and they hope and humbly pray that the President will accept the occasion here presented, and take early and effectual means to inform and reassure the whites, and to relieve them from possible misjudgment on the part of the Samoans.

ROBERT LOUIS STEVENSON.
E. W. GURR.
(And nine other signatures.)

III

Apia, September 30, 1891.

ROBERT LOUIS STEVENSON, ESQ., E. W. GURR, ESQ.

DEAR SIRS,—Thanking you for your kind letter dated 28th inst., which I received yesterday, together with the address in question, I beg to inform you that I am going to answer the address in writing as soon as possible.—I have the honour to be, dear Sirs, your obedient servant,

SENFFT.

IV

Apia, October 2, 1891.

ROBERT LOUIS STEVENSON, ESQ., E. W. GURR, ESQ.

GENTLEMEN,—I have the honour to acknowledge the receipt of an address without date which has been signed by you and some other foreign residents and handed to me on the 29th of September.

In this address my attention is directed to some rumours, specified therein, concerning which I am informed that "upon all and upon each of these points severally the white residents anxiously expect and respectfully beg information."

Generally, I beg to state that, with a view of successfully performing my official duties, I believe it is advisable for me to pay no attention to any anonymous rumour.

Further, I cannot forbear expressing my astonishment that in speaking to me so seriously in the name of "the white residents" the subscribers of the address have deemed it unnecessary to acquaint me with their authorisation for doing so. This omission is by no means a mere informality. There are white residents who in my presence have commented upon the rumours in question in a manner directly opposed to the meaning of the address.

This fact alone will justify me in objecting to the truth of the above-quoted statement so prominently set forth and so positively affirmed in the address. It will also justify me in abstaining from a reply to the further assertions of gentlemen who, in apostrophising me, care so little for the correctness of the facts they deal with.

If, in consequence, according to the apprehensions laid down in the address, those unexplained rumours will "damage the white races in the native mind," I think the signing parties will then remember that there are public authorities in Samoa officially and especially charged with the protection of "the white residents." If they present to them their complaints and their wishes I have no doubt by so doing they will get all information they may require.

I ask you, Gentlemen, to communicate this answer to the parties having signed the address in question.—I have the honour to be, Gentlemen, your obedient servant,   FRHR. SENFFT VON PILSACH.

v

October 9, 1891.

The signatories of the address are in receipt of the President's favour under date October 2. Much of his answer is occupied in dealing with a point foreign to the matter in hand, and in itself surprising to the signatories. Their address was an appeal for information on specific points and an appeal from specific persons, who correctly described themselves as "white residents," "the undersigned," and in the accompanying letter as the "signatories." They were so far from seeking to collect evidence in private that they applied frankly and directly to the person accused for explanation; and so far from seeking to multiply signatures or promote scandal that they kept the paper strictly to themselves. They see with regret that the President has failed to appreciate this delicacy. They see with sorrow and surprise that, in answer to a communication which they believe to have been temperately and courteously worded, the President has thought fit to make an imputation on their honesty. The trick of which he would seem to accuse them would have been useless, and even silly, if attempted; and on a candid re-examination of the address and the accompanying letter, the President will doubtless see fit to recall the imputation.

By way of answer to the questions asked the signatories can find nothing but what seems to be a recommendation to them to apply to their Consuls for "protection." It was not protection they asked, but information. It was not a sense of fear that moved them, but a sense of shame. It is their misfortune that they cannot address the President in his own language, or they would not now require to explain that the words "tend to damage the white races in the native mind," quoted and misapplied by the President, do not express any fear of suffering by the hands of the Samoans, but in their good opinion, and were not the expression of any concern for the duration of peace, but of a sense of shame under what they conceived to be disgraceful imputations. While agreeing generally with the President's expressed sentiment as to " anonymous rumours," they feel that a line has to be drawn. Certain rumours they would not suffer to remain uncontradicted for an hour. It was natural, therefore, that when they heard a man of their own white race accused of conspiring to blow up the jail and the prisoners who were there under the safeguard of his honour, they should attribute to the accused a similar impatience to be justified; and it is with a sense of painful surprise that they find themselves to have been mistaken.

(*Signatures as to No. 11.*)

VI

Apia, October 9, 1891.

GENTLEMEN,—Being in receipt of your communication under to-day's date, I have the honour to inform you that I have undertaken the re-examination of your first address, which you believe would induce me to recall the answer I have given on the 2nd inst.

From this re-examination I have learned again that your appeal begins with the following statement:

"Upon all and upon each of these points severally the white residents anxiously expect and respectfully beg information."

I have called this statement a seriously speaking to me in the name of the white residents, and I have objected to the truth of that statement.

If after a "candid re-examination" of the matter from your part you may refute me in either or both points, I shall be glad, indeed, in recalling my answer.

At present I beg to say that I see no reason for your supposing I misunderstood your expression of damaging the white races in the native mind, unless you have no other notion of protection than that applying to the body.

Concerning the assertion contained in the last clause of your second address, that five Samoan prisoners having been sentenced by a Samoan judge for destroying houses were in the jail of the Samoan Government "under the safeguard of my honour," I ask for your permission to recommend this statement also and especially to your re-examination.—I have the honour to be, Gentlemen, your obedient servant,

FRHR. SENFFT VON PILSACH.

III

Samoa, April 9, 1892.

SIR,—A sketch of our latest difficulty in Samoa will be interesting, at least to lawyers.

In the Berlin General Act there is one point on which, from the earliest moment, volunteer interpreters have been divided. The revenue arising from the customs was held by one party to belong to the Samoan Government, by another to the municipality; and the dispute was at last decided in favour of the municipality by Mr. Cedercrantz, Chief Justice. The decision was not given in writing; but it was reported by at least one of the Consuls to his Government, it was of public notoriety, it is not denied, and it was at once implicitly acted on by the parties. Before that decision, the revenue from customs was suffered to accumulate; ever since, to the knowledge of the Chief Justice, and with the daily countenance of the President, it has been preceived, administered, and spent by the municipality. It is the function of the Chief Justice to interpret the Berlin Act; its sense was thus supposed to be established beyond cavil; those who were dissatisfied with the result conceived their only recourse lay in a prayer to the Powers to have the treaty altered; and such a prayer was, but the other day, proposed, supported, and finally negatived, in a public meeting.

About a year has gone by since the decision, and the state of the Samoan Government has been daily growing more precarious. Taxes have not been paid, and the Government has not ventured to enforce them. Fresh taxes have fallen due, and the Government has not ventured to call for them. Salaries were running on, and that of the Chief Justice alone amounts to a considerable figure for these islands; the coffers had fallen low, at last it was believed they were quite empty, no resource seemed left, and bystanders waited with a smiling curiosity for the wheels to stop. I should add, to explain the epithet "smiling," that the Government has proved a still-born child; and except for some spasmodic movements which I have already made the subject of remark in your columns, it may be said to have done nothing but pay salaries.

In this state of matters, on March 28, the President of the Council, Baron Senfft von Pilsach, was suddenly and privately supplied by Mr.

Cedercrantz with a written judgment, reversing the verbal and public decision of a year before. By what powers of law was this result attained? And how was the point brought again before his Honour? I feel I shall here strain the credulity of your readers, but our authority is the President in person. The suit was brought by himself in his capacity (perhaps an imaginary one) of King's adviser; it was defended by himself in his capacity of President of the Council; no notice had been given, the parties were not summoned, they were advised neither of the trial nor the judgment; so far as can be learned, two persons only met and parted—the first was the plaintiff and defendant rolled in one, the other was a judge who had decided black a year ago, and had now intimated a modest willingness to decide white.

But it is possible to follow more closely these original proceedings. Baron von Pilsach sat down (he told us) in his capacity of adviser to the King, and wrote to himself, in his capacity of President of the Council, an eloquent letter of reprimand three pages long; an unknown English artist clothed it for him in good language; and nothing remained but to have it signed by King Malietoa, to whom it was attributed. "So long as he knows how to sign!"—a white official is said thus to have summed up, with a shrug, the qualifications necessary in a Samoan king. It was signed accordingly, though whether the King knew what he was signing is matter of debate; and thus regularised, it was forwarded to the Chief Justice enclosed in a letter of adhesion from the President. Such as they were, these letters appear to have been the pleadings on which the Chief Justice proceeded; such as they were, they seem to have been the documents in this unusual cause.

Suppose an unfortunate error to have been made, suppose a reversal of the Court's finding and the year's policy to have become immediately needful, wisdom would indicate an extreme frankness of demeanour. And our two officials preferred a policy of irritating dissimulation. While the revolution was being prepared behind the curtain, the President was holding night sessions of the municipal council. What was the business? No other than to prepare an ordinance regulating those very customs which he was secretly conspiring to withdraw from their control. And it was a piece of duplicity of a similar nature which first awoke the echoes of Apia by its miscarriage. The council had sent up for the approval of the Consular Board a project of several bridges, one of which, that of the Vaisingano, was of chief importance to the town. To sanction so much

464

fresh expense, at the very moment when, to his secret knowledge, the municipality was to be left bare of funds, appeared to one of the Consuls an unworthy act; and the proposal was accordingly disallowed. The people of Apia are extremely swift to guess. No sooner was the Vaisingano bridge denied them than they leaped within a measurable distance of the truth. It was remembered that the Chief Justice had but recently (this time by a decision regularly obtained) placed the municipal funds at the President's mercy; talk ran high of collusion between the two officials; it was rumoured the safe had been already secretly drawn upon; the newspaper being at this juncture suddenly and rather mysteriously sold, it was rumoured it had been bought for the officials with municipal money, and the Apians crowded in consequence to the municipal meeting on April 1, with minds already heated.

The President came on his side armed with the secret judgment; and the hour being now come, he unveiled his work of art to the municipal councillors. On the strength of the Chief Justice's decision, to his knowledge, and with the daily countenance of the President, they had for twelve months received and expended the revenue from customs. They learned now that this was wrong; they learned not only that they were to receive no more, but that they must refund what they had already spent; and the total sum amounting to about $25,000, and there being less than $20,000 in the treasury, they learned that they were bankrupt. And with the next breath the President reassured them; time was to be given to these miserable debtors, and the King in his clemency would even advance them from their own safe—now theirs no longer—a loan of $3000 against current expenses. If the municipal council of Apia be far from an ideal body, at least it makes roads and builds bridges, at least it does something to justify its existence and reconcile the ratepayer to the rates. This was to cease: all the funds husbanded for this end were to be transferred to the Government at Mulinuu, which has never done anything to mention but pay salaries, and of which men have long ceased to expect anything else but that it shall continue to pay salaries till it die of inanition. Let us suppose this raid on the municipal treasury to have been just and needful. It is plain, even if introduced in the most conciliatory manner, it could never have been welcome. And, as it was, the sting was in the manner—in the secrecy and the surprise, in the dissimulation, the dissonant decisions, the appearance of collusion between the officials, and the offer of a loan too small to help. Bitter words were spoken at the council-table; the public joined with shouts; it was openly proposed to overpower the President and seize the treasury key. Baron von Pilsach possesses the redeeming rudimentary virtue of courage. It required courage to come at all on such an errand to those he had deceived; and amidst violent voices and menacing hands he displayed a constancy worthy of a better cause. The council broke tumultuously up; the inhabitants crowded to a public meeting; the Consuls, acquainted with the alarming effervescency of feeling, communicated their willingness to meet the municipal councillors and arrange a compromise; and the inhabitants renewed by acclamation the mandate of their representatives. The same night these sat in council with the Consular Board, and a *modus vivendi* was agreed upon, which was rejected the next morning by the President.

The representations of the Consuls had, however, their effect; and when the council met again on April 6, Baron von Pilsach was found to have entirely modified his attitude. The bridge over the Vaisingano was conceded; the sum of $3000 offered to the council was increased to $9000, about one half of the existing funds; the Samoan Government, which was to profit by the customs, now agreed to bear the expenses of collection; the President, while refusing to be limited to a specific figure, promised an anxious parsimony in the Government expenditure, admitted his recent conduct had been of a nature to irritate the councillors, and frankly proposed it should be brought under the notice of the Powers. I should not be a fair reporter if I did not praise his bearing. In the midst of men whom he had grossly deceived, and who had recently insulted him in return, he behaved himself with tact and temper. And largely in consequence his *modus vivendi* was accepted under protest, and the matter in dispute referred without discussion to the Powers.

I would like to refer for one moment to my former letter. The Manono prisoners were solemnly sentenced to six months' imprisonment; and, by some unexplained and secret process, the sentence was increased to one of banishment. The fact seems to have rather amused the Governments at home. It did not at all amuse us here on the spot. But we sought consolation by remembering that the President was a layman, and the Chief Justice had left the islands but the day before. Let Mr. Cedercrantz return, we thought, and Arthur would be come again. Well, Arthur is come. And now we begin to think he was perhaps an approving, if an absent, party to the scandal. For do we not find, in the case of

466

the municipal treasury, the same disquieting features? A decision is publicly delivered, it is acted on for a year, and by some secret and inexplicable process we find it suddenly reversed. We are supposed to be governed by English law. Is this English law? Is it law at all? Does it permit a state of society in which a citizen can live and act with confidence? And when we are asked by natives to explain these peculiarities of white man's government and white man's justice, in what form of words are we to answer?

April 12.

Fresh news reaches me; I have once again to admire the accuracy of rumour in Apia, and that which I had passed over with a reference becomes the head and front of our contention. The *Samoa Times* was nominally purchased by a gentleman who, whatever be his other recommendations, was notoriously ill off. There was paid down for it £600 in gold, a huge sum of ready money for Apia, above all in gold, and all men wondered where it came from. It is this which has been discovered: The wrapper of each rouleau was found to be signed by Mr. Martin, collector for the municipality as well as for the Samoan Government, and countersigned by Mr. Savile, his assistant. In other words, the money had left either the municipal or the Government safe.

The position of the President is thus extremely exposed. His accounts up to January 1 are in the hands of auditors. The next term of March 31 is already past, and although the natural course has been repeatedly suggested to him, he has never yet permitted the verification of the balance in his safe. The case would appear less strong against the Chief Justice. Yet a month has not elapsed since he placed the funds at the disposal of the President, on the avowed ground that the population of Apia was unfit to be entrusted with its own affairs. And the very week of the purchase he reversed his own previous decision and liberated his colleague from the last remaining vestige of control. Beyond the extent of these judgments, I doubt if this astute personage will be found to have committed himself in black and white; and the more foolhardy President may thus be left in the top of the breach alone.

Let it be explained or apportioned as it may, this additional scandal is felt to have overfilled the measure. It may be argued that the President has great tact and the Chief Justice a fund of philosophy. Give us instead a judge who shall proceed according to the forms of justice, and a treasurer who shall permit the verification of his balances. Surely there can be found among the millions of Europe two frank and honest men, one of whom shall be acquainted with English law, and the other possess the ordinary virtues of a clerk, over whose heads, in the exercise of their duties, six months may occasionally pass without painful disclosures and dangerous scandals; who shall not weary us with their surprises and intrigues; who shall not amaze us with their lack of penetration; who shall not, in the hour of their destitution, seem to have diverted £600 of public money for the purchase of an inconsiderable sheet, or at a time when eight provinces of discontented natives threaten at any moment to sweep their ineffective Government into the sea to have sought safety and strength in gagging the local press of Apia. If it be otherwise—if we cannot be relieved, if the Powers are satisfied with the conduct of Mr. Cedercrantz and Baron Senfft von Pilsach; if these were sent here with the understanding that they should secretly purchase, perhaps privately edit, a little sheet of two pages, issued from a crazy wooden building at the mission gate; if it were, indeed, intended that, for this important end, they should divert (as it seems they have done) public funds and affront all the forms of law—we whites can only bow the head. We are here quite helpless. If we would complain of Baron Pilsach, it can only be to Mr. Cedercrantz; if we would complain of Mr. Cedercrantz, and the Powers will not hear us, the circle is complete. A nightly guard surrounds and protects their place of residence, while the house of the King is cynically left without the pickets. Secure from interference, one utters the voice of the law, the other moves the hands of authority; and now they seem to have sequestered in the course of a single week the only available funds and the only existing paper in the islands.

But there is one thing they forget. It is not the whites who menace the duration of their Government, and it is only the whites who read the newspaper. Mataafa sits hard by in his armed camp and sees. He sees the weakness, he counts the scandals of their Government. He sees his rival and "brother" sitting disconsidered at their doors, like Lazarus before the house of Dives, and, if he is not very fond of his "brother," he is very scrupulous of native dignities. He has seen his friends menaced with midnight destruction in the Government jail, and deported without form of law. He is not himself a talker, and his thoughts are hid from us; but what is said by his more hasty partisans we know. On March 29, the day after the Chief Justice signed the secret judgment, three days before it was made public, and while the purchase of the newspaper was yet in treaty, a native orator stood up in an assembly. "Who asked the Great Powers to make laws for us; to bring strangers here to rule us?" he cried. "We want no white officials to bind us in the bondage of taxation." Here is the changed spirit which these gentlemen have produced by a misgovernment of fifteen months. Here is their peril, which no purchase of newspapers and no subsequent editorial suppressions can avert.

It may be asked if it be still time to do anything. It is, indeed, already late; and these gentlemen, arriving in a golden moment, have fatally squandered opportunity and perhaps fatally damaged white prestige. Even the whites themselves they have not only embittered, but corrupted. We were pained the other day when our municipal councillors refused, by a majority, to make the production of invoices obligatory at the Custom-house. Yet who shall blame them, when the Chief Justice, with a smallness of capacity at which all men wondered, refused to pay, and, I believe, still withholds, the duties on his imports? He was above the law, being the head of it; and this was how he preached by example. He refused to pay his customs; the white councillors, following in his wake, refuse to take measures to enforce them against others; and the natives, following in his wake, refuse to pay their taxes. These taxes it may, perhaps, be never possible to raise again directly. Taxes have never been popular in Samoa; yet in the golden moment when this Government began its course, a majority of Samoans paid them. Every province should have seen some part of that money expended in its bounds; every nerve should have been strained to interest and gratify the natives in the manner of its expenditure. It has been spent instead on Mulinuu, to pay four white officials, two of whom came in the suite of the Chief Justice, and to build a so-called Government House, in which the President resides, and the very name of taxes is become abhorrent. What can still be done, and what must be done immediately, is to give us a new Chief Justice—a lawyer, a man of honour, a man who will not commit himself to one side, whether in politics or in private causes, and who shall not have the appearance of trying to coin money at every joint of our affairs. So much the better if he be a man of talent, but we do not ask so much. With an ordinary appreciation of law, an ordinary discretion, and ordinary generosity, he may still, in the course of time, and with good fortune, restore confidence and repair the breaches in the prestige of the whites. As for the President, there is much discussion. Some think the office is superfluous, still more the salary to be excessive; some regard the present man, who is young and personally pleasing, as a tool and scapegoat for another, and these are tempted to suppose that, with a new and firm Chief Justice, he might yet redeem his character. He would require at least to clear himself of the affair of the rouleaux, or all would be against him.—I am, Sir, your obedient servant, ROBERT LOUIS STEVENSON.

IV

TO THE EDITOR OF THE "TIMES"

Samoa, June 22, 1892.

SIR,—I read in a New Zealand paper that you published my last with misgiving. The writer then goes on to remind me that I am a novelist, and to bid me return to my romances and leave the affairs of Samoa to subeditors and distant quarters of the world. "We, in common with other journals, have correspondents in Samoa," he complains, "and yet we have no news from them of the curious conspiracy which Mr. Stevenson appears to have unearthed, and which, if it had any real existence, would be known to everybody on the island." As this is the only voice which has yet reached me from beyond the seas, I am constrained to make some answer. But it must not be supposed that, though you may perhaps have been alone to publish, I have been alone to write. The same story is now in the hands of the three Governments from their respective Consuls. Not only so, but the complaint to the municipal council, drawn by two able solicitors, has been likewise laid before them.

This at least is public, and I may say notorious: The solicitors were authorised to proceed with their task at a public meeting. The President (for I was there and heard him) approved the step, though he refrained from voting. But he seemed to have entertained a hope of burking, or, at least, indefinitely postponing, the whole business, and, when the meeting was over and its proceedings had been approved (as is necessary) by the Consular Board, he neglected to notify the two gentlemen appointed of that approval. In a large city the trick might have succeeded for a time; in a village like Apia, where all news leaks out and the King meets the cobbler daily, it did no more than to advertise his own artfulness. And the next he learned, the case for the municipal council had been prepared, approved by the Consuls, and despatched to the Great Powers. I am accustomed to have my word doubted in this matter, and must here look to have it doubted once again. But the fact is certain. The two solicitors (Messrs. Carruthers and Cooper) were actually cited to appear before the Chief Justice in the Supreme Court. I have seen the summons, and the summons was the first and last of this State trial. The proceeding, instituted in an hour of temper, was, in a moment of reaction, allowed to drop.

About the same date a final blow befell the Government of Mulinuu. Let me remind you, Sir, of the situation. The funds of the municipality had been suddenly seized, on what appears a collusive judgment, by the bankrupt Government of Mulinuu. The paper, the organ of opposition, was bought by a man of straw; and it was found the purchase-money had been paid in rouleaux from the Government safes. The Government consisted of two men. One, the President and treasurer, had a ready means to clear himself and dispose for ever of the scandal—that means, apart from any scandal, was his mere, immediate duty,—viz., to have his balance verified. And he has refused to do so, and he still refuses. But the other, though he sits abstruse, must not think to escape his share of blame. He holds a high situation; he is our chief magistrate, he has heard this miserable tale of the rouleaux, at which the Consuls looked so black, and why has he done nothing? When he found that the case against himself and his colleague had gone to the three Powers a little of the suddenest, he could launch summonses (which it seems he was afterwards glad to disavow) against Messrs. Cooper and Carruthers. But then, when the whole island murmured—then, when a large sum which could be traced to the Government treasuries was found figuring in the hands of a man of straw—where were his thunderbolts then? For more than a month the scandal has hung black about his colleague; for more than a month he has sat inert and silent; for more than a month, in consequence, the last spark of trust in him has quite died out.

It was in these circumstances that the Government of Mulinuu approached the municipal council with a proposal to levy fresh taxes from the whites. It was in these circumstances that the municipal council answered, No. Public works have ceased, the destination of public moneys is kept secret, and the municipal council resolved to stop supplies.

At this, it seems, the Government awoke to a sense of their position. The natives had long ceased to pay them; now the whites had followed suit. Destitution had succeeded to embarrassment. And they made haste to join with themselves another who did not share in their unpopularity. This

471

gentleman, Mr. Thomas Maben, Government surveyor, is himself deservedly popular, and the office created for him, that of Secretary of State, is one in which, under happier auspices, he might accomplish much.   He is promised a free hand; he has succeeded to, and is to exercise entirely, those vague functions claimed by the President under his style of adviser to the King.   It will be well if it is found to be so in the field of practice.   It will be well if Mr. Maben find any funds left for his not exorbitant salary.   It would doubtless have been better, in this day of their destitution and in the midst of growing Samoan murmurs against the high salaries of whites, if the Government could have fallen on some expedient which did not imply another.   And there is a question one would fain have answered.   The President claims to hold two offices—that of adviser to the King, that of President of the Municipal Council.   A year ago, in the time of the dynamite affair, he proposed to resign the second and retain his whole emoluments as adviser to the King.   He has now practically resigned the first; and we wish to know if he now proposes to retain his entire salary as President of the Council.—I am, etc.,

ROBERT LOUIS STEVENSON.

V

TO THE EDITOR OF THE "TIMES"

Apia, July 19, 1892.

SIR,—I am at last in receipt of your article upon my letter.   It was as I supposed; you had a difficulty in believing the events recorded; and, to my great satisfaction, you suggest an inquiry.   You observe the marks of passion in my letter, or so it seems to you.   But your summary shows me that I have not failed to communicate with a sufficient clearness the facts alleged.   Passion may have seemed to burn in my words; it has not, at least, impaired my ability to record with precision a plain tale.   The "cold language" of Consular reports (which you say you would prefer) is doubtless to be had upon inquiry in the proper quarter; I make bold to say it will be found to bear me out.   Of the law case for the municipality I can speak with more assurance; for, since it was sent, I have been shown a copy.   Its language is admirably cold, yet it tells (it is possible in a much better dialect) the same remarkable story.   But all these corroborations sleep in official keeping; and, thanks to the generosity with which you have admitted me to your columns, I stand alone before the public.   It is my prayer that this may cease as soon as possible.

There is other evidence gone home; let that be produced.   Or let us have (as you propose) an inquiry; give to the Chief Justice and the President an opportunity to clear their characters, and to myself that liberty (which I am so often requested to take) of returning to my private business.—I am, Sir, your obedient servant,   ROBERT LOUIS STEVENSON.

VI

TO THE EDITOR OF THE "TIMES"

Apia, September 14, 1892.

SIR,—The Peninsula of Mulinuu was claimed by the German firm; and in case their claim should be found good, they had granted to the Samoan Government an option to buy at a certain figure.   Hereon stand the houses of our officials, in particular that of the Chief Justice.   It has long been a problem here whether this gentleman paid any rent, and the problem is now solved; the Chief Justice of Samoa was a squatter.   On the ground that the Government was about to purchase the peninsula, he occupied a house; on the ground that the Germans were about to sell it, he refused to pay them any rent.   The firm seemed to have no remedy but to summon the squatter before himself, and hear over again from the official what they had heard already from the disastrous tenant.   But even in Samoa an ingenious man, inspired by annoyance, may find means of self-protection.   The house was no part of the land, nor included in the option; the firm put it up for sale; and the Government, under pain of seeing the Chief Justice houseless, was obliged to buy it.

In the meanwhile the German claim to Mulinuu was passed by the Land Commission and sent on to the Chief Justice on the 17th of May.   He ended by confirming the report; but though his judgment bears date the 9th of August, it was not made public till the 15th.   So far as we are aware, and certainly so far as Samoa has profited by his labours, his Honour may be said to have had nothing else to do but attend to this one piece of business; he was being paid to do so at the rate of £100 a month; and it took him ninety days, or about as long as it took Napoleon to recapture and to lose again his empire.   But better late than never; and the Germans, rejoicing in the decision, summoned the Government to complete the purchase or to waive their option.   There was again a delay in answering, for the policy of all parts of this extraordinary Government is on one model; and when the answer came it was only to announce a fresh deception.   The German claim had passed the Land Commission and the Supreme Court, it was good against objections, but it appeared it was not yet good for registration, and must still be resurveyed by a "Government surveyor." The option thus continues to brood over the land of Mulinuu, the Government to squat there without payment, and the German firm to stand helpless and dispossessed. What can they do? Their adversary is their only judge. I hear it calculated that the present state of matters may be yet spun out for months, at the end of which period there must come at last a day of reckoning; and the purchase-money will have to be found or the option to be waived and the Government to flit elsewhere. As for the question of arrears of rent, it will be in judicious hands, and his Honour may be trusted to deal with it in a manner suitable to the previous history of the case.

But why (it will be asked) spin out by these excessive methods a thread of such tenuity? Why go to such lengths for four months longer of fallacious solvency? I expect not to be believed, but I think the Government still hopes. A war-ship, under a hot-headed captain, might be decoyed into hostilities; the taxes might begin to come in again; the three Powers might become otherwise engaged and the little stage of Samoa escape observation—indeed, I know not what they hope, but they hope something. There lives on in their breasts a remainder coal of ambition still unquenched. Or it is only so that I can explain a late astonishing sally of his Honour's. In a long and elaborate judgment he has pared the nails, and indeed removed the fingers, of his only rival, the municipal magistrate. For eighteen months he has seen the lower Court crowded with affairs, the while his own stood unfrequented like an obsolete churchyard. He may have remarked with envy many hundred cases passing through his rival's hands, cases of assault, cases of larceny, ranging in the last four months from 2s. up to £1 12s.; or he may have viewed with displeasure that despatch of business which was characteristic of the Magistrate, Mr. Cooper. An end, at least, has been made of these abuses; Mr. Cooper is henceforth to draw his salary for the *minimum* of public service; and all larcenies and assaults, however trivial, must go, according to the nationality of those concerned, before the Consular or the Supreme Courts.

To this portentous judgment there are two sides—a practical and legal. And first as to the practical. For every blow struck or shilling stolen the parties must now march out to Mulinuu and place themselves at the mercy of a Court, which if Hamlet had known, he would have referred with more emotion to the law's delays. It is feared they will not do so, and that crime will go on in consequence unpunished, and increased by indulgence. But this is nothing. The Court of the municipal magistrate was a convenient common-ground and clearing-house for our manifold nationalities. It has now been, for all purpose of serious utility, abolished, and the result is distraction. There was a recent trumpery case, heard by Mr. Cooper amid shouts of mirth. It resolved itself (if I remember rightly) into three charges of assault with counter-charges, and three of abusive language with the same; and the parties represented only two nationalities—a small allowance for Apia. Yet in our new world, since the Chief Justice's decision, this vulgar shindy would have split up into six several suits before three different Courts; the charges must have been heard by one judge, the counter-charges by another; the whole nauseous evidence six times repeated, and the lawyers six times feed.

Remains the legal argument. His Honour admits the municipality to be invested "with such legislative powers as generally constitute a police jurisdiction"; he does not deny the municipality is empowered to take steps for the protection of the person, and it was argued this implied a jurisdiction in cases of assault. But this argument (observes his Honour) "proves too much, and consequently nothing. For like reasons the municipal council should have power to provide for the punishment of all felonies against the person, and I suppose the property as well." And, filled with a just sense that a merely police jurisdiction should be limited, he limits it with a vengeance by the exclusion of all assaults and all larcenies. A pity he had not looked into the Berlin Act! He would have found it already limited there by the same power which called it into being—limited to fines not exceeding $200 and imprisonment not extending beyond 180 days. Nay, and I think he might have even reasoned from this discovery that he was himself somewhat in error. For, assaults and larcenies being excluded, what kind of enormity is that which is to be visited with a fine of £40 or an imprisonment of half a year? It is perhaps childish to pursue further this childish controversialist. But there is one passage, if he had dipped into the Berlin Act, that well might have arrested his attention: that in which he is himself empowered to deal with "crimes and offences, . . . subject, however, to the provisions defining the jurisdiction of the municipal magistrate of Apia."

I trust, Sir, this is the last time I shall have to trouble you with these twopenny concerns. But until some step is taken by the three Powers, or until I have quite exhausted your indulgence, I shall continue to report our scandals as they arise. Once more, one thing or other: Either what I write is false, and I should be chastised as a calumniator; or else it is true, and these officials are unfit for their position.—I am, etc.,

ROBERT LOUIS STEVENSON.

P. S.—The mail is already closed when I receive at last decisive confirmation of the purchase of the *Samoa Times* by the Samoan Government. It has never been denied; it is now admitted. The paper which they bought so recently, they are already trying to sell; and have received and refused an offer of £150 for what they bought for upwards of £600. Surely we may now demand the attention of the three Powers.

VII

TO THE EDITOR OF THE "PALL MALL GAZETTE"

I

September 4, 1893.

In June it became clear that the King's Government was weary of waiting upon Europe, as it had been clear long before that Europe would do nothing. The last commentary on the Berlin Act was read. Malietoa Laupepa had been put in *ex auctoritate* by the Powers; the Powers would not support him even by a show of strength, and there was nothing left but to fall back on an "Election according to the Laws and Customs of Samoa"—by arbitrament of rifle-bullets and blackened faces. Instantly heaven was darkened by a brood of rumours, random calumnies, and idle tales. As we rode, late at night, through the hamlet near my house, we saw fires lighted in the houses, and eager talkers discussing the last report. The King was sick; he was dying; he was perfectly well; he was seen riding furiously by night in the back parts of Apia, and covering his face as he rode. Mataafa was in favour with the Germans; he was to be made a German king; he was secure of the support of all Samoa; he had no following whatsoever. The name of every chief and village (with many that were new to the hearer) came up in turn, to be dubbed Laupepa, or Mataafa, or both at the same time, or neither. Dr. George Brown, the missionary, had just completed a tour of the islands. There are few men in the world with a more mature knowledge of native character, and I applied to him eagerly for an estimate of the relative forces. "When the first shot is fired, and not before," said he, "you will know who is who." The event has shown that he might have gone yet further; for even after shots were fired and men slain, an important province was still hesitating and trimming.

Mataafa lay in Malie. He had an armed picket at a ford some two miles from Apia, where they sat in a prodigious state of vigilance and glee; and his whole troop, although not above five hundred strong, appeared animated with the most warlike spirit. For himself, he waited, as he had waited for two years; wrote eloquent letters, the time to answer which was quite gone by; and looked on while his enemies painfully collected their forces. Doubtless to the last he was assured and deceived by vain promises of help.

The process of gathering a royal army in Samoa is cumbrous and dilatory in the extreme. There is here none of the expedition of the fiery cross and the bale-fire; but every step is diplomatic. Each village, with a great expense of eloquence, has to be wiled with promises and spurred with threats, and the greater chieftains make stipulations ere they will march. Tamasese, son to the late German puppet, and heir of his ambitions, demanded the vice-kingship as the price of his accession, though I am assured that he demanded it in vain. The various provinces returned various and unsatisfactory answers. Atua was off and on; Tuamasaga was divided; Tutuila recalcitrant; and for long the King sat almost solitary under the windy palms of Mulinuu. It seemed indeed as if the war was off, and the whole archipelago unanimous (in the native phrase) to sit still and plant taro.

But at last, in the first days of July, Atua began to come in. Boats arrived, thirty and fifty strong, a drum and a very ill-played bugle giving time to the oarsmen, the whole crew uttering at intervals a savage howl; and on the decked fore-sheets of the boat the village champion, frantically capering and dancing. Parties were to be seen encamped in palm-groves with their rifles stacked. The shops were emptied of red handkerchiefs, the rallying-sign, or (as a man might say) the uniform of the Royal army. There was spirit shown; troops of handsome lads marched in a right manly fashion, with their guns on their shoulders, to the music of the drum and the bugle or the tin whistle. From a hamlet close to my own doors a contingent of six men marched out. Their leader's kit contained one stick of tobacco, four boxes of matches, and the inevitable red handkerchief; in his case it was of silk, for he had come late to the purchasing, and the commoner materials were exhausted. This childish band of braves marched one afternoon to a neighbouring hill, and the same night returned to their houses on the ground that it was "uncomfortable" in the bush. An excellent old fellow, who had had enough of war in many campaigns, took refuge in my service from the conscription, but in vain. The village had decided no warrior might hang back. One summoner arrived; and then followed some negotiations—I have no authority to say what: enough that the messenger departed and our friend remained. But, alas! a second envoy followed and proved to be of sterner composition; and with a basket full of food, kava, and tobacco, the reluctant hero proceeded to the wars. I am sure they had few handsomer soldiers, if, perhaps, some that were more willing. And he would have been better to be armed. His gun—but in Mr. Kipling's pleasant catchword, that is another story.

War, to the Samoan of mature years, is often an unpleasant necessity. To the young boy it is a heaven of immediate pleasures, as well as an opportunity of ultimate glory. Women march with the troops—even the Taupo-sa, or sacred maid of the village, accompanies her father in the field to carry cartridges, and bring him water to drink,—and their bright eyes are ready to "rain influence" and reward valour. To what grim deeds this practice may conduct I shall have to say later on. In the rally of their arms, it is at least wholly pretty; and I have one pleasant picture of a war-party marching out; the men armed and boastful, their heads bound with the red handkerchief, their faces blacked—and two girls marching in their midst under European parasols.

On Saturday, July 8, by the early morning, the troops began to file westward from Apia, and about noon found themselves face to face with the lines of Mataafa in the German plantation of Vaitele. The armies immediately fraternised; kava was made by the ladies, as who should say tea, at home, and partaken of by the braves with many truculent expressions. One chief on the King's side, revolted by the extent of these familiarities, began to beat his followers with a staff. But both parties were still intermingled between the lines, and the chiefs on either side were conversing, and even embracing, at the moment when an accidental, or perhaps a treacherous, shot precipitated the engagement. I cannot find there was any decisive difference in the numbers actually under fire; but the Mataafas appear to have been ill posted and ill led. Twice their flank was turned, their line enfiladed, and themselves driven, with the loss of about thirty, from two successive cattle walls. A third wall afforded them a more effectual shelter, and night closed on the field of battle without further advantage. All night the Royal troops hailed volleys of bullets at this obstacle. With the earliest light, a charge proved it to be quite deserted, and from farther down the coast smoke was seen rising from the houses of Malie. Mataafa had precipitately fled, destroying behind him the village, which, for two years, he had been raising and beautifying.

So much was accomplished: what was to follow? Mataafa took refuge in Manono, and cast up forts. His enemies, far from following up this advantage, held *fonos* and made speeches and found fault. I believe the majority of the King's army had marched in a state of continuous indecision, and maintaining an attitude of impartiality more to be admired in the cabinet of the philosopher than in the field of war. It is certain at least that only one province has as yet fired a shot for Malietoa Laupepa. The valour of the Tuamasaga was sufficient and prevailed. But Atua was in the rear, and has as yet done nothing. As for the men of Crana, so far from carrying out the plan agreed upon, and blocking the men of Malie, on the morning of the 8th, they were entertaining an embassy from Mataafa, and they suffered his fleet of boats to escape without a shot through certain dangerous narrows of the lagoon, and the chief himself to pass on foot and unmolested along the whole foreshore of their province. No adequate excuse has been made for this half-heartedness—or treachery. It was a piece of the whole which was a specimen. There are too many strings in a Samoan intrigue for the merely European mind to follow, and the desire to serve upon both sides, and keep a door open for reconciliation, was manifest almost throughout. A week passed in these divided counsels. Savaii had refused to receive Mataafa—it is said they now hesitated to rise for the King, and demanded instead a *fono* (or council) of both sides. And it seemed at least possible that the Royal army might proceed no farther, and the unstable alliance be dissolved.

On Sunday, the 16th, Her British Majesty's ship *Katoomba*, Captain Bickford, C.M.G., arrived in Apia with fresh orders. Had she but come ten days earlier the whole of this miserable business would have been prevented, for the three Powers were determined to maintain Malietoa Laupepa by arms, and had declared finally against Mataafa. Right or wrong, it was at least a decision, and therefore welcome. It may not be best—it was something. No honest friend to Samoa can pretend anything but relief that the three Powers should at last break their vacillating silence. It is of a piece with their whole policy in the islands that they should have hung in stays for upwards of two years—of a piece with their almost uniform ill-fortune that, eight days before their purpose was declared, war should have marked the country with burned houses and severed heads.

II

There is another side to the medal of Samoan warfare. So soon as an advantage is obtained, a new and (to us) horrible animal appears upon the scene—the Head-hunter. Again and again we have reasoned with our boys against this bestial practice; but reason and (upon this one point) even ridicule are vain. They admit it to be indefensible; they allege its imperative necessity. One young man, who had seen his father take a head in the late war, spoke of the scene with shuddering revolt, and yet said he must go and do likewise himself in the war which was to come. How else could a man prove he was brave ? and had not every country its own customs ?

Accordingly, as occasion offered, these same pleasing children, who had just been drinking kava with their opponents, fell incontinently on the dead and dying, and secured their grisly trophies. It should be said, in fairness, that the Mataafas had no opportunity to take heads, but that their chief, taught by the lesson of Fangalii, had forbidden the practice. It is doubtful if he would have been obeyed, and yet his power over his people was so great that the German plantation, where they lay some time, and were at last defeated, had not to complain of the theft of a single cocoanut. Hateful as it must always be to mutilate and murder the disabled, there were in this day's affray in Vaitele circumstances yet more detestable. Fifteen heads were brought in all to Mulinuu. They were carried with parade in front of the fine house which our late President built for himself before he was removed. Here, on the verandah, the King sat to receive them, and utter words of course and compliment to each successful warrior. They were *spoila opima* in the number. Leaupepe, Mataafa's nephew—or, as Samoans say, his son—had fallen by the first wall, and whether from those sentiments of kindred and friendship that so often unite the combatants in civil strife, or to mark by an unusual formality the importance of the conquest, not only his head but his mutilated body also was brought in. From the mat in which the corpse was enveloped a bloody hand protruded, and struck a chill in

480

white eye-witnesses. It were to attribute to (Malietoa) Laupepa sentiments entirely foreign to his race and training, if we were to suppose him
otherwise than gratified.

But it was not so throughout. Every country has its customs, say
native apologists, and one of the most decisive customs of Samoa ensures
the immunity of women. They go to the front, as our women of yore
went to a tournament. Bullets are blind; and they must take their risk
of bullets, but of nothing else. They serve out cartridges and water;
they jeer the faltering and defend the wounded. Even in this skirmish
of Vaitele they distinguished themselves on either side. One dragged her
skulking husband from a hole, and drove him to the front. Another,
seeing her lover fall, snatched up his gun, kept the head-hunters at bay,
and drew him unmutilated from the field. Such services they have been
accustomed to pay for centuries; and often, in the course of centuries, a
bullet or a spear must have despatched one of these warlike angels.
Often enough, too, the head-hunter, springing ghoul-like on fallen bodies,
must have decapitated a woman for a man. But, the case arising, there
was an established etiquette. So soon as the error was discovered the
head was buried, and the exploit forgotten. There had never yet, in the
history of Samoa, occurred an instance in which a man had taken a
woman's head and kept it and laid it at his monarch's feet.

Such was the strange and horrid spectacle, which must have immediately shaken the heart of Laupepa, and has since covered the faces of his
party with confusion. It is not quite certain if there were three, or only
two; a recent attempt to reduce the number to one must be received with
caution as an afterthought; the admissions in the beginning were too
explicit, the panic of shame and fear had been too sweeping. There is
scarce a woman of our native friends in Apia who can speak upon the
subject without terror; scarce any man without humiliation. And the
shock was increased out of measure by the fact that the head—or one of
the heads—was recognised; recognised for the niece of one of the greatest
of court ladies; recognised for a Taupo-sa, or sacred maid of a village
from Savaii. It seemed incredible that she—who had been chosen for virtue
and beauty, who went everywhere attended by the fairest maidens, and
watched over by vigilant duennas, whose part it was, in holiday costume,
to receive guests, to make kava, and to be the leader of the revels—
should become the victim of a brutal rally in a cow-park, and have her
race exposed for a trophy to the victorious king.

481

In all this muttering of aversion and alarm, no word has been openly said. No punishment, no disgrace, has been inflicted on the perpetrators of the outrage. King, Consuls, and mission appear to have held their peace alike. I can understand a certain apathy in whites. Head-hunting, they say, is a horrid practice: and will not stop to investigate its finer shades. But the Samoan himself does not hesitate; for him the act is portentous; and if it go unpunished, and set a fashion, its consequences must be damnable. This is not a breach of a Christian virtue, of something half-learned by rote, and from foreigners, in the last thirty years. It is a flying in the face of their own native, instinctive, and traditional standard: tenfold more ominous and degrading. And, taking the matter for all in all, it seems to me that head-hunting itself should be firmly and immediately suppressed. "How else can a man prove himself to be brave?" my friend asked. But often enough these are but fraudulent trophies. On the morrow of the fight at Vaitele, an Atua man discovered a body lying in the bush; he took the head. A day or two ago a party was allowed to visit Manono. The King's troops on shore, observing them put off from the rebel island, leaped to the conclusion that this must be the wounded going to Apia, launched off at once two armed boats and overhauled the others—after heads. The glory of such exploits is not apparent; their power for degradation strikes the eyes. Lieutenant Ulfsparre, our late Swedish Chief of Police and Commander of the forces, told his men that if any of them took a head his own hand should avenge it. That was talking; I should like to see all in the same story —King, Consuls, and missionaries—included.

III

The three Powers have at last taken hold here in Apia. But they came the day after the fair; and the immediate business on hand is very delicate. This morning, 18th, Captain Bickford, followed by two Germans, sailed for Manono. If he shall succeed in persuading Mataafa to surrender, all may be well. If he cannot, this long train of blunders may end in—what is so often the result of blundering in the field of politics—a horrible massacre. Those of us who remember the services of Mataafa, his unfailing generosity and moderation in the past, and his bereavement in the present—as well as those who are only interested in a mass of men and women, many of them our familiar friends, now pent up on an island, and beleaguered by three war-ships and a Samoan army —await the issue with dreadful expectation.

VIII

Vailima, Apia, April 23, 1894.

Sir,—I last addressed you on the misconduct of certain officials here, and I was so far happy as to have had my facts confirmed in every particular with but one exception. That exception, the affair of the dynamite, has been secretly smuggled away; you shall look in vain in either Bluebook or White-book for any mention even of the charge; it is gone like the conjurer's orange. I might have been tempted to inquire into the reason of this conspiracy of silence, whether the idea was conceived in the bosoms of the three Powers themselves, or whether in the breasts of the three Consuls, because one of their number was directly implicated. And I might have gone on to consider the moral effect of such suppressions, and to show how very idle they were, and how very undignified, in the face of a small and compact population, where everybody sees and hears, where everybody knows, and talks, and laughs. But only a personal question remained, which I judged of no interest to the public. The essential was accomplished. Baron Senfft was gone already. Mr. Cedercrantz still lingered among us in the character (I may say) of a private citizen, his Court at last closed, only his pocket open for the receipt of his salary, representing the dignity of the Berlin Act by sitting in the wind on Mulinuu Point for several consecutive months—a curious phantom or survival of a past age. The new officials were not as yet, because they had not been created. And we fell into our old estate of government by the three Consuls, as it was in the beginning before the Berlin Act existed; as it seems it will be to the end, after the Berlin Act has been swept away.

It was during the time of this triumvirate, and wholly at their instigation and under their conduct, that Mataafa was defeated, driven to Manono, and (three war-ships coming opportunely to hand) forced to surrender. I have been called a partisan of this chief's, and I accept the term. I thought him, on the whole, the most honest man in Samoa, not excepting white officials. I ventured to think he had been hardly used by the Treaty Powers; I venture to think so still. It was my opinion that he should have been conjoined with Malietoa as Vice-King; and I have seen no reason to change that opinion, except that the time for it is past. Mataafa has played and lost; an exile, and stripped of his titles, he walks the exiguous beach of Jaluit, sees the German flag over his head, and yearns for the land-wind of Upolu. In the politics of Samoa he is no longer a factor; and it only remains to speak of the manner in which his rebellion was suppressed and punished. Deportation is, to the Samoan mind, the punishment next to death, and thirteen of the chiefs engaged were deported with their leader. Twenty-seven others were cast into the jail. There they lie still; the Government makes almost no attempt to feed them, and they must depend on the activity of their families and the charity of pitying whites. In the meantime, these very families are overloaded with fines, the exorbitant sum of more than £6600 having been laid on the chiefs and villages that took part with Mataafa.

So far we can only complain that the punishments have been severe and the prison commissariat absent. But we have, besides, to regret the repeated scandals in connection with the conduct of the war, and we look in vain for any sign of punishment. The Consuls had to employ barbarous hands; we might expect outrages; we did expect them to be punished, or at least disowned. Thus, certain Mataafa chiefs were landed, and landed from a British man-of-war, to be shamefully abused, beaten, and struck with whips along the main street of Mulinuu. There was no punishment, there was even no inquiry; the three Consuls winked. Only one man was found honest and bold enough to open his mouth, and that was my old enemy, Mr. Cedercrantz. Walking in Mulinuu, in his character of disinterested spectator, gracefully desipient, he came across the throng of these rabblers and their victims. He had forgotten that he was an official, he remembered that he was a man. It was his last public appearance in Samoa to interfere; it was certainly his best. Again, the Government troops in the field took the heads of girls, a detestable felony even in Samoan eyes. They carried them in procession to Mulinuu, and made of them an oblation to that melancholy effigy the King, who (sore against his will) sat on the verandah of the Government building, publicly to receive this affront, publicly to utter the words of compliment and thanks which constitute the highest reward known to Samoan bravery, and crowned as heroes those who should have been hanged like dogs. And again the three Consuls unanimously winked. There was no punishment, there was even no inquiry.

Lastly, there is the story of Manono. Three hours were given to

Mataafa to accept the terms of the ultimatum, and the time had almost elapsed when his boats put forth, and more than elapsed before he came alongside the *Katoomba* and surrendered formally to Captain Bickford. In the dusk of the evening, when all the ships had sailed, flames were observed to rise from the island. Mataafa flung himself on his knees before Captain Bickford, and implored protection for his women and children left behind, and the captain put back the ship and despatched one of the Consuls to inquire. The *Katoomba* had been about seventy hours in the islands. Captain Bickford was a stranger; he had to rely on the Consuls implicitly. At the same time, he knew that the Government troops had been suffered to land for the purpose of restoring order, and with the understanding that no reprisals should be committed on the adherents of Mataafa; and he charged the emissary with his emphatic disapproval, threats of punishment on the offenders, and reminders that the war had now passed under the responsibility of the three Powers. I cannot condescend on what this Consul saw during his visit; I can only say what he reported on his return. He reported all well, and the chiefs on the Government side fraternising and making *ava* with those on Mataafa's. It may have been; at least it is strange. The burning of the island proceeded, fruit-trees were cut down, women stripped naked; a scene of brutal disorder reigned all night, and left behind it, over a quarter of the island, ruin. If they fraternised with Mataafa's chieftains they must have been singularly inconsistent, for, the next we learn of the two parties, they were beating, spitting upon, and insulting them along the highway. The next morning in Apia I asked the same Consul if there had not been some houses burned. He told me no. I repeated the question, alleging the evidence of officers on board the *Katoomba* who had seen the flames increase and multiply as they steamed away; whereupon he had this remarkable reply—" O! huts, huts, huts! There is n't a house, a frame house, on the island." The case to plain men stands thus: The people of Manono were insulted, their food-trees cut down, themselves left houseless; not more than ten houses—I beg the Consul's pardon, huts—escaped the rancour of their enemies; and to this day they may be seen to dwell in shanties on the site of their former residences, the pride of the Samoan heart. The ejaculation of the Consul was thus at least prophetic; and the traveller who revisits to-day the shores of the " Garden Island" may well exclaim in his turn, " Huts, huts, huts!"

The same measure was served out, in the mere wantonness of clan hatred, to Apolima, a nearly inaccessible islet in the straits of the same name; almost the only property saved there (it is amusing to remember) being a framed portrait of Lady Jersey, which its custodian escaped with into the bush, as it were the palladium and chief treasure of the inhabitants. The solemn promise passed by Consuls and captains in the name of the three Powers was thus broken; the troops employed were allowed their bellyful of barbarous outrage. And again there was no punishment, there was no inquiry; there was no protest, there was not a word said to disown the act or disengage the honour of the three Powers. I do not say the Consuls desired to be disobeyed, though the case looks black against one gentleman, and even he is perhaps only to be accused of levity and divided interest; it was doubtless important for him to be early in Apia, where he combines with his diplomatic functions the management of a thriving business as commission agent and auctioneer. I do say of all of them that they took a very nonchalant view of their duty.

I told myself that this was the government of the Consular Triumvirate. When the new officials came it would cease; it would pass away like a dream in the night; and the solid *Pax Romana* of the Berlin General Act would succeed. After all, what was there to complain of ? The Consuls had shown themselves no slovens and no sentimentalists. They had shown themselves not very particular, but in one sense very thorough. Rebellion was to be put down swiftly and rigorously, if need were with the hand of Cromwell; at least it was to be put down. And in these unruly islands I was prepared almost to welcome the face of Rhadamanthine severity.

And now it appears it was all a mistake. The government by the Berlin General Act is no more than a mask, and a very expensive one, for government by the Consular Triumvirate. Samoa pays (or tries to pay) £2200 a year to a couple of helpers; and they dare not call their souls their own. They take their walks abroad with an anxious eye on the three Consuls, like two well-behaved children with three nurses; and the Consuls, smiling superior, allow them to amuse themselves with the routine of business. But let trouble come, and the farce is suspended. At the whistle of a squall these heaven-born mariners seize the tiller, and the £2200 amateurs are knocked sprawling on the bilge. At the first beat of the drum, the treaty officials are sent below, gently protesting, like a pair of old ladies, and behold! the indomitable Consuls ready to clear the

486

wreck and make the deadly cutlass shine. And their method, studied under the light of a new example, wears another air. They are not so Rhadamanthine as we thought. Something that we can only call a dignified panic presides over their deliberations. They have one idea to lighten the ship. "Overboard with the ballast, the mainmast, and the chronometer!" is the cry. In the last war they got rid (first) of the honour of their respective countries, and (second) of all idea that Samoa was to be governed in a manner consistent with civilisation, or Government troops punished for any conceivable misconduct. In the present war they have sacrificed (first) the prestige of the new Chief Justice, and (second) the very principle for which they had contended so vigorously and so successfully in the war before—that rebellion was a thing to be punished.

About the end of last year, that war, a war of the Tupuas under Tamasese the younger, which was a necessary pendant to the crushing of Mataafa, began to make itself heard of in obscure grumblings. It was but a timid business. One half of the Tupua party, the whole province of Atua, never joined the rebellion, but sulked in their villages, and spent the time in indecisive eloquence and barren embassies. Tamasese, by a trick eminently Samoan, "went in the high bush and the mountains," carrying a gun like a private soldier—served, in fact, with his own troops *incognito*—and thus, to Samoan eyes, waived his dynastic pretensions. And the war, which was announced in the beginning with a long catalogue of complaints against the King and a distinct and ugly threat to the white population of Apia, degenerated into a war of defence by the province of Aána against the eminently brutal troops of Savaii, in which sympathy was generally and justly with the rebels. Savaii, raging with private clan hatred and the lust of destruction, was put at free quarters in the disaffected province, repeated on a wider scale the outrages of Manono and Apolima, cut down the food-trees, stripped and insulted the women, robbed the children of their little possessions, burned the houses, killed the horses, the pigs, the dogs, the cats, along one half the seaboard of Aána, and in the prosecution of these manly exploits managed (to the joy of all) to lose some sixty men killed, wounded, and drowned.

Government by the Treaty of Berlin was still erect when, one fine morning, in walked the three Consuls, totally uninvited, with a proclamation prepared and signed by themselves, without any mention of anybody else. They had awoke to a sense of the danger of the situation and their own indispensable merits. The two children knew their day was over; the nurses had come for them. Who can blame them for their timidity? The Consuls have the ears of the Governments; they are the authors of those despatches of which, in the ripeness of time, Blue-books and White-books are made up; they had dismissed (with some little assistance from yourself) MM. Cedercrantz and Senfft von Pilsach, and they had strangled, like an illegitimate child, the scandal of the dynamite. The Chief Justice and the President made haste to disappear between decks, and left the ship of the State to the three volunteers. There was no lack of activity. The Consuls went up to Atua, they went down to Aána; the oarsmen toiled, the talking men pleaded; they are said to have met with threats in Atua, and to have yielded to them —at least, in but a few days' time they came home to us with a new treaty of pacification. Of course, and as before, the Government troops were whitewashed; the Savaii ruffians had been stripping women and killing cats in the interests of the Berlin Treaty; there was to be no punishment and no inquiry; let them retire to Savaii with their booty and their dead. Offensive as this cannot fail to be, there is still some slight excuse for it. The King is no more than one out of several chiefs of clans. His strength resides in the willing obedience of the Tuamasaga, and a portion—I have to hope a bad portion—of the island of Savaii. To punish any of these supporters must always be to accept a risk; and the golden opportunity had been allowed to slip at the moment of the Mataafa war.

What was more original was the treatment of the rebels. They were under arms that moment against the Government; they had fought and sometimes vanquished; they had taken heads and carried them to Tamasese. And the terms granted were to surrender fifty rifles, to make some twenty miles of road, to pay some old fines—and to be forgiven! The loss of fifty rifles to people destitute of any shadow of a gunsmith to repair them when they are broken, and already notoriously short of ammunition, is a trifle; the number is easy to be made up of those that are out of commission; for there is not the least stipulation as to their value; any synthesis of old iron and smashed wood that can be called a gun is to be taken from its force. The road, as likely as not, will never be made. The fines have nothing to say to this war; in any reasonably governed country they should never have figured in the treaty; they had been inflicted before, and were due before. Before the rebellion

488

began, the beach had rung with I know not what indiscreet bluster: the natives were to be read a lesson; Tamasese (by name) was to be hanged; and after what had been done to Mataafa, I was so innocent as to listen with awe. And now the rebellion has come, and this was the punishment! There might well have been a doubt in the mind of any chief who should have been tempted to follow the example of Mataafa; but who is it that would not dare to follow Tamasese?

For some reason—I know not what, unless it be fear—there is a strong prejudice amongst whites against any interference with the bestial practice of head-hunting. They say it would be impossible to identify the criminals—a thing notoriously contrary to fact. A man does not take a head, as he steals an apple, for secret degustation; the essence of the thing is its publicity. After the girls' heads were brought into Mulinuu I pressed Mr. Cusack-Smith to take some action. He proposed a paper of protest, to be signed by the English residents. We made rival drafts; his was preferred, and I have heard no more of it. It has not been offered me to sign; it has not been published; under a paper-weight in the British Consulate I suppose it may yet be found! Meanwhile, his Honour, Mr. Ide, the new Chief Justice, came to Samoa and took spirited action. He engineered an ordinance through the House of Faipule, inflicting serious penalties on any who took heads, and the papers at the time applauded his success. The rebellion followed, the troops were passing to the front, and with excellent resolution Mr. Ide harangued the chiefs, reiterated the terms of the new law, and promised unfailing vengeance on offenders. It was boldly done, and he stood committed beyond possibility of retreat to enforce this his first important edict. Great was the commotion, great the division, in the Samoan mind. "O! we have had Chief Justices before," said a visitor to my house; "we know what they are; I will take a head if I can get one." Others were more doubtful, but thought none could be so bold as lay a hand on the peculiar institution of these islands. Yet others were convinced. Savaii took heads; but when they sent one to Mulinuu a messenger met them by the convent gates from the King; he would none of it, and the trophy must be ingloriously buried. Savaii took heads also, and Tamasese accepted the presentation. Tuamasaga, on the other hand, obeyed the Chief Justice, and (the occasion being thrust upon them) contented themselves with taking the dead man's ears. On the whole, about one third of the troops engaged, and our not very firm Monarch himself, kept the letter of the ordinance. And it was upon this scene of partial, but really cheering, success that the Consuls returned with their general pardon! The Chief Justice was not six months old in the islands. He had succeeded to a position complicated by the failure of his predecessor. Personally, speaking face to face with the chiefs, he had put his authority in pledge that the ordinance should be enforced. And he found himself either forgotten or betrayed by the three Consuls. These volunteers had made a liar of him; they had administered to him, before all Samoa, a triple buffet. I must not wonder, though I may still deplore, that Mr. Ide accepted the position thus made for him. There was a deal of alarm in Apia. To refuse the treaty thus hastily and shamefully cobbled up would have increased it tenfold. Already, since the declaration of war and the imminence of the results, one of the papers had ratted, and the white population were girding at the new ordinance. It was feared besides that the native Government, though they had voted, were secretly opposed to it. It was almost certain they would try to prevent its application to the loyalist offenders of Savaii The three Consuls in the negotiations of the treaty had fully illustrated both their want of sympathy with the ordinance and their want of regard for the position of the Chief Justice. " In short, I am to look for no support, whether physical or moral?" asked Mr. Ide; and I could make but the one answer—" Neither physical nor moral." It was a hard choice; and he elected to accept the terms of the treaty without protest. And the next war (if we are to continue to enjoy the benefits of the Berlin Act) will probably show us the result in an enlarged assortment of heads, and the next difficulty perhaps prove to us the diminished prestige of the Chief Justice. Mr. Ide announces his intention of applying the law in the case of another war; but I very much fear the golden opportunity has again been lost. About one third of the troops believed him this time; how many will believe him the next?

It will doubtless be answered that the Consuls were affected by the alarm in Apia and actuated by the desire to save white lives. I am far from denying that there may be danger; and I believe that the way we are going is the best way to bring it on. In the progressive de-civilisation of these islands—evidenced by the female heads taken in the last war and the treatment of white missionaries in this—our methods of pull devil, pull baker, general indecision, and frequent (though always dignified) panic are the best calculated in the world to bring on a massacre of whites. A consistent dignity, a consistent and independent figure of a Chief Justice, the enforcement of the laws, and, above all, of the laws against barbarity, a Consular Board the same in the presence as in the absence of war-ships, will be found our best defence.

Much as I have already occupied of your space, I would yet ask leave to draw two conclusions.

And first, Mataafa and Tamasese both made war. Both wars were presumably dynastic in character, though the Tupua not rallying to Tamasese as he had expected led him to cover his design. That he carried a gun himself, and himself fired, will not seem to European ears a very important alleviation. Tamasese received heads, sitting as a king, under whatever name; Mataafa had forbidden the taking of heads—of his own accord, and before Mr. Ide had taken office. Tamasese began with threats against the white population; Mataafa never ceased to reassure them and to extend an effectual protection to their property. What is the difference between their cases? That Mataafa was an old man, already famous, who had served his country well, had been appointed King of Samoa, had served in the office, and had been set aside—not, indeed, in the text, but in the protocols of the Berlin Act, by name? I do not grudge his good fortune to Tamasese, who is an amiable, spirited, and handsome young man; and who made a barbarous war, indeed, since heads were taken after the old Samoan practice, but who made it without any of the savagery which we have had reason to comment upon in the camp of his adversaries. I do not grudge the invidious fate that has befallen my old friend and his followers. At first I believed these judgments to be the expression of a severe but equal justice. I find them, on further experience, to be mere measures of the degree of panic in the Consuls, varying directly as the distance of the nearest war-ship. The judgments under which they fell have now no sanctity; they form no longer a precedent; they may perfectly well be followed by a pardon, or a partial pardon, as the authorities shall please. The crime of Mataafa is to have read strictly the first article of the Berlin Act, and not to have read at all (as how should he when it has never been translated?) the insidious protocol which contains its significance; the crime of his followers is to have practised clan fidelity, and to have in consequence raised an *imperium in impervio*, and fought against the Government. Their punishment is to be sent to a coral atoll and detained there prisoners. It does not sound much; it is a great deal. Taken from a mountain island, they must inhabit a narrow strip of reef sunk to the gunwale in the ocean. Sand, stone, and cocoanuts, stone, sand, and pandanus, make the scenery. There is no grass. Here these men, used to the cool, bright mountain rivers of Samoa, must drink with loathing even the brackish water of the coral. The food upon such islands is distressing even to the omnivorous white. To the Samoan, who has that shivering delicacy and ready disgust of the child or the rustic mountaineer, it is intolerable. I remember what our present King looked like, what a phantom he was, when he returned from captivity in the same place. Lastly, these fourteen have been divorced from their families. The daughter of Mataafa somehow broke the *consigne* and accompanied her father; but she only. To this day one of them, Palepa, the wife of Faamoina, is dunning the authorities in vain to be allowed to join her husband—she a young and handsome woman, he an old man and infirm. I cannot speak with certainty, but I believe they are allowed no communication with the prisoners, nor the prisoners with them. My own open experience is brief and conclusive—I have not been suffered to send my friends one stick of tobacco or one pound of *ava*. So much to show the hardships are genuine. I have to ask a pardon for these unhappy victims of untranslated protocols and inconsistent justice. After the case of Tamasese, I ask it almost as of right. As for the other twenty-seven in jail, let the doors be opened at once. They have shown their patience, they have proved their loyalty long enough. On two occasions, when the guards deserted in a body, and again when the Aána prisoners fled, they remained—one may truly say—voluntary prisoners. And at least let them be fed! I have paid taxes to the Samoan Government for some four years, and the most sensible benefit I have received in return has been to be allowed to feed their prisoners.

Second, if the farce of the Berlin Act is to be gone on with, it will be really necessary to moderate among our five Sovereigns—six if we are to count poor Malietoa, who represents to the life the character of the Hare and Many Friends. It is to be presumed that Mr. Ide and Herr Schmidt were chosen for their qualities; it is little good we are likely to get by them if, at every wind of rumour, the three Consuls are to intervene. The three Consuls are paid far smaller salaries, they have no right under the treaty to interfere with the government of autonomous Samoa, and they have contrived to make themselves all in all. The King and a majority of the Faipule fear them and look to them alone, while the legitimate adviser occupies a second place, if that. The misconduct of MM.

Cedercrantz and Senfft von Pilsach was so extreme that the Consuls were obliged to encroach; and now when these are gone the authority acquired in the contest remains with the encroachers. On their side they have no rights, but a tradition of victory, the ear of the Governments at home, and the *vis viva* of the war-ships. For the poor treaty officials, what have they but rights very obscurely expressed and very weakly defended by their predecessors? Thus it comes about that people who are scarcely mentioned in the text of the treaty are, to all intents and purposes, our only rulers. ROBERT LOUIS STEVENSON.

IX.

TO THE EDITOR OF THE "TIMES"

Vailima, Samoa, May 22, 1894.

SIR,—I told you in my last that the Consuls had tinkered up a treaty of peace with the rebels of Aána. A month has gone by, and I would not weary your readers with a story so intricate and purposeless. The Consuls seem to have gone backward and forward, to and fro. To periods of agitated activity, comparable to that of three ants about a broken nest, there succeeded seasons in which they rested from their labours and ruefully considered the result. I believe I am not overstating the case when I say that this treaty was at least twice rehandled, and the date of submission changed, in the interval. And yesterday at length we beheld the first-fruits of the Consular diplomacy. A boat came in from Aána bearing the promised fifty stand of arms—in other words, a talking man, a young chief, and some boatmen in charge of a boat-load of broken ironmongery. The Government (well advised for once) had placed the Embassy under an escort of German blue-jackets, or I think it must have gone ill with the Ambassadors.

So much for Aána and the treaty. With Atua, the other disaffected province, we have been and are on the brink of war. The woods have been patrolled, the army sent to the front, blood has been shed. It consists with my knowledge that the loyalist troops marched against the enemy under a hallucination. One and all believed, a majority of them still believe, that the war-ships were to follow and assist them. Who told them so? If I am to credit the rumours of the natives, as well as the gossip of official circles, a promise had been given to this effect by the Consuls, or at least by one of the Consuls. And when I say that a promise had been given, I mean that it had been sold. I mean that the natives had to buy it by submissions.

493

Let me take an example of these submissions. The native Government increased the salary of Mr. Gurr, the natives' advocate. It was not a largesse; it was rather an act of tardy justice, by which Mr. Gurr received at last the same emoluments as his predecessor in the office. At the same time, with a bankrupt treasury, all fresh expenses are and must be regarded askance. The President, acting under a so-called Treasury regulation, refused to honour the King's order. And a friendly suit was brought, which turned on the validity of this Treasury regulation. This was more than doubtful. The President was a treaty official; hence bound by the treaty. The three Consuls had been acting for him in his absence, using his powers and no other powers whatever under the treaty; and the three Consuls so acting had framed a regulation by which the powers of the President were greatly extended. This was a vicious circle with a vengeance. But the Consuls, with the ordinary partiality of parents for reformed offspring, regarded the regulation as the apple of their eye. They made themselves busy in its defence, they held interviews, it is reported they drew pleas; and it seemed to all that the Chief Justice hesitated. It is certain at least that he long delayed sentence. And during this delay the Consuls showed their power. The native Government was repeatedly called together, and at last forced to rescind the order in favour of Mr. Gurr. It was not done voluntarily, for the Government resisted. It was not done by conviction, for the Government has taken the first opportunity to restore it. If the Consuls did not appear personally in the affair—and I do not know that they did not—they made use of the President as a mouthpiece; and the President delayed the deliberations of the Government until he should receive further instructions from the Consuls. Ten pounds is doubtless a considerable affair to a bankrupt Government. But what were the Consuls doing in this matter of inland administration? What was their right to interfere? What were the arguments with which they overcame the resistance of the Government? I am either very much misinformed, or these gentlemen were trafficking in a merchandise which they did not possess, and selling at a high price the assistance of the war-ships over which (as now appears) they have no control.

Remark the irony of fate. This affair had no sooner been settled, Mr. Gurr's claim cut at the very root, and the Treasury regulation apparently set beyond cavil, than the Chief Justice pulled himself together, and, taking his life in his right hand, delivered sentence in the case. Great was the surprise. Because the Chief Justice had balked so long, it was supposed he would never have taken the leap. And here, upon a sudden, he came down with a decision flat against the Consuls and their Treasury regulation. The Government have, I understand, restored Mr. Gurr's salary in consequence. The Chief Justice, after giving us all a very severe fright, has reinstated himself in public opinion by this tardy boldness; and the Consuls find their conduct judicially condemned.

It was on a personal affront that the Consuls turned on Mr. Cedercrantz. Here is another affront, far more galling and public! I suppose it is but a coincidence that I should find at the same time the clouds beginning to gather about Mr. Ide's head. In a telegram, dated from Auckland, March 30, and copyrighted by the Associated Press, I find the whole blame of the late troubles set down to his account. It is the work of a person worthy of no trust. In one of his charges, and in one only, he is right. The Chief Justice fined and imprisoned certain chiefs of Aána under circumstances far from clear; the act was, to say the least of it, susceptible of misconstruction, and by natives will always be thought of as an act of treachery. But, even for this, it is not possible for me to split the blame justly between Mr. Ide and the three Consuls. In these early days, as now, the three Consuls were always too eager to interfere where they had no business, and the Chief Justice was always too patient or too timid to set them in their place. For the rest of the telegram no qualification is needed. "The Chief Justice was compelled to take steps to disarm the natives." He took no such steps; he never spoke of disarmament except publicly and officially to disown the idea; it was during the days of the Consular Triumvirate that the cry began. "The Chief Justice called upon Malietoa to send a strong force," etc.; the Chief Justice "disregarded the menacing attitude assumed by the Samoans," etc. —these are but the delusions of a fever. The Chief Justice has played no such part; he never called for forces; he never disregarded menacing attitudes, not even those of the Consuls. What we have to complain of in Mr. Ide and Mr. Schmidt is strangely different. We complain that they have been here since November, and the three Consuls are still allowed, when they are not invited, to interfere in the least and the greatest; that they have been here for upwards of six months, and government under the Berlin Treaty is still overridden—and I may say overlaid—by the government of the Consular Triumvirate.

This is the main foundation of our present discontents. This it is that

495

we pray to be relieved from. Out of six Sovereigns, exercising incongruous rights or usurpations on this unhappy island, we pray to be relieved of three. The Berlin Treaty was not our choice; but if we are to have it at all, let us have it plain. Let us have the text, and nothing but the text. Let the three Consuls who have no position under the treaty cease from troubling, cease from raising war and making peace, from passing illegal regulations in the face of day, and from secretly blackmailing the Samoan Government into renunciations of its independence. Afterwards, when we have once seen it in operation, we shall be able to judge whether government under the Berlin Treaty suits or does not suit our case.—I am, Sir, etc.,   ROBERT LOUIS STEVENSON.

X

FROM THE "DAILY CHRONICLE," MARCH 18, 1895

(Subjoined is the full text of the late Robert Louis Stevenson's last letter to Mr. J. F. Hogan, M.P. Apart from its pathetic interest as one of the final compositions of the distinguished novelist, its eloquent terms of pleading for his exiled friend Mataafa, and the light it sheds on Samoan affairs, make it a very noteworthy and instructive document.—ED. D C.)

Vailima, October 7, 1894.

J. F. HOGAN, ESQ., M.P.

DEAR SIR,—My attention was attracted the other day by the thoroughly pertinent questions which you put in the House of Commons, and which the Government failed to answer. It put an idea in my head that you were perhaps the man who might take up a task which I am almost ready to give up. Mataafa is now known to be my hobby. People laugh when they see any mention of his name over my signature, and the *Times*, while it still grants me hospitality, begins to lead the chorus. I know that nothing can be more fatal to Mataafa's cause than that he should be made ridiculous, and I cannot help feeling that a man who makes his bread by writing fiction labours under the disadvantage of suspicion when he touches on matters of fact. If I were even backed up before the world by one other voice, people might continue to listen, and in the end something might be done. But so long as I stand quite alone, telling the same story, which becomes, apparently, not only more tedious, but less credible by repetition, I feel that I am doing nothing good, possibly even some evil.

Now, Sir, you have shown by your questions in the House, not only that you remember Mataafa, but that you are instructed in his case, and this exposes you to the trouble of reading this letter.

Mataafa was made the prisoner of the three Powers. He had been guilty of rebellion; but surely rather formally than really. He was the appointed King of Samoa. The treaty set him aside, and he obeyed the three Powers. His successor — or I should rather say his successor's advisers and surroundings — fell out with him. He was disgusted by the spectacle of their misgovernment. In this humour he fell to the study of the Berlin Act, and was misled by the famous passage, "His successor shall be duly elected according to the laws and customs of Samoa." It is to be noted that what I will venture to call the infamous protocol — a measure equally of German vanity, English cowardice, and American *incuria* — had not been and *has never yet been* translated into the Samoan language. They feared light because their works were darkness. For what he did during what I can only call his candidature, I must refer you to the last chapter of my book. It was rebellion to the three Powers; to him it was not rebellion. The troops of the King attacked him first. The sudden arrival and sudden action of Captain Bickford concluded the affair in the very beginning. Mataafa surrendered. He surrendered to Captain Bickford. He was brought back to Apia on Captain Bickford's ship. I shall never forget the captain pointing to the British ensign and saying, "Tell them they are safe under that." And the next thing we learned, Mataafa and his chiefs were transferred to a German war-ship and carried to the Marshalls.

Who was responsible for this? Who is responsible now for the care and good treatment of these political prisoners? I am far from hinting that the Germans actually maltreat him. I know even that many of the Germans regard him with respect. But I can only speak of what I know here. It is impossible to send him or any of his chiefs either a present or a letter. I believe the mission (Catholic) has been allowed some form of communication. On the same occasion I sent down letters and presents. They were refused; and the officer of the deck on the German war-ship had so little reticence as to pass the remark, " O, you see, you like Mataafa; we don't." In short, communication is so completely sundered that for anything we can hear in Samoa, they may all have been hanged at the yard-arm two days out.

To take another instance. The high chief Faamoina was recently married to a young and pleasing wife. She desired to follow her husband, an old man, in bad health, and so deservedly popular that he had been given the by-name of "*Papalagi Mativa*," or "Poor White Man," on account of his charities to our countrymen. She was refused. Again and again she has renewed her applications to be allowed to rejoin him, and without the least success.

It has been decreed by some one, I know not whom, that Faamoina must have no one to nurse him, and that his wife must be left in the anomalous and dangerous position which the Treaty Powers have made for her. I have wearied myself, and I fear others, by my attempts to get a passage for her or to have her letters sent. Every one sympathises. The German ships now in port are loud in expressions of disapproval and professions of readiness to help her. But to whom can we address ourselves? Who is responsible? Who is the unknown power that sent Mataafa in a German ship to the Marshalls, instead of in an English ship to Fiji? that has decreed since that he shall receive not even inconsiderable gifts and open letters? and that keeps separated Faamoina and his wife?

Now, dear Sir, these are the facts, and I think that I may be excused for being angry. At the same time, I am well aware that an angry man is a bore. I am a man with a grievance, and my grievance has the misfortune to be very small and very far away. It is very small, for it is only the case of under a score of brown-skinned men who have been dealt with in the dark by I know not whom. And I want to know. I want to know by whose authority Mataafa was given over into German hands. I want to know by whose authority, and for how long a term of years, he is condemned to the miserable exile of a low island. And I want to know how it happens that what is sauce for the goose is not sauce for the gander in Samoa?—that the German enemy Mataafa has been indefinitely exiled for what is after all scarce more than constructive rebellion, and the German friend Tamasese, for a rebellion which has lasted long enough to threaten us with famine, and was disgraced in its beginning by ominous threats against the whites, has been punished by a fine of one hundred rifles?

True, I could sympathise with the German officers in their embarrassment. Here was the son of the old King whom they had raised, and whom they had deserted. What an unenviable office was theirs when they must make war upon, suppress, and make a feint of punishing, this man to whom they stood bound by a hereditary alliance, and to whose father they had already failed so egregiously. They were loyal all round. They were loyal to their Tamasese, and got him off with his fine. And shall I not be a little loyal to Mataafa? And will you not help me? He is now an old man, very piously inclined, and I believe he would enter at least the lesser orders of the Church if he were suffered to come back. But I do not even ask so much as this, though I hope it. It would be enough if he were brought back to Fiji, back to the food and fresh water of his childhood, back into the daylight from the darkness of the Marshalls, where some of us could see him, where we could write to him and receive answers, where he might pass a tolerable old age. If you can help me to get this done, I am sure that you will never regret it. In its small way, this is another case of *Toussaint L'Ouverture*, not so monstrous if you like, not on so large a scale, but with circumstances of small perfidy that make it almost odious.

I may tell you in conclusion that, circumstances co-operating with my tedious insistence, the last of the Mataafa chiefs here in Apia has been liberated from jail. All this time they stayed of their own freewill, thinking it might injure Mataafa if they escaped when others did. And you will see by the enclosed paper how these poor fellows spent the first hours of their liberty.[1] You will see also that I am not the firebrand that I am sometimes painted, and that in helping me, if you shall decide to do so, you will be doing nothing against the peace and prosperity of Samoa.

With many excuses for having occupied so much of your valuable time, I remain, yours truly, ROBERT LOUIS STEVENSON.

P. S.— On revisal, I observe some points: in the first place, I do not believe Captain Bickford was to blame; I suspect him to have been a victim. I have been told, but it seems incredible, that he underwent

---

[1] I.e., in building a section of a new road to Mr. Stevenson's house. The paper referred to is a copy of the *Samoa Times*, containing a report of the dinner given by Mr. Stevenson at Vailima to inaugurate this new road. (See Appendix to *Vailima Letters*.)

an examination about Mataafa's daughter having been allowed to accompany him. Certainly he liked his job little, and some of his colleagues less.   R. L. S.

October 9.

Latest intelligence. We have received at last a letter from Mataafa. He is well treated and has good food; only complains of not hearing from Samoa. This has very much relieved our minds. But why were they previously left in the dark?   R. L. S.

LETTERS TO YOUNG PEOPLE

I

TO MISS B——

Vailima Plantation (Spring, 1892).

DEAR FRIEND,[1]— Please salute your pupils in my name, and tell them that a long, lean, elderly man who lives right through on the under side of the world, so that down in your cellar you are nearer him than the people in the street, desires his compliments.

This man lives on an island which is not very long and is extremely narrow. The sea beats round it very hard, so that it is difficult to get to shore. There is only one harbour where ships come, and even that is very wild and dangerous; four ships of war were broken there a little while ago, and one of them is still lying on its side on a rock clean above water, where the sea threw it as you might throw your fiddle-bow upon the table. All round the harbour the town is strung out: it is nothing but wooden houses, only there are some churches built

---

[1] The lady to whom the first three of these letters are addressed "used to hear" (writes Mr. Lloyd Osbourne) "so frequently of the 'boys' in Vailima that she wrote and asked Mr. Stevenson for news of them, as it would so much interest her little girls. In the tropics, for some reason or other that it is impossible to understand, servants and work-people are always called 'boys,' though the years of Methuselah may have whitened their heads, and great-grandchildren prattle about their knees. Mr. Stevenson was amused to think that his 'boys,' who ranged from eighteen years of age to threescore and ten, should be mistaken for little youngsters; but he was touched to hear of the sick children his friend tried so hard to entertain, and gladly wrote a few letters to them. He would have written more but for the fact that his friend left the home, being transferred elsewhere."

of stone. They are not very large, but the people have never seen such fine buildings. Almost all the houses are of one story. Away at one end of the village lives the king of the whole country. His palace has a thatched roof which rests upon posts; there are no walls, but when it blows and rains, they have Venetian blinds which they let down between the posts, making all very snug. There is no furniture, and the king and the queen and the courtiers sit and eat on the floor, which is of gravel; the lamp stands there too, and every now and then it is upset.

These good folks wear nothing but a kilt about their waists, unless to go to church or for a dance on the New Year or some great occasion. The children play marbles all along the street; and though they are generally very jolly, yet they get awfully cross over their marbles, and cry and fight just as boys and girls do at home. Another amusement in country places is to shoot fish with a little bow and arrow. All round the beach there is bright shallow water, where the fishes can be seen darting or lying in shoals. The child trots round the shore, and whenever he sees a fish, lets fly an arrow, and misses, and then wades in after his arrow. It is great fun (I have tried it) for the child, and I never heard of it doing any harm to the fishes: so what could be more jolly?

The road to this lean man's house is up hill all the way, and through forests; the trees are not so much unlike those at home, only here and there some very queer ones are mixed with them — cocoanut-palms, and great trees that are covered with bloom like red hawthorn but not near so bright; and from them all thick creepers hang down like ropes, and ugly-looking weeds that they call orchids grow in the forks of the branches; and on the ground many prickly things are dotted, which they call pineapples. I suppose every one has eaten pineapple drops.

On the way up to the lean man's house, you pass a little village, all of houses like the king's house, so that as you ride by you can see everybody sitting at dinner, or, if it is night, lying in their beds by lamplight; because all the people are terribly afraid of ghosts, and would not lie in the dark for anything. After the village, there is only one more house, and that is the lean man's. For the people are not very many, and live all by the sea, and the whole inside of the island is desert woods and mountains. When the lean man goes into the forest, he is very much ashamed to own it, but he is always in a terrible fright. The wood is so great, and empty, and hot, and it is always filled with curious noises: birds cry like children, and bark like dogs; and he can hear people laughing and felling trees; and the other day (when he was far in the woods) he heard a sound like the biggest mill-wheel possible, going with a kind of dot-and-carry-one movement like a dance. That was the noise of an earthquake away down below him in the bowels of the earth; and that is the same thing as to say away up towards you in your cellar in Kilburn. All these noises make him feel lonely and scared, and he does n't quite know what he is scared of. Once when he was just about to cross a river, a blow struck him on the top of his head, and knocked him head-foremost down the bank and splash into the water. It was a nut, I fancy, that had fallen from a tree, by which accident people are sometimes killed. But at the time he thought it was a Black Boy.

"Aha," say you, "and what is a Black Boy?" Well, there are a lot of poor people here who are brought to Samoa from distant islands to labour for the Germans. They are not at all like the king and his people, who are brown and very pretty; for these are black as negroes and as ugly as sin, poor souls, and in their own land they live all the time at war, and cook and eat men's flesh. The Germans make them work; and every now and then some run away into the Bush, as the forest is called, and build little sheds of leaves, and eat nuts and roots and fruits, and dwell there by themselves. Sometimes they are bad, and wild, and people whisper to each other that some of them have gone back to their horrid old habits, and catch men and women in order to eat them. But it is very likely not true; and the most of them are poor, half-starved, pitiful creatures, like frightened dogs. Their life is all very well when the sun shines, as it does eight or nine months in the year. But it is very different the rest of the time. The wind rages then most violently. The great trees thrash about like whips; the air is filled with leaves and branches flying like birds; and the sound of the trees falling shakes the earth. It rains, too, as it never rains at home. You can hear a shower while it is yet half a mile away, hissing like a shower-bath in the forest; and when it comes to you, the water blinds your eyes, and the cold drenching takes your breath away as though some one had struck you. In that kind of weather it must be dreadful indeed to live in the woods, one man alone by himself. And you must know that if the lean man feels afraid to be in

503

the forest, the people of the island and the Black Boys are much more afraid than he; for they believe the woods to be quite filled with spirits; some like pigs, and some like flying things; but others (and these are thought the most dangerous) in the shape of beautiful young women and young men, beautifully dressed in the island manner, with fine kilts and fine necklaces, and crosses of scarlet seeds and flowers. Woe betide him or her who gets to speak with one of these! They will be charmed out of their wits, and come home again quite silly, and go mad and die. So that the poor runaway Black Boy must be always trembling, and looking about for the coming of the demons.

Sometimes the women-demons go down out of the woods into the villages; and here is a tale the lean man heard last year: One of the islanders was sitting in his house, and he had cooked fish. There came along the road two beautiful young women, dressed as I told you, who came into his house, and asked for some of his fish. It is the fashion in the islands always to give what is asked, and never to ask folks' names. So the man gave them fish, and talked to them in the island jesting way. Presently he asked one of the women for her red necklace; which is good manners and their way: he had given the fish, and he had a right to ask for something back. "I will give it you by-and-by," said the woman, and she and her companion went away; but he thought they were gone very suddenly, and the truth is they had vanished. The night was nearly come, when the man heard the voice of the woman crying that he should come to her, and she would give the necklace. He looked out, and behold! she was standing calling him from the top of the sea, on which she stood as you might stand on the table. At that, fear came on the man; he fell on his knees and prayed, and the woman disappeared.

It was said afterwards that this was once a woman, indeed, but she should have died a thousand years ago, and has lived all that while as an evil spirit in the woods beside the spring of a river. Sau-mai-afe [1] is her name, in case you want to write to her.

Ever your friend (for whom I thank the stars),

TUSITALA (Tale-writer).

[1] " Come-a-thousand."

II

Vailima Plantation, 14 Aug., 1892.

. . . The lean man is exceedingly ashamed of himself, and offers his apologies to the little girls in the cellar just above. If they will be so good as to knock three times upon the floor, he will hear it on the other side of his floor, and will understand that he is forgiven.

I left you and the children still on the road to the lean man's house, where a great part of the forest has now been cleared away. It comes back again pretty quick, though not quite so high; but everywhere, except where the weeders have been kept busy, young trees have sprouted up, and the cattle and the horses cannot be seen as they feed. In this clearing there are two or three houses scattered about, and between the two biggest I think the little girls in the cellar would first notice a sort of thing like a gridiron on legs, made of logs of wood. Sometimes it has a flag flying on it, made of rags of old clothes. It is a fort (as I am told) built by the person here who would be much the most interesting to the girls in the cellar. This is a young gentleman of eleven years of age, answering to the name of Austin. It was after reading a book about the Red Indians that he thought it more prudent to create this place of strength. As the Red Indians are in North America, and this fort seems to me a very useless kind of building, I anxiously hope that the two may never be brought together. When Austin is not engaged in building forts, nor on his lessons, which are just as annoying to him as other children's lessons are to them, he walks sometimes in the Bush, and if anybody is with him, talks all the time. When he is alone I don't think he says anything, and I dare say he feels very lonely and frightened, just as the Samoan does, at the queer noises and the endless lines of trees.

He finds the strangest kinds of seeds, some of them bright-coloured like lollipops, or really like precious stones; some of them in odd cases like tobacco-pouches. He finds and collects all kinds of little shells, with which the whole ground is scattered, and that, though they are the shells of land creatures like our snails, are of nearly as many shapes and colours as the shells on our sea-beaches. In the streams that come runnmg down out of our mountains, all as clear and bright as mirror-glass, he sees eels and little bright fish that sometimes jump together out of the surface of the brook in a spray of silver, and fresh-water prawns which lie close under the stones, looking up at him through the water with eyes the colour of a jewel. He sees all kinds of beautiful birds, some of them blue and white, and some of them coloured like our pigeons at home; and these last, the little girls in the cellar may like to know, live almost entirely on wild nutmegs as they fall ripe off the trees. Another little bird he may sometimes see, as the lean man saw him only this morning: a little fellow not so big as a man's hand, exquisitely neat, of a pretty bronzy black like ladies' shoes, who sticks up behind him (much as a peacock does) his little tail, shaped and fluted like a scallop-shell.

Here there are a lot of curious and interesting things that Austin sees all round him every day; and when I was a child at home in the old country I used to play and pretend to myself that I saw things of the same kind — that the rooms were full of orange and nutmeg trees, and the cold town gardens outside the windows were alive with parrots and with lions. What do the little girls in the cellar think that Austin does? He makes believe just the other way; he pretends that the strange great trees with their broad leaves and slab-sided roots are European oaks; and the places on the road up (where you and I and the little girls in the cellar have already gone) he calls old-fashioned, faraway European names, just as if you were to call the cellar-stair and the corner of the next street — if you could only manage to pronounce their names — Upolu and Savaii. And so it is with all of us, with Austin, and the lean man, and the little girls in the cellar: wherever we are, it is but a stage on the way to somewhere else, and whatever we do, however well we do it, it is only a preparation to do something else that shall be different.

But you must not suppose that Austin does nothing but build forts, and walk among the woods, and swim in the rivers. On the contrary, he is sometimes a very busy and useful fellow; and I think the little girls in the cellar would have admired him very nearly as much as he admired himself, if they had seen him setting off on horseback, with his hand on his hip, and his pocket full of letters and orders, at the head of quite a procession of huge white cart-horses with pack-saddles, and big, brown native men with nothing on but gaudy kilts. Mighty well he managed all his commissions; and those who saw him ordering and eating his single-handed luncheon in the queer little Chinese restaurant on the beach declare he looked as if the place, and the town, and the whole archipelago belonged to him.

But I am not going to let you suppose that this great gentleman at the head of all his horses and his men, like the King of France in the old rhyme, would be thought much of a dandy on the streets of London. On the contrary, if he could be seen with his dirty white cap and his faded purple shirt, and his little brown breeks that do not reach his knees, and the bare shanks below, and the bare feet stuck in the stirrup-leathers — for he is not quite long enough to reach the irons — I am afraid the little girls and boys in your part of the town might be very much inclined to give him a penny in charity. So you see that a very big man in one place might seem very small potatoes in another, just as the king's palace here (of which I told you in my last) would be thought rather a poor place of residence by a Surrey gipsy. And if you come to that, even the lean man himself, who is no end of an important person, if he were picked up from the chair where he is now sitting, and slung down, feet-foremost, in the neighbourhood of Charing Cross, would probably have to escape into the nearest shop, or take the risk of being mobbed. And the ladies of his family, who are very pretty ladies, and think themselves uncommonly well dressed for Samoa, would (if the same thing were to be done to them) be extremely glad to get into a cab. . . .   TUSITALA.

III

UNDER COVER TO MISS B——

Vailima, 4 Sept., 1892.

DEAR CHILDREN IN THE CELLAR,— I told you before something of the Black Boys who come here to work on the plantations, and some of whom run away and live a wild life in the forests of the island.[1] Now

1 The German company, from which we got our black boy Arick, owns and cultivates many thousands of acres in Samoa, and keeps at least a thousand black people to work on its plantations. Two schooners are always busy in bringing fresh batches to Samoa, and in taking home to their own islands the men who have worked out their three years' term of labour. This traffic in human beings is called the "labour trade," and is the life's blood, not only of the great German company, but of all the planters in Fiji, Queensland, New Caledonia, German New Guinea, the

I want to tell you of one who lived in the house of the lean man. Like the rest of them here, he is a little fellow, and when he goes about in old battered cheap European clothes, looks very small and shabby When first he came he was as lean as a tobacco-pipe, and his smile (like that of almost all the others) was the sort that half makes you wish to smile yourself, and half wish to cry. However, the boys in the kitchen took him in hand and fed him up. They would set him down alone to table, and wait upon him till he had his fill, which was a good long time to wait. The first thing we noticed was that his little stomach began to stick out like a pigeon's breast; and then the food got a little wider spread, and he started little calves to his legs; and last of all, he began to get quite saucy and impudent. He is really what you ought to call a young man, though I suppose nobody in the whole wide world has any idea of his age; and so far as his behaviour goes, you can only think of him as a big little child with a good deal of sense.

When Austin built his fort against the Indians, Arick (for that is the Black Boy's name) liked nothing so much as to help him. And this is very funny, when you think that of all the dangerous savages in this island Arick is one of the most dangerous. The other day, besides, he made Austin a musical instrument of the sort they use in his own country—a harp with only one string. He took a stick about three feet long and perhaps four inches round. The under side he hollowed out in a deep trench to serve as a sounding-box; the two ends of the upper side he made to curve upward like the ends of a canoe, and between these he stretched the single string. He plays upon it with a match or a little piece of stick, and sings to it songs of his own country, of which no person here can understand a single word, and which are, very likely, all about fighting with his enemies in battle, and killing

Solomon Islands, and the New Hebrides. The difference between the labour trade, as it is now carried on under Government supervision, and the slave trade is a great one, but not great enough to please sensitive people. In Samoa the missionaries are not allowed by the company to teach these poor savages religion, or to do anything to civilise them and raise them from their monkey-like ignorance. But in other respects the company is not a bad master, and treats its people pretty well. The system, however, is one that cannot be defended and must sooner or later be suppressed.—[L. O.]

them, and, I am sorry to say, cooking them in a ground-oven, and eating them for supper when the fight is over.

For Arick is really what you call a savage, though a savage is a very different sort of a person, and very much nicer than he is made to appear in little books. He is the kind of person that everybody smiles to, or makes faces at, or gives a smack as he goes by; the sort of person that all the girls on the plantation give the best seat to and help first, and love to decorate with flowers and ribbons, and yet all the while are laughing at him; the sort of person who likes best to play with Austin, and whom Austin, perhaps (when he is allowed), likes best to play with. He is all grins and giggles and little steps out of dances, and little droll ways to attract people's attention and set them laughing. And yet, when you come to look at him closely, you will find that his body is all covered with *scars!* This happened when he was a child. There was war, as is the way in these wild islands, between his village and the next, much as if there were war in London between one street and another; and all the children ran about playing in the middle of the trouble, and, I dare say, took no more notice of the war than you children in London do of a general election. But sometimes, at general elections, English children may get run over by processions in the street; and it chanced that as little Arick was running about in the Bush, and very busy about his playing, he ran into the midst of the warriors on the other side. These speared him with a poisoned spear; and his own people, when they had found him, in order to cure him of the poison scored him with knives that were probably made of fishbone.

This is a very savage piece of child-life; and Arick, for all his good-nature, is still a very savage person. I have told you how the Black Boys sometimes run away from the plantations, and live alone in the forest, building little sheds to protect them from the rain, and sometimes planting little gardens for food; but for the most part living the best they can upon the nuts of the trees and the yams that they dig with their hands out of the earth. I do not think there can be anywhere in the world people more wretched than these runaways. They cannot return, for they would only return to be punished; they can never hope to see again their own people—indeed, I do not know what they can hope, but just to find enough yams every day to keep them from starvation. And in the wet season of the year, which is our summer and your winter, when the rain falls day after day far harder and louder than the loudest thunder-plump that ever fell in England, and the room is so dark that the lean man is sometimes glad to light his lamp to write by, I can think of nothing so dreary as the state of these poor runaways in the houseless Bush. You are to remember, besides, that the people of the island hate and fear them because they are cannibals; sit and tell tales of them about their lamps at night in their own comfortable houses, and are sometimes afraid to lie down to sleep if they think there is a lurking Black Boy in the neighbourhood. Well, now, Arick is of their own race and language, only he is a little more lucky because he has not run away; and how do you think that he proposed to help them? He asked if he might not have a gun. "What do you want with a gun, Arick?" was asked. He answered quite simply, and with his nice, good-natured smile, that if he had a gun he would go up into the High Bush and shoot Black Boys as men shoot pigeons. He said nothing about eating them, nor do I think he really meant to; I think all he wanted was to clear the plantation of vermin, as gamekeepers at home kill weasels or rats.

The other day he was sent on an errand to the German company where many of the Black Boys live. It was very late when he came home. He had a white bandage around his head, his eyes shone, and he could scarcely speak for excitement. It seems some of the Black Boys who were his enemies at home had attacked him, one with a knife. By his own account, he had fought very well; but the odds were heavy. The man with the knife had cut him both in the head and back; he had been struck down; and if some Black Boys of his own side had not come to the rescue, he must certainly have been killed. I am sure no Christmas box could make any of you children so happy as this fight made Arick. A great part of the next day he neglected his work to play upon the one-stringed harp and sing songs about his great victory. To-day, when he is gone upon his holiday, he has announced that he is going back to the German firm to have another battle and another triumph. I do not think he will go, all the same, or I should be uneasy; for I do not want to have my Arick killed; and there is no doubt that if he begin this fight again, he will be likely to go on with it very far. For I have seen him once when he saw, or thought he saw, an enemy.

It was one of those dreadful days of rain, the sound of it like a great waterfall, or like a tempest of wind blowing in the forest; and there came to our door two runaway Black Boys seeking refuge. In such weather as that my enemy's dog (as Shakespeare says) should have had a right to shelter. But when Arick saw the two poor rogues coming with their empty stomachs and drenched clothes, one of them with a stolen cutlass in his hand, through that world of falling water, he had no thought of any pity in his heart. Crouching behind one of the pillars of the verandah, to which he clung with his two hands, his mouth drew back into a strange sort of smile, his eyes grew bigger and bigger, and his whole face was just like the one word MURDER in big capitals.

But I have told you a great deal too much about poor Arick's savage nature, and now I must tell you of a great amusement he had the other day. There came an English ship of war into the harbour, and the officers good-naturedly gave an entertainment of songs and dances and a magic lantern, to which Arick and Austin were allowed to go. At the door of the hall there were crowds of Black Boys waiting and trying to peep in, as children at home lie about and peep under the tent of a circus; and you may be sure Arick was a very proud person when he passed them all by, and entered the hall with his ticket.

I wish I knew what he thought of the whole performance; but a friend of the lean man, who sat just in front of Arick, tells me what seemed to startle him most. The first thing was when two of the officers came out with blackened faces, like minstrels, and began to dance. Arick was sure that they were really black, and his own people, and he was wonderfully surprised to see them dance in this new European style.

But the great affair was the magic lantern. The hall was made quite dark, which was very little to Arick's taste. He sat there behind my friend, nothing to be seen of him but eyes and teeth, and his heart was beating finely in his little scarred breast. And presently there came out of the white sheet that great big eye of light that I am sure all of you children must have often seen. It was quite new to Arick; he had no idea what would happen next, and in his fear and excitement he laid hold with his little slim black fingers like a bird's claw on the neck of the friend in front of him. All through the rest of the show, as one picture followed another on the white sheet, he sat there grasping and clutching, and goodness knows whether he were more pleased or frightened.

Doubtless it was a very fine thing to see all those bright pictures coming out and dying away again, one after another; but doubtless it was rather alarming also, for how was it done? At last when there appeared upon the screen the head of a black woman (as it might be his own mother or sister), and this black woman of a sudden began to roll her eyes, the fear or the excitement, whichever it was, wrung out of him a loud, shuddering sob. I think we all ought to admire his courage when, after an evening spent in looking at such wonderful miracles, he and Austin set out alone through the forest to the lean man's house. It was late at night and pitch-dark when some of the party overtook the little white boy and the big black boy, marching among the trees with their lantern. I have told you this wood has an ill name, and all the people of the island believe it to be full of evil spirits; it is a pretty dreadful place to walk in by the moving light of a lantern, with nothing about you but a curious whirl of shadows, and the black night above and beyond. But Arick kept his courage up, and I dare say Austin's too, with a perpetual chatter, so that the people coming after heard his voice long before they saw the shining of the lantern.   TUSITALA.

IV

TO AUSTIN STRONG

Vailima, November 2, 1892.

MY DEAR AUSTIN,— First and foremost I think you will be sorry to hear that our poor friend Arick has gone back to the German firm. He had not been working very well, and we had talked of sending him off before; but remembering how thin he was when he came here, and seeing what fat little legs and what a comfortable little stomach he had laid on in the meanwhile, we found we had not the heart. The other day, however, he set up chat to Henry, the Samoan overseer, asking him who he was and where he came from, and refusing to obey his orders. I was in bed in the workmen's house, having a fever. Uncle Lloyd came over to me, told me of it, and I had Arick sent up. I told him I would give him another chance. He was taken out and asked to apologise to Henry, but he would do no such thing. He preferred to go back to the German firm. So we hired a couple of Samoans who were up here on a visit to the boys, and packed him off in their charge to the firm, where he arrived safely, and a receipt was given for him like a parcel.[1]

Sunday last the *Alameda* returned. Your mother was off bright and early with Palema, for it is a very curious thing, but is certainly the case, that she was very impatient to get news of a young person by the name of Austin. Mr. Gurr lent a horse for the Captain — it was a pretty big horse, but our handsome Captain, as you know, is a very big Captain indeed. Now, do you remember Misifolo — a tall, thin Hovea boy that came shortly before you left? He had been riding up this same horse of Gurr's just the day before, and the horse threw him off at Motootua corner, and cut his hip. So Misifolo called out to the Captain as he rode by that that was a very bad horse, that it ran away and threw people off, and that he had best be careful; and the funny thing is, that the Captain did not like it at all. The foal might as well have tried to run away with Vailima as that horse with Captain Morse, which is poetry, as you see, into the bargain; but the Captain was not at all in that way of thinking, and was never really happy until he had got his foot on ground again. It was just then that the horse began to be happy too, so they parted in one mind. But the horse is still wondering what kind of piece of artillery he had brought up to Vailima last Sunday morning. So far it was all right. The Captain was got safe off the wicked horse, but how was he to get back again to Apia and the *Alameda*?

Happy thought — there was Donald, the big pack-horse! The last time Donald was ridden he had upon him a hair-pin and a pea — by which I mean (once again to drop into poetry) you and me. Now he was to have a rider more suited to his size. He was brought up to the

[1] When Arick left us and went back to the German company, he had grown so fat and strong and intelligent that they deemed he was made for better things than cotton-picking or plantation work, and handed him over to their surveyor, who needed a man to help him. I used often to meet him after this, tripping at his master's heels with the theodolite, or scampering about with tapes and chains like a kitten with a spool of thread. He did not look then as though he were destined to die of a broken heart, though that was his end not so many months afterwards. The plantation manager told me that Arick and a New Ireland boy went crazy with homesickness, and died in the hospital together.— [L. O].

door — he looked a mountain. A step-ladder was put alongside of him. The Captain approached the step-ladder, and he looked an Alp. I was n't as much afraid for the horse as I was for the step-ladder, but it bore the strain, and with a kind of sickening smash that you might have heard at Monterey, the Captain descended to the saddle. Now don't think that I am exaggerating, but at the moment when that enormous Captain settled down upon Donald, the horse's hind legs gave visibly under the strain. What the couple looked like, one on top of t' other, no words can tell you, and your mother must here draw a picture. — Your respected Uncle,   O TUSITALA.

V

TO AUSTIN STRONG

Vailima, November 15, 1892.

MY DEAR AUSTIN, — The new house is begun. It stands out nearly half-way over towards Pineapple Cottage — the lower floor is laid and the uprights of the wall are set up; so that the big lower room wants nothing but a roof over its head. When it rains (as it does mostly all the time) you never saw anything look so sorry for itself as that room left outside. Beyond the house there is a work-shed roofed with sheets of iron, and in front, over about half the lawn, the lumber for the house lies piled. It is about the bringing up of this lumber that I want to tell you.

For about a fortnight there were at work upon the job two German overseers, about a hundred Black Boys, and from twelve to twenty-four draught-oxen. It rained about half the time, and the road was like lather for shaving. The Black Boys seemed to have had a new rig-out. They had almost all shirts of scarlet flannel, and lavalavas, the Samoan kilt, either of scarlet or light blue. As the day got warm they took off the shirts; and it was a very curious thing, as you went down to Apia on a bright day, to come upon one tree after another in the empty forest with these shirts stuck among the branches like vermilion birds.

I observed that many of the boys had a very queer substitute for a pocket. This was nothing more than a string which some of them tied about their upper arms and some about their necks, and in which they stuck their clay pipes; and as I don't suppose they had anything else to carry, it did very well. Some had feathers in their hair, and some long stalks of grass through the holes in their noses. I suppose this was intended to make them look pretty, poor dears; but you know what a Black Boy looks like, and these Black Boys, for all their blue, and their scarlet, and their grass, looked just as shabby and small, and sad, and sorry for themselves, and like sick monkeys as any of the rest.

As you went down the road you came upon them first working in squads of two. Each squad shouldered a couple of planks and carried them up about two hundred feet, gave them to two others, and walked back empty-handed to the places they had started from. It was n't very hard work, and they did n't go about it at all lively; but, of course, when it rained, and the mud was deep, the poor fellows were unhappy enough. This was in the upper part about Trood's. Below, all the way down to Tanugamanono, you met the bullock-carts coming and going, each with ten or twenty men to attend upon it, and often enough with one of the overseers near. Quite a far way off through the forest you could hear the noise of one of these carts approaching. The road was like a bog, and though a good deal wider than it was when you knew it, so narrow that the bullocks reached quite across it with the span of their big horns. To pass by, it was necessary to get into the Bush on one side or the other. The bullocks seemed to take no interest in their business; they looked angry and stupid, and sullen beyond belief; and when it came to a heavy bit of road, as often as not they would stop.

As long as they were going the Black Boys walked in the margin of the Bush on each side, pushing the cart-wheels with hands and shoulders, and raising the most extraordinary outcry. It was strangely like some very big kind of bird. Perhaps the great flying creatures that lived upon the earth long before man came, if we could have come near one of their meeting-places, would have given us just such a concert.

When one of the bullamacows [1] stopped altogether the fun was

[1] "Bullamacow" is a word that always amuses the visitor to Samoa. When the first pair of cattle was brought to the islands, and the natives asked the missionaries what they must call these strange creatures, they were told that the English name was "a bull and a cow." But the Samoans thought that "a bull and a cow" was the name of each of the animals, and they soon corrupted the English words into "bullamacow," which has remained the name for beef or cattle ever since.—[L. O.]

highest. The bullamacow stood on the road, his head fixed fast in the yoke, chewing a little, breathing very hard, and showing in his red eye that if he could get rid of the yoke he would show them what a circus was. All the Black Boys tailed on to the wheels and the back of the cart stood there getting their spirits up, and then of a sudden set to shooing and singing out. It was these outbursts of shrill cries that it was so curious to hear in the distance. One such stuck cart I came up to and asked what was the worry. " Old fool bullamacow stop same place," was the reply. I never saw any of the overseers near any of the stuck carts; you were a very much better overseer than either of these.

While this was going on, I had to go down to Apia five or six different times, and each time there were a hundred Black Boys to say " Good-morning " to. This was rather a tedious business; and, as very few of them answered at all, and those who did, only with a grunt like a pig's, it was several times in my mind to give up this piece of politeness. The last time I went down, I was almost decided ; but when I came to the first pair of Black Boys, and saw them looking so comic and so melancholy, I began the business over again. This time I thought more of them seemed to answer, and when I got down to the tail-end where the carts were running, I received a very pleasant surprise, for one of the boys, who was pushing at the back of a cart, lifted up his head, and called out to me in wonderfully good English, " You good man — always say ' Good-morning.' " It was sad to think that these poor creatures should think so much of so small a piece of civility, and strange that (thinking so) they should be so dull as not to return it.   UNCLE LOUIS.

VI

TO AUSTIN STRONG

June 18, 1893.

RESPECTED HOPKINS,[1]— This is to inform you that the Jersey cow had an elegant little cow-calf Sunday last. There was a great deal of rejoicing, of course; but I don't know whether or not you remember

---

[1] In the letters that were sent to Austin Strong you will be surprised to see his name change from Austin to Hoskyns, and from Hopkins to Hutchinson. It was the penalty Master Austin had to pay for being the particular and bosom friend of each of the one hundred and eighty blue

the Jersey cow. Whatever else she is, the Jersey cow is *not* good-natured, and Dines, who was up here on some other business, went down to the paddock to get a hood and to milk her. The hood is a little wooden board with two holes in it, by which it is hung from her horns. I do not know how he got it on, and I don't believe *he* does. Anyway, in the middle of the operation, in came Bull Bazett, with his head down, and roaring like the last trumpet. Dines and all his merry men hid behind trees in the paddock and skipped. Dines then got upon a horse, plied his spurs, and cleared for Apia. The next time he is asked to meddle with our cows, he will probably want to know the reason why. Meanwhile, there was the cow, with the board over her eyes, left tied by a pretty long rope to a small tree in the paddock, and who was to milk her? She roared,—I was going to say like a bull, but it was Bazett who did that, walking up and down, switching his tail, and the noise of the pair of them was perfectly dreadful.

Palema went up to the Bush to call Lloyd; and Lloyd came down in one of his know-all-about-it moods. "It was perfectly simple," he said. "The cow was hooded; anybody could milk her. All you had to do was to draw her up to the tree, and get a hitch about it." So he untied the cow, and drew her up close to the tree, and got a hitch about it right enough. And then the cow brought her intellect to bear on the subject, and proceeded to walk round the tree to get the hitch off.

Now, this is geometry, which you 'll have to learn some day. The tree is the centre of two circles. The cow had a "radius" of about two feet, and went leisurely round a small circle; the man had a "radius" of about thirty feet, and either he must let the cow get the hitch unwound, or else he must take up his two feet to about the height of his eyes and race round a big circle. This was racing and chasing.

The cow walked quietly round and round the tree to unwind herself; and first Lloyd, and then Palema, and then Lloyd again, scampered round the big circle, and fell, and got up again, and bounded like a deer, to keep her hitched.

jackets that made up the crew of the British man-of-war *Curaçoa;* for, whether it was due to some bitter memories of the Revolutionary war, or to some rankling reminiscences of 1812, that even friendship could not altogether stifle (for Austin was a true American boy), they annoyed him by giving him, each one of them, a separate name.—[L. O.]

It was funny to see, but we could n't laugh with a good heart; for every now and then (when the man who was running tumbled down) the cow would get a bit ahead; and I promise you there was then no sound of any laughter, but we rather edged away towards the gate,

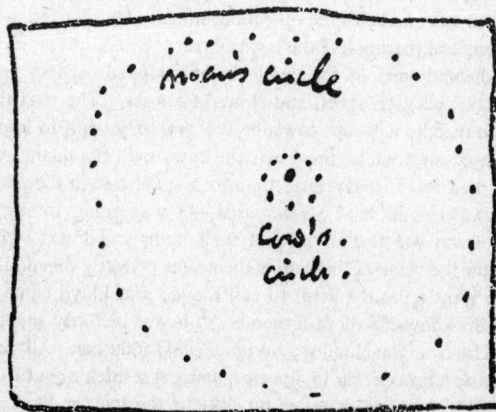

looking to see the crazy beast loose, and charging us. To add to her attractions, the board had fallen partly off, and only covered one eye, giving her the look of a crazy old woman in a Sydney slum. Meanwhile, the calf stood looking on, a little perplexed, and seemed to be saying: " Well, now, is this life? It does n't seem as if it was all it was cracked up to be. And is this my mamma? What a very impulsive lady! "

All the time, from the lower paddock, we could hear Bazett roaring like the deep seas, and if we cast our eye that way, we could see him switching his tail, as a very angry gentleman may sometimes switch his cane. And the Jersey would every now and then put up her head, and low like the pu[1] for dinner. And take it for all in all, it was a very striking scene. Poor Uncle Lloyd had plenty of time to regret having been in such a hurry; so had poor Palema, who was let into the business, and ran until he was nearly dead. Afterwards Palema

1 The big conch-shell that was blown at certain hours every day.— [L. O.]

went and sat on a gate where your mother sketched him, and she is going to send you the sketch. And the end of it? Well, we got her tied again, I really don't know how; and came stringing back to the house with our tails between our legs. That night at dinner, the Tamaitai [1] bid us tell the boys to be very careful "not to frighten the cow." It was too much; the cow had frightened us in such fine style that we all broke down and laughed like mad.

General Hoskyns, there is no further news, your Excellency, that I am aware of. But it may interest you to know that Mr. Christian held his twenty-fifth birthday yesterday — a quarter of a living century old; think of it, drink of it, innocent youth! — and asked down Lloyd and Daplyn to a feast at one o'clock, and Daplyn went at seven, and got nothing to eat at all. Whether they had anything to drink, I know not — no, not I; but it 's to be hoped so. Also, your Uncle Lloyd has stopped smoking, and he does n't like it much. Also, that your mother is most beautifully gotten up to-day, in a pink gown with a topaz stone in front of it; and is really looking like an angel, only that she is n't like an angel at all — only like your mother herself.

Also that the Tamaitai has been waxing the floor of the big room, so that it shines in the most ravishing manner; and then we insisted on coming in, and she would n't let us, and we came anyway, and have made the vilest mess of it — but still it shines.

Also, that I am, your Excellency's obedient servant,

UNCLE LOUIS.

VII

TO AUSTIN STRONG

MY DEAR HUTCHINSON, — This is not going to be much of a letter, so don't expect what can't be had. Uncle Lloyd and Palema made a malanga [2] to go over the island to Siumu, and Talolo was anxious to go also; but how could we get along without him? Well, Misifolo, the Maypole, set off on Saturday, and walked all that day down the island to beyond Faleasiu with a letter for Iopu; and Iopu and Tali and Misifolo rose very early on the Sunday morning, and walked all that day up the island, and came by seven at night — all pretty tired,

---

[1] Mrs. R. L. S., as she is called in Samoan, "the Lady." — [L. O.]
[2] A visiting party.

and Misifolo most of all — to Tanugamanono.[1] We at Vailima knew nothing at all about the marchings of the Saturday and Sunday, but Uncle Lloyd got his boys and things together and went to bed.

A little after five in the morning I woke and took the lantern, and went out of the front door and round the verandahs. There was never a spark of dawn in the east, only the stars looked a little pale; and I expected to find them all asleep in the workhouse. But no! the stove was roaring, and Talolo and Fono, who was to lead the party, were standing together talking by the stove, and one of Fono's young men was lying asleep on the sofa in the smoking-room, wrapped in his lava-lava. I had my breakfast at half-past five that morning, and the bell rang before six, when it was just the grey of dawn. But by seven the feast was spread — there was Iopu coming up, with Tali at his heels, and Misifolo bringing up the rear — and Talolo could go the malanga.

Off they set with two guns and three porters, and Fono and Lloyd and Palema, and Talolo himself with his best Sunday-go-to-meeting lavalava rolled up under his arm, and a very sore foot; but much he cared — he was smiling from ear to ear, and would have gone to Siumu over red-hot coals. Off they set round the corner of the cook-house, and into the Bush beside the chicken-house, and so good-bye to them.

But you should see how Iopu has taken possession! "Never saw a place in such a state!" is written on his face. "In my time," says he, "we did n't let things go ragging along like this, and I 'm going to show you fellows." The first thing he did was to apply for a bar of soap, and then he set to work washing everything (that had all been washed last Friday in the regular course). Then he had the grass cut all round the cook-house, and I tell you but he found scraps, and odds and ends, and grew more angry and indignant at each fresh discovery.

1 Talolo was the Vailima cook; Sina, his wife; Tauilo, his mother; Mi-taele and Sosimo, his brothers. Lafaele, who was married to Faauma, was a middle-aged Futuna Islander, and had spent many years of his life on a whale-ship, the captain of which had kidnapped him when a boy. Misi-folo was one of the "housemaids." Iopu and Tali, man and wife, had long been in our service, but had left it after they had been married some time; but, according to Samoan deas, they were none the less members of Tusi-tala's family, because, though they were no longer working for him, they still owed him allegiance. "Aunt Maggie" is Mr. Stevenson's mother; Palema, Mr. Graham Balfour.—[L. O.]

"If a white chief came up here and smelt this, how would you feel?" he asked your mother. "It is enough to breed a sickness!"

And I dare say you remember this was just what your mother had often said to himself; and did say the day she went out and cried on the kitchen steps in order to make Talolo ashamed. But Iopu gave it all out as little new discoveries of his own. The last thing was the cows, and I tell you he was solemn about the cows. They were all destroyed, he said, nobody knew how to milk except himself — where he is about right. Then came dinner and a delightful little surprise. Perhaps you remember that long ago I used not to eat mashed potatoes, but always had two or three boiled in a plate. This has not been done for months, because Talolo makes such admirable mashed potatoes that I have caved in. But here came dinner, mashed potatoes for your mother and the Tamaitai, and then boiled potatoes in a plate for me!

And there is the end of the Tale of the return of Iopu, up to date. What more there may be is in the lap of the gods, and, Sir, I am yours considerably,   UNCLE LOUIS.

VIII

TO AUSTIN STRONG

MY DEAR HOSKYNS, — I am kept away in a cupboard because everybody has the influenza; I never see anybody at all, and never do anything whatever except to put ink on paper up here in my room. So what can I find to write to you? — you, who are going to school, and getting up in the morning to go bathing, and having (it seems to me) rather a fine time of it in general?

You ask if we have seen Arick? Yes, your mother saw him at the head of a gang of boys, and looking fat, and sleek, and well-to-do. I have an idea that he misbehaved here because he was homesick for the other Black Boys, and did n't know how else to get back to them. Well, he has got them now, and I hope he likes it better than I should.

I read the other day something that I thought would interest so great a sea-bather as yourself. You know that the fishes that we see, and catch, go only a certain way down into the sea. Below a certain depth there is no life at all. The water is as empty as the air is above a certain height. Even the shells of dead fishes that come down there are crushed into nothing by the huge weight of the water. Lower still, in the places where the sea is profoundly deep, it appears that life begins again. People fish up in dredging-buckets loose rags and tatters of creatures that hang together all right down there with the great weight holding them in one, but come all to pieces as they are hauled up. Just what they look like, just what they do or feed upon, we shall never find out. Only that we have some flimsy fellow-creatures down in the very bottom of the deep seas, and cannot get them up except in tatters. It must be pretty dark where they live, and there are no plants or weeds, and no fish come down there, or drowned sailors either, from the upper parts, because these are all mashed to pieces by the great weight long before they get so far, or else come to a place where perhaps they float. But ! dare say a cannon sometimes comes careering solemnly down, and circling about like a dead leaf or thistledown; and then the ragged fellows go and play about the cannon and tell themselves all kinds of stories about the fish higher up and their iron houses, and perhaps go inside and sleep, and perhaps dream of it all like their betters.

Of course you know a cannon down there would be quite light. Even in shallow water, where men go down with a diving-dress, they grow so light that they have to hang weights about their necks, and have their boots loaded with twenty pounds of lead—as I know to my sorrow. And with all this, and the helmet, which is heavy enough of itself to any one up here in the thin air, they are carried about like gossamers, and have to take every kind of care not to be upset and stood upon their heads. I went down once in the dress, and speak from experience. But if we could get down for a moment near where the fishes are, we should be in a tight place. Suppose the water not to crush us (which it would), we should pitch about in every kind of direction; every step we took would carry us as far as if we had seven-league boots; and we should keep flying head over heels, and top over bottom, like the liveliest clowns in the world.

Well, Sir, here is a great deal of words put down upon a piece of paper, and if you think that makes a letter, why, very well! And if you don't, I can't help it. For I have nothing under heaven to tell you.

So, with kindest wishes to yourself, and Louie, and Aunt Nellie, believe me, your affectionate   UNCLE LOUIS.

Now here is something worth telling you. This morning at six o'clock I saw all the horses together in the front paddock, and in a terrible ado about something. Presently I saw a man with two buckets on the march, and knew where the trouble was—the cow! The whole lot cleared to the gate but two—Donald, the big white horse, and my Jack. They stood solitary, one here, one there. I began to get interested, for I thought Jack was off his feed. In came the man with the bucket and all the ruck of curious horses at his tail. Right round he went to where Donald stood (*D*) and poured out a feed, and the majestic Donald ate it, and the ruck of common horses followed the man. On he went to the second station, Jack's (*J* in the plan), and poured out a feed, and the fools of horses went in with him to the next place (*A* in the plan). And behold as the train swung round, the last of them came curiously too near Jack; and Jack left his feed and rushed upon this fool with a kind of outcry, and the fool fled, and Jack returned to his feed; and he and Donald ate theirs with glory, while the others were still circling round for fresh feeds.

Glory be to the name of Donald and to the name of Jack, for they had found out where the foods were poured, and each took his station and waited there, Donald at the first of the course for his, Jack at the second station, while all the impotent fools ran round and round after the man with his buckets!   R. L. S.

IX

TO AUSTIN STRONG
Vailima.

MY DEAR AUSTIN,—Now when the overseer is away [1] I think it my duty to report to him anything serious that goes on on the plantation.

Early the other afternoon we heard that Sina's foot was very bad, and soon after that we could have heard her cries as far away as the front balcony. I think Sina rather enjoys being ill, and makes as much of it

1 While Austin was in Vailima many little duties about the plantation fell to his share, so that he was often called the "overseer"; and, small as he was, he sometimes took charge of a couple of big men, and went into town

as she possibly can; but all the same it was painful to hear the cries; and there is no doubt she was at least very uncomfortable. I went up twice to the little room behind the stable, and found her lying on the floor, with Tali and Faauma and Talolo all holding on different bits of her. I gave her an opiate; but whenever she was about to go to sleep one of these silly people would be shaking her, or talking in her ear, and then she would begin to kick about again and scream.

Palema and Aunt Maggie took horse and went down to Apia after the doctor. Right on their heels off went Mitaele on Musu to fetch Tauilo, Talolo's mother. So here was all the island in a bustle over Sina's foot. No doctor came, but he told us what to put on. When I went up at night to the little room, I found Tauilo there, and the whole plantation boxed into the place like little birds in a nest. They were sitting on the bed, they were sitting on the table, the floor was full of them, and the place as close as the engine-room of a steamer. In the middle lay Sina, about three parts asleep with opium; two able-bodied work-boys were pulling at her arms, and whenever she closed her eyes calling her by name, and talking in her ear.

I really did n't know what would become of the girl before morning. Whether or not she had been very ill before, this was the way to make her so, and when one of the work-boys woke her up again, I spoke to him very sharply, and told Tauilo she must put a stop to it.

Now I suppose this was what put it into Tauilo's head to do what she did next. You remember Tauilo, and what a fine, tall, strong Madame Lafarge sort of person she is? And you know how much afraid the natives are of the evil spirits in the wood, and how they think all sickness comes from them? Up stood Tauilo, and addressed the spirit in Sina's foot, and scolded it, and the spirit answered and promised to be a good boy and go away. I do not feel so much afraid of the demons after this. It was Faauma told me about it. I was going out into the pantry after soda-water, and found her with a lantern drawing water from the tank. "Bad spirit he go away," she told me.

"That 's first-rate," said I. "Do you know what the name of that spirit was? His name was *tautala* [talking]."

"O, no!" she said; "his name is *Tu*."

with the pack-horses. It was not all play, either; for he had to see that the barrels and boxes did not chafe the horses' backs, and that they were not allowed to come home too fast up the steep road.— [L. O.]

You might have knocked me down with a straw. "How on earth do you know that?" I asked.

"Hear him tell Tauilo," she said.

As soon as I heard that, I began to suspect Mrs. Tauilo was a little bit of a ventriloquist; and imitating as well as I could the sort of voice they make, asked her if the bad spirit did not talk like that. Faauma was very much surprised, and told me that was just his voice.

Well, that was a very good business for the evening. The people all went away because the demon was gone away, and the circus was over, and Sina was allowed to sleep. But the trouble came after. There had been an evil spirit in that room and his name was Tu. No one could say when he might come back again; they all voted it was *Tu* much; and now Talolo and Sina have had to be lodged in the Soldier Room.[1] As for the little room by the stable, there it stands empty; it is too small to play soldiers in, and I do not see what we can do with it, except to have a nice brass name-plate engraved in Sydney, or in "Frisco," and stuck upon the door of it—*Mr. Tu.*

So you see that ventriloquism has its bad side as well as its good sides; and I don't know that I want any more ventriloquists on this plantation. We shall have *Tu* in the cook-house next, and then *Tu* in Lafaele's, and *Tu* in the workman's cottage; and the end of it all will be that we shall have to take the Tamaitai's room for the kitchen, and my room for the boys' sleeping-house, and we shall all have to go out and camp under umbrellas.

Well, where you are there may be schoolmasters, but there is no such thing as Mr. *Tu!*

Now, it's all very well that these big people should be frightened out of their wits by an old wife talking with her mouth shut; that is one of the things we happen to know about. All the old women in the world might talk with their mouths shut, and not frighten you or me, but there are plenty of other things that frighten us badly. And if we only knew about them, perhaps we should find them no more worthy to be feared than an old woman talking with her mouth shut. And the names of some of these things are Death, and Pain, and Sorrow.

UNCLE LOUIS.

---

[1] A room set apart to serve as the theatre for an elaborate war-game. which was one of Mr. Stevenson's favourite recreations.

TO AUSTIN STRONG

January 27, 1893.

DEAR GENERAL HOSKYNS,—I have the honour to report as usual. Your giddy mother having gone planting a flower-garden, I am obliged to write with my own hand, and, of course, nobody will be able to read it. This has been a very mean kind of a month. Aunt Maggie left with the influenza. We have heard of her from Sydney, and she is all right again; but we have inherited her influenza, and it made a poor place of Vailima. We had Talolo, Mitaele, Sosimo, Iopu, Sina, Misifolo, and myself, all sick in bed at the same time; and was not that a pretty dish to set before the king! The big hall of the new house having no furniture, the sick pitched their tents in it,—I mean their mosquito-nets,—like a military camp. The Tamaitai and your mother went about looking after them, and managed to get us something to eat. Henry, the good boy! though he was getting it himself, did housework, and went round at night from one mosquito-net to another, praying with the sick. Sina, too, was as good as gold, and helped us greatly. We shall always like her better. All the time—I do not know how they managed—your mother found the time to come and write for me; and for three days, as I had my old trouble on, and had to play dumb man, I dictated a novel in the deaf-and-dumb alphabet. But now we are all recovered, and getting to feel quite fit. A new paddock has been made; the wires come right up to the top of the hill, pass within twenty yards of the big clump of flowers (if you remember that) and by the end of the pineapple patch. The Tamaitai and your mother and I all sleep in the upper story of the new house. Uncle Lloyd is alone in the workman's cottage; and there is nobody at all at night in the old house, but ants and cats and mosquitos. The whole inside of the new house is varnished. It is a beautiful golden-brown by day, and in lamplight all black, and sparkle. In the corner of the hall the new safe is built in, and looks as if it had millions of pounds in it; but I do not think there is much more than twenty dollars and a spoon or two; so the man that opens it will have a great deal of trouble for nothing. Our great fear is lest we should forget how to open it; but it will look just as well if we can't. Poor Misifolo—you remember the thin boy, do you not?—had a desperate attack of influenza; and he was in a great taking. You would not like to be very sick in some savage place in the islands, and have only the savages to doctor you. Well, that was just the way he felt. "It is all very well," he thought, "to let these childish white people doctor a sore foot or a toothache, but this is serious—I might die of this! For goodness' sake, let me get away into a draughty native house, where I can lie in cold gravel, eat green bananas, and have a real grown-up, tattooed man to raise spirits and say charms over me." A day or two we kept him quiet, and got him much better. Then he said he *must* go. He had had his back broken in his own island, he said; it had come broken again, and he must go away to a native house, and have it mended. "Confound your back!" said we; "lie down in your bed." At last, one day, his fever was quite gone, and he could give his mind to the broken back entirely. He lay in the hall; I was in the room alone; all morning and noon I heard him roaring like a bull calf, so that the floor shook with it. It was plainly humbug; it had the humbugging sound of a bad child crying; and about two of the afternoon we were worn out, and told him he might go. Off he set. He was in some kind of a white wrapping, with a great white turban on his head, as pale as clay, and walked leaning on a stick. But, O, he was a glad boy to get away from these foolish, savage, childish white people, and get his broken back put right by somebody with some sense. He nearly died that night, and little wonder! but he has now got better again, and long may it last! All the others were quite good, trusted us wholly, and stayed to be cured where they were. But then he was quite right, if you look at it from his point of view; for, though we may be very clever, we do not set up to cure broken backs. If a man has his back broken, we white people can do nothing at all but bury him. And was he not wise, since that was his complaint, to go to folks who could do more?

Best love to yourself, and Louie, and Aunt Nellie, and apologies for so dull a letter, from your respectful and affectionate

UNCLE LOUIS.

LAY MORALS

The following chapters of a projected treatise on ethics, here printed for the first time, were drafted at Edinburgh in the spring of 1879. They are unrevised, and must not be taken as representing, either as to matter or form, their author's final thoughts; but they contain much that is essentially characteristic of his mind.

LAY MORALS

CHAPTER I

THE problem of education is twofold: first to know, and then to utter. Every one who lives any semblance of an inner life thinks more nobly and profoundly than he speaks; and the best of teachers can impart only broken images of the truth which they perceive. Speech which goes from one to another between two natures, and, what is worse, between two experiences, is doubly relative. The speaker buries his meaning; it is for the hearer to dig it up again; and all speech, written or spoken, is in a dead language until it finds a willing and prepared hearer. Such, moreover, is the complexity of life, that when we condescend upon details in our advice, we may be sure we condescend on error; and the best of education is to throw out some magnanimous hints. No man was ever so poor that he could express all he has in him by words, looks, or actions; his true knowledge is eternally incommunicable, for it is a knowledge of himself; and his best wisdom comes to him by no process of the mind, but in a supreme self-dictation, which keeps varying from hour to hour in its dictates with the variation of events and circumstances.

A few men of picked nature, full of faith, courage, and contempt for others, try earnestly to set forth as much as they can grasp of this inner law; but the vast majority, when they come to advise the young, must be content to retail certain doctrines which have been already retailed to them in their own youth. Every generation has to educate another which it has brought upon the stage. People who readily accept the responsibility of parentship, having very different matters in their eye, are apt to feel rueful when that responsibility falls due. What are they to tell the child about life and conduct, subjects on which they have themselves so few and such confused opinions? Indeed, I do not know; the least said, perhaps, the soonest mended; and yet the child keeps asking, and the parent must find some words to say in his own defence. Where does he find them? and what are they when found?

As a matter of experience, and in nine hundred and ninety-nine cases out of a thousand, he will instil into his wide-eyed brat three bad things; the terror of public opinion, and, flowing from that as a fountain, the desire of wealth and applause. Besides these, or what might be deduced as corollaries from these, he will teach not much else of any effective value: some dim notions of divinity, perhaps, and book-keeping, and how to walk through a quadrille.

But, you may tell me, the young people are taught to be Christians. It may be want of penetration, but I have not yet been able to perceive it. As an honest man, whatever we teach, and be it good or evil, it is not the doctrine of Christ. What he taught (and in this he is like all other teachers worthy of the name) was not a code of rules, but a ruling spirit; not truths, but a spirit of truth; not views, but a view. What he showed us was an attitude of mind. Towards the many considerations on which conduct is built, each man stands in a certain relation. He takes life on a certain principle. He has a compass in his spirit which points in a certain direction. It is the attitude, the relation, the point of the compass, that is the whole body and gist of what he has to teach us; in this, the details are comprehended; out of this the specific precepts issue, and by this, and this only, can they be explained and applied. And thus, to learn aright from any teacher, we must first of all, like a historical artist, think ourselves into sympathy with his position and, in the technical phrase, create his character. A historian confronted with some ambiguous politician, or an actor charged with a part, have but one preoccupation; they must search all round and upon every side, and grope for some central conception which is to explain and justify the most extreme details; until that is found, the politician is an enigma, or perhaps a quack, and the part a tissue of fustian sentiment and big words; but once that is found, all enters into a plan, a human nature appears, the politician or the stage-king is understood from point to point, from end to end. This is a degree of trouble which will be gladly taken by a very humble artist; but not even the terror of eternal fire can teach a business man to bend his imagination to such athletic efforts. Yet without this, all is vain;

until we understand the whole, we shall understand none of the parts; and otherwise we have no more than broken images and scattered words; the meaning remains buried; and the language in which our prophet speaks to us is a dead language in our ears.

Take a few of Christ's sayings and compare them with our current doctrines.

" *Ye cannot,*" he says, " *serve God and Mammon.*" Cannot? And our whole system is to teach us how we can!

" *The children of this world are wiser in their generation than the children of light.*" Are they? I had been led to understand the reverse: that the Christian merchant, for example, prospered exceedingly in his affairs; that honesty was the best policy; that an author of repute had written a conclusive treatise " How to make the best of both worlds." Of both worlds indeed! Which am I to believe then—Christ or the author of repute?

" *Take no thought for the morrow.*" Ask the Successful Merchant; interrogate your own heart; and you will have to admit that this is not only a silly but an immoral position. All we believe, all we hope, all we honour in ourselves or our contemporaries, stands condemned in this one sentence, or, if you take the other view, condemns the sentence as unwise and inhumane. We are not then of the "same mind that was in Christ." We disagree with Christ. Either Christ meant nothing, or else he or we must be in the wrong. Well says Thoreau, speaking of some texts from the New Testament, and finding a strange echo of another style which the reader may recognise: " Let

534

but one of these sentences be rightly read from any pulpit in the land, and there would not be left one stone of that meeting-house upon another."

It may be objected that these are what are called "hard sayings"; and that a man, or an education, may be very sufficiently Christian although it leave some of these sayings upon one side. But this is a very gross delusion. Although truth is difficult to state, it is both easy and agreeable to receive, and the mind runs out to meet it ere the phrase be done. The universe, in relation to what any man can say of it, is plain, patent, and staringly comprehensible. In itself, it is a great and travailing ocean, unsounded, unvoyageable, an eternal mystery to man; or, let us say, it is a monstrous and impassable mountain, one side of which, and a few near slopes and foot-hills, we can dimly study with these mortal eyes. But what any man can say of it, even in his highest utterance, must have relation to this little and plain corner, which is no less visible to us than to him. We are looking on the same map; it will go hard if we cannot follow the demonstration. The longest and most abstruse flight of a philosopher becomes clear and shallow, in the flash of a moment, when we suddenly perceive the aspect and drift of his intention. The longest argument is but a finger pointed; once we get our own finger rightly parallel, and we see what the man meant, whether it be a new star or an old street-lamp. And briefly, if a saying is hard to understand, it is because we are thinking of something else.

But to be a true disciple is to think of the same things as our prophet, and to think of different things in the

same order. To be of the same mind with another is
to see all things in the same perspective; it is not to
agree in a few indifferent matters near at hand and not
much debated; it is to follow him in his farthest flights,
to see the force of his hyperboles, to stand so exactly
in the centre of his vision that whatever he may express,
your eyes will light at once on the original, that whatever he may see to declare, your mind will at once
accept. You do not belong to the school of any philosopher because you agree with him that theft is, on
the whole, objectionable, or that the sun is overhead
at noon. It is by the hard sayings that discipleship is
tested. We are all agreed about the middling and indifferent parts of knowledge and morality; even the
most soaring spirits too often take them tamely upon
trust. But the man, the philosopher or the moralist,
does not stand upon these chance adhesions; and the
purpose of any system looks towards those extreme
points where it steps valiantly beyond tradition and
returns with some covert hint of things outside. Then
only can you be certain that the words are not words of
course, nor mere echoes of the past; then only are you
sure that if he be indicating anything at all, it is a star
and not a street-lamp; then only do you touch the heart
of the mystery, since it was for these that the author
wrote his book.

Now, every now and then, and indeed surprisingly
often, Christ finds a word that transcends all commonplace morality; every now and then he quits the
beaten track to pioneer the unexpressed, and throws
out a pregnant and magnanimous hyperbole; for it
is only by some bold poetry of thought that men can

be strung up above the level of every-day conceptions to take a broader look upon experience or accept some higher principle of conduct. To a man who is of the same mind that was in Christ, who stands at some centre not too far from his, and looks at the world and conduct from some not dissimilar or, at least, not opposing attitude—or, shortly, to a man who is of Christ's philosophy—every such saying should come home with a thrill of joy and corroboration; he should feel each one below his feet as another sure foundation in the flux of time and chance; each should be another proof that in the torrent of the years and generations, where doctrines and great armaments and empires are swept away and swallowed, he stands immovable, holding by the eternal stars. But alas! at this juncture of the ages it is not so with us; on each and every such occasion our whole fellowship of Christians falls back in disapproving wonder and implicitly denies the saying. Christians! the farce is impudently broad. Let us stand up in the sight of heaven and confess. The ethics that we hold are those of Benjamin Franklin. *Honesty is the best policy*, is perhaps a hard saying; it is certainly one by which a wise man of these days will not too curiously direct his steps; but I think it shows a glimmer of meaning to even our most dimmed intelligences; I think we perceive a principle behind it; I think, without hyperbole, we are of the same mind that was in Benjamin Franklin.

CHAPTER II

But, I may be told, we teach the ten commandments, where a world of morals lies condensed, the very pith and epitome of all ethics and religion; and a young man with these precepts engraved upon his mind must follow after profit with some conscience and Christianity of method. A man cannot go very far astray who neither dishonours his parents, nor kills, nor commits adultery, nor steals, nor bears false witness; for these things, rightly thought out, cover a vast field of duty.

Alas! what is a precept? It is at best an illustration; it is case law at the best which can be learned by precept. The letter is not only dead, but killing; the spirit which underlies, and cannot be uttered, alone is true and helpful. This is trite to sickness; but familiarity has a cunning disenchantment; in a day or two she can steal all beauty from the mountain-tops; and the most startling words begin to fall dead upon the ear after several repetitions. If you see a thing too often, you no longer see it; if you hear a thing too often, you no longer hear it. Our attention requires to be surprised; and to carry a fort by assault, or to gain a thoughtful hearing from the ruck of mankind, are feats of about an equal difficulty and must be tried by not dissimilar means. The whole Bible has thus lost its message for the common run of hearers; it has become mere words of course; and the parson may bawl himself scarlet and beat the pulpit like a thing possessed, but his hearers will continue to nod; they are strangely at peace; they know all he has to say; ring the old bell as you choose, it is still the old bell and it cannot startle their composure. And so with this by-word about the letter and the spirit. It is quite true, no doubt; but it has no meaning in the world to any man of us. Alas! it has just this meaning, and neither more nor less: that while the spirit is true, the letter is eternally false.

The shadow of a great oak lies abroad upon the ground at noon, perfect, clear, and stable like the earth. But let a man set himself to mark out the boundary with cords and pegs, and were he never so nimble and never so exact, what with the multiplicity of the leaves and the progression of the shadow as it flees before the travelling sun, long ere he has made the circuit the whole figure will have changed. Life may be compared, not to a single tree, but to a great and complicated forest; circumstance is more swiftly changing than a shadow, language much more inexact than the tools of a surveyor; from day to day the trees fall and are renewed; the very essences are fleeting as we look; and the whole world of leaves is swinging tempest-tossed among the winds of time. Look now for your shadows. O man of formulæ, is this a place for you? Have you fitted the spirit to a single case? Alas, in the cycle of the ages when shall such another be proposed for the judgment of man? Now when the sun shines and the winds blow, the wood is filled with an innumerable multitude of shadows, tumultuously tossed and changing; and at every gust the whole carpet leaps and becomes new. Can you or your heart say more?

Look back now, for a moment, on your own brief experience of life; and although you lived it feelingly in your own person, and had every step of conduct burned in by pains and joys upon your memory, tell me what definite lesson does experience hand on from youth to manhood, or from both to age? The settled tenor which first strikes the eye is but the shadow of a delusion. This is gone; that never truly was; and you yourself are altered beyond recognition. Times and men and circumstances change about your changing character, with a speed of which no earthly hurricane affords an image. What was the best yesterday, is it still the best in this changed theatre of a to-morrow? Will your own Past truly guide you in your own violent and unexpected Future? And if this be questionable, with what humble, with what hopeless eyes, should we not watch other men driving beside us on their unknown careers, seeing with unlike eyes, impelled by different gales, doing and suffering in another sphere of things?

And as the authentic clue to such a labyrinth and change of scene, do you offer me these twoscore words? these five bald prohibitions? For the moral precepts are no more than five; the first four deal rather with matters of observance than of conduct; the tenth, *Thou shalt not covet*, stands upon another basis, and shall be spoken of ere long. The Jews, to whom they were first given, in the course of years began to find these precepts insufficient; and made an addition of no less than six hundred and fifty others! They hoped to make a pocket-book of reference on morals, which should stand to life in some such relation, say, as Hoyle stands in to the scientific game of whist. The comparison is just, and condemns the design; for those who play by rule will never be more than tolerable players; and you and I would like to play our game in life to the noblest and the most divine advantage. Yet if the Jews took a petty and huckstering view of conduct, what view do we take ourselves, who callously leave youth to go forth into the enchanted forest, full of spells and dire chimeras, with no guidance more complete than is afforded by these five precepts?

Honour thy father and thy mother. Yes, but does that mean to obey? and if so, how long and how far? *Thou shalt not kill.* Yet the very intention and purport of the prohibition may be best fulfilled by killing. *Thou shalt not commit adultery.* But some of the ugliest adulteries are committed in the bed of marriage and under the sanction of religion and law. *Thou shalt not bear false witness.* How? by speech or by silence also? or even by a smile? *Thou shalt not steal.* Ah, that indeed! But what is *to steal?*

To steal? It is another word to be construed; and who is to be our guide? The police will give us one construction, leaving the word only that least minimum of meaning without which society would fall in pieces; but surely we must take some higher sense than this; surely we hope more than a bare subsistence for mankind; surely we wish mankind to prosper and go on from strength to strength, and ourselves to live rightly in the eye of some more exacting potentate than a policeman. The approval or the disapproval of the police must be eternally indifferent to a man who is both valorous and good. There is extreme discomfort, but no shame, in the condemnation of the law. The law represents that modicum of morality which can be squeezed out of the ruck of mankind; but what is that to me, who aim higher and seek to be my own more stringent judge? I observe with pleasure that no brave man has ever given a rush for such considerations. The Japanese have a nobler and more sentimental feeling for this social bond into which we all are born when we come into the world, and whose comforts and protection we all indifferently share throughout our lives:—but even to them, no more than to our Western saints and heroes, does the law of the state supersede the higher law of duty. Without hesitation and without remorse, they transgress the stiffest enactments rather than abstain from doing right. But the accidental superior duty being thus fulfilled, they at once return in allegiance to the common duty of all citizens; and hasten to denounce themselves; and value at an equal rate their just crime and their equally just submission to its punishment.

The evading of the police will not long satisfy an active conscience or a thoughtful head. But to show you how one or the other may trouble a man, and what a vast extent of frontier is left unridden by this invaluable eighth commandment, let me tell you a few pages out of a young man's life.

He was a friend of mine; a young man like others; generous, flighty, as variable as youth itself, but always with some high motions and on the search for higher thoughts of life. I should tell you at once that he thoroughly agrees with the eighth commandment. But he got hold of some unsettling works, the New Testament among others, and this loosened his views of life and led him into many perplexities. As he was the son of a man in a certain position, and well off, my friend had enjoyed from the first the advantages of education, nay, he had been kept alive through a sickly childhood by constant watchfulness, comforts, and change of air; for all of which he was indebted to his father's wealth.

At college he met other lads more diligent than himself, who followed the plough in summer-time to pay their college fees in winter; and this inequality struck him with some force. He was at that age of a conversable temper, and insatiably curious in the aspects of life; and he spent much of his time scraping acquaintance with all classes of man- and womankind. In this way he came upon many depressed ambitions, and many intelligences stunted for want of opportunity; and this also struck him. He began to perceive that life was a handicap upon strange, wrong-sided principles; and not, as he had been told, a fair and equal race. He began to tremble that he himself had been unjustly favoured, when he saw all the avenues of wealth and power and comfort closed against so many of his superiors and equals, and held unwearyingly open before so idle, so desultory, and so dissolute a being as himself. There sat a youth beside him on the college benches, who had only one shirt to his back, and, at intervals sufficiently far apart, must stay at home to have it washed. It was my friend's principle to stay away as often as he dared; for I fear he was no friend to learning. But there was something that came home to him sharply, in this fellow who had to give over study till his shirt was washed, and the scores of others who had never an opportunity at all. *If one of these could take his place*, he thought; and the thought tore away a bandage from his eyes. He was eaten by the shame of his discoveries, and despised himself as an unworthy favourite and a creature of the backstairs of Fortune. He could no longer see without confusion one of these brave young fellows battling up hill against adversity. Had he not filched that fellow's birthright? At best was he not coldly profiting by the injustice of society, and greedily devouring stolen goods? The money, indeed, belonged to his father, who had worked, and thought, and given up his liberty to earn it; but by what justice could the money belong to my friend, who had, as yet, done nothing but help to squander it? A more sturdy honesty, joined to a more even and impartial temperament, would have drawn from these considerations a new force of industry, that this equivocal position might be brought as swiftly as possible to an end, and some good services to mankind justify the appropriation of expense. It was not so with my friend, who was only unsettled and discouraged, and filled full of that trumpeting anger with which young men regard injustices in the first blush of youth; although in a few years they will tamely acquiesce in their existence, and knowingly profit by their complications. Yet all this while he suffered many indignant pangs. And once, when he put on his boots, like any other unripe donkey, to run away from home, it was his best consolation that he was now, at a single plunge, to free himself from the responsibility of this wealth that was not his, and do battle equally against his fellows in the warfare of life.

Some time after this, falling into ill health, he was sent at great expense to a more favourable climate; and then I think his perplexities were thickest. When he thought of all the other young men of singular promise, upright, good, the prop of families, who must remain at home to die, and with all their possibilities be lost to life and mankind; and how he, by one more unmerited favour, was chosen out from all these others to survive; he felt as if there were no life, no labour, no devotion of soul and body, that could repay and justify these partialities. A religious lady, to whom he communicated these reflections, could see no force in them whatever. "It was God's will," said she. But he knew it was by God's will that Joan of Arc was burnt at Rouen, which cleared neither Bedford nor Bishop Cauchon; and again, by God's will that Christ was crucified outside Jerusalem, which excused neither the rancour of the priests nor the timidity of Pilate. He knew, moreover, that although the possibility of this favour he was now enjoying issued from his circumstances, its acceptance was the act of his own will; and he had accepted it greedily, longing for rest and sunshine. And hence this allegation of God's providence did little to relieve his scruples. I promise you he had a very troubled mind. And I would not laugh if I were you, though while he was thus making mountains out of what you think mole-hills, he were still (as perhaps he was) contentedly practising many other things that to you seem black as hell. Every man is his own judge and mountain-guide through life. There is an old story of a mote and a beam, apparently not true, but worthy perhaps of some consideration. I should, if I were you, give some consideration to these scruples of his, and if I were he, I should do the like by yours; for it is not unlikely that there may be something under both. In the meantime you must hear how my friend acted. Like many invalids, he supposed that he would die. Now should he die, he saw no means of repaying this huge loan which, by the hands of his father, mankind had advanced him for his sickness. In that case it would be lost money. So he determined that the advance should be as small as possible; and, so long as he continued to doubt his recovery, lived in an upper room, and grudged himself all but necessaries. But so soon as he began to perceive a change for the better, he felt justified in spending more freely, to speed and brighten his return to health, and trusted in the future to lend a help to mankind, as mankind, out of its treasury, had lent a help to him.

I do not say but that my friend was a little too curious and partial in his view; nor thought too much of himself and too little of his parents; but I do say that here are some scruples which tormented my friend in his youth, and still, perhaps, at odd times give him a prick in the midst of his enjoyments, and which after all have some foundation in justice, and point, in their confused way, to some more honourable honesty within the reach of man. And at least, is not this an unusual gloss upon the eighth commandment? And what sort of comfort, guidance, or illumination did that precept afford my friend throughout these contentions? "Thou shalt not steal." With all my heart! But *am* I stealing?

The truly quaint materialism of our view of life disables us from pursuing any transaction to an end. You can make no one understand that his bargain is anything more than a bargain, whereas in point of fact it is a link in the policy of mankind, and either a good or an evil to the world. We have a sort of blindness which prevents us from seeing anything but sovereigns. If one man agrees to give another so many shillings for so many hours' work, and then wilfully gives him a certain proportion of the price in bad money and only the remainder in good, we can see with half an eye that this man is a thief. But if the other spends a certain proportion of the hours in smoking a pipe of tobacco, and a certain other proportion in looking at the sky, or the clock, or trying to recall an air, or in meditation on his own past adventures, and only the remainder in downright work such as he is paid to do, is he, because the theft is one of time and not of money,—is he any the less a thief ? The one gave a bad shilling, the other an imperfect hour; but both broke the bargain, and each is a thief. In piece-work, which is what most of us do, the case is none the less plain for being even less material. If you forge a bad knife, you have wasted some of mankind's iron, and then, with unrivalled cynicism, you pocket some of mankind's money for your trouble. Is there any man so blind who cannot see that this is theft ? Again, if you carelessly cultivate a farm, you have been playing fast and loose with mankind's resources against hunger; there will be less bread in consequence, and for lack of that bread somebody will die next winter: a grim consideration. And you must not hope to shuffle out of blame because you got less money for your less quantity of bread; for although a theft be partly punished, it is none the less a theft for that. You took the farm against competitors; there were others ready to shoulder the responsibility and be answerable for the tale of loaves; but it was you who took it. By the act you came under a tacit bargain with mankind to cultivate that farm with your best endeavour; you were under no superintendence, you were on parole; and you have broke your bargain, and to all who look closely, and yourself among the rest if you have moral eyesight, you are a thief. Or take the case of men of letters. Every piece of work which is not as good as you can make it, which you have palmed off imperfect, meagrely thought, niggardly in execution, upon mankind who is your paymaster on parole and in a sense your pupil, every hasty or slovenly or untrue performance, should rise up against you in the court of your own heart and condemn you for a thief. Have you a salary? If you trifle with your health, and so render yourself less capable for duty, and still touch and still greedily pocket the emolument—what are you but a thief? Have you double accounts? do you by any time-honoured juggle, deceit, or ambiguous process, gain more from those who deal with you than if you were bargaining and dealing face to face in front of God?—What are you but a thief? Lastly, if you fill an office, or produce an article, which, in your heart of hearts, you think a delusion and a fraud upon mankind, and still draw your salary and go through the sham manœuvres of this office, or still book your profits and keep on flooding the world with these injurious goods? —though you were old, and bald, and the first at church, and a baronet, what are you but a thief ? These may seem hard words and mere curiosities of the intellect, in an age when the spirit of honesty is so sparingly cultivated that all business is conducted upon lies and so-called customs of the trade, that not a man bestows two thoughts on the utility or honourableness of his pursuit. I would say less if I thought less. But looking to my own reason and the right of things, I can only avow that I am a thief myself, and that I passionately suspect my neighbours of the same guilt.

Where did you hear that it was easy to be honest ? Do you find that in your Bible ? Easy ? It is easy to be an ass and follow the multitude like a blind, besotted bull in a stampede; and that, I am well aware, is what you and Mrs. Grundy mean by being honest. But it will not bear the stress of time nor the scrutiny of conscience. Even before the lowest of all tribunals—before a court of law, whose business it is, not to keep men right, or within a thousand miles of right, but to withhold them from going so tragically wrong that they will pull down the whole jointed fabric of society by their misdeeds—even before a court of law, as we begin to see in these last days, our easy view of following at each other's tails, alike to good and evil, is beginning to be reproved and punished, and declared no honesty at all, but open theft and swindling; and simpletons who have gone on through life with a quiet conscience may learn suddenly, from the lips of a judge, that the custom of the trade may be a custom of the devil. You thought it was easy to be honest. Did you think it was easy to be just and kind and truthful ? Did you think the whole duty of aspiring man was as simple as a hornpipe? and you could walk through life like a gentleman and a hero, with no more concern than it takes to go to church or to address a circular? And yet all this time you had the eighth commandment! and, what makes it richer, you would not have broken it for the world!

The truth is, that these commandments by themselves are of little use in private judgment. If compression is what you want, you have their whole spirit compressed into the golden rule; and yet there expressed with more significance, since the law is there spiritually and not materially stated. And in truth, four out of these ten commands, from the sixth to the ninth, are rather legal than ethical. The police court is their proper home. A magistrate cannot tell whether you love your neighbour as yourself, but he can tell more or less whether you have murdered, or stolen, or committed adultery, or held up your hand and testified to that which was not; and these things, for rough practical tests, are as good as can be found. And perhaps, therefore, the best condensation of the Jewish moral law is in the maxims of the priests, "neminem lædere" and "suum cuique tribunere." But all this granted, it becomes only the more plain that they are inadequate in the sphere of personal morality; that while they tell the magistrate roughly when to punish, they can never direct an anxious sinner what to do.

Only Polonius, or the like solemn sort of ass, can offer us a succinct proverb by way of advice, and not burst out blushing in our faces. We grant them one and all, and for all that they are worth; it is something above and beyond that we desire. Christ was in gen-

eral a great enemy to such a way of teaching; we rarely
find him meddling with any of these plump commands
but it was to open them out, and lift his hearers from
the letter to the spirit. For morals are a personal affair;
in the war of righteousness every man fights for his own
hand; all the six hundred precepts of the Mishna cannot
shake my private judgment; my magistracy of myself
is an indefeasible charge, and my decisions absolute
for the time and case. The moralist is not a judge of
appeal, but an advocate who pleads at my tribunal.
He has to show not the law, but that the law applies.
Can he convince me? then he gains the cause. And
thus you find Christ giving various counsels to varying
people, and often jealously careful to avoid definite
precept. Is he asked, for example, to divide a heritage?
He refuses: and the best advice that he will offer is but
a paraphrase of that tenth commandment which figures
so strangely among the rest. *Take heed, and beware
of covetousness.* If you complain that this is vague, I
have failed to carry you along with me in my guar-
ment. For no definite precept can be more than an
illustration, though its truth were resplendent like the
sun, and it was announced from heaven by the voice
of God. And life is so intricate and changing, that
perhaps not twenty times, or perhaps not twice in the
ages, shall we find that nice consent of circumstances
to which alone it can apply.

CHAPTER III

ALTHOUGH the world and life have in a sense become commonplace to our experience, it is but in an external torpor; the true sentiment slumbers within us; and we have but to reflect on ourselves or our surroundings to rekindle our astonishment. No length of habit can blunt our first surprise. Of the world I have but little to say in this connection; a few strokes shall suffice. We inhabit a dead ember swimming wide in the blank of space, dizzily spinning as it swims, and lighted up from several million miles away by a more horrible hell-fire than was ever conceived by the theological imagination. Yet the dead ember is a green, commodious dwelling-place; and the reverberation of this hell-fire ripens flower and fruit and mildly warms us on summer eves upon the lawn. Far off on all hands other dead embers, other flaming suns, wheel and race in the apparent void; the nearest is out of call, the farthest so far that the heart sickens in the effort to conceive the distance. Shipwrecked seamen on the deep, though they bestride but the truncheon of a boom, are safe and near at home compared with mankind on its bullet. Even to us who have known no other, it seems a strange, if not an appalling, place of residence.

But far stranger is the resident, man, a creature compact of wonders that, after centuries of custom, is still wonderful to himself. He inhabits a body which he is continually outliving, discarding, and renewing. Food and sleep, by an unknown alchemy, restore his spirits and the freshness of his countenance. Hair grows on him like grass; his eyes, his brain, his sinews, thirst for action; he joys to see and touch and hear, to partake the sun and wind, to sit down and intently ponder on his astonishing attributes and situation, to rise up and run to perform the strange and revolting round of physical functions. The sight of a flower, the note of a bird, will often move him deeply; yet he looks unconcerned on the impassable distances and portentous bonfires of the universe. He comprehends, he designs, he tames nature, rides the sea, ploughs, climbs the air in a balloon, makes vast inquiries, begins interminable labours, joins himself into federations and populous cities, spends his days to deliver the ends of the earth or to benefit unborn posterity; and yet knows himself for a piece of unsurpassed fragility and the creature of a few days. His sight, which conducts him, which takes notice of the farthest stars, which is miraculous in every way and a thing defying explanation or belief, is yet lodged in a piece of jelly, and can be extinguished with a touch. His heart, which all through life so indomitably, so athletically labours, is but a capsule, and may be stopped with a pin. His whole body, for all its savage energies, its leaping and its winged desires, may yet be tamed and conquered by a draught of air or a sprinkling of cold dew. What he calls death, which is the seeming arrest of everything, and the ruin and hateful transformation of the visible body, lies in wait for him outwardly in a thousand accidents, and grows up in secret diseases from within. He is still learning to be a man when his faculties are already beginning to decline; he has not yet understood himself or his position before he inevitably dies. And yet this mad, chimerical creature can take no thought of his last end, lives as though he were eternal, plunges with his vulnerable body into the shock of war, and daily affronts death with unconcern. He cannot take a step without pain or pleasure. His life is a tissue of sensations, which he distinguishes as they seem to come more directly from himself or his surroundings. He is conscious of himself as a joyer or a sufferer, as that which craves, chooses, and is satisfied; conscious of his surroundings as it were of an inexhaustible purveyor, the source of aspects, inspirations, wonders, cruel knocks and transporting caresses. Thus he goes on his way, stumbling among delights and agonies.

Matter is a far-fetched theory, and materialism is without a root in man. To him everything is important in the degree to which it moves him. The telegraph wires and posts, the electricity speeding from clerk to clerk, the clerks, the glad or sorrowful import of the message, and the paper on which it is finally brought to him at home, are all equally facts, all equally exist for man. A word or a thought can wound him as acutely as a knife of steel. If he thinks he is loved, he will rise up and glory to himself, although he be in a distant land and short of necessary bread. Does he think he is not loved?—he may have the woman at his beck, and there is not a joy for him in all the world. Indeed, if we are to make any account of this figment of reason, the distinction between material and immaterial, we shall conclude that the life of each man as an individual is immaterial, although the continuation and prospects of mankind as a race turn upon material conditions. The physical business of each man's body is transacted for him; like a Sybarite, he has attentive valets in his own viscera; he breathes, he sweats, he digests without an effort, or so much as a consenting volition; for the most part he even eats, not with a wakeful consciousness, but as it were between two thoughts. His life is centred among other and more important considerations; touch him in his honour or his love, creatures of the imagination which attach him to mankind or to an individual man or woman; cross him in his piety which connects his soul with heaven; and he turns from his food, he loathes his breath, and with a magnanimous emotion cuts the knots of his existence and frees himself at a blow from the web of pains and pleasures.

It follows that man is twofold at least; that he is not a rounded and autonomous empire; but that in the same body with him there dwell other powers, tributary but independent. If I now behold one walking in a garden, curiously coloured and illuminated by the sun, digesting his food with elaborate chemistry, breathing, circulating blood, directing himself by the sight of his eyes, accommodating his body by a thousand delicate balancings to the wind and the uneven surface of the path, and all the time, perhaps, with his mind engaged about America, or the dog-star, or the attributes of God —what am I to say, or how am I to describe the thing I see? Is that truly a man, in the rigorous meaning of the word? or is it not a man and something else? What, then, are we to count the centre-bit and axle of a being so variously compounded? It is a question much debated. Some read his history in a certain intricacy of nerve and the success of successive digestions; others find him an exiled piece of heaven blown upon and determined by the breath of God; and both schools of theorists will scream like scalded children at a word of doubt. Yet either of these views, however plausible, is beside the question; either may be right; and I care not; I ask a more particular answer, and to a more immediate point. What is the man? There is Something that was before hunger and that remains behind after a meal. It may or may not be engaged in any given act or passion, but when it is, it changes, heightens, and sanctifies. Thus it is not engaged in lust, where satisfaction ends the chapter; and it is engaged in love, where no satisfaction can blunt the edge of the desire, and where age, sickness, or alienation may deface what was desirable without diminishing the sentiment. This something, which is the man, is a permanence which abides through the vicissitudes of passion, now overwhelmed and now triumphant, now unconscious of itself in the immediate distress of appetite or pain, now rising unclouded above all. So, to the man, his own central self fades and grows clear again amid the tumult of the senses, like a revolving Pharos in the night. It is forgotten; it is hid, it seems, for ever; and yet in the next calm hour he shall behold himself once more, shining and unmoved among changes and storm.

Mankind, in the sense of the creeping mass that is born and eats, that generates and dies, is but the aggregate of the outer and lower sides of man. This inner consciousness, this lantern alternately obscured and shining, to and by which the individual exists and must order his conduct, is something special to himself and not common to the race. His joys delight, his sorrows wound him, according as *this* is interested or indifferent in the affair; according as they arise in an imperial war or in a broil conducted by the tributary chieftains of the mind. He may lose all, and *this* not suffer; he may lose what is materially a trifle, and *this* leap in his bosom with a cruel pang. I do not speak of it to hardened theorists: the living man knows keenly what it is I mean.

"Perceive at last that thou hast in thee something better and more divine than the things which cause the various effects, and, as it were, pull thee by the strings. What is that now in thy mind? is it fear, or suspicion, or desire, or anything of that kind?" Thus far Marcus Aurelius, in one of the most notable passages in any book. Here is a question worthy to be answered. What is in thy mind? What is the utterance of your inmost self when, in a quiet hour, it can be heard intelligibly? It is something beyond the compass of your thinking, inasmuch as it is yourself; but is it not of a higher spirit than you had dreamed betweenwhiles, and erect above all base considerations? This soul seems hardly touched with our infirmities; we can find in it certainly no fear, suspicion, or desire; we are only conscious—and that as though we read it in the eyes of some one else—of a great and unqualified readiness. A readiness to what? to pass over and look beyond the objects of desire and fear, for something else. And this something else? this something which is apart from desire and fear, to which all the kingdoms of the world and the immediate death of the body are alike indifferent and beside the point, and which yet regards conduct— by what name are we to call it? It may be the love of God; or it may be an inherited (and certainly well-concealed) instinct to preserve self and propagate the race; I am not, for the moment, averse to either theory; but it will save time to call it righteousness. By so doing I intend no subterfuge to beg a question; I am indeed ready, and more than willing, to accept the rigid consequence, and lay aside, as far as the treachery of the reason will permit, all former meanings attached to the word *righteousness*. What is right is that for which a man's central self is ever ready to sacrifice immediate or distant interests; what is wrong is what the central self discards or rejects as incompatible with the fixed design of righteousness.

To make this admission is to lay aside all hope of definition. That which is right upon this theory is intimately dictated to each man by himself, but can never be rigorously set forth in language, and never, above all, imposed upon another. The conscience has, then, a vision like that of the eyes, which is incommunicable, and for the most part illuminates none but its possessor. When many people perceive the same or any cognate facts, they agree upon a word as symbol; and hence we have such words as *tree, star, love, honour*, or *death;* hence also we have this word *right*, which, like the others, we all understand, most of us understand differently, and none can express succinctly otherwise. Yet even on the straitest view, we can make some steps towards comprehension of our own superior thoughts. For it is an incredible and most bewildering fact that a man, through life, is on variable terms with himself; he is aware of tiffs and reconciliations; the intimacy is at times almost suspended, at times it is renewed again with joy. As we said before, his inner self or soul appears to him by successive revelations, and is frequently obscured. It is from a study of these alternations that we can alone hope to discover, even dimly, what seems right and what seems wrong to this veiled prophet of ourself.

All that is in the man in the larger sense, what we call impression as well as what we call intuition, so far as my argument looks, we must accept. It is not wrong to desire food, or exercise, or beautiful surroundings, or the love of sex, or interest which is the food of the mind. All these are craved; all these should be craved; to none of these in itself does the soul demur; where there comes an undeniable want, we recognise a demand of nature. Yet we know that these natural demands may be superseded; for the demands which are common to mankind make but a shadowy consideration in comparison to the demands of the individual soul. Food is almost the first prerequisite; and yet a high character will go without food to the ruin and death of the body rather than gain it in a manner which the spirit disavows. Pascal laid aside mathematics; Origen doctored his body with a knife; every day some one is thus mortifying his dearest interests and desires, and, in Christ's words, entering maim into the kingdom of heaven. This is to supersede the lesser and less harmonious affections by renunciation; and though by this ascetic path we may get to heaven, we cannot get thither a whole and perfect man. But there is another way, to supersede them by reconciliation, in which the soul and all the faculties and senses pursue a common route and share in one desire. Thus, man is tormented by a very imperious physical desire; it spoils his rest, it is not to be denied; the doctors will tell you, not I, how it is a physical need, like the want of food or slumber. In the satisfaction of this desire, as it first appears, the soul sparingly takes part; nay, it oft unsparingly regrets and disapproves the satisfaction. But let the man learn to love a woman as far as he is capable of love; and for this random affection of the body there is substituted a steady determination, a consent of all his powers and faculties, which supersedes, adopts, and commands the other. The desire survives, strengthened, perhaps, but taught obedience, and changed in scope and character. Life is no longer a tale of betrayals and regrets; for the man now lives as a whole; his consciousness now moves on uninterrupted like a river; through all the extremes and ups and downs of passion, he remains approvingly conscious of himself.

Now to me, this seems a type of that rightness which the soul demands. It demands that we shall not live alternately with our opposing tendencies in continual seesaw of passion and disgust, but seek some path on which the tendencies shall no longer oppose, but serve each other to a common end. It demands that we shall not pursue broken ends, but great and comprehensive purposes, in which soul and body may unite like notes in a harmonious chord. That were indeed a way of peace and pleasure, that were indeed a heaven upon earth. It does not demand, however, or, to speak in measure, it does not demand of me, that I should starve my appetites for no purpose under heaven but as a purpose in itself; or, in a weak despair, pluck out the eye that I have not yet learned to guide and enjoy with wisdom. The soul demands unity of purpose, not the dismemberment of man; it seeks to roll up all his strength and sweetness, all his passion and wisdom, into one, and make of him a perfect man exulting in perfection. To conclude ascetically is to give up, and not to solve, the problem. The ascetic and the creeping hog, although they are at different poles, have equally failed in life. The one has sacrificed his crew; the other brings back his seamen in a cock-boat, and has lost the ship. I believe there are not many sea-captains who would plume themselves on either result as a success.

But if it is righteousness thus to fuse together our divisive impulses and march with one mind through life, there is plainly one thing more unrighteous than all others, and one declension which is irretrievable and draws on the rest. And this is to lose consciousness of oneself. In the best of times, it is but by flashes, when our whole nature is clear, strong, and conscious, and events conspire to leave us free, that we enjoy communion with our soul. At the worst, we are so fallen and passive that we may say shortly we have none. An arctic torpor seizes upon men. Although built of nerves, and set adrift in a stimulating world, they develop a tendency to go bodily to sleep; consciousness becomes engrossed among the reflex and mechanical parts of life, and soon loses both the will and power to look higher considerations in the face.

This is ruin; this is the last failure in life; this is temporal damnation, damnation on the spot and without
the form of judgment. "What shall it profit a man if
he gain the whole world and *lose himself?*"

It is to keep a man awake, to keep him alive to his
own soul and its fixed design of righteousness, that the
better part of moral and religious education is directed;
not only that of words and doctors, but the sharp ferule
of calamity under which we are all God's scholars till
we die. If, as teachers, we are to say anything to the
purpose, we must say what will remind the pupil of
his soul; we must speak that soul's dialect; we must
talk of life and conduct as his soul would have him
think of them. If, from some conformity between us
and the pupil, or perhaps among all men, we do in truth
speak in such a dialect and express such views, beyond
question we shall touch in him a spring; beyond question he will recognise the dialect as one that he himself has spoken in his better hours; beyond question he
will cry, "I had forgotten, but now I remember; I too
have eyes, and I had forgot to use them! I too have a
soul of my own, arrogantly upright, and to that I will
listen and conform." In short, say to him anything
that he has once thought, or been upon the point of
thinking, or show him any view of life that he has once
clearly seen, or been upon the point of clearly seeing;
and you have done your part and may leave him to
complete the education for himself.

Now the view taught at the present time seems to
me to want greatness; and the dialect in which alone
it can be intelligibly uttered is not the dialect of my
soul. It is a sort of postponement of life; nothing

quite is, but something different is to be; we are to keep our eyes upon the indirect from the cradle to the grave. We are to regulate our conduct not by desire, but by a politic eye upon the future; and to value acts as they will bring us money or good opinion; as they will bring us, in one word, *profit*. We must be what is called respectable, and offend no one by our carriage; it will not do to make oneself conspicuous—who knows? even in virtue? says the Christian parent! And we must be what is called prudent and make money; not only because it is pleasant to have money, but because that also is a part of respectability, and we cannot hope to be received in society without decent possessions. Received in society! as if that were the kingdom of heaven! There is dear Mr. So-and-so;—look at him! —so much respected—so much looked up to—quite the Christian merchant! And we must cut our conduct as strictly as possible after the pattern of Mr. So-and-so; and lay our whole lives to make money and be strictly decent. Besides these holy injunctions, which form by far the greater part of a youth's training in our Christian homes, there are at least two other doctrines. We are to live just now as well as we can, but scrape at last into heaven, where we shall be good. We are to worry through the week in a lay, disreputable way, but, to make matters square, live a different life on Sunday.

The train of thought we have been following gives us a key to all these positions, without stepping aside to justify them on their own ground. It is because we have been disgusted fifty times with physical squalls, and fifty times torn between conflicting impulses, that we teach people this indirect and tactical procedure in life, and to judge by remote consequences instead of the immediate face of things. The very desire to act as our own souls would have us, coupled with a pathetic disbelief in ourselves, moves us to follow the example of others; perhaps, who knows? they may be on the right track; and the more our patterns are in number, the better seems the chance; until, if we be acting in concert with a whole civilised nation, there are surely a majority of chances that we must be acting right. And again, how true it is that we can never behave as we wish in this tormented sphere, and can only aspire to different and more favourable circumstances, in order to stand out and be ourselves wholly and rightly! And yet once more, if in the hurry and pressure of affairs and passions you tend to nod and become drowsy, here are twenty-four hours of Sunday set apart for you to hold counsel with your soul and look around you on the possibilities of life.

This is not, of course, all that is to be, or even should be, said for these doctrines. Only, in the course of this chapter, the reader and I have agreed upon a few catchwords, and been looking at morals on a certain system; it was a pity to lose an opportunity of testing the catchwords, and seeing whether, by this system as well as by others, current doctrines could show any probable justification. If the doctrines had come too badly out of the trial, it would have condemned the system. Our sight of the world is very narrow; the mind but a pedestrian instrument; there's nothing new under the sun, as Solomon says, except the man himself; and though that changes the aspect of everything else, yet he must see the same things as other people, only from a different side.

And now, having admitted so much, let us turn to criticism.

If you teach a man to keep his eyes upon what others think of him, unthinkingly to lead the life and hold the principles of the majority of his contemporaries, you must discredit in his eyes the one authoritative voice of his own soul. He may be a docile citizen; he will never be a man. It is ours, on the other hand, to disregard this babble and chattering of other men better and worse than we are, and to walk straight before us by what light we have. They may be right; but so, before heaven, are we. They may know; but we know also, and by that knowledge we must stand or fall. There is such a thing as loyalty to a man's own better self; and from those who have not that, God help me, how am I to look for loyalty to others? The most dull, the most imbecile, at a certain moment turn round, at a certain point will hear no further argument, but stand unflinching by their own dumb, irrational sense of right. It is not only by steel or fire, but through contempt and blame, that the martyr fulfils the calling of his dear soul. Be glad if you are not tried by such extremities. But although all the world ranged themselves in one line to tell you " This is wrong," be you your own faithful vassal and the ambassador of God—throw down the glove and answer, " This is right." Do you think you are only declaring yourself? Perhaps in some dim way, like a child who delivers a message not fully understood, you are opening wider the straits of prejudice and preparing mankind for some truer and more spiritual grasp of truth; perhaps, as you stand forth for your own judgment, you are covering a thousand weak ones with your body; perhaps, by this declaration alone, you have avoided the guilt of false witness against humanity and the little ones unborn. It is good, I believe, to be respectable, but much nobler to respect oneself and utter the voice of God. God, if there be any God, speaks daily in a new language by the tongues of men; the thoughts and habits of each fresh generation and each new-coined spirit throw another light upon the universe and contain another commentary on the printed Bibles; every scruple, every true dissent, every glimpse of something new, is a letter of God's alphabet; and though there is a grave responsibility for all who speak, is there none for those who unrighteously keep silence and conform? Is not that also to conceal and cloak God's counsel? And how should we regard the man of science who suppressed all facts that would not tally with the orthodoxy of the hour?

Wrong? You are as surely wrong as the sun rose this morning round the revolving shoulder of the world. Not truth, but truthfulness, is the good of your endeavour. For when will men receive that first part and prerequisite of truth, that, by the order of things, by the greatness of the universe, by the darkness and partiality of man's experience, by the inviolate secrecy of God, kept close in His most open revelations, every man is, and to the end of the ages must be, wrong? Wrong to the universe; wrong to mankind; wrong to God. And yet in another sense, and that plainer and nearer, every man of men, who wishes truly, must be right. He is right to himself, and in the measure of

his sagacity and candour. That let him do in all sincerity and zeal, not sparing a thought for contrary
opinions; that, for what it is worth, let him proclaim.
Be not afraid; although he be wrong, so also is the
dead, stuffed Dagon he insults. For the voice of God,
whatever it is, is not that stammering, inept tradition
which the people holds. These truths survive in travesty, swamped in a world of spiritual darkness and
confusion; and what a few comprehend and faithfully
hold, the many, in their dead jargon, repeat, degrade,
and misinterpret.

So far of Respectability: what the Covenanters used
to call "rank conformity": the deadliest gag and wet
blanket that can be laid on men. And now of Profit.
And this doctrine is perhaps the more redoubtable, because it harms all sorts of men; not only the heroic and
self-reliant, but the obedient, cowlike squadrons. A
man, by this doctrine, looks to consequences at the
second, or third, or fiftieth turn. He chooses his end,
and for that, with wily turns and through a great sea of
tedium, steers this mortal bark. There may be political
wisdom in such a view; but I am persuaded there can
spring no great moral zeal. To look thus obliquely
upon life is the very recipe for moral slumber. Our
intention and endeavour should be directed, not on
some vague end of money or applause, which shall
come to us by a ricochet in a month or a year, or twenty
years, but on the act itself; not on the approval of others,
but on the rightness of that act. At every instant, at
every step in life, the point has to be decided, our soul
has to be saved, heaven has to be gained or lost. At
every step our spirits must applaud, at every step we

must set down the foot and sound the trumpet. "This have I done," we must say; "right or wrong, this have I done, in unfeigned honour of intention, as to myself and God." The profit of every act should be this, that it was right for us to do it. Any other profit than that, if it involved a kingdom or the woman I love, ought, if I were God's upright soldier, to leave me untempted.

It is the mark of what we call a righteous decision, that it is made directly and for its own sake. The whole man, mind and body, having come to an agreement, tyrannically dictates conduct. There are two dispositions eternally opposed: that in which we recognise that one thing is wrong and another right, and that in which, not seeing any clear distinction, we fall back on the consideration of consequences. The truth is, by the scope of our present teaching, nothing is thought very wrong and nothing very right, except a few actions which have the disadvantage of being disrespectable when found out; the more serious part of men inclining to think all things *rather wrong*, the more jovial to suppose them *right enough for practical purposes*. I will engage my head, they do not find that view in their own hearts; they have taken it up in a dark despair; they are but troubled sleepers talking in their sleep. The soul, or my soul at least, thinks very distinctly upon many points of right and wrong, and often differs flatly with what is held out as the thought of corporate humanity in the code of society or the code of law. Am I to suppose myself a monster? I have only to read books, the Christian Gospels for example, to think myself a monster no longer; and instead I think the mass of people are merely speaking in their sleep.

It is a commonplace, enshrined, if I mistake not, even in school copy-books, that honour is to be sought and not fame. I ask no other admission; we are to seek honour, upright walking with our own conscience every hour of the day, and not fame, the consequence, the far-off reverberation of our footsteps. The walk, not the rumour of the walk, is what concerns righteousness. Better disrespectable honour than dishonourable fame. Better useless or seemingly hurtful honour, than dishonour ruling empires and filling the mouths of thousands. For the man must walk by what he sees, and leave the issue with God who made him and taught him by the fortune of his life. You would not dishonour yourself for money; which is at least tangible; would you do it, then, for a doubtful forecast in politics, or another person's theory in morals ?

So intricate is the scheme of our affairs, that no man can calculate the bearing of his own behaviour even on those immediately around him, how much less upon the world at large or on succeeding generations! To walk by external prudence and the rule of consequences would require, not a man, but God. All that we know to guide us in this changing labyrinth is our soul with its fixed design of righteousness, and a few old precepts which commend themselves to that. The precepts are vague when we endeavour to apply them; consequences are more entangled than a wisp of string, and their confusion is unrestingly in change; we must hold to what we know and walk by it. We must walk by faith, indeed, and not by knowledge.

You do not love another because he is wealthy or wise or eminently respectable: you love him because you

love him; that is love, and any other only a derision
and grimace. It should be the same with all our actions. If we were to conceive a perfect man, it should
be one who was never torn between conflicting impulses,
but who, on the absolute consent of all his parts and
faculties, submitted in every action of his life to a self-
dictation as absolute and unreasoned as that which bids
him love one woman and be true to her till death. But
we should not conceive him as sagacious, ascetical,
playing off his appetites against each other, turning the
wing of public respectable immorality instead of riding
it directly down, or advancing towards his end through
a thousand sinister compromises and considerations.
The one man might be wily, might be adroit, might be
wise, might be respectable, might be gloriously useful;
it is the other man who would be good.

The soul asks honour and not fame; to be upright,
not to be successful; to be good, not prosperous; to
be essentially, not outwardly, respectable. Does your
soul ask profit? Does it ask money? Does it ask the
approval of the indifferent herd? I believe not. For
my own part, I want but little money, I hope; and I
do not want to be decent at all, but to be good.

CHAPTER IV

We have spoken of that supreme self-dictation which keeps varying from hour to hour in its dictates with the variation of events and circumstances. Now, for us, that is ultimate. It may be founded on some reasonable process, but it is not a process which we can follow or comprehend. And moreover the dictation is not continuous, or not continuous except in very lively and well-living natures; and betweenwhiles we must brush along without it. Practice is a more intricate and desperate business than the toughest theorising; life is an affair of cavalry, where rapid judgment and prompt action are alone possible and right. As a matter of fact, there is no one so upright but he is influenced by the world's chatter; and no one so headlong but he requires to consider consequences and to keep an eye on profit. For the soul adopts all affections and appetites without exception, and cares only to combine them for some common purpose which shall interest all. Now respect for the opinion of others, the study of consequences and the desire of power and comfort, are all undeniably factors in the nature of man; and the more undeniably since we find that, in our current doctrines, they have swallowed up the others and are thought to conclude in themselves all the worthy parts of man. These, then, must also be suffered to affect

conduct in the practical domain, much or little according as they are forcibly or feebly present to the mind
of each.

Now a man's view of the universe is mostly a view
of the civilised society in which he lives. Other men
and women are so much more grossly and so much
more intimately palpable to his perceptions, that they
stand between him and all the rest; they are larger to
his eye than the sun, he hears them more plainly than
thunder; with them, by them, and for them, he must
live and die. And hence the laws that affect his intercourse with his fellow-men, although merely customary
and the creatures of a generation, are more clearly and
continually before his mind than those which bind him
into the eternal system of things, support him in his
upright progress on this whirling ball, or keep up the
fire of his bodily life. And hence it is that money
stands in the first rank of considerations and so powerfully affects the choice. For our society is built with
money for mortar; money is present in every joint of
circumstance; it might be named the social atmosphere,
since, in society, it is by that alone that men continue
to live, and only through that or chance that they can
reach or affect one another. Money gives us food,
shelter, and privacy; it permits us to be clean in person,
opens for us the doors of the theatre, gains us books for
study or pleasure, enables us to help the distresses of
others, and puts us above necessity so that we can
choose the best in life. If we love, it enables us to
meet and live with the loved one, or even to prolong her
health and life; if we have scruples, it gives us an opportunity to be honest; if we have any bright designs,

here is what will smooth the way to their accomplishment. Penury is the worst slavery, and will soon lead to death.

But money is only a means; it presupposes a man to use it. The rich can go where he pleases, but perhaps please himself nowhere. He can buy a library or visit the whole world, but perhaps has neither patience to read nor intelligence to see. The table may be loaded, and the appetite wanting; the purse may be full, and the heart empty. He may have gained the world and lost himself; and with all his wealth around him, in a great house and spacious and beautiful demesne, he may live as blank a life as any tattered ditcher. Without an appetite, without an aspiration, void of appreciation, bankrupt of desire and hope, there, in his great house, let him sit and look upon his fingers. It is perhaps a more fortunate destiny to have a taste for collecting shells than to be born a millionaire. Although neither is to be despised, it is always better policy to learn an interest than to make a thousand pounds; for the money will soon be spent, or perhaps you may feel no joy in spending it; but the interest remains imperishable and ever new. To become a botanist, a geologist, a social philosopher, an antiquary, or an artist, is to enlarge one's possessions in the universe by an incalculably higher degree, and by a far surer sort of property, than to purchase a farm of many acres. You had perhaps two thousand a year before the transaction; perhaps you have two thousand five hundred after it. That represents your gain in the one case. But in the other, you have thrown down a barrier which concealed significance and beauty. The blind man has learned to see. The prisoner has opened up a window in his cell and beholds enchanting prospects; he will never again be a prisoner as he was; he can watch clouds and changing seasons, ships on the river, travellers on the road, and the stars at night; happy prisoner! his eyes have broken jail! And again he who has learned to love an art or science has wisely laid up riches against the day of riches; if prosperity come, he will not enter poor into his inheritance; he will not slumber and forget himself in the lap of money, or spend his hours in counting idle treasures, but be up and briskly doing; he will have the true alchemic touch, which is not that of Midas, but which transmutes dead money into living delight and satisfaction. *Être et pas avoir*—to be, not to possess—that is the problem of life. To be wealthy, a rich nature is the first requisite and money but the second. To be of a quick and healthy blood, to share in all honourable curiosities, to be rich in admiration and free from envy, to rejoice greatly in the good of others, to love with such generosity of heart that your love is still a dear possession in absence or unkindness—these are the gifts of fortune which money cannot buy and without which money can buy nothing. For what can a man possess, or what can he enjoy, except himself? If he enlarge his nature, it is then that he enlarges his estates. If his nature be happy and valiant, he will enjoy the universe as if it were his park and orchard.

But money is not only to be spent; it has also to be earned. It is not merely a convenience or a necessary in social life; but it is the coin in which mankind pays his wages to the individual man. And from this side, the question of money has a very different scope and application. For no man can be honest who does not work. Service for service. If the farmer buys corn, and the labourer ploughs and reaps, and the baker sweats in his hot bakery, plainly you who eat must do something in your turn. It is not enough to take off your hat, or to thank God upon your knees for the admirable constitution of society and your own convenient situation in its upper and more ornamental stories. Neither is it enough to buy the loaf with a sixpence; for then you are only changing the point of the inquiry; and you must first have *bought the sixpence*. Service for service: how have you bought your sixpences? A man of spirit desires certainty in a thing of such a nature; he must see to it that there is some reciprocity between him and mankind; that he pays his expenditure in service; that he has not a lion's share in profit and a drone's in labour; and is not a sleeping partner and mere costly incubus on the great mercantile concern of mankind.

Services differ so widely with different gifts, and some are so inappreciable to external tests, that this is not only a matter for the private conscience, but one which even there must be leniently and trustfully considered. For remember how many serve mankind who do no more than meditate; and how many are precious to their friends for no more than a sweet and joyous temper. To perform the function of a man of letters it is not necessary to write; nay, it is perhaps better to be a living book. So long as we love we serve; so long as we are loved by others, I would almost say that we are indispensable; and no man is useless while he has a friend. The true services of life are inestimable in money, and are never paid. Kind words and caresses, high and wise thoughts, humane designs, tender behaviour to the weak and suffering, and all the charities of man's existence, are neither bought nor sold.

Yet the dearest and readiest, if not the most just, criterion of a man's services, is the wage that mankind pays him or, briefly, what he earns. There at least there can be no ambiguity. St. Paul is fully and freely entitled to his earnings as a tent-maker, and Socrates fully and freely entitled to his earnings as a sculptor, although the true business of each was not only something different, but something which remained unpaid. A man cannot forget that he is not superintended, and serves mankind on parole. He would like, when challenged by his own conscience, to reply: "I have done so much work, and no less, with my own hands and brain, and taken so much profit, and no more, for my own personal delight." And though St. Paul, if he had possessed a private fortune, would probably have scorned to waste his time in making tents, yet of all sacrifices to public opinion none can be more easily pardoned than that by which a man, already spiritually useful to the world, should restrict the field of his chief usefulness to perform services more apparent, and possess a livelihood that neither stupidity nor malice could call in question. Like all sacrifices to public opinion and mere external decency, this would certainly be wrong; for the soul should rest contented with its own approval and indissuadably pursue its own calling. Yet, so grave and delicate is the question, that a man may well hesitate before he decides it for himself; he may well fear that he sets too high a valuation on his own endeavours after good; he may well condescend upon a humbler duty, where others than himself shall judge the service and proportion the wage.

And yet it is to this very responsibility that the rich are born. They can shuffle off the duty on no other; they are their own paymasters on parole; and must pay themselves fair wages and no more. For I suppose that in the course of ages, and through reform and civil war and invasion, mankind was pursuing some other and more general design than to set one or two Englishmen of the nineteenth century beyond the reach of needs and duties. Society was scarce put together, and defended with so much eloquence and blood, for the convenience of two or three millionaires and a few hundred other persons of wealth and position. It is plain that if mankind thus acted and suffered during all these generations, they hoped some benefit, some ease, some well-being, for themselves and their descendants; that if they supported law and order, it was to secure fair-play for all; that if they denied themselves in the present, they must have had some designs upon the future. Now a great hereditary fortune is a miracle of man's wisdom and mankind's forbearance; it has not only been amassed and handed down, it has been suffered to be amassed and handed down; and surely in such a consideration as this, its possessor should find only a new spur to activity and honour, that with all this power of service he should not prove unserviceable, and that this mass of treasure should return in benefits upon the race. If he had twenty, or thirty, or a hundred thousand at his banker's, or if all Yorkshire or all California were his to manage or to sell, he would still be morally penniless, and have the world to begin like Whittington, until he had found some way of serving mankind. His wage is physically in his own hand; but, in honour, that wage must still be earned. He is only steward on parole of what is called his fortune. He must honourably perform his stewardship. He must estimate his own services and allow himself a salary in proportion, for that will be one among his functions. And while he will then be free to spend that salary, great or little, on his own private pleasures, the rest of his fortune he but holds and disposes under trust for mankind; it is not his, because he has not earned it; it cannot be his, because his services have already been paid; but year by year it is his to distribute, whether to help individuals whose birthright and outfit have been swallowed up in his, or to further public works and institutions.

At this rate, short of inspiration, it seems hardly possible to be both rich and honest; and the millionaire is under a far more continuous temptation to thieve than the labourer who gets his shilling daily for despicable toils. Are you surprised? It is even so. And you repeat it every Sunday in your churches. "It is easier for a camel to pass through the eye of a needle than for a rich man to enter the kingdom of God." I have heard this and similar texts ingeniously explained away and brushed from the path of the aspiring Christian by the tender Great-heart of the parish. One excellent clergyman told us that the "eye of a needle" meant a low, Oriental postern through which camels could not pass till they were unloaded—which is very

likely just; and then went on, bravely confounding the
"kingdom of God" with heaven, the future paradise,
to show that of course no rich person could expect to
carry his riches beyond the grave—which, of course,
he could not and never did. Various greedy sinners of
the congregation drank in the comfortable doctrine with
relief. It was worth the while having come to church
that Sunday morning! All was plain. The Bible, as
usual, meant nothing in particular; it was merely an
obscure and figurative school copy-book; and if a man
were only respectable, he was a man after God's own
heart.

Alas! I fear not. And though this matter of a man's
services is one for his own conscience, there are some
cases in which it is difficult to restrain the mind from
judging. Thus I shall be very easily persuaded that
a man has earned his daily bread; and if he has but a
friend or two to whom his company is delightful at
heart, I am more than persuaded at once. But it will
be very hard to persuade me that any one has earned
an income of a hundred thousand. What he is to his
friends, he still would be if he were made penniless
to-morrow; for as to the courtiers of luxury and power,
I will neither consider them friends, nor indeed consider
them at all. What he does for mankind there are most
likely hundreds who would do the same, as effectually
for the race and as pleasurably to themselves, for the
merest fraction of this monstrous wage. Why it is
paid, I am, therefore, unable to conceive, and as the
man pays it himself, out of funds in his detention, I
have a certain backwardness to think him honest.

At least, we have gained a very obvious point: that

LAY MORALS

*what a man spends upon himself, he shall have earned
by services to the race.* Thence flows a principle for the
outset of life, which is a little different from that taught
in the present day. I am addressing the middle and
the upper classes; those who have already been fostered
and prepared for life at some expense; those who have
some choice before them, and can pick professions;
and above all, those who are what is called independent,
and need do nothing unless pushed by honour or ambition. In this particular the poor are happy; among
them, when a lad comes to his strength, he must take
the work that offers, and can take it with an easy conscience. But in the richer classes the question is complicated by the number of opportunities and a variety
of considerations. Here, then, this principle of ours
comes in helpfully. The young man has to seek, not
a road to wealth, but an opportunity of service; not
money, but honest work. If he has some strong pro-
pensity, some calling of nature, some overweening
interest in any special field of industry, inquiry, or art,
he will do right to obey the impulse; and that for two
reasons: the first external, because there he will render
the best services; the second personal, because a demand of his own nature is to him without appeal
whenever it can be satisfied with the consent of his
other faculties and appetites. If he has no such elec-
tive taste, by the very principle on which he chooses
any pursuit at all he must choose the most honest and
serviceable, and not the most highly remunerated. We
have here an external problem, not from or to ourself,
but flowing from the constitution of society; and we
have our own soul with its fixed design of righteous-

ness. All that can be done is to present the problem
in proper terms, and leave it to the soul of the individual.
Now the problem to the poor is one of necessity: to
earn wherewithal to live, they must find remunerative
labour. But the problem to the rich is one of honour:
having the wherewithal, they must find serviceable
labour. Each has to earn his daily bread: the one,
because he has not yet got it to eat; the other, who
has already eaten it, because he has not yet earned it.

Of course, what is true of bread is true of luxuries
and comforts, whether for the body or the mind. But
the consideration of luxuries leads us to a new aspect
of the whole question, and to a second proposition no
less true, and maybe no less startling, than the last.

At the present day, we, of the easier classes, are in
a state of surfeit and disgrace after meat. Plethora has
filled us with indifference; and we are covered from
head to foot with the callosities of habitual opulence.
Born into what is called a certain rank, we live, as the
saying is, up to our station. We squander without
enjoyment, because our fathers squandered. We eat
of the best, not from delicacy, but from brazen habit.
We do not keenly enjoy or eagerly desire the presence
of a luxury; we are unaccustomed to its absence. And
not only do we squander money from habit, but still
more pitifully waste it in ostentation. I can think of
no more melancholy disgrace for a creature who pro-
fesses either reason or pleasure for his guide, than to
spend the smallest fraction of his income upon that
which he does not desire; and to keep a carriage in
which you do not wish to drive, or a butler of whom
you are afraid, is a pathetic kind of folly. Money, being

a means of happiness, should make both parties happy when it changes hands; rightly disposed, it should be twice blessed in its employment; and buyer and seller should alike have their twenty shillings' worth of profit out of every pound. Benjamin Franklin went through life an altered man, because he once paid too dearly for a penny whistle. My concern springs usually from a deeper source, to wit, from having bought a whistle when I did not want one. I find I regret this, or would regret it if I gave myself the time, not only on personal but on moral and philanthropical considerations. For, first, in a world where money is wanting to buy books for eager students and food and medicine for pining children, and where a large majority are starved in their most immediate desires, it is surely base, stupid, and cruel to squander money when I am pushed by no appetite and enjoy no return of genuine satisfaction. My philanthropy is wide enough in scope to include myself; and when I have made myself happy, I have at least one good argument that I have acted rightly; but where that is not so, and I have bought and not enjoyed, my mouth is closed, and I conceive that I have robbed the poor. And, second, anything I buy or use which I do not sincerely want or cannot vividly enjoy, disturbs the balance of supply and demand, and contributes to remove industrious hands from the production of what is useful or pleasurable and to keep them busy upon ropes of sand and things that are a weariness to the flesh. That extravagance is truly sinful, and a very silly sin to boot, in which we impoverish mankind and ourselves. It is another question for each man's heart. He knows if he can enjoy what he buys and uses; if he cannot, he is a dog in the manger; nay, if he cannot, I contend he is a thief, for nothing really belongs to a man which he cannot use. Proprietor is connected with propriety; and that only is the man's which is proper to his wants and faculties.

A youth, in choosing a career, must not be alarmed by poverty. Want is a sore thing, but poverty does not imply want. It remains to be seen whether with half his present income, or a third, he cannot, in the most generous sense, live as fully as at present. He is a fool who objects to luxuries; but he is also a fool who does not protest against the waste of luxuries on those who do not desire and cannot enjoy them. It remains to be seen, by each man who would live a true life to himself and not a merely specious life to society, how many luxuries he truly wants and to how many he merely submits as to a social propriety; and all these last he will immediately forswear. Let him do this, and he will be surprised to find how little money it requires to keep him in complete contentment and activity of mind and senses. Life at any level among the easy classes is conceived upon a principle of rivalry, where each man and each household must ape the tastes and emulate the display of others. One is delicate in eating, another in wine, a third in furniture or works of art or dress; and I, who care nothing for any of these refinements, who am perhaps a plain athletic creature and love exercise, beef, beer, flannel shirts and a camp bed, am yet called upon to assimilate all these other tastes and make these foreign occasions of expenditure my own. It may be cynical: I am sure I shall be told it is selfish; but I will spend my money as I please and for my own intimate personal gratification, and should count myself a nincompoop indeed to lay out the colour of a halfpenny on any fancied social decency or duty. I shall not wear gloves unless my hands are cold, or unless I am born with a delight in them. Dress is my own affair, and that of one other in the world; that, in fact and for an obvious reason, of any woman who shall chance to be in love with me. I shall lodge where I have a mind. If I do not ask society to live with me, they must be silent; and even if I do, they have no further right but to refuse the invitation.

There is a kind of idea abroad that a man must live up to his station, that his house, his table, and his toilette shall be in a ratio of equivalence, and equally imposing to the world. If this is in the Bible, the passage has eluded my inquiries. If it is not in the Bible, it is nowhere but in the heart of the fool. Throw aside this fancy. See what you want, and spend upon that; distinguish what you do not care about, and spend nothing upon that. There are not many people who can differentiate wines above a certain and that not at all a high price. Are you sure you are one of these? Are you sure you prefer cigars at sixpence each to pipes at some fraction of a farthing? Are you sure you wish to keep a gig? Do you care about where you sleep, or are you not as much at your ease in a cheap lodging as in an Elizabethan manor-house? Do you enjoy fine clothes? It is not possible to answer these questions without a trial; and there is nothing more obvious to my mind than that a man who has not experienced some ups and downs, and been forced to live more cheaply than in his father's house, has still his education to begin. Let the experiment be made, and he will find to his surprise that he has been eating beyond his appetite up to that hour; that the cheap lodging, the cheap tobacco, the rough country clothes, the plain table, have not only no power to damp his spirits, but perhaps give him as keen pleasure in the using as the dainties that he took, betwixt sleep and waking, in his former callous and somnambulous submission to wealth.

The true Bohemian, a creature lost to view under the imaginary Bohemians of literature, is exactly described by such a principle of life. The Bohemian of the novel, who drinks more than is good for him and prefers anything to work, and wears strange clothes, is for the most part a respectable Bohemian, respectable in disrespectability, living for the outside, and an adventurer. But the man I mean lives wholly to himself, does what he wishes and not what is thought proper, buys what he wants for himself and not what is thought proper, works at what he believes he can do well and not what will bring him in money or favour. You may be the most respectable of men, and yet a true Bohemian. And the test is this: a Bohemian, for as poor as he may be, is always open-handed to his friends; he knows what he can do with money and how he can do without it, a far rarer and more useful knowledge; he has had less, and continued to live in some contentment; and hence he cares not to keep more, and shares his sovereign or his shilling with a friend. The poor, if they are generous, are Bohemian in virtue of their birth. Do you know where beggars go? Not to the great houses where people sit dazed among their thousands, but to the doors of poor men who have seen the world;

and it was the widow who had only two mites, who cast half her fortune into the treasury.

But a young man who elects to save on dress or on lodging, or who in any way falls out of the level of expenditure which is common to his level in society, falls out of society altogether. I suppose the young man to have chosen his career on honourable principles; he finds his talents and instincts can be best contented in a certain pursuit; in a certain industry, he is sure that he is serving mankind with a healthy and becoming service; and he is not sure that he would be doing so, or doing so equally well, in any other industry within his reach. Then that is his true sphere in life; not the one in which he was born to his father, but the one which is proper to his talents and instincts. And suppose he does fall out of society, is that a cause of sorrow? Is your heart so dead that you prefer the recognition of many to the love of a few? Do you think society loves you? Put it to the proof. Decline in material expenditure, and you will find they care no more for you than for the Khan of Tartary. You will lose no friends. If you had any, you will keep them. Only those who were friends to your coat and equipage will disappear; the smiling faces will disappear as by enchantment; but the kind hearts will remain steadfastly kind. Are you so lost, are you so dead, are you so little sure of your own soul and your own footing upon solid fact, that you prefer before goodness and happiness the countenance of sundry diners-out, who will flee from you at a report of ruin, who will drop you with insult at a shadow of disgrace, who do not know you and do not care to know you but by sight, and whom you in your turn

neither know nor care to know in a more human manner? Is it not the principle of society, openly avowed,
that friendship must not interfere with business; which
being paraphrased, means simply that a consideration
of money goes before any consideration of affection
known to this cold-blooded gang, that they have not
even the honour of thieves, and will rook their nearest
and dearest as readily as a stranger? I hope I would go
as far as most to serve a friend; but I declare openly I
would not put on my hat to do a pleasure to society.
I may starve my appetites and control my temper for
the sake of those I love; but society shall take me as
I choose to be, or go without me. Neither they nor I
will lose; for where there is no love, it is both laborious
and unprofitable to associate.

But it is obvious that if it is only right for a man to
spend money on that which he can truly and thoroughly
enjoy, the doctrine applies with equal force to the rich
and to the poor, to the man who has amassed many
thousands as well as to the youth precariously beginning life. And it may be asked, Is not this merely
preparing misers, who are not the best of company?
But the principle was this: that which a man has not
fairly earned, and, further, that which he cannot fully
enjoy, does not belong to him, but is a part of mankind's treasure which he holds as steward on parole.
To mankind, then, it must be made profitable; and how
this should be done is, once more, a problem which
each man must solve for himself, and about which none
has a right to judge him. Yet there are a few considerations which are very obvious and may here be stated.
Mankind is not only the whole in general, but every

one in particular. Every man or woman is one of mankind's dear possessions; to his or her just brain, and kind heart, and active hands, mankind entrusts some of its hopes for the future; he or she is a possible wellspring of good acts and source of blessings to the race. This money which you do not need, which, in a rigid sense, you do not want, may therefore be returned not only in public benefactions to the race, but in private kindnesses. Your wife, your children, your friends stand nearest to you, and should be helped the first. There at least there can be little imposture, for you know their necessities of your own knowledge. And consider, if all the world did as you did, and according to their means extended help in the circle of their affections, there would be no more crying want in times of plenty and no more cold, mechanical charity given with a doubt and received with confusion. Would not this simple rule make a new world out of the old and cruel one which we inhabit? Have you more money after this is done? are you so wealthy in gold, so poor in friends who need your help, that having done all you can among your own circle, you have still much of mankind's treasure undisposed upon your hands? There are still other matters to be done where you need not fear imposition; and what is over you may hand over without fear to the children whom you have taught; they may be unfaithful to the trust, but you will have done your best and told them on what a solemn responsibility they must accept and deal with this money. . . .

At this point the fragment breaks off. —[ED.]

PRAYERS

WRITTEN FOR FAMILY USE AT VAILIMA

From the author's unpublished MSS

PRAYERS

For Success

LORD, behold our family here assembled. We thank Thee for this place in which we dwell; for the love that unites us; for the peace accorded us this day; for the hope with which we expect the morrow; for the health, the work, the food, and the bright skies, that make our lives delightful; for our friends in all parts of the earth, and our friendly helpers in this foreign isle. Let peace abound in our small company. Purge out of every heart the lurking grudge. Give us grace and strength to forbear and to persevere. Offenders, give us the grace to accept and to forgive offenders. Forgetful ourselves, help us to bear cheerfully the forgetfulness of others. Give us courage and gaiety and the quiet mind. Spare to us our friends, soften to us our enemies. Bless us, if it may be, in all our innocent endeavours. If it may not, give us the strength to encounter that which is to come, that we be brave in peril, constant in tribulation, temperate in wrath, and in all changes of fortune, and down to the gates of death, loyal and loving one to another. As the clay to the potter, as the windmill to the wind, as children of their sire, we beseech of Thee this help and mercy for Christ's sake.

For Grace

GRANT that we here before Thee may be set free from the fear of vicissitude and the fear of death, may finish what remains before us of our course without dishonour to ourselves or hurt to others, and, when the day comes, may die in peace. Deliver us from fear and favour: from mean hopes and cheap pleasures. Have mercy on each in his deficiency; let him be not cast down; support the stumbling on the way, and give at last rest to the weary.

At Morning

THE day returns and brings us the petty round of irritating concerns and duties. Help us to play the man, help us to perform them with laughter and kind faces, let cheerfulness abound with industry. Give us to go blithely on our business all this day, bring us to our resting beds weary and content and undishonoured, and grant us in the end the gift of sleep.

Evening

WE come before Thee, O Lord, in the end of thy day with thanksgiving.

Our beloved in the far parts of the earth, those who are now beginning the labours of the day what time we end them, and those with whom the sun now stands at the point of noon, bless, help, console, and prosper them.

Our guard is relieved, the service of the day is over, and the hour come to rest. We resign into thy hands our sleeping bodies, our cold hearths and open doors.

Give us to awake with smiles, give us to labour smiling. As the sun returns in the east, so let our patience be renewed with dawn; as the sun lightens the world, so let our loving-kindness make bright this house of our habitation.

Another for Evening

LORD, receive our supplications for this house, family, and country. Protect the innocent, restrain the greedy and the treacherous, lead us out of our tribulation into a quiet land.

Look down upon ourselves and upon our absent dear ones. Help us and them; prolong our days in peace and honour. Give us health, food, bright weather, and light hearts. In what we meditate of evil, frustrate our will; in what of good, further our endeavours. Cause injuries to be forgot and benefits to be remembered.

Let us lie down without fear and awake and arise with exultation. For his sake, in whose words we now conclude.

In Time of Rain

WE thank Thee, Lord, for the glory of the late days and the excellent face of thy sun. We thank Thee for good news received. We thank Thee for the pleasures we have enjoyed and for those we have been able to confer. And now, when the clouds gather and the rain impends over the forest and our house, permit us not to be cast down; let us not lose the savour of past mercies and past pleasures; but, like the voice of a bird singing in the rain, let grateful memory survive in the hour of darkness. If there be in front of us any painful duty, strengthen us with the grace of courage; if any act of mercy, teach us tenderness and patience.

Another in Time of Rain

LORD, Thou sendest down rain upon the uncounted millions of the forest, and givest the trees to drink exceedingly. We are here upon this isle a few handfuls of men, and how many myriads upon myriads of stalwart trees! Teach us the lesson of the trees. The sea around us, which this rain recruits, teems with the race of fish; teach us, Lord, the meaning of the fishes. Let us see ourselves for what we are, one out of the countless number of the clans of thy handiwork. When we would despair, let us remember that these also please and serve Thee.

Before a Temporary Separation

TO-DAY we go forth separate, some of us to pleasure, some of us to worship, some upon duty. Go with us, our guide and angel; hold Thou before us in our divided paths the mark of our low calling, still to be true to what small best we can attain to. Help us in that, our maker, the dispenser of events—Thou, of the vast designs, in which we blindly labour, suffer us to be so far constant to ourselves and our beloved.

For Friends

FOR our absent loved ones we implore thy loving-kindness. Keep them in life, keep them in growing honour; and for us, grant that we remain worthy of their love.   For Christ's sake, let not our beloved blush for us, nor we for them.   Grant us but that, and grant us courage to endure lesser ills unshaken, and to accept death, loss, and disappointment as it were straws upon the tide of life.

For the Family

AID us, if it be thy will, in our concerns.   Have mercy on this land and innocent people.   Help them who this day contend in disappointment with their frailties.   Bless our family, bless our forest house, bless our island helpers.   Thou who hast made for us this place of ease and hope, accept and inflame our gratitude; help us to repay, in service one to another, the debt of thine unmerited benefits and mercies, so that when the period of our stewardship draws to a conclusion, when the windows begin to be darkened, when the bond of the family is to be loosed, there shall be no bitterness of remorse in our farewells.

Help us to look back on the long way that Thou hast brought us, on the long days in which we have been served not according to our deserts but our desires; on the pit and the miry clay, the blackness of despair, the horror of misconduct, from which our feet have been plucked out.   For our sins forgiven or prevented, for our shame unpublished, we bless and thank Thee, O God.   Help us yet again and ever.   So order events, so strengthen our frailty, as that day by day we shall come before Thee with this song of gratitude, and in the end we be dismissed with honour.   In their weakness and their fear, the vessels of thy handiwork so pray to Thee, so praise Thee.   Amen.

PRAYERS

Sunday

WE beseech Thee, Lord, to behold us with favour, folk of many families and nations gathered together in the peace of this roof, weak men and women subsisting under the covert of thy patience. Be patient still; suffer us yet awhile longer;—with our broken purposes of good, with our idle endeavours against evil, suffer us awhile longer to endure and (if it may be) help us to do better. Bless to us our extraordinary mercies; if the day come when these must be taken, brace us to play the man under affliction. Be with our friends, be with ourselves. Go with each of us to rest; if any awake, temper to them the dark hours of watching; and when the day returns, return to us, our sun and comforter, and call us up with morning faces and with morning hearts—eager to labour—eager to be happy, if happiness shall be our portion—and if the day be marked for sorrow, strong to endure it.

We thank Thee and praise Thee; and in the words of him to whom this day is sacred, close our oblation.

For Self-blame

LORD, enlighten us to see the beam that is in our own eye, and blind us to the mote that is in our brother's. Let us feel our offences with our hands, make them great and bright before us like the sun, make us eat them and drink them for our diet. Blind us to the offences of our beloved, cleanse them from our memories, take them out of our mouths for ever. Let all here before Thee carry and measure with the false balances

596

of love, and be in their own eyes and in all conjunctures the most guilty. Help us at the same time with the grace of courage, that we be none of us cast down when we sit lamenting amid the ruins of our happiness or our integrity: touch us with fire from the altar, that we may be up and doing to rebuild our city: in the name and by the method of him in whose words of prayer we now conclude.

For Self-forgetfulness

LORD, the creatures of thy hand, thy disinherited children, come before Thee with their incoherent wishes and regrets: Children we are, children we shall be, till our mother the earth hath fed upon our bones. Accept us, correct us, guide us, thy guilty innocents. Dry our vain tears, wipe out our vain resentments, help our yet vainer efforts. If there be any here, sulking as children will, deal with and enlighten him. Make it day about that person, so that he shall see himself and be ashamed. Make it heaven about him, Lord, by the only way to heaven, forgetfulness of self, and make it day about his neighbours, so that they shall help, not hinder him.

For Renewal of Joy

WE are evil, O God, and help us to see it and amend. We are good, and help us to be better. Look down upon thy servants with a patient eye, even as Thou sendest sun and rain; look down, call upon the dry bones, quicken, enliven; re-create in us the soul of service, the spirit of peace; renew in us the sense of joy.

ADDENDA

NOTE

THESE Addenda are matters which either came to the knowledge of Mr. Stevenson's literary executor after the collection of the main body of his writings, or they are pieces which, although already printed in a fugitive form, it had not been thought best to include, until during the publication of the more important volumes some curiosity was found to exist about them among collectors and others who had learned of their existence. They were therefore brought together in a small volume and added as supplementary to the Edinburgh Edition of Mr. Stevenson's works. They are included in the Thistle Edition in order that nothing important of whatever kind may be omitted from it.

In speaking of the appendix volume, Mr. Sidney Colvin, the Editor of the Edinburgh Edition, said:

"It is a medley, made up of items, some serious and some trifling, which for one reason or another were not included in the main edition. Among them are things which various subscribers have already expressed a desire to possess. Such are *The Charity Bazaar* and the two papers on *Lighthouse Illumination* and *The Thermal Influence of Forests*. . . . The first-named of these, which opens the volume, is a boyish skit privately printed on a charity occasion at Edinburgh, I believe in *1868,* and in its original form has for some time been a rarity competed for by collectors. The other two were contributed to the Transactions of the Royal Scottish Society of Arts for *1871* and the Proceedings of the Royal Society of Edinburgh for *1873* respectively. They are not literature, and do not proceed from any natural bias of the writer's mind. They do, however, represent the circumstances of his origin and early training as a member of a distinguished family of civil engineers; one of them gained the silver medal of the Royal Scottish Society of Arts: and it has been ascertained that to some of those interested in his career their inclusion in this place will be welcome. I have prefixed to them two sets of lighthouse verses from his note-books of *1869* and *1870,* one written in a sentimental, the other in somewhat of a cynic mood, which show what used to be the private thoughts and real preoccupations of the youthful engineer on his professional rounds. Next follow three pieces not before printed from his later note-books. In *Reflections and Remarks on Human Life* we have the draft of some chapters of an unfinished treatise on morals and conduct, subjects on which he always wrote in the spirit of a keen and thoughtful soldier in the battle of life: in one of these chapters it will be noticed that he deals with the problems of free-will and rewards and punishments on the same lines as in the brilliant little apologue already published as No. *1* of his *Fables,* but at greater length. *The Ideal House* belongs to the winter of *1884–5,* and sets forth the predilections, as to the site and arrangements of a home, of one who had for years been a vagrant, priding himself on his freedom from local ties and the burden of the world's gear. But by this time he had become the head of a household, and having tried two domiciles in Provence, was about to take possession of a new one on the English coast at Bournemouth. Then follows the *Preface to "The Master of Ballantrae,"* written in the Pacific in 1889, with reminiscences of the office in Edinburgh of his old friend Mr. Charles Baxter, W.S. When he published the book in that year, he decided to suppress his preface, as being too much in the vein of Jedediah Cleishbotham and Mr. Peter Pattieson; but afterwards he expressed a wish that it should be given with the Edinburgh Edition. At that time, however, the manuscript had gone astray, and the text has now been recovered from his original draft."

THE CHARITY BAZAAR:

AN ALLEGORICAL DIALOGUE

PERSONS OF THE DIALOGUE

The Ingenuous Public.
His Wife.
The Tout.

The Tout, in an allegorical costume, holding a silver trumpet in his right hand, is discovered on the steps in front of the Bazaar. He sounds a preliminary flourish.

The Tout. Ladies and Gentlemen, I have the honour to announce a sale of many interesting, beautiful, rare, quaint, comical, and necessary articles. Here you will find objects of taste, such as Babies' Shoes, Children's Petticoats, and Shetland Wool Cravats; objects of general usefulness, such as Tea-cosies, Bangles, Brahmin Beads, and Madras Baskets; and objects of imperious necessity, such as Pen-wipers, Indian Figures carefully repaired with glue, and Sealed Envelopes, containing a surprise. And all this is not to be sold by your common Shopkeepers, intent on small and legitimate profits, but by Ladies and Gentlemen, who would as soon think of picking your pocket of a cotton handkerchief, as of selling a single one of these many interesting, beautiful, rare, quaint, comical, and necessary articles at less than twice its market value.

(He sounds another flourish.)

The Wife. This seems a very fair-spoken young man.

The Ingenuous Public (addressing the Tout). Sir, I am a man of simple and untutored mind; but I apprehend that this sale, of which you give us so glowing a description, is neither more nor less than a Charity Bazaar?

ADDENDA

The Tout. Sir, your penetration has not deceived you.

The Ingenuous Public. Into which you seek to entice unwary passengers?

The Tout. Such is my office.

The Ingenuous Public. But is not a Charity Bazaar, Sir, a place where, for ulterior purposes, amateur goods are sold at a price above their market value?

The Tout. I perceive you are no novice. Let us sit down, all three, upon the door-steps, and reason this matter at length. The position is a little conspicuous, but airy and convenient.

    (*The Tout seats himself on the second step, the Ingenuous Public and his Wife to right and left of him, one step below.*)

The Tout. Shopping is one of the dearest pleasures of the human heart.

The Wife. Indeed, Sir, and that it is.

The Tout. The choice of articles, apart from their usefulness, is an appetising occupation, and to exchange bald, uniform shillings for a fine big, figurative knick-knack, such as a windmill, a gross of green spectacles, or a cocked hat, gives us a direct and emphatic sense of gain. We have had many shillings before, as good as these; but this is the first time we have possessed a windmill. Upon these principles of human nature, Sir, is based the theory of the Charity Bazaar. People were doubtless charitably disposed. The problem was to make the exercise of charity entertaining in itself—you follow me, Madam?—and in the Charity Bazaar a satisfactory solution was attained. The act of giving away money for charitable purposes is, by this admirable invention, transformed into an amusement, and puts on the externals of profitable commerce. You play at shopping awhile; and in order to keep up the illusion, sham goods do actually change hands. Thus, under the similitude of a game, I have seen children confronted with the horrors of arithmetic, and even taught to gargle.

The Ingenuous Public. You expound this subject very magisterially, Sir. But tell me, would it not be possible to carry this element of play still further? and after I had remained a proper time in the Bazaar, and negotiated a sufficient number of sham bargains, would it not be possible to return me my money in the hall?

The Tout. I question whether that would not impair the humour of the situation. And besides, my dear Sir, the pith of the whole device is 'o take that money from you.

The Ingenuous Public. True. But at least the Bazaar might take back the tea-cosies and pen-wipers.

The Tout. I have no doubt, if you were to ask it handsomely, that you would be so far accommodated. Still it is out of the theory. The sham goods, for which, believe me, I readily understand your disaffection —the sham goods are well adapted for their purpose. Your lady wife will lay these tea-cosies and pen-wipers aside in a safe place, until she is asked to contribute to another Charity Bazaar. There the tea-cosies and pen-wipers will be once more charitably sold. The new purchasers, in their turn, will accurately imitate the dispositions of your lady wife. In short, Sir, the whole affair is a cycle of operations. The tea-cosies and pen-wipers are merely counters; they come off and on again like a stage army; and year after year people pretend to buy and pretend to sell them, with a vivacity that seems to indicate a talent for the stage. But in the course of these illusory manœuvres, a great deal of money is given in charity, and that in a picturesque, bustling, and agreeable manner. If you have to travel somewhere on business, you would choose the prettiest route, and desire pleasant companions by the way. And why not show the same spirit in giving alms?

The Ingenuous Public. Sir, I am profoundly indebted to you for all you have said. I am, Sir, your absolute convert.

The Wife. Let us lose no time, but enter the Charity Bazaar.

The Ingenuous Public. Yes; let us enter the Charity Bazaar.

Both (*singing*). Let us enter, let us enter, let us enter,
Let us enter the Charity Bazaar!

(*An interval is supposed to elapse. The Ingenuous Public and his Wife are discovered issuing from the Charity Bazaar.*)

The Wife. How fortunate you should have brought your cheque-book!

The Ingenuous Public. Well, fortunate in a sense. (*Addressing the Tout*). Sir, I shall send a van in the course of the afternoon for the little articles I have purchased. I shall not say good-bye; because I shall probably take a lift in the front seat, not from any solicitude, believe me, about the little articles, but as the last opportunity I may have for some time of enjoying the costly entertainment of a drive.

THE SCENE CLOSES.

THE LIGHT-KEEPER

I

The brilliant kernel of the night,
   The flaming lightroom circles me:
I sit within a blaze of light
   Held high above the dusky sea.
Far off the surf doth break and roar
Along bleak miles of moonlit shore,
   Where through the tides the tumbling wave
Falls in an avalanche of foam
And drives its churnèd waters home
   Up many an undercliff and cave.

The clear bell chimes: the clockworks strain:
   The turning lenses flash and pass,
Frame turning within glittering frame
   With frosty gleam of moving glass:
Unseen by me, each dusky hour
The sea-waves welter up the tower
   Or in the ebb subside again;
And ever and anon all night,
Drawn from afar by charm of light,
   A sea-bird beats against the pane.

And lastly when dawn ends the night
   And belts the semi-orb of sea,
The tall, pale pharos in the light
   Looks white and spectral as may be.
The early ebb is out: the green
Straight belt of sea-weed now is seen,
   That round the basement of the tower
Marks out the interspace of tide;
And watching men are heavy-eyed,
   And sleepless lips are dry and sour.

ADDENDA

The night is over like a dream:
  The sea-birds cry and dip themselves;
And in the early sunlight, steam
  The newly bared and dripping shelves,
Around whose verge the glassy wave
With lisping wash is heard to lave;
  While, on the white tower lifted high,
With yellow light in faded glass
The circling lenses flash and pass,
  And sickly shine against the sky.

1869.

II

As the steady lenses circle
With a frosty gleam of glass;
And the clear bell chimes,
And the oil brims over the lip of the burner,
Quiet and still at his desk,
The lonely Light-Keeper
Holds his vigil.

Lured from afar,
The bewildered sea-gull beats
Dully against the lantern;
Yet he stirs not, lifts not his head
From the desk where he reads,
Lifts not his eyes to see
The chill blind circle of night
Watching him through the panes.
This is his country's guardian,
The outmost sentry of peace.
This is the man,
Who gives up all that is lovely in living
For the means to live.

Poetry cunningly gilds
The life of the Light-Keeper,
Held on high in the blackness

ADDENDA

In the burning kernel of night,
The seaman sees and blesses him:
The Poet, deep in a sonnet,
Numbers his inky fingers
Fitly to praise him;
Only we behold him,
Sitting, patient and stolid,
Martyr to a salary.

1870.

ON A NEW FORM OF INTERMITTENT LIGHT
FOR LIGHTHOUSES [1]

The necessity for marked characteristics in coast illumination increases
with the number of lights.   The late Mr. Robert Stevenson, my grandfather, contributed two distinctions, which he called respectively the
intermittent and the *flashing* light.   It is only to the former of these
that I have to refer in the present paper.   The intermittent light was first
introduced at Tarbetness in 1830, and is already in use at eight stations
on the coasts of the United Kingdom.   As constructed originally, it was
an arrangement by which a fixed light was alternately eclipsed and revealed.   These recurrent occultations and revelations produce an effect
totally different from that of the revolving light, which comes gradually
into its full strength, and as gradually fades away.   The changes in the
intermittent, on the other hand, are immediate; a certain duration of
darkness is followed at once and without the least gradation by a certain
period of light.   The arrangement employed by my grandfather to effect
this object consisted of two opaque cylindric shades or extinguishers, one
of which descended from the roof, while the other ascended from below
to meet it, at a fixed interval.   The light was thus entirely intercepted.

At a later period, at the harbour light of Troon, Mr. Wilson, C. E.,
produced an intermittent light by the use of gas, which leaves little to
be desired, and which is still in use at Troon harbour.   By a simple mechanical contrivance, the gas-jet was suddenly lowered to the point of
extinction, and, after a set period, as suddenly raised again.   The chief

[1] Read before the Royal Scottish Society of Arts on 27th March, 1871,
and awarded the Society's Silver Medal.

608

superiority of this form of intermittent light is economy in the consumption of gas. In the original design, of course, the oil continues uselessly to illuminate the interior of the screens during the period of occultation.

Mr. Wilson's arrangement has been lately resuscitated by Mr. Wigham of Dublin, in connection with his new gas-burner.

Gas, however, is inapplicable to many situations; and it has occurred to me that the desired result might be effected with strict economy with oil lights, in the following manner:

In Fig. 1, *AAA* represents in plan an ordinary Fresnel's dioptric fixed light apparatus, and *BB'* a hemispherical mirror (either metallic or dioptric on my father's principle) which is made to revolve with uniform speed about the burner. This mirror, it is obvious, intercepts the rays of one hemisphere, and, returning them through the

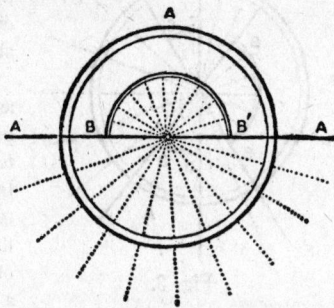

Fig. 1.

flame (less loss by absorption, etc.), spreads them equally over the other. In this way 180° of light pass regularly the eye of the seaman; and are followed at once by 180° of darkness. As the hemispherical mirror begins to open, the observer receives the full light, since the whole lit hemisphere is illuminated with strict equality; and as it closes again, he passes into darkness.

Other characteristics can be produced by different modifications of the above. In Fig. 2 the original hemispherical mirror is shown broken up into three different sectors, *BB'*, *CC'*, and

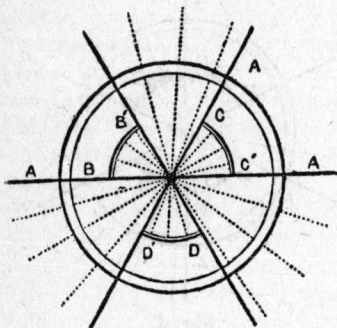

Fig. 2.

DD'; so that with the same velocity of revolution the periods of light and darkness will be produced in quicker succession. In this figure (Fig. 2)

the three sectors have been shown as subtending equal angles, but if one of them were increased in size and the other two diminished (as in Fig. 3), we should have one long steady illumination and two short flashes at each revolution. Again, the number of sectors may be increased; and by varying both their number and their relative size, a number of additional characteristics are attainable.

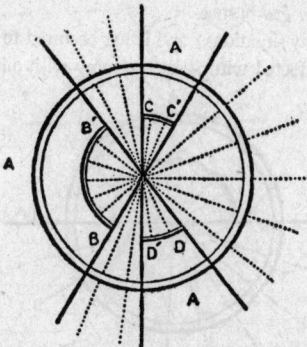

Fig. 3.

Colour may also be introduced as a means of distinction. Coloured glass may be set in the alternate spaces; but it is necessary to remark that these coloured sectors will be inferior in power to those which remain white. This objection is, however, obviated to a large extent (especially where the dioptric spherical mirror is used) by such an arrangement as is shown in Fig. 4; where the two sectors, WW, are left unassisted, while the two

with the red screens are reinforced respectively by the two sectors of mirror, MM.

Another mode of holophotally producing the intermittent light has been suggested by my father, and is shown in Fig. 5. It consists of alternate and opposite sectors of dioptric spherical mirror, MM, and of Fresnel's fixed light apparatus, AA. By the revolution of this composite frame about the burner, the same immediate

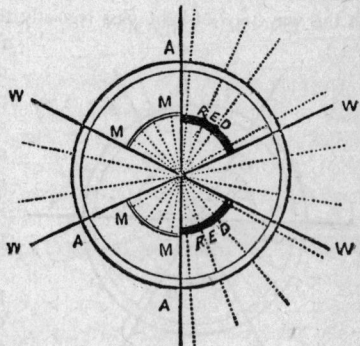

Fig. 4.

alternation of light and darkness is produced, the first when the front of the fixed panel, and the second when the back of the mirror, is presented to the eye of the sailor.

One advantage of the method that I propose is this, that while we are able to produce a plain intermittent light; an intermittent light of variable period, ranging from a brief flash to a steady illumination of half the revolution; and finally, a light combining the immediate occultation of the intermittent with combination and change of colour, we can yet preserve comparative lightness in the revolving parts, and consequent economy in the driving machinery. It must, however, be noticed, that none of these last methods are applicable to cases where

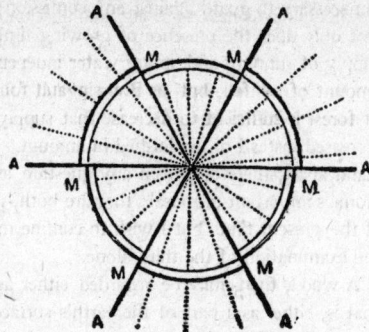

Fig. 5.

more than one radiant is employed: for these cases, either my grandfather's or Mr. Wilson's contrivance must be resorted to.

1871.

ON THE THERMAL INFLUENCE OF FORESTS[1]

The opportunity of an experiment on a comparatively large scale, and under conditions of comparative isolation, can occur but rarely in such a science as Meteorology. Hence Mr. Milne Home's proposal for the plantation of Malta seemed to offer an exceptional opportunity for progress. Many of the conditions are favourable to the simplicity of the result; and it seemed natural that, if a searching and systematic series of observations were to be immediately set afoot, and continued during the course of the plantation and the growth of the wood, some light would be thrown on the still doubtful question of the climatic influence of forests.

Mr. Milne Home expects, as I gather, a threefold result: 1st, an increased and better-regulated supply of available water; 2nd, an increased rainfall; and, 3rd, a more equable climate, with more temperate summer

[1] Read before the Royal Society, Edinburgh, 19th May, 1873, and reprinted from the *Proceedings* R. S. E.

heat and winter cold.[1] As to the first of these expectations, I suppose there can be no doubt that it is justified by facts; but it may not be unnecessary to guard against any confusion of the first with the second. Not only does the presence of growing timber increase and regulate the supply of running and spring water independently of any change in the amount of rainfall, but, as Boussingault found at Marmato,[2] denudation of forest is sufficient to decrease that supply, even when the rainfall has increased instead of diminished in amount. The second and third effects stand apart, therefore, from any question as to the utility of Mr. Milne Home's important proposal; they are both, perhaps, worthy of discussion at the present time, but I wish to confine myself in the present paper to the examination of the third alone.

A wood, then, may be regarded either as a *superficies* or as a *solid;* that is, either as a part of the earth's surface slightly elevated above the rest, or as a diffused and heterogeneous body displacing a certain portion of free and mobile atmosphere. It is primarily in the first character that it attracts our attention, as a radiating and absorbing surface, exposed to the sun and the currents of the air; such that, if we imagine a plateau of meadow-land or bare earth raised to the mean level of the forest's exposed leaf-surface, we shall have an agent entirely similar in kind, although perhaps widely differing in the amount of action. Now, by comparing a tract of wood with such a plateau as we have just supposed, we shall arrive at a clear idea of the specialties of the former. In the first place, then, the mass of foliage may be expected to increase the radiating power of each tree. The upper leaves radiate freely towards the stars and the cold interstellar spaces, while the lower ones radiate to those above and receive less heat in return; consequently, during the absence of the sun, each tree cools gradually downward from top to bottom. Hence we must take into account not merely the area of leaf-surface actually exposed to the sky, but, to a greater or less extent, the surface of every leaf in the whole tree or the whole wood. This is evidently a point in which the action of the forest may be expected to differ from that of the meadow or naked earth; for though, of course, inferior strata tend to a certain extent to follow somewhat the same course as the mass of inferior leaves, they do so to a less degree—conduction, and the conduction of a very slow conductor, being substituted for radiation.

1 *Jour. Scot. Met. Soc.*, New Ser., xxvi. 35.
2 Quoted by Mr. Milne Home.

We come next, however, to a second point of difference. In the case of the meadow, the chilled air continues to lie upon the surface, the grass, as Humboldt says, remaining all night submerged in the stratum of lowest temperature; while in the case of trees, the coldest air is continually passing down to the space underneath the boughs, or what we may perhaps term the crypt of the forest. Here it is that the consideration of any piece of woodland conceived as a solid comes naturally in; for this solid contains a portion of the atmosphere, partially cut off from the rest, more or less excluded from the influence of wind, and lying upon a soil that is screened all day from isolation by the impending mass of foliage. In this way (and chiefly, I think, from the exclusion of winds), we have underneath the radiating leaf-surface a stratum of comparatively stagnant air, protected from many sudden variations of temperature, and tending only slowly to bring itself into equilibrium with the more general changes that take place in the free atmosphere.

Over and above what has been mentioned, thermal effects have been attributed to the vital activity of the leaves in the transudation of water, and even to the respiration and circulation of living wood. The whole actual amount of thermal influence, however, is so small that I may rest satisfied with the mere mention. If these actions have any effect at all, it must be practically insensible; and the others that I have already stated are not only sufficient validly to account for all the observed differences, but would lead naturally to the expectation of differences very much larger and better marked. To these observations I proceed at once. Experience has been acquired upon the following three points: 1, The relation between the temperature of the trunk of a tree and the temperature of the surrounding atmosphere; 2, The relation between the temperature of the air under a wood and the temperature of the air outside; and, 3, The relation between the temperature of the air above a wood and the temperature of the air above cleared land.

As to the first question, there are several independent series of observations; and I may remark in passing, what applies to all, that allowance must be made throughout for some factor of specific heat. The results were as follows: The seasonal and monthly means in the tree and in the air were not sensibly different. The variations in the tree, in M. Becquerel's own observations, appear as considerably less than a fourth of those in the atmosphere, and he has calculated, from observations made at Geneva between 1796 and 1798, that the variations in the tree were less than a fifth of those in the air; but the tree in this case, besides being of a different species, was seven or eight inches thicker than the one experimented on by himself.[1] The variations in the tree, therefore, are always less than those in the air, the ratio between the two depending apparently on the thickness of the tree in question and the rapidity with which the variations followed upon one another. The times of the maxima, moreover, were widely different: in the air, the maximum occurs at 2 P. M. in winter, and at 3 P. M. in summer; in the tree, it occurs in winter at 6 P. M., and in summer between 10 and 11 P. M. At nine in the morning in the month of June, the temperatures of the tree and of the air had come to an equilibrium. A similar difference of progression is visible in the means, which differ most in spring and autumn, and tend to equalise themselves in winter and in summer. But it appears most strikingly in the case of variations somewhat longer in period than the daily ranges. The following temperatures occurred during M. Becquerel's observations in the Jardin des Plantes:

Date, 1859.	Temperature of the Air.	Temperature in the Tree.
Dec. 15	26.78°	32°
" 16	19.76°	32°
" 17	17.78°	31.46°
" 18	13.28°	30.56°
" 19	12.02°	28.40°
" 20	12.54°	25.34°
" 21	38.30°	27.86°
" 22	43.34°	30.92°
" 23	44.06°	31.46°

A moment's comparison of the two columns will make the principle apparent. The temperature of the air falls nearly fifteen degrees in five days; the temperature of the tree, sluggishly following, falls in the same time less than four degrees. Between the 19th and 20th the temperature of the air has changed its direction of motion, and risen nearly a degree; but the temperature of the tree persists in its former course, and continues to fall nearly three degrees farther. On the 21st there comes a sudden increase of heat, a sudden thaw; the temperature of the air rises twenty-five and a half degrees; the change at last reaches the tree, but only raises

[1] *Atlas Météorologique de l'Observatoire Impérial*, 1867.

its temperature by less than three degrees; and even two days afterwards when the air is already twelve degrees above freezing-point, the tree is still half a degree below it. Take, again, the following case:

Date, 1859.	Temperature of the Air.		Temperature in the Tree.
July 13	84.92°	....	76.28°
" 14	82.58°	....	78.62°
" 15	80.42°	....	77.72°
" 16	79.88°	....	78.44°
" 17	73.22°	....	75.92°
" 18	68.54°	....	74.30°
" 19	65.66°	....	70.70°

The same order reappears. From the 13th to the 19th the temperature of the air steadily falls, while the temperature of the tree continues apparently to follow the course of previous variations, and does not really begin to fall, is not really affected by the ebb of heat, until the 17th, three days at least after it had been operating in the air.[1] Hence we may conclude that all variations of the temperature of the air, whatever be their period, from twenty-four hours up to twelve months, are followed in the same manner by variations in the temperature of the tree; and that those in the tree are always less in amount and considerably slower of occurrence than those in the air. The *thermal sluggishness*, so to speak, seems capable of explaining all the phenomena of the case without any hypothetical vital power of resisting temperatures below the freezing-point, such as is hinted at even by Becquerel.

Réaumur, indeed, is said to have observed temperatures in slender trees nearly thirty degrees higher than the temperature of the air in the sun; but we are not informed as to the conditions under which this observation was made, and it is therefore impossible to assign to it its proper value. The sap of the ice-plant is said to be materially colder than the surrounding atmosphere; and there are several other somewhat incongruous facts, which tend, at first sight, to favour the view of some inherent power of resistance in some plants to high temperatures, and in others to low temperatures.[2] But such a supposition seems in the meantime to be

[1] *Comptes Rendus de l'Académie,* 29th March, 1869.
[2] *Professor Balfour's Class Book of Botany,* Physiology, chap. xii. p. 670.

gratuitous. Keeping in view the thermal redispositions, which must be greatly favoured by the ascent of the sap, and the difference between the condition as to temperature of such parts as the root, the heart of the trunk, and the extreme foliage, and never forgetting the unknown factor of specific heat, we may still regard it as possible to account for all anomalies without the aid of any such hypothesis. We may, therefore, I think, disregard small exceptions, and state the result as follows:

If, after every rise or fall, the temperature of the air remained stationary for a length of time proportional to the amount of the change, it seems probable—setting aside all question of vital heat—that the temperature of the tree would always finally equalise itself with the new temperature of the air, and that the range in tree and atmosphere would thus become the same. This pause, however, does not occur: the variations follow each other without interval; and the slow-conducting wood is never allowed enough time to overtake the rapid changes of the more sensitive air. Hence, so far as we can see at present, trees appear to be simply bad conductors, and to have no more influence upon the temperature of their surroundings than is fully accounted for by the consequent tardiness of their thermal variations.

Observations bearing on the second of the three points have been made by Becquerel in France, by La Cour in Jutland and Iceland, and by Rivoli at Posen. The results are perfectly congruous. Becquerel's observations [1] were made under wood, and about a hundred yards outside in open ground, at three stations in the district of Montargis, Loiret. There was a difference of more than one degree Fahrenheit between the mean annual temperatures in favour of the open ground. The mean summer temperature in the wood was from two to three degrees lower than the mean summer temperature outside. The mean maxima in the wood were also lower than those without by a little more than two degrees. Herr La Cour [2] found the daily range consistently smaller inside the wood than outside. As far as regards the mean winter temperatures, there is an excess in favour of the forests, but so trifling in amount as to be unworthy of much consideration. Libri found that the minimum winter temperatures were not sensibly lower in Florence, after the Apennines had been denuded of forest, than they had been before. [3] The disheartening contradictori-

[1] *Comptes Rendus*, 1867 and 1869.
[2] See his paper.
[3] *Annales de Chimie et de Physique*, xlv., 1830. A more detailed com-

ness of his observations on this subject led Herr Rivoli to the following ingenious and satisfactory comparison.[1] Arranging his results according to the wind that blew on the day of observation, he set against each other the variation of the temperature under wood from that without, and the variation of the temperature of the wind from the local mean for the month:

Wind......................	N.	N.E.	E.	S.E.	S.	S.W.	W.	N.W.
Var. in Wood	+0.60	+0.26	+0.26	+0.04	−0.04	−0.20	+0.16	+0.07
Var. in Wind.............	−0.30	−2.60	−3.30	−1.20	+1.00	+1.30	+1.00	+1.00

From this curious comparison, it becomes apparent that the variations of the difference in question depend upon the amount of variations of temperature which take place in the free air, and on the slowness with which such changes are communicated to the stagnant atmosphere of woods; in other words, as Herr Rivoli boldly formulates it, a forest is simply a bad conductor. But this is precisely the same conclusion as we have already arrived at with regard to individual trees; and in Herr Rivoli's table, what we see is just another case of what we saw in M. Becquerel's —the different progression of temperatures. It must be obvious, however, that the thermal condition of a single tree must be different in many ways from that of a combination of trees and more or less stagnant air, such as we call a forest. And accordingly we find, in the case of the latter, the following new feature: The mean yearly temperature of woods is lower than the mean yearly temperature of free air, while they are decidedly colder in summer, and very little, if at all, warmer in winter. Hence, on the whole,. forests are colder than cleared lands. But this is just what might have been expected from the amount of evaporation, the continued descent of cold air, and its stagnation in the close and sunless crypt of a forest; and one can only wonder here, as elsewhere, that the resultant difference is so insignificant and doubtful.

We come now to the third point in question, the thermal influence of woods upon the air above them. It will be remembered that we have seen reason to believe their effect to be similar to that of certain other surfaces, except in so far as it may be altered, in the case of the forest,

parison of the climate in question would be a most interesting and important contribution to the subject.

[1] Reviewed in the *Austrian Meteorological Magazine*, vol. iv. p. 543.

by the greater extent of effective radiating area, and by the possibility of generating a descending cold current as well as an ascending hot one. M. Becquerel is (so far as I can learn) the only observer who has taken up the elucidation of this subject. He placed his thermometers at three points:[1] A and B were both about seventy feet above the surface of the ground; but A was at the summit of a chestnut-tree, while B was in the free air, fifty feet away from the other. C was four or five feet above the ground, with a northern exposure; there was also a fourth station to the south, at the same level as this last, but its readings are very seldom referred to. After several years of observation, the mean temperature at A was found to be between one and two degrees higher than that at B. The order of progression of differences is as instructive here as in the two former investigations. The maximum difference in favour of station A occurred between three and five in the afternoon, later or sooner according as there had been more or less sunshine, and ranged sometimes as high as seven degrees. After this the difference kept declining until sunrise, when there was often a difference of a degree, or a degree and a half, upon the other side. On cloudy days the difference tended to a minimum. During a rainy month of April, for example, the difference in favour of station A was less than half a degree; the first fifteen days of May following, however, were sunny, and the difference rose to more than a degree and a half.[2] It will be observed that I have omitted up to the present point all mention of station C. I do so because M. Becquerel's language leaves it doubtful whether the observations made at this station are logically comparable with those made at the other two. If the end in view were to compare the progression of temperatures above the earth, above a tree, and in free air, removed from all such radiative and absorptive influences, it is plain that all three should have been equally exposed to the sun or kept equally in shadow. As the observations were made, they give us no notion of the relative action of the earth-surface and forest-surface upon the temperature of the contiguous atmosphere; and this, as it seems to me, was just the *crux* of the problem. So far, however, as they go, they seem to justify the view that all these actions are the same in kind, however they may differ in degree. We find the forest heating the air during the day, and heating it more or less according as there has been more or less sunshine for it to absorb, and we find it also

[1] *Comptes Rendus*, 28th May, 1860.
[2] *Ibid.*, 20th May, 1861.

618

chilling it during the night; both of which are actions common to any radiating surface, and would be produced, if with differences of amount and time, by any other such surface raised to the mean level of the exposed foliage.

To recapitulate:

1st. We find that single trees appear to act simply as bad conductors.

2nd. We find that woods, regarded as solids, are, on the whole, slightly lower in temperature than the free air which they have displaced, and that they tend slowly to adapt themselves to the various thermal changes that take place without them.

3rd. We find forests regarded as surfaces acting like any other part of the earth's surface, probably with more or less difference in amount and progression, which we still lack the information necessary to estimate.

All this done, I am afraid that there can be little doubt that the more general climatic investigations will be long and vexatious. Even in South America, with extremely favourable conditions, the result is far from being definite. Glancing over the table published by M. Becquerel in his book on climates, from the observations of Humboldt, Hall, Boussingault, and others, it becomes evident, I think, that nothing can be founded upon the comparisons therein instituted; that all reasoning, in the present state of our information, is premature and unreliable. Strong statements have certainly been made; and particular cases lend themselves to the formation of hasty judgments. "From the Bay of Cupica to the Gulf of Guayaquil," says M. Boussingault, "the country is covered with immense forests and traversed by numerous rivers; it rains there almost ceaselessly; and the mean temperature of this moist district scarcely reaches 78.8° F. . . . At Payta commence the sandy deserts of Priura and Sechura; to the constant humidity of Choco succeeds almost at once an extreme of dryness; and the mean temperature of the coast increases at the same time by 1.8° F." [1] Even in this selected favourable instance it might be argued that the part performed in the change by the presence or absence of forest was comparatively small; there seems to have been, at the same time, an entire change of soil; and, in our present ignorance, it would be difficult to say by how much this of itself is able to affect the climate. Moreover, it is possible that the humidity of the one district is due to other causes besides the presence of wood, or even that the presence of wood is itself only an effect of some more general difference or combination of differ-

[1] Becquerel, *Climats*, p. 141.

ences. Be that as it may, however, we have only to look a little longer at the table before referred to, to see how little weight can be laid on such special instances. Let us take five stations, all in this very district of Choco. Hacquita is eight hundred and twenty feet above Novita, and their mean temperatures are the same. Alto de Mombu, again, is five hundred feet higher than Hacquita, and the mean temperature has here fallen nearly two degrees. Go up another five hundred feet to Tambo de la Orquita, and again we find no fall in the mean temperature. Go up some five hundred farther to Chami, and there is a fall in the mean temperature of nearly six degrees. Such numbers are evidently quite untrustworthy; and hence we may judge how much confidence can be placed in any generalisation from these South American mean temperatures.

The question is probably considered too simply — too much to the neglect of concurrent influences. Until we know, for example, somewhat more of the comparative radiant powers of different soils, we cannot expect any very definite result. A change of temperature would certainly be effected by the plantation of such a marshy district as the Sologne, because, if nothing else were done, the roots might pierce the impenetrable subsoil, allow the surface-water to drain itself off, and thus dry the country. But might not the change be quite different if the soil planted were a shifting sand, which, *fixed* by the roots of the trees, would become gradually covered with a vegetable earth, and thus be changed from dry to wet? Again, the complication and conflict of effects arises, not only from the soil, vegetation, and geographical position of the place of the experiment itself, but from the distribution of similar or different conditions in its immediate neighbourhood, and probably to great distances on every side. A forest, for example, as we know from Herr Rivoli's comparison, would exercise a perfectly different influence in a cold country subject to warm winds, and in a warm country subject to cold winds; so that our question might meet with different solutions even on the east and west coasts of Great Britain.

The consideration of such a complexity points more and more to the plantation of Malta as an occasion of special importance; its insular position and the unity of its geological structure both tend to simplify the question. There are certain points about the existing climate, moreover, which seem specially calculated to throw the influence of woods into a strong relief. Thus, during four summer months, there is practically no rainfall. Thus, again, the northerly winds when stormy, and especially in winter, tend to depress the temperature very suddenly; and thus, too, the southerly and south-westerly winds, which raise the temperature during their prevalence to from eighty-eight to ninety-eight degrees, seldom last longer than a few hours; insomuch that "their disagreeable heat and dryness may be escaped by carefully closing the windows and doors of apartments at their onset."[1] Such sudden and short variations seem just what is wanted to accentuate the differences in question. Accordingly, the opportunity seems one not lightly to be lost, and the British Association or this Society itself might take the matter up and establish a series of observations, to be continued during the next few years. Such a combination of favourable circumstances may not occur again for years; and when the whole subject is at a standstill for want of facts, the present occasion ought not to go past unimproved.

Such observations might include the following:

The observation of maximum and minimum thermometers in three different classes of situation — *videlicet*, in the areas selected for plantation themselves, at places in the immediate neighbourhood of those areas where the external influence might be expected to reach its maximum, and at places distant from those areas where the influence might be expected to be least.

The operation of rain-gauges and hygrometers at the same three descriptions of locality.

In addition to the ordinary hours of observation, special readings of the thermometers should be made as often as possible at a change of wind and throughout the course of the short hot breezes alluded to already, in order to admit of the recognition and extension of Herr Rivoli's comparison.

Observation of the periods and forces of the land and sea breezes.

Gauging of the principal springs, both in the neighbourhood of the areas of plantation and at places far removed from those areas.

1873.

[1] Scoresby-Jackson's *Medical Climatology*.

ADDENDA

REFLECTION AND REMARKS ON HUMAN LIFE

I. *Justice and Justification.*—(1) It is the business of this life to make excuses for others, but none for ourselves. We should be clearly persuaded of our own misconduct, for that is the part of knowledge in which we are most apt to be defective. (2) Even justice is no right of a man's own, but a thing, like the king's tribute, which shall never be his, but which he should strive to see rendered to another. None was ever just to me; none ever will be. You may reasonably aspire to be chief minister or sovereign pontiff; but not to be justly regarded in your own character and acts. You know too much to be satisfied. For justice is but an earthly currency, paid to appearances; you may see another superficially righted; but be sure he has got too little or too much; and in your own case rest content with what is paid you. It is more just than you suppose; that your virtues are misunderstood is a price you pay to keep your meannesses concealed. (3) When you seek to justify yourself to others, you may be sure you will plead falsely. If you fail, you have the shame of the failure; if you succeed, you will have made too much of it, and be unjustly esteemed upon the other side. (4) You have perhaps only one friend in the world, in whose esteem it is worth while for you to right yourself. Justification to indifferent persons is, at best, an impertinent intrusion. Let them think what they please; they will be the more likely to forgive you in the end. (5) It is a question hard to be resolved, whether you should at any time criminate another to defend yourself. I have done it many times, and always had a troubled conscience for my pains.

II. *Parent and Child.*—(1) The love of parents for their children is, of all natural affections, the most ill-starred. It is not a love for the person, since it begins before the person has come into the world, and founds on an imaginary character and looks. Thus it is foredoomed to disappointment; and because the parent either looks for too much, or at least for something inappropriate, at his offspring's hands, it is too often insufficiently repaid. The natural bond, besides, is stronger from parent to child than from child to parent; and it is the side which confers benefits, not which receives them, that thinks most of a relation. (2) What do we owe our parents? No man can *owe* love; none can *owe* obedience. We owe, I think, chiefly pity; for we are the pledge of their dear and joyful union, we have been the solicitude of their days and the anxiety of their nights, we have made them, though by no will of ours, to carry the burthen of our sins, sorrows, and physical infirmities; and too many of us grow up at length to disappoint the purpose of their lives and requite their care and piety with cruel pangs. (3) *Mater Dolorosa.* It is the particular cross of parents that when the child grows up and becomes himself instead of that pale ideal they had preconceived, they must accuse their own harshness or indulgence for this natural result. They have all been like the duck and hatched swan's eggs, or the other way about; yet they tell themselves with miserable penitence that the blame lies with them; and had they sat more closely, the swan would have been a duck, and home-keeping, in spite of all. (4) A good son, who can fulfil what is expected of him, has done his work in life. He has to redeem the sins of many, and restore the world's confidence in children.

III. *Dialogue on Character and Destiny between Two Puppets.*—At the end of Chapter xxxiii. Count Spada and the General of the Jesuits were left alone in the pavilion, while the course of the story was turned upon the doings of the virtuous hero. Profiting by this moment of privacy, the Jesuit turned with a very warning countenance upon the peer.

" Have a care, my lord," said he, raising a finger. " You are already no favourite with the author; and for my part, I begin to perceive from a thousand evidences that the narrative is drawing near a close. Yet a chapter or two at most, and you will be overtaken by some sudden and appalling judgment."

" I despise your womanish presentiments," replied Spada, " and count firmly upon another volume; I see a variety of reasons why my life should be prolonged to within a few pages of the end; indeed, I permit myself to expect resurrection in a sequel, or second part. You will scarce suggest that there can be any end to the newspaper; and you will certainly never convince me that the author, who cannot be entirely without sense, would have been at so great pains with my intelligence, gallant exterior, and happy and natural speech, merely to kick me hither and thither for two or three paltry chapters and then drop me at the end like a dumb personage. I know you priests are often infidels in secret. Pray, do you believe in an author at all?"

" Many do not, I am aware," replied the General, softly; " even in the last chapter we encountered one, the self-righteous David Hume, who goes so far as to doubt the existence of the newspaper in which our adventures are now appearing; but it would neither become my cloth, nor do credit to my great experience, were I to meddle with these dangerous opinions. My alarm for you is not metaphysical, it is moral in its origin: You must be aware, my poor friend, that you are a very bad character—the worst, indeed, that I have met with in these pages. The author hates you, Count; and difficult as it may be to connect the idea of immortality—or, in plain terms, of a sequel—with the paper and printer's ink of which your humanity is made, it is yet more difficult to foresee anything but punishment and pain for one who is justly hateful in the eyes of his creator."

"You take for granted many things that I shall not be easily persuaded to allow," replied the villain. "Do you really so far deceive yourself in your imagination as to fancy that the author is a friend to good? Read; read the book in which you figure; and you will soon disown such crude vulgarities. Lelio is a good character; yet only two chapters ago we left him in a fine predicament. His old servant was a model of the virtues, yet did he not miserably perish in that ambuscade upon the road to Poitiers? And as for the family of the bankrupt merchant, how is it possible for greater moral qualities to be alive with more irremediable misfortunes? And yet you continue to misrepresent an author to yourself, as a deity devoted to virtue and inimical to vice? Pray, if you have no pride in your intellectual credit for yourself, spare at least the sensibilities of your associates."

"The purposes of the serial story," answered the Priest, "are, doubtless for some wise reason, hidden from those who act in it. To this limitation we must bow. But I ask every character to observe narrowly his own personal relations to the author. There, if nowhere else, we may glean some hint of his superior designs. Now I am myself a mingled personage, liable to doubts, to scruples, and to sudden revulsions of feeling; I reason continually about life, and frequently the result of my reasoning is to condemn or even to change my action. I am now convinced, for example, that I did wrong in joining your plot against the innocent and most unfortunate Lelio. I told you so, you will remember, in the chapter which has just been concluded; and though I do not know whether you perceived the ardour and fluency with which I expressed myself, I am still confident in my own heart that I spoke at that moment not only with the warm approval, but under the direct inspiration, of the author of the tale. I know, Spada, I tell you I *know* that he loved me as I uttered these words; and yet at other periods of my career I have been conscious of his indifference and dislike. You must not seek to reason me from this conviction; for it is supplied me from higher authority than that of reason, and is, indeed, a part of my experience. It may be an illusion that I drove last night from Saumur; it may be an illusion that we are now in the garden chamber of the château; it may be an illusion that I am conversing with Count Spada; you may be an illusion, Count, yourself; but of three things I will remain eternally persuaded, that the author exists not only in the newspaper but in my own heart, that he loves me when I do well, and that he hates and despises me when I do otherwise."

"I too believe in the author," returned the Count. "I believe likewise in a sequel, written in finer style and probably cast in a still higher rank of society than the present story; although I am not convinced that we shall then be conscious of our pre-existence here. So much of your argument is, therefore, beside the mark; for to a certain point I am as orthodox as yourself. But where you begin to draw general conclusions from your own private experience, I must beg pointedly and finally to differ. You will not have forgotten, I believe, my daring and single-handed butchery of the five secret witnesses? Nor the sleight of mind and dexterity of language with which I separated Lelio from the merchant's family? These were not virtuous actions; and yet, how am I to tell you? I was conscious of a troubled joy, a glee, a hellish gusto in my author's bosom, which seemed to renew my vigour with every sentence, and which has indeed made the first of these passages accepted for a model of spirited narrative description, and the second for a masterpiece of wickedness and wit. What result, then, can be drawn from two experiences so contrary as yours and mine? For my part, I lay it down as a principle, no author can be moral in a merely human sense. And, to pursue the argument higher, how can you, for one instant, suppose the existence of free-will in puppets situated as we are in the thick of a novel which we do not even understand? And how, without free-will upon our parts, can you justify blame or approval on that of the author? We are in his hands; by a stroke of the pen, to speak reverently, he made us what we are; by a stroke of the pen he can utterly undo and transmute what he has made. In the very next chapter, my dear General, you may be shown up for an impostor, or I be stricken down in the tears of penitence and hurried into the retirement of a monastery!"

"You use an argument old as mankind, and difficult of answer," said the Priest. "I cannot justify the free-will of which I am usually conscious; nor will I ever seek to deny that this consciousness is interrupted. Sometimes events mount upon me with such swiftness and pressure that my choice is overwhelmed, and even to myself I seem to obey a will external to my own; and again I am sometimes so paralysed and impotent between alternatives that I am tempted to imagine a hesitation on the part of my author. But I contend, upon the other hand, for a limited free-will in the sphere of consciousness; and as it is in and by my consciousness that I exist to myself, I will not go on to inquire whether that free-will is valid as against the author, the newspaper, or even the readers of the story. And I contend, further, for a sort of empire or independence of our own characters when once created, which the author cannot or at least does not choose to violate. Hence Lelio was conceived upright, honest, courageous, and headlong; to that first idea all his acts and speeches must of necessity continue to answer; and the same, though with such different defects and qualities, applies to you, Count Spada, and to myself. We must act up to our characters; it is these characters that the author loves or despises; it is on account of them that we must suffer or triumph, whether in this work or in a sequel. Such is my belief."

"It is pure Calvinistic election, my dear sir, and, by your leave, a very heretical position for a churchman to support," replied the Count. "Nor can I see how it removes the difficulty. I was not consulted as to my character; I might have chosen to be Lelio; I might have chosen to be yourself; I might even have preferred to figure in a different romance, or not to enter into the world of literature at all. And am I to be blamed or hated, because some one else wilfully and inhumanely made me what I am, and has continued ever since to encourage me in what are called my vices? You may say what you please, my dear sir, but if that is the case, I had rather be a telegram from the seat of war than a reasonable and conscious character in a romance; nay, and I have a perfect right to repudiate, loathe, curse, and utterly condemn the ruffian who calls himself the author."

"You have, as you say, a perfect right," replied the Jesuit; "and I am convinced that it will not affect him in the least."

"He shall have one slave the fewer for me," added the Count. "I discard my allegiance once for all."

"As you please," concluded the other; "but at least be ready, for I perceive we are about to enter on the scene."

And indeed, just at that moment, Chapter xxxiv. being completed, Chapter xxxv., "The Count's Chastisement," began to appear in the columns of the newspaper.

IV. *Solitude and Society*.—(1) A little society is needful to show a man his failings; for if he lives entirely by himself, he has no occasion to fall, and, like a soldier in time of peace, becomes both weak and vain. But a little solitude must be used, or we grow content with current virtues and forget the ideal. In society we lose scrupulous brightness of honour; in solitude we lose the courage necessary to face our own imperfections. (2) As a question of pleasure, after a man has reached a certain age, I can hardly perceive much room to choose between them: each is in a way delightful, and each will please best after an experience of the other. (3) But solitude for its own sake should surely never be preferred. We are bound by the strongest obligations to busy ourselves amid the world of men, if it be only to crack jokes. The finest trait in the character of St. Paul was his readiness to be damned for the salvation of anybody else. And surely we should all endure a little weariness to make one face look brighter or one hour go more pleasantly in this mixed world. (4) It is our business here to speak, for it is by the tongue that we multiply ourselves most influentially. To speak kindly, wisely, and pleasantly is the first of duties, the easiest of duties, and the duty that is most blessed in its performance. For it is natural, it whiles away life, it spreads intelligence; and it increases the acquaintance of man with man. (5) It is, besides, a good investment, for while all other pleasures decay, and even the delight in nature, Grandfather William is still bent to gossip. (6) Solitude is the climax of the negative virtues. When we go to bed after a solitary day we can tell ourselves that we have not been unkind nor dishonest nor untruthful; and the negative virtues are agreeable to that dangerous faculty we call the conscience. That they should ever be admitted for a part of virtue is what I cannot explain. I do not care two straws for all the *nots*. (7) The positive virtues are imperfect; they are even ugly in their imperfection : for man's acts, by the necessity of his being, are coarse and mingled.

The kindest, in the course of a day of active kindnesses, will say some things rudely, and do some things cruelly; the most honourable, perhaps, trembles at his nearness to a doubtful act. (8) Hence the solitary recoils from the practice of life, shocked by its unsightliness. But if I could only retain that superfine and guiding delicacy of the sense that grows in solitude, and still combine with it that courage of performance which is never abashed by any failure, but steadily pursues its right and human design in a scene of imperfection, I might hope to strike in the long run a conduct more tender to others and less humiliating to myself.

V. *Selfishness and Egoism.*—An unconscious, easy, selfish person shocks less, and is more easily loved, than one who is laboriously and egoistically unselfish. There is at least no fuss about the first; but the other parades his sacrifices, and so sells his favours too dear. Selfishness is calm, a force of nature: you might say the trees were selfish. But egoism is a piece of vanity; it must always take you into its confidence; it is uneasy, troublesome, seeking; it can do good, but not handsomely; it is uglier, because less dignified, than selfishness itself. But here I perhaps exaggerate to myself, because I am the one more than the other, and feel it like a hook in my mouth, at every step I take. Do what I will, this seems to spoil all.

VI. *Right and Wrong.*—It is the mark of a good action that it appears inevitable in the retrospect. We should have been cut-throats to do otherwise. And there's an end. We ought to know distinctly that we are damned for what we do wrong; but when we have done right, we have only been gentlemen, after all. There is nothing to make a work about.

VII. *Discipline of Conscience.*—(1) Never allow your mind to dwell on your own misconduct; that is ruin. The conscience has morbid sensibilities; it must be employed but not indulged, like the imagination or the stomach. (2) Let each stab suffice for the occasion; to play with this spiritual pain turns to penance; and a person easily learns to feel good by dallying with the consciousness of having done wrong. (3) Shut your eyes hard against the recollection of your sins. Do not be afraid, you will not be able to forget them. (4) You will always do wrong: you must try to get used to that, my son. It is a small matter to make a work about, when all the world is in the same case. I meant when I was a young man to write a great poem; and now I am cobbling little prose articles and in excellent good spirits, I thank you. So, too, I meant to lead a life that should keep mounting from the first; and though I have been repeatedly down again below sea-level, and am scarce higher than when I started, I am as keen as ever for that enterprise. Our business in this world is not to succeed, but to continue to fail, in good spirits. (5) There is but one test of a good life: that the man shall continue to grow more difficult about his own behaviour. That is to be good: there is no other virtue attainable. The virtues we admire in the saint and the hero are the fruits of a happy constitution. You, for your part, must not think you will ever be a good man, for these are born and not made. You will have your own reward, if you keep on growing better than you were—how do I say? if you do not keep on growing worse. (6) A man is one thing, and must be exercised in all his faculties. Whatever side of you is neglected, whether it is the muscles, or the taste for art, or the desire for virtue, that which is cultivated will suffer in proportion. —— was greatly tempted, I remember, to do a very dishonest act, in order that he might pursue his studies in art. When he consulted me, I advised him not (putting it that way for once), because his art would suffer. (7) It might be fancied that if we could only study all sides of our being in an exact proportion, we should attain wisdom. But in truth a chief part of education is to exercise one set of faculties à outrance—one, since we have not the time so to practise all; thus the dilettante misses the kernel of the matter; and the man who has wrung forth the secret of one part of life knows more about the others than he who has tepidly circumnavigated all. (8) Thus, one must be your profession, the rest can only be your delights; and virtue had better be kept for the latter, for it enters into all, but none enters by necessity into it. You will learn a great deal of virtue by studying any art; but nothing of any art in the study of virtue. (9) The study of conduct has to do with grave problems; not every action should be higgled over; one of the leading virtues therein is to let oneself alone. But if you make it your chief employment, you are sure to meddle too much. This is the great error of those who are called pious. Although the war of virtue be unending except with life, hostilities are frequently suspended, and the troops go into winter quarters; but the pious will not profit by these times of truce; where their conscience can perceive no sin, they will find a sin in that very innocency; and so they pervert, to their annoyance, those seasons which God gives to us for repose and a reward. (10) The nearest approximation to sense in all this matter lies with the Quakers. There must be no *will*-worship; how much more, no *will*-repentance. The damnable consequences of set seasons, even for prayer, is to have a man continually posturing to himself, till his conscience is taught as many tricks as a pet monkey, and the gravest expressions are left with a perverted meaning. (11) For my part, I should try to secure some part of every day for meditation, above all in the early morning and the open air; but how that time was to be improved I should leave to circumstance and the inspiration of the hour. Nor if I spent it in whistling or numbering my footsteps, should I consider it misspent for that. I should have given my conscience a fair field; when it has anything to say, I know too well it can speak daggers; therefore, for this time, my hard taskmaster has given me a holy day, and I may go in again rejoicing to my breakfast and the human business of the day.

VIII. *Gratitude to God.*—(1) To the gratitude that becomes us in this life, I can set no limit. Though we steer after a fashion, yet we must sail according to the winds and currents. After what I have done, what might I not have done? That I have still the courage to attempt my life, that I am not now overladen with dishonours, to whom do I owe it but to the gentle ordering of circumstances in the great design? More has not been done to me than I can bear; I have been marvellously restrained and helped: not unto us, O Lord! (2) I cannot forgive God for the suffering of others; when I look abroad upon His world and behold its cruel destinies, I turn from Him with disaffection; nor do I conceive that He will blame me for the impulse. But when I consider my own fates, I grow conscious of His gentle dealing: I see Him chastise with helpful blows, I feel His stripes to be caresses; and this knowledge is my comfort that reconciles me to the world. (3) All those whom I now pity with indignation are perhaps not less fatherly dealt with than myself. I do right to be angry: yet they, perhaps, if they lay aside heat and temper, and reflect with patience on their lot, may find everywhere, in their worst trials, the same proofs of a divine affection. (4) While we have little to try us, we are angry with little; small annoyances do not bear their justification on their faces; but when we are overtaken by a great sorrow or perplexity, the greatness of our concern sobers us so that we see more

630

clearly and think with more consideration. I speak for myself; nothing grave has yet befallen me but I have been able to reconcile my mind to its occurrence, and see in it, from my own little and partial point of view, an evidence of a tender and protecting God. Even the misconduct into which I have been led has been blessed to my improvement. If I did not sin, and that so glaringly that my conscience is convicted on the spot, I do not know what I should become, but I feel sure I should grow worse. The man of very regular conduct is too often a prig, if he be not worse—a rabbi. I, for my part, want to be startled out of my conceits; I want to be put to shame in my own eyes; I want to feel the bridle in my mouth, and be continually reminded of my own weakness and the omnipotence of circumstances. (5) If I from my spy-hole, looking with purblind eyes upon the least part of a fraction of the universe, yet perceive in my own destiny some broken evidences of a plan and some signals of an overruling goodness; shall I then be so mad as to complain that all cannot be deciphered? Shall I not rather wonder, with infinite and grateful surprise, that in so vast a scheme I seem to have been able to read, however little, and that that little was encouraging to faith?

IX. *Blame.*— What comes from without and what comes from within, how much of conduct proceeds from the spirit or how much from circumstances, what is the part of choice and what the part of the selection offered, where personal character begins or where, if anywhere, it escapes at all from the authority of nature, these are questions of curiosity and eternally indifferent to right and wrong. Our theory of blame is utterly sophisticated and untrue to man's experience. We are as much ashamed of a pimpled face that came to us by natural descent as of one that we have earned by our excesses, and rightly so; since the two cases, in so much as they unfit us for the easier sort of pleasing and put an obstacle in the path of love, are exactly equal in their consequences. We look aside from the true question. We cannot blame others at all; we can only punish them; and ourselves we blame indifferently for a deliberate crime, a thoughtless brusquerie, or an act done without volition in an ecstasy of madness. We blame ourselves from two considerations: first, because another has suffered; and second, because, in so far as we have again done wrong, we can look forward with the less confidence to what remains of our career. Shall we repent this failure? It is there that the consciousness of sin most cruelly affects us; it is in view of this that a man cries out, in exaggeration, that his heart is desperately wicked and deceitful above all things. We all tacitly subscribe this judgment: Woe unto him by whom offences shall come! We accept palliations for our neighbours; we dare not, in the sight of our own soul, accept them for ourselves. We may not be to blame; we may be conscious of no free-will in the matter, of a possession, on the other hand, of an irresistible tyranny of circumstances,—yet we know, in another sense, we are to blame for all. Our right to live, to eat, to share in mankind's pleasures, lies precisely in this: that we must be persuaded we can on the whole live rather beneficially than hurtfully to others. Remove this persuasion, and the man has lost his right. That persuasion is our dearest jewel, to which we must sacrifice the life itself to which it entitles us. For it is better to be dead than degraded.

X. *Marriage.*—(1) No considerate man can approach marriage without deep concern. I, he will think, who have made hitherto so poor a business of my own life, am now about to embrace the responsibility of another's. Henceforth, there shall be two to suffer from my faults; and that other is the one whom I most desire to shield from suffering. In view of our impotence and folly, it seems an act of presumption to involve another's destiny with ours. We should hesitate to assume command of an army or a trading-smack; shall we not hesitate to become surety for the life and happiness, now and henceforward, of our dearest friend? To be nobody's enemy but one's own, although it is never possible to any, can least of all be possible to one who is married. (2) I would not so much fear to give hostages to fortune, if fortune ruled only in material things; but fortune, as we call those minor and more inscrutable workings of providence, rules also in the sphere of conduct. I am not so blind but that I know I might be a murderer or even a traitor to-morrow; and now, as if I were not already too feelingly alive to my misdeeds, I must choose out the one person whom I most desire to please, and make her the daily witness of my failures, I must give a part in all my dishonours to the one person who can feel them more keenly than myself. (3) In all our daring, magnanimous human way of life, I find nothing more bold than this. To go into battle is but a small thing by comparison. It is the last act of committal. After that, there is no way left, not even suicide, but to be a good man. (4) She will help you, let us pray. And yet she is in the same case; she, too, has daily made shipwreck of her own happiness and worth; it is with a courage no less irrational than yours, that she also ventures on this new experiment of life. Two who have failed severally now join their fortunes with a wavering hope. (5) But it is from the boldness of the enterprise that help springs. To take home to your hearth that living witness whose blame will most affect you, to eat, to sleep, to live with your most admiring and thence most exacting judge, is not this to domesticate the living God? Each becomes a conscience to the other, legible like a clock upon the chimney-piece. Each offers to his mate a figure of the consequence of human acts. And while I may still continue by my inconsiderate or violent life to spread far-reaching havoc throughout man's confederacy, I can do so no more, at least, in ignorance and levity; one face shall wince before me in the flesh; I have taken home the sorrows I create to my own hearth and bed; and though I continue to sin, it must be now with open eyes.

XI. *Idleness and Industry.*— I remember a time when I was very idle; and lived and profited by that humour. I have no idea why I ceased to be so, yet I scarce believe I have the power to return to it; it is a change of age. I made consciously a thousand little efforts, but the determination from which these arose came to me while I slept and in the way of growth. I have had a thousand skirmishes to keep myself at work upon particular mornings, and sometimes the affair was hot; but of that great change of campaign, which decided all this part of my life, and turned me from one whose business was to shirk into one whose business was to strive and persevere,— it seems as though all that had been done by some one else. The life of Goethe affected me; so did that of Balzac; and some very noble remarks by the latter in a pretty bad book, the *Cousine Bette.* I dare say I could trace some other influences in the change. All I mean is, I was never conscious of a struggle, nor registered a vow, nor seemingly had anything personally to do with the matter. I came about like a well-handled ship. There stood at the wheel that unknown steersman whom we call God.

XII. *Courage.*— Courage is the principal virtue, for all the others presuppose it. If you are afraid, you may do anything. Courage is to be cultivated, and some of the negative virtues may be sacrificed in the cultivation.

XIII. *Results of Action.*—The result is the reward of actions, not the test. The result is a child born; if it be beautiful and healthy, well: if club-footed or crook-back, perhaps well also. We cannot direct . . .
[1878?]

THE IDEAL HOUSE

Two things are necessary in any neighbourhood where we propose to spend a life: a desert and some living water.

There are many parts of the earth's surface which offer the necessary combination of a certain wildness with a kindly variety. A great prospect is desirable, but the want may be otherwise supplied; even greatness can be found on the small scale; for the mind and eye measure differently. Bold rocks near at hand are more inspiriting than distant Alps, and the thick fern upon a Surrey heath makes a fine forest for the imagination, and the dotted yew-trees noble mountains. A Scottish moor with birches and firs grouped here and there upon a knoll, or one of those rocky sea-side deserts of Provence overgrown with rosemary and thyme and smoking with aroma, are places where the mind is never weary. Forests, being more enclosed, are not at first sight so attractive, but they exercise a spell; they must, however, be diversified with either heath or rock, and are hardly to be considered perfect without conifers. Even sand-hills, with their intricate plan, and their gulls and rabbits, will stand well for the necessary desert.

The house must be within hail of either a little river or the sea. A great river is more fit for poetry than to adorn a neighbourhood; its sweep of waters increases the scale of the scenery and the distance of one notable object from another; and a lively burn gives us, in the space of a few yards, a greater variety of promontory and islet, of cascade, shallow goil, and boiling pool, with answerable changes both of song and colour, than a navigable stream in many hundred miles. The fish, too, make a more considerable feature of the brook-side, and the trout plumping in the shadow takes the ear. A stream should, besides, be narrow enough to cross, or the burn hard by a bridge, or we are at once shut out of Eden. The quantity of water need be of

634

no concern, for the mind sets the scale, and can enjoy a Niagara Fall of thirty inches. Let us approve the singer of

> "Shallow rivers, by whose fall
> Melodious birds sing madrigals.

If the sea is to be our ornamental water, choose an open seaboard with a heavy beat of surf; one much broken in outline, with small havens and dwarf headlands; if possible a few islets; and as a first necessity, rocks reaching out into deep water. Such a rock on a calm day is a better station than the top of Teneriffe or Chimborazo. In short, both for the desert and the water, the conjunction of many near and bold details is bold scenery for the imagination and keeps the mind alive.

Given these two prime luxuries, the nature of the country where we are to live is, I had almost said, indifferent; after that, inside the garden, we can construct a country of our own. Several old trees, a considerable variety of level, several well-grown hedges to divide our garden into provinces, a good extent of old well-set turf, and thickets of shrubs and evergreens to be cut into and cleared at the new owner's pleasure, are the qualities to be sought for in your chosen land. Nothing is more delightful than a succession of small lawns, opening one out of the other through tall hedges; these have all the charm of the old bowling-green repeated, do not require the labour of many trimmers, and afford a series of changes. You must have much lawn against the early summer, so as to have a great field of daisies, the year's morning frost; as you must have a wood of lilacs, to enjoy to the full the period of their blossoming. Hawthorn is another of the Spring's ingredients; but it is even best to have a rough public lane at one side of your enclosure, which, at the right season, shall become an avenue of bloom and odour. The old flowers are the best and should grow carelessly in corners. Indeed, the ideal fortune is to find an old garden, once very richly cared for, since sunk into neglect, and to tend, not repair, that neglect; it will thus have a smack of nature and wildness which skilful dispositions cannot overtake. The gardener should be an idler, and have a gross partiality to the kitchen plots; an eager or toilful gardener misbecomes the garden landscape; a tasteful gardener will be ever meddling, will keep the borders raw, and take the bloom off nature. Close adjoining, if you are in the south, an olive-yard, if in the north, a swarded apple-orchard reaching to the stream, completes your miniature domain; but this is perhaps best entered through a door in the high fruit-wall; so that you close the door behind you on your sunny plots, your hedges and evergreen jungle, when you go down to watch the apples falling in the pool. It is a golden maxim to cultivate the garden for the nose, and the eyes will take care of themselves. Nor must the ear be forgotten: without birds, a garden is a prison-yard. There is a garden near Marseilles on a steep hill-side, walking by which, upon a sunny morning, your ear will suddenly be ravished with a burst of small and very cheerful singing: some score of cages being set out there to sun their occupants. This is a heavenly surprise to any passer-by; but the price paid, to keep so many ardent and winged creatures from their liberty, will make the luxury too dear for any thoughtful pleasure-lover. There is only one sort of bird that I can tolerate caged, though even then I think it hard, and that is what is called in France the Bec-d'Argent. I once had two of these pigmies in captivity; and in the quiet, bare house upon a silent street where I was then living, their song, which was not much louder than a bee's, but airily musical, kept me in a perpetual good-humour. I put the cage upon my table when I worked, carried it with me when I went for meals, and kept it by my head at night: the first thing in the morning these *maestrini* would pipe up. But these, even if you can pardon their imprisonment, are for the house. In the garden the wild birds must plant a colony, a chorus of the lesser warblers that should be almost deafening, a blackbird in the lilacs, a nightingale down the lane, so that you must stroll to hear it, and yet a little farther, tree-tops populous with rooks.

Your house should not command much outlook; it should be set deep and green, though upon rising ground, or, if possible, crowning a knoll, for the sake of drainage. Yet it must be open to the east, or you will miss the sunrise; sunset occurring so much later, you can go up a few steps and look the other way. A house of more than two stories is a mere barrack; indeed the ideal is of one story, raised upon cellars. If the rooms are large, the house may be small: a single room, lofty, spacious, and lightsome, is more palatial than a castleful of cabinets and cupboards. Yet size in a house, and some extent and intricacy of corridor, is certainly delightful to the flesh. The reception-room should be, if possible, a place of many recesses, which are "petty retiring-places for conference"; but it must have one long wall with a divan: for a day spent upon a divan, among a world of cushions, is as full of diversion as to travel. The eating-room, in the French mode, should be *ad hoc :* unfurnished, but with a buffet, the table, necessary chairs, one or two of Canaletto's etchings, and a tile fireplace for the winter. In neither of these public places should there be anything beyond a shelf or two of books; but the passages may be one library from end to end, and the stair, if there be one, lined with volumes in old leather, very brightly carpeted, and leading half-way up, and by the way of landing, to a windowed recess with a fireplace; this window, almost alone in the house, should command a handsome prospect. Husband and wife must each possess a studio; on the woman's sanctuary I hesitate to dwell, and turn to the man's. The walls are shelved waist-high for books, and the top thus forms a continuous table running round the wall. Above are prints, a large map of the neighbourhood, a Corot and a Claude or two. The room is very spacious, and the five tables and two chairs are but as islands. One table is for actual work; one close by for references in use; one, very large, for MSS. or proofs that wait their turn; one kept clear for an occasion; and the fifth is the map table, groaning under a collection of large-scale maps and charts. Of all books these are the least wearisome to read and the richest in matter; the course of roads and rivers, the contour-lines and the forests in the maps — the reefs, soundings, anchors, sailing-marks, and little pilot-pictures in the charts — and, in both, the bead-roll of names, make them of all printed matter the most fit to stimulate and satisfy the fancy. The chair in which you write is very low and easy, and backed into a corner; at one elbow the fire twinkles; close at the other, if you are a little inhumane, your cage of silver-bills are twittering into song.

Joined along by a passage, you may reach the great, sunny, glass-roofed, and tiled gymnasium, at the far end of which, lined with bright marble, is your plunge and swimming bath, fitted with a capacious boiler.

The whole loft of the house from end to end makes one undivided chamber; here are set forth tables on which to model imaginary countries in putty or plaster, with tools and hardy pigments; a carpenter's bench; and a spared corner for photography, while at the far end a space is kept for playing soldiers. Two boxes contain the two armies of some five hundred horse and foot; two others the ammunition of each side, and a fifth the foot-rules and the three colours of chalk, with which you lay down, or, after a day's play, refresh the outlines of the country; red or white for the two kinds of road (according as they are suitable or not for the passage of ordnance), and blue for the course of the obstructing rivers. Here I foresee that you may pass much happy time; against a good adversary a game may well continue for a month; for with armies so considerable three moves will occupy an hour. It will be found to set an excellent edge on this diversion if one of the players shall, every day or so, write a report of the operations in the character of army correspondent.

I have left to the last the little room for winter evenings. This should be furnished in warm positive colours, and sofas and floor thick with rich furs. The hearth, where you burn wood of aromatic quality on silver dogs, tiled round with Bible pictures; the seats deep and easy; a single Titian in a gold frame; a white bust or so upon a bracket; a rack for the journals of the week; a table for the books of the year; and close in a corner the three shelves full of eternal books that never weary: Shakespeare, Molière, Montaigne, Lamb, Sterne, De Musset's comedies (the one volume open at *Carmosine* and the other at *Fantasio*); the *Arabian Nights*, and kindred stories, in Weber's solemn volumes; Borrow's *Bible in Spain*, the *Pilgrim's Progress*, *Guy Mannering* and *Rob Roy*, *Monte Cristo* and the *Vicomte de Bragelonne*, immortal Boswell sole among biographers, Chaucer, Herrick, and the *State Trials*.

The bedrooms are large, airy, with almost no furniture, floors of varnished wood, and at the bed-head, in case of insomnia, one shelf of books of a particular and dippable order, such as *Pepys*, the *Paston Letters*, Burt's *Letters from the Highlands*, or the *Newgate Calendar* . . .

[1884 ?]

PREFACE TO
"THE MASTER OF BALLANTRAE"

Although an old, consistent exile, the editor of the following pages revisits now and again the city of which he exults to be a native; and there are few things more strange, more painful, or more salutary, than such revisitations. Outside, in foreign spots, he comes by surprise and awakens more attention than he had expected; in his own city, the relation is reversed, and he stands amazed to be so little recollected. Elsewhere he is refreshed to see attractive faces, to remark possible friends; there he scouts the long streets, with a pang at heart, for the faces and friends that are no more. Elsewhere he is delighted with the presence of what is new, there tormented by the absence of what is old. Elsewhere he is content to be his present self; there he is smitten with an equal regret for what he once was and for what he once hoped to be.

He was feeling all this dimly, as he drove from the station, on his last visit; he was feeling it still as he alighted at the door of his friend, Mr. Johnstone Thomson, W. S., with whom he was to stay. A hearty welcome, a face not altogether changed, a few words that sounded of old days, a laugh provoked and shared, a glimpse in passing of the snowy cloth and bright decanters and the Piranesis on the dining-room wall, brought him to his bedroom with a somewhat lightened cheer, and when he and Mr. Thomson sat down a few minutes later, cheek by jowl, and pledged the past in a preliminary bumper, he was already almost consoled, he had already almost forgiven himself his two unpardonable errors, that he should ever have left his native city, or ever returned to it.

"I have something quite in your way," said Mr. Thomson. "I wished to do honour to your arrival; because, my dear fellow, it is my own youth that comes back along with you; in a very tattered and withered state, to be sure, but—well!—all that 's left of it."

"A great deal better than nothing," said the editor. "But what is this which is quite in my way?"

"I was coming to that," said Mr. Thomson: "Fate has put it in my power to honour your arrival with something really original by way of dessert. A mystery."

"A mystery?" I repeated.

"Yes," said his friend, "a mystery. It may prove to be nothing, and it may prove to be a great deal. But in the meanwhile it is truly mysterious, no eye having looked on it for near a hundred years; it is highly genteel, for it treats of a titled family; it ought to be melodramatic, for (according to the superscription) it is concerned with death."

"I think I rarely heard a more obscure or a more promising annunciation," the other remarked. "But what is It?"

"You remember my predecessor's, old Peter M'Brair's business?"

"I remember him acutely; he could not look at me without a pang of reprobation, and he could not feel the pang without betraying it. He was to me a man of a great historical interest, but the interest was not returned."

"Ah, well, we go beyond him," said Mr. Thomson. "I dare say old Peter knew as little about this as I do. You see, I succeeded to a prodigious accumulation of old law-papers and old tin boxes, some of them of Peter's hoarding, some of his father's, John, first of the dynasty, a great man in his day. Among other collections, were all the papers of the Durrisdeers."

"The Durrisdeers!" cried I. "My dear fellow, these may be of the greatest interest. One of them was out in the '45; one had some strange passages with the devil—you will find a note of it in Law's *Memorials*, I think; and there was an unexplained tragedy, I know not what, much later, about a hundred years ago —"

"More than a hundred years ago," said Mr. Thomson. "In 1783."

"How do you know that? I mean some death."

"Yes, the lamentable deaths of my lord Durrisdeer and his brother, the Master of Ballantrae (attainted in the troubles)," said Mr. Thomson, with something the tone of a man quoting. "Is that it?"

"To say truth," said I, "I have only seen some dim reference to the things in memoirs; and heard some traditions dimmer still, through my uncle (whom I think you knew). My uncle lived when he was a boy in the neighbourhood of St. Bride's; he has often told me of the avenue closed up and grown over with grass, the great gates never opened, the last lord and his old-maid sister who lived in the back parts of the house, a quiet, plain, poor, humdrum couple it would seem—but pathetic too, as the last of that stirring and brave house —and, to the country folk, faintly terrible from some deformed traditions."

"Yes," said Mr. Thomson. "Henry Graeme Durie, the last lord, died in 1820; his sister, the Honourable Miss Katherine Durie, in '27; so much I know; and by what I have been going over the last few days, they were what you say, decent, quiet people and not rich. To say truth, it was a letter of my lord's that put me on the search for the packet we are going to open this evening. Some papers could not be found; and he wrote to Jack M'Brair suggesting they might be among those sealed up by a Mr. Mackellar. M'Brair answered, that the papers in question were all in Mackellar's own hand, all (as the writer understood) of a purely narrative character; and besides, said he, 'I am bound not to open them before the year 1889.' You may fancy if these words struck me: I instituted a hunt through all the M'Brair repositories; and at last hit upon that packet which (if you have had enough wine) I propose to show you at once."

In the smoking-room, to which my host now led me, was a packet, fastened with many seals and enclosed in a single sheet of strong paper thus endorsed:

"Papers relating to the lives and lamentable deaths of the late Lord Durrisdeer, and his elder brother James, commonly called Master of Ballantrae, attainted in the troubles: entrusted into the hands of John M'Brair in the Lawnmarket of Edinburgh, W. S.; this 20th day of September Anno Domini 1789; by him to be kept secret until the revolution of one hundred years complete, or until the 20th day of September 1889: the same compiled and written by me,

"Ephraim Mackellar,

"*For near forty years Land Steward on the estates of His Lordship.*"

As Mr. Thomson is a married man, I will not say what hour had struck when we laid down the last of the following pages; but I will give a few words of what ensued.

"Here," said Mr. Thomson, "is a novel ready to your hand: all you have to do is to work up the scenery, develop the characters, and improve the style."

"My dear fellow," said I, "they are just the three things that I would rather die than set my hand to. It shall be published as it stands."

" But it 's so bald," objected Mr. Thomson.

"I believe there is nothing so noble as baldness," replied I, " and I am sure there is nothing so interesting. I would have all literature bald, and all authors (if you like) but one."

" Well, well," said Mr. Thomson, "we shall see."

1889.